D0214017

OXFORD STUDIES IN
SOCIAL AND CULTURAL ANTHROPOLOGY

Editorial Board

John Davis   Luc de Heusch   Caroline Humphrey
Emily Martin   Peter Rivière   Marilyn Strathern

THE HEAT OF THE HEARTH

WITHDRAWN
ITHACA COLLEGE LIBRARY

OXFORD STUDIES IN SOCIAL AND CULTURAL ANTHROPOLOGY

Oxford Studies in Social and Cultural Anthropology represents the work of authors, new and established, which will set the criteria of excellence in ethnographic description and innovation in analysis. The series serves as an essential source of information about the world and the discipline.

OTHER TITLES IN THE SERIES

Organizing Jainism in India and England
Marcus Banks

Sea Hunters of Indonesia: Fishers and Weavers of Lamalera
R. H. Barnes

Society and Exchange in Nias
Andrew Beatty

Global Migrants, Local Lives: Travel and Transformation in Rural Bangladesh
Katy Gardner

Contested Hierarchies: A Collaborative Ethnography of Caste among the Newars of the Kathmandu Valley, Nepal
David N. Gellner and Declan Quigley

The Culture of Coincidence: Accident and Absolute Liability in Huli
Laurence Goldman

The Female Bridegroom: A Comparative Study of Life-Crisis Rituals in South India and Sri Lanka
Anthony Good

Of Mixed Blood: Kinship and History in Peruvian Amazonia
Peter Gow

The Archetypal Actions of Ritual: A Theory of Ritual Illustrated by the Jain Rite of Worship
Caroline Humphrey and James Laidlaw

Shamans and Elders:
Experience, Knowledge, and Power among the Daur Mongols
Caroline Humphrey with Urgunge Onon

The People of the Alas Valley: A Study of an Ethnic Group of Northern Sumatra
Akifumi Iwabuchi

Nuer Prophets: A History of Prophecy from the Upper Nile in the Nineteenth and Twentieth Centuries
Douglas H. Johnson

Knowledge and Secrecy in an Aboriginal Religion: Yolngu of North-East Arnhem Land
Ian Keen

Riches and Renunciation: Religion, Economy, and Society among the Jains
James Laidlaw

The Interpretation of Caste
Declan Quigley

The Arabesk Debate: Music and Musicians in Modern Turkey
Martin Stokes

Inside The Cult: Religious Innovation and Transmission in Papua New Guinea
Harvey Whitehouse

THE HEAT OF THE HEARTH

THE PROCESS OF KINSHIP IN A MALAY FISHING COMMUNITY

JANET CARSTEN

CLARENDON PRESS · OXFORD
1997

ADA - 2588

GN
635
.M4
C39
1997

Oxford University Press, Great Clarendon Street, Oxford OX2 6DP

Oxford New York
Athens Auckland Bangkok Bogota Bombay
Buenos Aires Calcutta Cape Town Dar es Salaam
Delhi Florence Hong Kong Istanbul Karachi
Kuala Lumpur Madras Madrid Melbourne
Mexico City Nairobi Paris Singapore
Taipei Tokyo Toronto

and associated companies in
Berlin Ibadan

Oxford is a trade mark of Oxford University Press

Published in the United States
by Oxford University Press Inc., New York

© Janet Carsten 1997

All rights reserved. No part of this publication may be reproduced, stored in a retrieval system, or transmitted, in any form or by any means, without the prior permission in writing of Oxford University Press. Within the UK, exceptions are allowed in respect of any fair dealing for the purpose of research or private study, or criticism or review, as permitted under the Copyright, Designs and Patents Act, 1988, or in the case of reprographic reproduction in accordance with the terms of the licences issued by the Copyright Licensing Agency. Enquiries concerning reproduction outside these terms and in other countries should be sent to the Rights Department, Oxford University Press, at the address above

This book is sold subject to the condition that it shall not, by way of trade or otherwise, be lent, re-sold, hired out or otherwise circulated without the publisher's prior consent in any form of binding or cover other than that in which it is published and without a similar condition including this condition being imposed on the subsequent purchaser

British Library Cataloguing in Publication Data
Data available

Library of Congress Cataloging in Publication Data

Carsten, Janet.
The heat of the hearth: the process of kinship in a Malay fishing community/Janet Carsten.
— (Oxford studies in social and cultural anthropology)
Includes bibliographical references and index.
1. Kinship—Malaysia—Langkawi Island (Kedah) 2. Langkawi Island (Kedah)—Social life and customs. 3. Fishing villages—Malaysia—Langkawi Island (Kedah) 4. Malaysia—Social life and customs. I. Title. II. Series.
GN635.M4C39 1997 306.83'09595'1—dc20 96-35165

ISBN 0–19–828045–9
ISBN 0–19–828046–7 (Pbk.)

Typeset by Best-set Typesetter Ltd., Hong Kong
Printed in Great Britain
on acid-free paper by
Biddles Ltd., Guildford and King's Lynn

For Francis Carsten
and in memory of
Ruth Carsten
1911–1994

ACKNOWLEDGEMENTS

Writing this book has been a long process. It began with fieldwork in Langkawi in 1980–2, which was followed by writing a doctoral thesis at the London School of Economics, and then by further fieldwork in 1988–9, and was finally completed by substantially rewriting the thesis. The length of the process has been paralleled by the burgeoning debts I have acquired along the way. In one way or another, there is hardly a single friend or member of my family who has not given their intellectual stimulation or moral support. I thank them all.

It is with a particularly deep sense of obligation that I thank the many people in Malaysia on whom I had no claim but who gave me their help during my original fieldwork. I owe a profound debt to Hatijah Hussin, Senawi Bakar, Hasnah Senawi, and to Bahador Nanyan. Wazir Jahan Karim sponsored my research, and gave her encouragement and enthusiasm on the many occasions when I was in danger of losing mine. I am grateful to her and to others then at Universiti Sains Malaysia, in particular, Otome Hutheesing, Razha Rashid, Jean de Bernardi, Cornelius Simoons, and members of the KANITA project for their advice and support. The School of Comparative Social Sciences at the university generously provided facilities which enabled me to work in the most productive and pleasant surroundings. Fahariah Wahab and her family gave me the pleasure of their hospitality in Kuala Lumpur. I owe a special debt to Zainol Che Din in Langkawi for introducing me into the village, providing welcome respites, and giving me the benefit of his good humour and perceptive insights on many occasions. Farzin Bakar and the late Che Rus Kassim assisted me in the collection of a household census and other data.

On my return to Malaysia in 1988, I once again drew on the support of Wazir Jahan Karim and Razha Rashid. I was given help and advice on the historical aspects of this work by Cheah Boon Kheng of the Department of History, and Khoo Kay Jin of the School of Social Sciences, at Universiti Sains Malaysia. I also had many thought-provoking and enjoyable discussions with Robert McKinley. The material on history of migration was collected with the help of Sharifah Masniah, Ibrahim Takip, and Cik Jamaliyah, who were then third-year history students at Universiti Sains Malaysia.

I am grateful to both the Socio-Economic Research Unit of the Prime Minister's Department (SERU) and the State Government of Kedah for permitting this work to be carried out. The original research was supported by a Social Science Research Council (now ESRC) studentship. Additional funds were provided by the Central Research Fund of the University of London. My second fieldwork was financed by grants from the Evans Fund of the University of Cambridge, the Wenner–Gren Foundation for Anthropological Research, and the British Academy. Final revisions of the manuscript were carried out during the tenure of a Poste Rouge at the Institut de Recherche sur le Sud-Est Asiatique (IRSEA—UMR 9962) of the Centre National de la Recherche Scientifique and the Université de Provence. I am indebted to all these institutions for making this research possible.

In places, I have drawn on previously published material. I am grateful to the Royal Anthropological Institute of Great Britain and Ireland, the American Anthropological Association, and the publishers and editors of the following articles for permission to make use of them here: 'Cooking Money: Gender and the Symbolic Transformation of Means of Exchange in a Malay Fishing Community', in J. P. Parry and M. Bloch (eds.), *Money and the Morality of Exchange* (Cambridge: Cambridge University Press, 1989). 'Children in between: Fostering and the Process of Kinship on Pulau Langkawi, Malaysia', *Man* (NS) 26: 425–43, 1991. 'The Substance of Kinship and the Heat of the Hearth: Feeding, Personhood and Relatedness among Malays in Pulau Langkawi', *American Ethnologist*, 22 (2): 223–41, 1995 (copyright American Anthropological Association, 1995). 'The Politics of Forgetting: Migration, Kinship and Memory on the Periphery of the Southeast Asian State', *Journal of the Royal Anthropological Institute* (NS) 1: 317–35, 1995.

Fellow postgraduate students, and members of staff of the Department of Anthropology at the London School of Economics have been a constant source of encouragement, intellectual stimulus, and supportive friendship—both during the writing of the thesis and since. I am especially grateful to Tom Gibson, Michael Stewart, and Maria Phylactou.

Sally Laird, Paul Laird, and Charles Stafford made contributions which have gone well beyond the normal expectations of friendship. Nicholas Wright and David Lan housed me in the south of France while I wrote the final chapters, and David Lan read and commented on a draft of the Introduction. I am grateful to all of them.

I owe to Akis Papataxiarchis a particular debt too complex to record here. Those readers who have a knowledge of Greek ethnography may detect some of his influence in my rendering of Malay personhood.

My colleagues in the Department of Anthropology at the University of Manchester generously gave me a term off teaching in 1990 to write this book. But between 1989 and 1993 all of them in different ways also contributed their support and intellectual stimulation. The difference between this book and my thesis is in a large part a measure of that. In Manchester I also drew on the support, interest, and suggestions of John Pickstone. For her constant encouragement during this period, I am particularly indebted to Marilyn Strathern, whose influence on my thinking (often silently incorporated) will be evident to readers familiar with her work.

Finally, I come to the obligations of which I am most deeply conscious because making a return would be quite impossible. Ruth and Francis Carsten gave their constant support, material and moral, over many years of research and writing. They are a part of this work in more ways than I could possibly have imagined when I began it. Jonathan Spencer meticulously edited a draft of the manuscript. His creative expertise and clarity of thought helped to bring an unruly and amorphous creature into shape. I am grateful to him for that, and for much else besides.

Maurice Bloch, who supervised my thesis, has given his unstinting encouragement, support, and inspiration at every stage. Like the very best of teachers, he has enabled me to go beyond what I was taught.

In order to protect people's privacy, I have with great regret used pseudonyms for villagers throughout this book, and disguised the identity of the village where I conducted fieldwork. Many people in Langkawi tolerated my intrusive presence with good humour, patience, and hospitality. My thanks to them are anonymous but no less deeply felt for that. My warmest appreciation goes to my foster mother, *mak*, and to her family for allowing me into their domestic life and for teaching me what it means to be a proper daughter in Malay terms. They and many others responded to their uninvited guest with imagination, warmth, and humour. This is their story. I hope they would not be embarrassed or ashamed by the way I have told it.

CONTENTS

LIST OF PLATES

LIST OF FIGURES

LIST OF MAPS

NOTE ON ORTHOGRAPHY

This study uses a number of Malay terms which are given in italics in the text. Malays in Langkawi normally speak in Kedah dialect. Unless otherwise stated, the Malay terms in the text follow these local usages. Spellings are in accordance with the conventions of Standard Malay (as set out in the supplement to Teuku Iskandar's 1970 *Kamus Dewan*).

Introduction

Langkawi Island (*Pulau Langkawi*) is situated about thirty miles off the west coast of Malaysia, just south of the Thai border. Some of the most vivid images from beginning my fieldwork there in 1980 are of the many everyday occurrences for young women inside a Malay house. Being left to look after a small baby during the daytime; taking a midday meal of rice and fish on the floor of the kitchen with my foster family; being sent to make the coffee when unexpected visitors arrive; the intense heat of houses in the middle of the day; the quiet, easy familiarity of the cooler evenings when friends and neighbours drop by for a chat and a betel quid. The joking, story-telling, and affection between women of one house and their immediate neighbours while they attend to household tasks; their unpleasant quarrels and recriminations. The men's comings and goings from fishing, the coffee-shop, or the mosque; older ones perched on the edge of a doorsill cutting dried *nipah* leaves for cigarettes; younger men engaging in jocular banter on their less frequent appearances. The quiet of night when children drop to the floor and are carefully covered to protect them from mosquitoes; adults of the house eventually taking their regular sleeping places among them.

These, on the whole peaceful and pleasant, images from more than ten years ago are accompanied still today by a more unnerving and powerful sensation of claustrophobia and intrusion. The absence of privacy was more than just that; it was a feeling of being taken over and controlled, of having every gesture and movement monitored and corrected. Clothing changed and adjusted; eating habits altered; bathing and toilet habits checked. A never-ending round of commentary, re-education, and improvement that left my senses battered and identity assaulted. An overwhelming sense of powerlessness—this is the most vivid and painful memory from those first months of life in a Malay house.

The tension between the warmth and intimacy that life with a family afforded and the more negative feelings of lack of control over what was happening to me is at the heart of this book. The experience of fieldwork encouraged me to focus on what might be called the 'anthropology of

Map 1. Southeast Asia

1. Becoming kin: child and her maternal great-grandmother sitting on a house ladder

everyday life'—on the house and the everyday and seemingly unmarked activities that take place within houses, such as eating a meal or looking after children. These activities involve women and what I have called the process of kinship—that is, feeding, hospitality, exchanges, marriage, children, fostering, and grandparenthood—all the ways in which Malay people on the island of Langkawi become kin. Kinship and personhood in Langkawi have to be understood in processual terms. Identity is always mutable and fluid; it is both given at birth through ties of procreation, but perhaps more importantly, it is also acquired throughout life by living together in one house and sharing food. Notions about bodily substance, in which blood is central, stress the changeability and fluidity of blood, which is altered through the consumption of different foods. Eating together creates shared blood, that is, kinship.

The closest of kin are siblings, and mothers and their children, who share blood to a remarkable degree. But others can become kin too. The birth of children in Langkawi creates a consanguineal link between their two sets of grandparents; long-term fostering relations (which are common) eventually lead to the foster child sharing substance with its foster family and coming to acquire their physical characteristics together with close emotional ties. The long process of becoming kin in Langkawi is thus one in which I myself was involved, albeit unwittingly, from the first days in which I lived with a family as a foster daughter.

At the end of 1988, after nearly seven years' absence, I returned to Langkawi for four months further fieldwork focusing on the history of migration. After writing my thesis, I was aware that the activities and ideas that I described there laid remarkable stress on incorporation. Hospitality, exchanges, marriage, and having children could all be considered as means of incorporation, of making people similar. The paradox I uncovered was that this stress on conformity and similarity has its roots in a history of diversity and difference.

What my second fieldwork revealed was the striking degree of demographic mobility in Langkawi. In almost every house people recalled recent ancestors who had come from mainland Malaysia, Thailand, or Indonesia. Many life histories involved several moves back and forth between the mainland and Langkawi. Just as striking as the extent of this mobility was its 'invisibility'. Not only are present-day inhabitants of the island whose recent ancestors have come from elsewhere quite indistinguishable in their dialect, dress, or house styles from each other, so too are most of those who have themselves migrated to Langkawi. The processes of incorporation at work are highly effective; the conformity in patterns of behaviour very great. And women's activities which are at the heart of this incorporative process have a particular 'political' significance in this context. It is through these activities that village communities are established and reproduce themselves. In this way, I have come to understand the sense of lack of control which characterized my own experience of life as a foster daughter as part of a more general process of 'coercive incorporation' through which outsiders of diverse origins are transformed into kin who are thought of as essentially similar. These are the themes running through this book. I elucidate them through the particular example of one village in Langkawi which I came to know well. I have called this village 'Sungai Cantik'.

Living in Sungai Cantik

Fieldwork is always a complex process of interaction. The variable course it takes depends on both the culture and preconceptions of the fieldworker and those of the people she lives amongst. The preferences which shaped the way I was to work were naïvely idealistic—but probably no more so than for most young graduate students whose ideas and training are based in the post-colonial era and who are quick to criticize the methods of their anthropological predecessors. I was anxious to minimize the distance between myself and those I was to study, to integrate myself as far as possible into village life, to cultivate informal modes of inquiry, and to live among Malay villagers much as they themselves lived. Above all, I wished to perform everyday domestic tasks myself rather than have them performed for me, and to be treated by villagers without deference and in a spirit of equality.

I could not have foreseen the manner in which these desires were to be met or the particular preconceptions which governed the way in which the Malay villagers I lived amongst accepted or tolerated my presence. The cultural logic which I believe lies behind the way I was received is one that I unpack in the following chapters. In Chapter 9 I address the issue of my own experience in Langkawi directly, and link it to the processes of kinship and history which are described in this book. However, my own understanding of these processes was acquired slowly and painfully—much of it after I had finished my initial fieldwork.

I was introduced into Sungai Cantik by a young man who held a clerical post in the local hospital, and who had close friendships with a large family in the village. The house of this family was already crowded, and they in turn recommended me to their kin in a neighbouring house. It was agreed I would lodge and take my meals there in return for a small rent. The family, whose income and standing were in the middle to upper range of the village, comprised an elderly couple, their married daughter and husband, and the daughter's three young children. I was to become 'foster daughter' (*anak angkat*) to the senior couple. The young son-in-law was the chief income earner of the household, his father-in-law being no longer strong enough to go fishing. Over time, I developed a particularly close attachment to my foster mother. I accompanied her as she cultivated the family's rice fields and vegetable garden and in her round of social visits, and under her supervision I learnt about Malay culture and about the proper behaviour expected of a young adult daughter.

I had anticipated a struggle to gain acceptance on terms which fitted my own ideological stance, but the reality was very different. The more closely my mode of life conformed to the ideals of behaviour for young Malay women, the better pleased were those I lived with. Living together with a family of seven (which grew to eight when my foster sister gave birth soon after my arrival) in a two-room house, there was little chance of privacy or secrets on either side. Nor was there a struggle to become integrated or to be treated without deference. On the contrary, I quickly found myself subject to the kind of behavioural constraints befitting the modesty of a young Malay woman. Such constraints often seemed a

2. The author at a rice-harvesting

hindrance to my mobility and my ability to carry out anthropological fieldwork. Similarly, I was strongly encouraged to perform all the normal tasks of household work—cleaning, laundering clothes, drawing water at the well, washing dishes, minding babies, as well as agricultural labour in the rice fields and vegetable gardens. My relationship with my foster mother and with the senior woman and her adult daughters in the neighbouring house to which I had originally been introduced grew emotionally close during my eighteen months in the village. The two senior women would not hesitate to tell me how to behave or to give me instructions about domestic tasks.

On the whole, I welcomed the chance to learn about women's labour through participation, although at times I found the less sociable tasks tedious and the behavioural constraints demanded by Malay etiquette irksome. I learnt the hard way that there were limits to my own desire or capacity to integrate myself into village life. A failure to live up to my own idealistic expectations often left me depressed and lonely. It was partly to alleviate such feelings that I returned for a few days every month to Penang, where I made use of university facilities and drew upon the support of academic colleagues and friends.

After I had lived in the village for about six months, I was visited by my Ph.D. supervisor. The visit was timely because it occurred at a point when I was becoming quite anxious about my inadequacies as a fieldworker. It is a mark of my own naïvety that I was utterly astonished to be told that I was unusually integrated into domestic life, that anthropological research does not necessarily involve living in such close proximity to those one studies, and that it may even be carried out through interpreters and with the help of assistants. While I felt I was unable to live up to the standards of proper participant observation (with the emphasis on participation), my supervisor became anxious that I was becoming too caught up in domestic processes to be able to carry out research properly. The visit was a kind of turning-point in that it marked a first step in putting my own preconceptions into perspective as well as beginning a long process of reflection on the kind of relationships that were developing between people in Sungai Cantik and myself.

In the months that followed, I developed a network of friends and foster kin (mainly but not exclusively through the connections of my foster mother) whose houses I would visit regularly on an informal basis. I became close to the women in about half a dozen houses, and would feel comfortable sitting chatting with them and asking them about their lives and work. In these houses I was treated in a relaxed and open way. Women of different ages would sit together gossiping, chewing betel, and taking snacks sometimes more or less ignoring my presence, sometimes answering my direct questions about labour in the rice fields, marriage, childbirth, or whatever. On the whole, I found middle-aged and older women to be more informative than younger ones on matters in which I was interested. Four or five women over 40 (including my foster mother) became particular favourites, and I learnt which of them enjoyed talking about different topics—marriage, labour arrangements, sentiments of kinship, etc., and would go to these 'specialists' for particular kinds of instruction. But I also visited a much wider circle of households on a more irregular basis, and in these I might or might not be treated in a more formal manner. I very rarely conducted formal interviews or used a tape recorder but all my conversations were conducted in the vernacular—my own highly imperfect Malay quite quickly came to acquire the tones of the local Kedah dialect.

Although the circle of people whom I knew well seemed relatively narrow, I was familiar enough with a number of households to judge that the representativeness of what I record here was not a major problem. I checked details of what I learnt with different people in different houses, and there were many women who were comfortable enough in my presence to give me frank opinions about particular practices or people. Indeed, several older women who knew me well often gave me small lectures on particular topics, demanding that I write things down, and then drilling me to make sure I had properly understood or scolding me when I clearly had not. I also accompanied my foster mother and other kin on visits to other villages in Langkawi on numerous occasions when they might be visiting relatives, helping with agricultural labour, or attending a wedding.

While I got to know a variety of women of different ages and incomes, my familiarity with men in the village was more restricted. As I have emphasized, what is written here is on the whole gained from conversations with women. However, I was on relatively relaxed terms with the men in the household in which I lived and in a few other houses, and these men would often participate in conversations with me. I also had frequent conversations with several of the male village elders. In this way, I gained a more rounded impression of relations between men and women but my knowledge of relations between men is restricted to what I could witness or learn about indirectly and is certainly more fragmentary. I did not spend time in the coffee-shops, and only once went out on a fishing trip.

Towards the end of my first fieldwork, I conducted a household survey of sixty houses in the village with the help of two local assistants. I had not previously used assistants in the field, and the purpose of this survey was to acquire more general information about residence and marriage patterns. I decided to use male assistants, partly because of my restricted access to matters pertaining to men in the village, but also because the young women whom I knew would have been too shy to conduct the inquiries I had in mind. The first of these assistants, Che Rus Kassim, who died tragically in a motorcycle accident not long after we began work, was a young man who had recently completed training as a teacher and was awaiting employment. The second, Farzin Bakar, had finished secondary school, and was recommended to me as not too shy to ask women about their households and marital histories. Before returning to Britain in 1982, I also spent one week in a village in mainland Kedah for comparative purposes.

In 1988–9 I returned to Malaysia for four months to conduct research on historical migration in Langkawi. For part of this time I again used assistants. But this time, because I wished to take quite detailed and standardized household migration histories, I gained the help of three undergraduates in history studying at Universiti Sains Malaysia. Together we interviewed married couples in 110 households about their family migration histories using interview schedules. During this visit I also spent a considerable time in conversation with a village midwife, and collected quite a lot of the material on childbirth presented in Chapter 4.

I began this Introduction by describing my most vivid memories of the early months of fieldwork in Sungai Cantik. These memories encapsulate a contrast between the warmth and intimacy afforded by being inside a house and an intense feeling of suffocation and lack of control. In time, I came to see this contrast as at the heart of my research and of the themes which I develop here. I return to it again in Chapter 9, where I discuss the historical process of incorporation more generally, and place my own experience in the context of this kinship and history.

Langkawi in Southeast Asia

The village of Sungai Cantik is a large coastal community composed of several sub-villages whose boundaries are somewhat unclear. The village is densely populated; its houses are of various styles and materials (mainly wooden and raised on posts), built close to each other in compounds which are connected to each other by a network of paths. The houses in compounds often face inwards, towards each other, and the area between them is one where children play and where neighbourhood women congregate and chat when they are not at work. Coconut trees are planted close to houses—they are a distinctive marker of any rural Malay settlement and provide an essential ingredient in local cuisine. Otherwise, the area close to houses is used for keeping chickens and ducks, small rice granaries, and wells for bathing and washing clothes. At most times of day (except the early afternoon when people tend to nap indoors) this area is lively with women performing domestic tasks, children running about, and neighbours chatting to each other.

The commercial area of the village is situated near the seafront. Here there are numerous 'sundry shops' and coffee-shops, as well as a barber's, and the premises of the Chinese middlemen who are prominent in buying and reselling local fish. This is the area of the village where men who are not out fishing tend to meet—taking drinks and snacks in the coffee-shops or chatting to each other outside the barber's shop. Women tend to come and go rather quickly with a particular errand in view.

In 1980 Sungai Cantik's population numbered about 3,000; the great majority of these were Malays. The village economy is extensively monetized. The occupation of most men and the main source of cash for most families was fishing. Much of the fish was destined for export to the mainland and to Singapore. Some Chinese families lived in Sungai Cantik, where they worked as shopkeepers and middlemen. They had very little social interaction outside their commercial relations with Malay villagers. Many Malay villagers grew rice for home consumption as well as some fruit and vegetables. This agricultural activity was dominated by women.

The village has experienced profound demographic change during this century. Its population has expanded rapidly: maps of the area show Sungai Cantik as a small settlement in the 1940s. Increase in population has resulted in an extremely dense pattern of housing by rural Malay standards and a fragmentation of landholdings. In the early 1980s there were no big landowners in the village and very few people owned enough land to sell surplus rice. The economy of the village was based primarily on fishing and secondarily on rice cultivation. Many households grew enough rice to meet their subsistence needs, either wholly or in part, although some owned no rice land at all.

Langkawi Island is an administrative district (*daerah*) of the mainland state of Kedah, with a population of 28,340 in 1980.[1] The Malay population of Langkawi is bound economically, socially, and politically to the mainland. While agricultural activities in the early 1980s were mainly concerned with subsistence, the local market for fish absorbed only a small proportion of the produce. Fish were exported, mainly through the intervention of Chinese middlemen, to Penang and Singapore. Further, almost all adolescent men spent the years between leaving school and marriage engaged in migrant work on the fishing trawlers that operated from the mainland coast of Kedah. Occasionally adolescent women too worked as domestic servants or factory workers on the mainland.

The steady flow of traffic to and from the mainland reflects villagers' multiple links with peninsular society. The state capital of Kedah is Alor Setar, where the state government offices and regional headquarters are located. Villagers from Langkawi with administrative or legal problems often have cause to visit these. But visits to the mainland often have more sociable aims: weddings, the birth of a child, funerals, or just a desire to spend time with kin, regularly cause women and men, often accompanied by children, to travel to distant villages and towns on the peninsula and spend time there. The local population in Langkawi is bound through ties of kinship with far-flung communities on the mainland.

Economically significant activities on Langkawi in the early 1980s included tourism, marble-quarrying, and private rubber plantations worked by ethnic Indians, all of which were restricted to the eastern side of the island. In the early 1980s tourism was a small but growing part of the island economy. On the whole it impinged very little on the lives of the people I lived with. Tourists at that time were lodged in a few hotels in the main town of the island, Kuah, about fifteen miles from Sungai Cantik. Since that period, the Malaysian government has encouraged tourist development on an intensive scale in Langkawi. The effects of this were evident in 1989. By that time, several large hotels had been built around the coast (some of which had been abandoned while still unfinished), new roads crossed the island, and other development projects were planned. Perhaps most significant of all was the inflation in land prices. Land on the coast which had previously been of little economic value was now a precious commodity.

The significance of these developments can hardly be overestimated.

[1] Jabatan Perangkaan Malaysia (June 1984: 49).

Apart from the profound shift in the island's economic base, the influx of people, and the new cultural influences, the inflation in the price of land might be expected to directly alter relations between villagers. In this book I describe how villagers tend to phrase their relations with each other in an idiom of equality, and I link this to long-term historical processes in the region. In the early 1980s Sungai Cantik villagers characterized themselves as poor people and as fishing people in contrast to mainland rice-growers or urban workers. Ownership of land and its inheritance was not a means for wealth differences to become entrenched and perpetuated. Tourism will profoundly alter villagers' relationship to land and to each other as very marked wealth differences come between them. In 1989 the beginnings of these effects could be felt. In the future it remains to be seen whether coastal communities such as Sungai Cantik manage to persist in anything like the form described here or whether their inhabitants will be forced to succumb to the logic of development plans and move to a new location altogether.

The main fieldwork on which this book is based took place before the Malaysian government's development plans were put into effect. Most of the material presented here is drawn from the early 1980s. Unless otherwise stated, my use of the ethnographic present refers to that time, and should not be taken to imply a timeless and unchanging order. In the circumstances which villagers in Langkawi face today that would be highly misleading. An account of the effects of tourism on Langkawi is one worth telling but it must be the subject of another volume (see Bird 1989 for a preliminary account).

The History of Incorporation

Three themes emerge very clearly in the chapters which follow. The first is that of incorporation. Langkawi people are not necessarily born kin, but may become so. Kinship is a process of becoming, not a fixed state. The process is brought about through a variety of means which include feeding, living together, fostering, and marriage. Through these processes people gradually become kin to each other; they become similar. At the core of these ideas is a model of incorporation: difference which marks the outside world can be negated by subsuming it to, and incorporating it into, the uniformity and similarity which constitute domestic life.

The second theme which I stress is the prominence of women and of houses (with which women are strongly associated) in practical and symbolic elaborations of kinship. Women's centrality is not only very marked in domestic organization, it also applies to wider neighbourhood and village groupings which are in many respects also modelled on the house. The symbolic reproduction of the community occurs largely through activities in which women dominate. The prominence of women must be understood as part of the emphasis on incorporation. Or, put another way, women's activities are to a great extent the means by which this incorporation occurs.

The third theme can be understood as an effect of the emphasis on incorporation. People in Langkawi place a strong emphasis on equality. In many ways and contexts they stress their similarity to each other and deny the differences between them. However much they recognize the salience of political and economic realities which may seem to divide them, people in Sungai Cantik always assert their kinship to each other in terms of shared substance, attributes, and way of life.

The problems with which I am concerned here involve not only a description of the way these three themes are elaborated in Langkawi and of the interconnections between them. I am also concerned with explanations of why these themes should emerge so strongly in an account of Langkawi kinship. I seek to understand the historical conditions in which they have developed. For while aspects of kinship in Langkawi fall within a broad range of Southeast Asian patterns, they are also historically and geographically specific—they have their own particularity.

In looking to history to 'explain' the phenomena I describe, I am aligning myself with a growing number of anthropologists who have given a major historical dimension to their work. Anthropologists such as Rosaldo (1980), Wolf (1982), Bloch (1986), and Dirks (1987) have shown the fruitfulness of combining history with anthropology. While history can never be said to begin at a zero point, anthropologists may at least shed light on their subject by tracing the historical conditions for the emergence of present phenomena. In most cases this task is constrained by the evidence available and the capacities and time of the researcher. This is certainly true in the present case.

Most of the historical material which I present in Chapter 9 is history from the point of view of the people of Sungai Cantik as they remember it. Put another way, it is the history of their kinship. As anthropologists from Evans-Pritchard (1940) on the Nuer to Peter Gow (1991) on Amazonia have pointed out, for many people time and history are understood in the idiom of kinship and ideas about relatedness.[2] In Langkawi the symbolization of kinship is seen in terms of the erasing of difference, the construction of similarity. In the nineteenth century Langkawi was a 'frontier' region of the Malay state of Kedah, geographically and politically peripheral to the centres of power on the mainland. In Chapter 9 I use family histories to show how, from the late nineteenth century onwards (and probably for very much longer than that), peasants have migrated to Langkawi motivated by poverty, land shortage, heavy taxation, and warfare on the mainland, or simply a desire, familiar from other Southeast Asian societies, to move about (see, for example, Freeman 1970; Kato 1982). In the outlying regions of hierarchical Malay states land was relatively abundant, and the social order was characteristically more egalitarian; peasants were less constrained by the exactions of their superiors (see Banks 1983; Sharom 1984; Kratoska 1985; Cheah 1988).

The extent of population mobility is very great. Almost every family that was interviewed had members who had migrated from the mainland, or back and forth between the mainland and Langkawi, in the recent past. Many had several ancestors who had done so over a number of generations. There is enormous variation in geographic origins of the present-day population of Sungai Cantik. While certain localities appear frequently in villagers' accounts, what is more surprising is the size of the area involved: mainland Kedah, Penang, Siam and present-day Thailand, Aceh, Melaka, the east coast of Malaysia, more distant parts of Indonesia are all mentioned. This then is truly regional migration operating on a pan-Southeast Asian scale. It recalls Braudel's (1976) classic analysis of another renowned trading region of the world, the Mediterranean (see Coedès 1968; Reid 1988; Wolters 1982).

Another striking feature of the history of migration to Langkawi is more paradoxical. In spite of the diversity of their origins, what people stress about themselves is their similarity. They endlessly assert 'we are all kin here, we are all the same'. These statements are borne out in behaviour to a remarkable degree. Not only did I fail to detect differences of origin in accent, dress, or comportment (which I at first put down to my own lack

[2] Peter Gow has written of the people of the Bajo Urubamba river of the Peruvian Amazon, 'For native people, history is kinship. History is not experienced by native people as a force which enters from outside to disrupt a timeless structure of kinship duties and obligations. Kinship relations are created and dissolved in historical time, and historical time draws its meaning and power for native people by being structured by kinship relations' (Gow 1991: 3). Although geographically far from the Amazon, ways of thinking about and enacting kinship in Langkawi show some surprising similarities with those of the people of the Bajo Urubamba.

Map 2. Peninsular Malaysia

of sensitivity to local variations), but the Malaysian students who assisted me in my research on the history of migration had the same experience. Incorporation is a rapid process in Langkawi; people do not cling to regional customs or attributes.

The rapid erasing of differences of origin leads to obvious difficulties in conducting such research. People's memory of where their ancestors have come from is short once these ancestors are dead. Such information has little importance to them. This brings to mind the 'structural amnesia' which Freeman (1961) long ago associated with cognatic kinship and which has often been noted by other Southeast Asian ethnographers. Even if local people can remember where their own parents and grandparents came from, they are usually quite unaware that their neighbours originate from anywhere other than Langkawi. However, rather than seeing this as a simple absence of knowledge, I understand it as the outcome of a particular interweaving of kinship and history in which the emphasis is not on where people have come from in the past, but on the process of transforming them into Langkawi people in the present and future.

I have already said that the process of incorporation occurs through feeding, fostering, and marriage and having children—often these are stages by which strangers can be gradually transformed into kin. In Chapter 7 I show how marriage in Langkawi is thought to occur between people who are 'close' (*dekat*). This may be in terms of kinship—although people are always ambivalent about the advantages of marrying close kin. The notion of closeness conflates genealogical relatedness, geographic proximity, similarity of backgrounds, appearance, and attributes. In the end, people who are 'close' are people who are similar and therefore well matched. Through this notion of endogamy, people who marry each other become kin whether or not they were so previously. The idea that like marries like, that people should marry those they are close to, has clearly been historically significant in the creation of a community of people who, in spite of their diverse origins, conceive themselves to be similar to each other.

There are other practical realities behind the symbolic elaborations of kinship in Langkawi. One of the most important factors motivating migration to Langkawi both today and in the past has been poverty. Many migrants have come to Langkawi because of a shortage of rice land. In Sungai Cantik the main means of gaining a livelihood is fishing, with rice cultivation providing an important source of subsistence. In comparison with rice-growing villages on the mainland, the emphasis on equality in Langkawi is very marked. This may be attributable to the fact that fishing does not entail the entrenchment of economic differentiation through the inheritance of land which is a prominent feature of mainland agricultural communities (see, for example, Scott 1985). Economic differentiation does of course occur in Langkawi; however, it is clear from villagers' accounts that an absence of large landholdings, and the fact that most villagers were engaged in small-scale fishing, has contributed to their perception of themselves as 'poor people' (*orang susah*), without significant property.

These historical circumstances have resulted in an image of the outside world as divisive and threatening. In the past Langkawi may have appeared as a refuge where it was possible to gain a living relatively free from the demands imposed by Malay chiefs or colonial authorities. Today the state is more intrusive. In Chapter 5 I discuss how Langkawi people view the outside world as fragmented and fragmenting. Within Langkawi it is men rather than women who are associated with the divisiveness of the outside world. Fishing involves men in competitive exchange relations with each other. It also involves them in dealings with Chinese middlemen and the Malaysian state over the sale of fish for export, the negotiation of loans, obtaining licences, and taxation. Men also involve themselves far more than women in local political activities. Politics not only associates them with party organizations which are often closely associated with the state and with practices that are regarded by many as corrupt, it also involves them in local disputes. Political differences in Malaysia are often articulated in a religious idiom, and it is significant that men's political activities often turn into disputes over religious orthodoxy. Women and men associate politics with divisiveness within the village.

The Political Implications of Gendered Domains

The historical and contemporary features of life which I have outlined give women's activities their particular significance. However, this book is not just an ethnography of women in Langkawi. Gender differences in Langkawi, as in many other Southeast Asian societies, are in fact remarkably unelaborated (see Atkinson and Errington 1990). Malay women, like women elsewhere in Southeast Asia (see van Esterik 1982), are known for their high status and 'autonomy'.[3] Compared to some other regions of the world, the differences between men and women are not to any great extent the basis of other classificatory schemes. Age, rank, and class are more important markers of social difference than gender (see Wazir Jahan Karim 1992). Gender is not a particular problem for people in Langkawi. In fact, I would argue that it is partly *because* gender difference is not especially problematic for those concerned that the things women do can emerge as central to the political process.

The everyday tasks in which women engage: cooking a meal, looking after children, running the house, visiting their neighbours and affines, calling on the sick and the dying, cultivating rice, organizing rotating credit associations, arranging marriages, attending communal feasts, do not simply reflect their engagement in domestic organization. Because men's activities are associated with an external and fragmenting world, women come to have a centrality that is not purely domestic. It is true that the tasks mentioned above are all associated with domestic reproduction and with the house. However, the house itself is not simply a domestic unit. In the context I have described, the house has a communal and political significance which goes beyond what anthropologists conventionally label 'the domestic'. One representation of the community is in fact that of an enlarged house, a group of people who are all related to each other and who eat food together. When women carry out their everyday activities they reproduce the wider community as much as the domestic hearth. Further, the process of incorporation which I describe, and which is crucial to the construction of an image of community composed of similar people who are united against a threatening and divisive external world, is one that occurs very largely through the actions of women. Feeding, fostering, marriage, and having children are all processes in which women dominate.

These are circumstances in which the women's activities rather than men's are central to the symbolic reproduction of the community. Men may dominate in the fishing economy, and in political and religious activities, but these are all processes that have their focus outside the village.

[3] Rudie (1993) has a sensitive discussion of the problematic implications of the term 'autonomy'. She stresses how in a Western context female autonomy implies 'free-floating, culturally "complete" and potentially single individuals', while in the Malay context women may seem 'autonomous' in relation to their husbands but nevertheless gain their 'most basic identity as complementary family persons' (1993: 103). I would strongly support the view that women are thoroughly embedded in kin relationships. On the other hand, because of the importance of siblingship in Langkawi, I hesitate to describe kinship there as 'matrifocal' as H. Geertz (1961) and Tanner (1974) have suggested for other Southeast Asian societies.

Because of Langkawi's history and geographic peripherality, and the fact that fishing is primarily for export and that rice production and consumption (to which women are central) are far more significant in the symbolic economy of the village, men are not the symbolic reproducers of their society in Langkawi as they are elsewhere in Southeast Asia (see, for example, Freeman 1970; Kahn 1980). On the contrary, the activities they engage in are often seen as divisive and potentially threatening.

In the most important of village rituals, the marriage feast, which I describe in Chapter 6, men, women, and children eat a large rice meal together. The everyday domestic meal is transformed into a communal event. The boundaries between different houses and their inhabitants are negated as the community projects itself as a single expansive domestic hearth which keeps the external world at bay. This 'domesticated' community does of course include men; it is a world composed of men and women. But gender differences are not particularly significant in this symbolic community.

Women's prominence in the symbolism of social reproduction has complex historical and social roots which perhaps have little to do with issues of gender *per se*. However, this does not mean that the contemporary forms of this symbolism and the conditions which have produced them will not be of interest to feminist scholars. On the contrary, my argument is central to feminist concerns. Examples of societies in which women's activities are given symbolic prominence are rare enough in the anthropological literature. My account goes beyond this: I show how these activities may be linked to wider political and historical processes, and why they must be understood as central to these processes rather than of peripheral interest. The complex interrelationship that Malay *adat* (custom), and the bilateral principles enshrined in it, have historically developed with Islam, and the effect of this articulation on women and Malay culture, have recently been examined by Wazir Jahan Karim. The present study bears out her conclusion that 'Malay women in history were not passive receivers of authority; they were active participants of the political process' (Karim 1992: 220).

In showing that the actions of women in Langkawi are symbolically elaborated in particular ways that go beyond their 'domestic' importance, I would, of course, challenge the division that anthropologists often assume to exist between the 'domestic' and 'political' domains. Not only can we say that in Langkawi what is commonly labelled 'domestic' has a 'political' import, but the very definition of these two spheres is called into question. In the context described here, are visiting between female affines, offering hospitality to a stranger, or fostering an unrelated child domestic or political acts? Like Yanagisako (1979; 1987), Strathern (1984), and Moore (1988), I would suggest that while the division between the domestic and the political may be central to Western thought and to anthropological analysis, we cannot assume this division to exist in the same way in the societies anthropologists study. In the Southeast Asian cases examined by Karim (1992), Rudie (1994), and Wikan (1990) this division has been shown to be particularly problematic.

A focus on things which women do and views which women hold leads me to suggest that we cannot predict either the meaning or the significance of seemingly simple domestic acts. In the historical conditions that have produced contemporary social organization in Langkawi these acts have come to be valued in particular ways. I believe this may well be true in other contexts. I hope this book will encourage all anthropologists, not just Southeast Asianists, kinship specialists, or feminists, to reconsider the value of what we claim to know best. Throughout the book I try to show how central processes of social life can be discerned in the apparently mundane details of everyday activities.

A new approach to the ethnography of so-called domestic life and everyday activities, to the unformalized and non-ritualized aspects of life that anthropologists sometimes ignore because they assume they know their meaning, may not only prove ethnographically refreshing. Bloch (1991) has argued that, in ignoring everyday knowledge and practices, anthropologists privilege certain other kinds of knowledge and behaviour, thereby exoticizing their subject and contributing to a misleading view of cognitive processes. The argument is relevant not just in terms of certain actors and activities which have tended to be less visible than others, but also has implications for the analysis of social space. Much of this book is concerned with what happens inside houses, with the symbolic elaboration of the house, and with what it means to be of one house in Langkawi. Houses, I have suggested, are not just domestic units. They are the sites of the incorporative process I have described, and they may come to symbolize the wider community.

Although there are several excellent accounts of Malay villages which focus on their political and economic life, and several more which focus on kinship and household organization, these aspects of social life have on the whole been treated as analytically distinct. Studies such as those of Firth (1966 [1946]), Wilson (1967), Syed Husin Ali (1975), Scott (1985), constitute a rich source of information on fishing and agricultural practices, property ownership and transmission, political and administrative structures and the way these are perceived and dealt with by Malay peasants. Some of these works and a number of other important studies address class antagonisms and local politics in a context of rapid economic and social change (Syed Husin Ali 1975; Rogers 1977, 1993; Scott 1985; Shamsul 1986; Wan Hashim 1978). The effects of the 'green revolution' on rice-growing peasants have been examined by Scott (1985) and by Wong (1987) amongst others, while Aihwa Ong (1987) has focused attention on the important issues raised by increasing capitalist penetration of the rural labour market and women's participation in factory work.

From the time of Rosemary Firth's (1966 [1943]) classic study of household organization onwards, there has also been a growing corpus of detailed information on the Malay household and kinship structures (see, for example, Djamour 1965; Wilder 1982; Banks 1983; Massard 1983*a*; Peletz 1988; Li 1989; Rudie 1994). It is clear from these studies that women occupy a central and dominant position within the home and are often economically active outside it. In these studies, however, the emotional texture of life within houses, or of relations between close kin, is not always easy to discern. Furthermore, studies of Southeast Asian societies in the 1950s and 1960s tended to see structural features of kinship as operating at the level of the household (see Murdock 1960). The connections between the 'domestic' world and the wider political or economic context have rarely been explored.

Many of the studies undertaken in the 1960s and 1970s assumed a division between the domestic and political rather than attempting to connect them. This approach, deriving from Fortes's (1958; 1969) classic formulations, has carried with it an implicit androcentrism. The 'domestic' is by definition the world of women, a world that is marginal to, and separated from, the political and economic spheres that are dominated by men. Even if women did seem remarkably dominant in their domestic lives (which was usually but not always acknowledged), it was difficult to attribute a wider significance to this.

A paradox in the study of Malay kinship is that, given Murdock's (1960) stress on the importance of the domestic group and the pioneering work carried out by Rosemary Firth, analysis of the way in which houses actually function and their symbolic significance has been quite fragmentary. This may in part be due to the fact that the house constitutes female space while many of the studies of Malay kinship have been carried out by male ethnographers. This can produce misleading results. In spite of the stimulating historical approach that Banks adopts in the introduction to his 1983 study, his ethnography is flawed by a strong male bias, which produces a picture of Malay society 'in which women play a subordinate, passive and nurturant role. They are deferential and shy in public, submissive in private' (1983: 68).[4] This image not only contradicts the observations of many other writers but also at times his own.[5] The lack of any systematic study of the symbolic and practical importance of the house in Malay rural society is also, I suspect, due to the tendency in anthropology, to which I referred above, to concentrate on the seemingly exotic and bizarre. Everyday spaces and activities are ignored because we assume we know their meaning.

This book is an attempt to restore some of these omissions. First, in describing life inside houses, I seek to capture the emotional resonance of everyday existence and of relations between people who are close to each other. It is this tenor of life which is often missing in anthropological accounts of kinship. Secondly, my account places women at the centre. But the world I describe is not so much the world of women as distinct from men. Rather, it is the world of women and men described from the point of view of women. For these worlds are not rigidly separated. Indeed, to a remarkable extent, men and women in Langkawi interact with each other in a friendly and relaxed spirit. And this spirit is part of what I seek to convey. Thirdly, then, I place the lack of separation between women's and men's worlds at the centre of the analysis. I connect the everyday activities of women with the wider political processes that have shaped life in Langkawi. I show how the significance of these activities is determined within a particular historical context.

In describing the way a Malay family sits down to a daily meal in Langkawi, or how the household furniture is arranged, or the kind of joking and teasing that occurs during co-operative rice-harvesting, I am describing a very internal world. This is not the one that formal visitors are allowed to see. It deserves to be written about in its own right. But its significance extends beyond the internal. That the domestic is political has become a feminist truism. But how and why that is the case within specific cultural contexts requires detailed investigation.

The approach I have adopted has also involved rethinking what anthropologists mean by kinship. I have tried to capture the texture of relations

[4] See also Banks (1983: 62–9; 88–104, 131, 132, 160).

[5] e.g. Banks (1983: 63, 89, 93, 99, 163). Koentjaraningrat (1960: 104) has observed how the custom of women retiring to the back of the house when strangers come gives foreigners 'the erroneous impression' that Javanese women have an inferior status in the household.

between those who live together, and to show how kinship, far from being an analytic abstraction, is part of the fabric of people's lives. Kinship is not a lifeless and pre-given force which in some mysterious way determines the form of people's relations with each other. On the contrary, it consists of the many small actions, exchanges, friendships and enmities that people themselves create in their everyday lives. For most people it is perhaps the heart of their creativity. But the content of these relations is not only continuously created anew, it is also shaped by long-term political processes. And this has also involved rethinking what kinship is—from a different angle.[6]

The kinship I describe here cannot be separated off from politics or economics or history but is embedded in them. The meanings of kinship cannot be separately analysed. This of course is another truism—this time of anthropology—but it is more often avowed than actually demonstrated. Since Fortes, we have been accustomed to assert these connections but then to describe domestic life as though it were a quite separate sphere. In this book I seek to demonstrate the connectedness between what goes on inside houses and the external world.

House Societies

Like other ethnographers of Southeast Asia, I have been struck by the centrality of the house to the social organization I describe. In trying to place this feature of Langkawi in its regional context, I have found Lévi-Strauss's writings on the house (1983*a*; 1983*b*; 1987) extremely helpful. Lévi-Strauss draws attention to the importance of the house as a native category in a variety of societies including the Kwakiutl, medieval Europe, feudal Japan, and various Southeast Asian groups. Bringing together material, social, and symbolic aspects of the house, he suggests that analysis of social organization and kinship in these societies has been hampered by the fact that anthropologists have tried to apply rigid analytical categories, such as 'lineage', rather than trying to understand them in indigenous terms.

Lévi-Strauss emphasizes the centrality of alliance in what he calls

[6] It seems to me that the evidence for Banks's assertion that Malay kinship in Sik is now 'in crisis' (1983: 174–7) due to excessive population pressure and a shortage of land, and, further, that it 'has acted as a residual structure of meaning, a remnant of a past reality that is no longer applicable' (1972: 1272) is questionable. I would argue that it is the malleability and adaptability of Malay kinship under different historical, economic, and social conditions that is one of its defining features.

'house-based societies'. Discussing Indonesian societies specifically, he argues that marriage is a principle both of unity and of antagonism where criteria such as descent, property, and residence, taken alone, are not sufficient for the constitution of groups. The married couple is both central to the house and also a source of tension between houses, since a lack of clear residence rules (a common feature of these societies) means that each marriage generates tension over where the couple will live. The house, then, 'transfixes' an unstable union, becoming '*the objectification of a relation*: the unstable relation of alliance which, as an institution, the house functions to solidify, if only in an illusory form' (1987: 155, original emphasis).

The centrality of the house as category, building, and social group in Langkawi is one of the main features of the analysis I present here. As Lévi-Strauss suggests, and as I show in Chapter 8, marriage in Langkawi is a tense and unstable relation, particularly in its initial phases—precisely when locality of residence is an issue. But conjugality is also a core principle of houses and is necessary for their establishment.

In spite of problems with Lévi-Strauss's analysis, in the regional context of Southeast Asia his ideas have clearly borne fruit.[7] Barraud (1979), Errington (1987; 1989), Macdonald (1987), Waterson (1990), and McKinnon (1991), amongst others, have taken up his approach and shown its usefulness in the study of specific societies and, perhaps even more significantly, have revealed its comparative potential.

Malay people of Langkawi conform to a familiar pattern in Southeast Asia. Their kinship is cognatic with broadly endogamous marriage; they are relatively egalitarian; women are characteristically rather independent. These and other features recall not only Malays elsewhere (Fraser 1960; Raymond Firth 1966; Rosemary Firth 1966; Djamour 1965; Syed Husin Ali 1975; Massard 1983*a*) as well as Javanese peasants (Hildred Geertz 1961; Jay 1969) but also other Southeast Asian cognatic groups which practise swidden cultivation, such as the Iban of Sarawak (Freeman 1970) or the Buid of Mindoro (Gibson 1986).

Amongst these cognatic, endogamous groups siblingship is central to notions of kinship (see Errington 1989). The significance of siblingship, however, has often been unemphasized or ignored in the ethnographic literature on Malays. Notable exceptions here include McKinley's (1975; 1981) brilliant analysis of kinship among urban Malays which I draw on in

[7] See Macdonald 1987; Carsten and Hugh-Jones 1995. For an attempt to apply these ideas to Langkawi, see Carsten 1987*b*; 1995*b*.

Chapter 3, and Peletz's (1988) meticulous historical study of the matrilineal Malays of Negeri Sembilan. Both these authors reject the characterization of Southeast Asian kinship as 'loosely structured' (Embree 1950) and underline the importance of siblingship rather than descent as a structuring principle. Both have shown the significance of child transfers and informal adoption, and how these must be understood in the context of close bonds between sisters. Siblingship is not simply an undifferentiated principle—ties between brothers differ markedly from those between sisters, or between cross-sex siblings (see also Bowen 1991; 1993 on the Gayo of Sumatra).

In Chapter 3 I show how siblingship is the core of kinship in Langkawi—taking logical precedence, I argue, over filiation. All relations may be traced back to a sibling tie, and siblingship embodies the core values of kinship morality. Siblingship above all connotes unity and similarity; more distant kin have these qualities to a weaker degree. Even relations between husbands and wives are modelled on those between older brother and younger sister. Marriage is thought of in the idiom of siblingship, and also produces new sets of siblings in the future. This concept of marriage always involves mild connotations of incest and is prone to tensions. One aspect of the power of siblingship relates to the process of incorporation I have referred to above. The qualities of siblingship may be more or less present, depending on the closeness of the relation; they are not simply present or absent, Strangers who come to live in Langkawi become kin through fostering and marriage which in turn imply siblingship.

Drawing together these features of kinship within a regional framework, I have found Errington's (1987; 1989) comparative model of Southeast Asian societies particularly useful. Errington discusses a range of societies in the region in terms of their houses, marriage systems, and concepts of siblingship. She draws a distinction between societies of 'Eastern Indonesia', such as the Rotinese and others, which have asymmetric alliance and are underlain by a thoroughgoing symbolic dualism (see Fox 1980), and those of the 'Centrist Archipelago' which, like Langkawi, have cognatic kinship and endogamous marriage.[8] While Eastern Indonesian societies have clearly bounded houses between which marital exchanges operate, the societies of the Centrist Archipelago exhibit a strong centripetal tendency. Here,

[8] Errington (1987: 404) notes that this distinction does not operate within strictly defined geographic boundaries.

the 'Houses' or social groupings tend either to coincide with the whole society, and hence be wishfully complete and autonomous as in the Indic States, or to be centred on an Ego or set of full siblings and to stretch indefinitely from that center, with no clear boundaries. (1987: 405)

What is illuminated by Errington's analysis is the way these two forms, which seem very different, can be seen as transformations of each other. Both principles—that of dualism and centrism—are present in Eastern Indonesia *and* in the Centrist Archipelago. In Eastern Indonesia, the difference between brother and sister and their enforced separation at marriage ensures the whole system of exchange between houses. In the Centrist Archipelago, cross-sex siblings epitomize unity and similarity. Here, the hierarchical states conceive themselves in an image of encompassment and unity which is often envisaged in terms of siblingship. Unity, however, is threatened by the outside: the centrist societies are shot through with dualism between 'us' and 'them'. As Errington puts it, 'Eastern Indonesia postulates unity but institutes fracture' (1987: 435), while the Centrist Archipelago 'institutionalises unity but is haunted by duality' (ibid.: 435). The fractured houses of Eastern Indonesia would disappear were marriage to be endogamous; while in the Centrist Archipelago, it is the incest taboo which prevents the whole system from collapsing in on itself.

In suggesting that the Centrist societies are haunted by the principle of dualism, and the dualist ones by the principle of centrism, Errington unites these very different Southeast Asian forms within one model. She captures both their more obvious features and their underlying tensions. I have been struck by many points of similarity between Errington's study of Luwu in South Sulawesi and the material presented here. In Langkawi the image of unity and encompassment is projected in an idiom of siblingship which is central to the house—as I show in the first chapters of the book. But this seems to fit uneasily with an opposition between 'us' and 'them' which characterizes local people's relations with the external world which are described in the second part of the book. This draws attention to the problematic status of boundaries. In Langkawi it is always difficult to make hard and fast distinctions between one kind of people and another without permanently excluding certain people from social intercourse, as happens between the Malays and the Chinese. Within the Malay community, boundaries are much more fluid. In fact, the nature of boundaries in the context I describe is a central theme of this book.

Malay Boundaries

I suggest in the Conclusion that Malay culture can be read as a product of a very subtle speculation on the nature of boundaries between that which is similar and that which is different. In these ideas, the line between the inside and the outside, the similar and the different, is always of immense concern. Boundaries are drawn only to be erased or redrawn in another place. This has implications for notions of personhood and the body as well as ideas about relatedness.

I argue that concepts of the person in Langkawi reveal a constant play between single and multiple identity. However, I also suggest that these ideas do not necessarily imply highly exotic notions of personhood and the body such as have been described in recent Melanesian and Indian ethnographic accounts. Rather, the ideas described here would suggest the possibility of holding different notions of personhood simultaneously.

Drawing on ideas about relatedness in Langkawi, I also take a critical look at the anthropological study of kinship, arguing for an approach which begins with indigenous ideas rather than models derived from the analysis of very different cultures. The definition of kinship I use here is a very broad one—in keeping with the enormous flexibility of notions of kinship in Langkawi, and the different ways in which people there create a sense of relatedness to each other. Rather than sharply distinguishing kin from non-kin, what is stressed in Langkawi is that people may become kin to each other through living and eating together, even if they start out unrelated. Kinship itself is always being created and transformed.

Taking up Schneider's (1984) *Critique of the Study of Kinship* in the Conclusion, I use ethnographic evidence from Langkawi to question the conventional definition of kinship. Like Schneider, I view the distinction between the biological and the social as fundamental to anthropological definitions of kinship. In Langkawi this distinction makes little sense. However, the conclusions I draw from this do not involve the abandonment of kinship as a subject of study as Schneider suggests, but rather adopting a more flexible approach to its study.

The structure of this book problematizes boundaries in other ways. The book takes the form of a journey from inside the house to the outside world. As such, it naïvely emulates the way a child might learn about its environment in Langkawi or, more to the point, it reflects the way the anthropologist learnt her way around. The first half of the book, then, is concerned with the house and life inside houses. It is about the reproduction of a warm, nurturing, ideal world where the tense, competitive exchanges that characterize the world outside can be kept at bay. The second half of the book examines this external world seen, as it were, from inside the house. It looks at relations between houses—visits, exchanges, marriage, and relations between affines. Information about the impingement of the present-day state, politics, and the economy is provided in Chapter 5, which links these two halves.

The process of incorporation which I describe continues to operate in the present-day context, and is one I myself experienced. I was fed and fostered in a Malay family and it was clear that these processes were, in indigenous terms, the logical preliminaries to marriage, having children, and settling on the island—to 'becoming a Langkawi person'. I thus came to understand the process I call 'coercive incorporation' through being myself a kind of immigrant. In Chapter 9 I draw on this experience and use it as a further illustration of the processes I describe here.

The island of Langkawi is situated on the Malaysian side of a modern international border with Thailand. In the past, the state of Kedah, which Langkawi is part of, was at various times a tributary of Siam. The heterogeneous origins of people in Langkawi, to which I have referred, and its location 'on the border' suggest yet another sense in which the notion of boundary is pertinent. Historically, the Malay world of which Langkawi was part was geographically extensive, and boundaries between states were fluid. My analysis has had to take cognizance of this wider world. I have tried to tread a middle path between situating this study in the field of 'Malay studies', defined in its narrowest sense, and taking on a much broader literature on Southeast Asia more generally. In attempting both strategies, I am of course vulnerable to the charge that I have succeeded in neither.

It should by now be clear that my account of life in Langkawi is broadly a 'culturalist' one. In places, readers may feel that I have taken undue liberties with the material I present. But I hope they will be able to distinguish the explanations and interpretations supplied by villagers from my own interpretations. The material I discuss is culled from many months of participation in, observation of, and conversations about everyday life in a fishing village in Langkawi. The ethnographic evidence for the analysis I present would not necessarily be more weighty if it were presented in a 'weightier' manner. Some readers may be disappointed to find relatively few detailed 'case studies' presented; others may find this a relief.

Finally, I want to emphasize my awareness that the ethnography I have written is a partial one. Since much of the material I present was gathered in conversations with women, the analysis of kinship given here might be said to apply particularly to women. However, I argue that for specific historical and social reasons women's perspective on kinship in Langkawi has a wider significance which pertains to men and to children too. This is not to say that men might not in some circumstances phrase matters differently. But then women too differ among themselves about how they view particular aspects of kinship. There is no single version of the complex matters I discuss. I have tried to present a reasonably coherent account that is true to the way I understand Langkawi people to think on these matters. Men would recognize this account as much as women even if they themselves would perhaps emphasize other aspects. They would, I think, not deny the broad outlines of the picture I have drawn.

One could tell the story of Langkawi people, or even write a study of their kinship, in many different ways. I have left much out of the account. I am especially conscious that I have not done justice to one very important aspect of the lives of people in Langkawi: Islam. This is a result of the difficulties I had with this topic during fieldwork and in no way reflects on the religiosity of the people I lived with. There is another story to be told which would have much to say about religion and politics and the world of men. It is not one I feel competent to tell, but then I do not take completeness to be an appropriate aim for an anthropologist.

PART 1

Inside the House

1

The House

The Way In

Malay houses always have more than one door. There are many ways to enter the house.

What is it that gives the house in Langkawi its significance? What makes a house a house? Is it its spatial layout, its physical structure as a building, the rituals which are enacted in it and which are part of the process of building? Or is the social significance of the house an aspect of the quality and types of relations of the people who live within it and of the activities which they engage in there?

I could begin by describing the appearance of houses outside and in, their structure, design, and furnishings, the division of space within them. I could give an account of the process of house-building, beginning with the ritual choosing of a site by an expert. I could evoke the people who live together in one house, their relations in terms of kinship, their shared activities, the texture and quality of their way of being together inside houses.

All of these are different aspects of what makes houses house-like. All involve detailed description which refers to many other domains of social life: kinship, religion, economy, gender divisions. And they would all be legitimate 'beginnings' to a story which—like all anthropological stories—has no beginning because everything connects with everything else.

Early in 1989, after nearly ten years' acquaintance with the village of Sungai Cantik I was sitting talking to an old woman whom I knew well. She was the senior woman in a neighbouring house to the one in which I lived. Humorous, lively, and opinionated, Aisyah was always willing to offer her hospitality and share her knowledge. And I was always grateful for her gifts. We were in a classificatory aunt and niece relation and she took her duty of informing me about life in Langkawi seriously. I have had some of my most enjoyable moments of fieldwork in her house, learnt much of what I know about this society from her, and her daughters are among my closest friends in the village.

During this return visit to the village our discussions tended to be rather specific. I was trying to clear up particular points or test some idea; my questions would often be narrowly focused. On this occasion, however, I simply asked how one establishes a house. It was a question to which I already knew many different answers but hers was illuminating.

In fact what I asked Aisyah was the meaning of the Malay term *berumah tangga*. Like many Malay usages, this is a concise expression which requires a lot of unpacking. *Rumah* means house; *tangga* the ladder leading up to it; *rumah tangga* can be used for household, or the house and its land. The prefix *ber* signifies a verbal form. *Berumah tangga* might be translated as to make or establish a house. But in parts of Malaysia (though not generally in Langkawi) it means to marry, implying of course that the two processes are inseparable.

Aisyah told me that *berumah tangga* was what happened after a couple marry, when they separate from the parental household. I asked what exactly happens, expecting to be told about the process of house-building, the saving of money, buying furnishings. Instead, to my surprise, she listed the ingredients of a chicken curry. Rice, salt, chilli, onions, garlic, ginger, pepper, turmeric, and other spices must all be bought. All the things you need for a curry, and then coffee and sugar.[1] The contents of a kitchen (*dapur*). These are all bought by a mother for her daughter.

It was only after she had gone through what might have been a shopping list for a family meal in some detail that Aisyah got on to the furnishings of the house, what she called the contents of the inner room. Then she talked of the curtains, bedding, mats that a mother buys for a daughter. What made a vivid impression was the idea that the establishment of a house starts with the equipping of a kitchen, specifically with the food to be cooked there. And that these ingredients are bought with money which comes from a woman's mother's house.

And so I was given an image of a succession of hearths generating each other, as mothers generate daughters. The process of reproduction of hearths parallels and contains the reproduction of people in the house; it generates further houses and further people. To both these reproductive processes women are central.

We have stepped into the house in a particular way. Not into its formal reception area where outside visitors are greeted but directly into its

[1] In fact, these are the ingredients required for the feast when a new house is established. Meat must be served rather than fish, which is eaten on normal occasions.

symbolic centre and most intimate space, the *dapur*, hearth. In the following sections of this chapter I suggest that houses can be viewed as expanded hearths and I draw out some of the meanings of the processes of cooking and eating that take place there. The chapters which follow this one broaden out the picture of the *dapur* as the transforming centre of social life in Langkawi so that the reason for choosing this way into the house rather than another will become clear. But before we can understand how houses reproduce themselves we must first look at their construction.

The House as a Building

House structure in Langkawi, as elsewhere in Malaysia, shows considerable variation in style and design.[2] Hilton (1956) has noted the susceptibility of Malay house-building to changes in fashion, and in Langkawi the marked variation in style and quality of housing is one of the clearest indicators of wealth. From the point of view of the developmental cycle of the domestic group, perhaps the most significant feature of the more traditional type of Malay house is that it can be easily enlarged and that it is movable from place to place (ibid.: 144). These features of their design permit flexibility and mobility in the residence patterns of their occupants.

When a new house is to be built, a *bomoh* (traditional curer, diviner) is consulted to make sure that the site and time of building are propitious. I did not witness these rites in the village, but was told that this procedure was necessary before building could commence.[3] The *bomoh* throws a piece of wood which then becomes the site for the central house post (*tiang seri*). Houses are usually orientated so that the roofs are on an east–west axis, following the direction of the sun's rising and setting and also that of Mecca. The *dapur* is traditionally to the north and the hills (*bukit*), although today it is of equal importance that it should be to the far side of any road. People sleep with their heads to the south and the sea. They are

[2] See Carsten (1987*b*; 1995*b*) for a discussion of the symbolic elaboration of houses in Langkawi, particularly with reference to Lévi-Strauss's ideas.

[3] See Endicott (1970: 113); Skeat (1900: 144–5) for a description of house-building rites at the end of the 19th cent. Gullick (1987: 181–8) summarizes some historical descriptions of Malay houses in this period. He begins his chapter on 'The Malay Style of Living' with the observation that 'The Malay house is a useful introduction to the general subject of the Malay style of living, since the house stands at the centre of Malay traditional culture and reflects many of its facets' (p. 181).

buried with their heads to the north. While they are still inside the house the dead are placed with their heads to the east.

There is a strong association between the house and women which is ritually expressed during house-building. The mother of the house (*ibu rumah*) must hold the central house post (*tiang seri*) when it is erected. Villagers make clear that this is a symbolic action; women wear their best clothes for the occasion; it is men who do the real lifting, women just hold the post, they say. This central post is the abode of the house spirit (*semangat rumah* or *manya rumah*), which is also believed to be female. Like other women, the house spirit must be suitably adorned. The top of the *tiang seri* is wrapped around with red, black, and white cloths known as *bunga alang* or *bunga tiang* (from *bunga*, flower). These are sometimes described as the clothes of the house spirit, associated with different parts of her body, in which she is dressed to 'look pretty' (*bagi elok*).[4] The spirit as well as the occupants of the house are vulnerable to attack from other spirits which are less benevolent and may cause sickness. To protect them from this, gold, silver, money, and an alloy of gold and copper (*suasa*) are placed in the top of the *tiang seri*, and iron is buried in the ground at its base.

While the amount of building activity going on in the village is striking, very little of it involves the construction of new houses; instead old ones may be repaired, extended, improved, or partly rebuilt, creating the impression that the village is under continuous reconstruction. Houses are built in stages—renovated or extended as the need arises and resources become available.

Building involves a combination of household labour and skilled, hired workmen (*tukang*). Both male and female members of the household participate in construction work. Weaving of *nipah* palm leaves for *atap* roofing is done by women; men do the heavier building work. In the past they also made the plaited bamboo walls which are becoming rarer today. Neighbours and kin are also expected to participate in house demolition and construction. Major improvements or extensions to a house (for example, building a new room) are often undertaken by parents at the time of a child's marriage. Frequent changes in residence after marriage are normal: a couple may move house (*pindah rumah*) several times during

[4] One man described how white was for her heart, *hati*; red for her body, *badan*; and black for her head, *kepala*. He went on to describe the colours as those of the Malay flag, *bendera Melayu*, which could not be shown at the time of the Dutch colonial regime when Indonesia and Malaya were united. In this description the house, the body, and the state have become conflated in mythic-historical time.

3. Village house with *ibu rumah* in centre

4. Older *dapur* of same house

the first years of their married life. House-moving also emphasizes the strong connection between women and houses. After a move the mother of the house spends three days in the house (defined to include its compound). She is, as it were, physically attached to the house.

Rosemary Firth has commented that a Malay 'will think nothing of buying a house, taking it to pieces and re-erecting it elsewhere' (1966: 23). In Langkawi, villagers may simply omit taking it to pieces. The practice of 'lifting the house' (*usung rumah*), which may involve moving to another site within the same compound or to an entirely different area of the village, is another aspect of the flexibility of residence. These are occasions of some festivity requiring the co-operation of neighbours and kin who are given food in return for their effort. A house may be transported in this way when village land is bought or sold, after a death, or the birth of a child which leads to the reorganization of the household or setting up a new one.

The nature of house construction (the fact that it is a continuously ongoing process) and the physical mobility of houses are thus related to stages in the developmental cycle of the domestic group, but they also underline the traditional impermanence of the house structure itself and its loose relation to a specific site. Rodman's (1985) observations on a Melanesian society, in which 'houses that symbolize kinship are not firmly rooted in place' (p. 69), and where both houses and residence are also strikingly mobile, are highly relevant here. She stresses how residence is in constant flux, and this process 'becomes part of the interweaving of place and people that creates Longana kinship' (ibid.). A similar interweaving of locality and persons lies at the heart of kinship and community

5. House deconstruction

in Langkawi. Today, however, these features of the house are changing. Houses are becoming both significant items of property (with implications for inheritance practices) and more permanent structures.

The fact that houses are constantly improved and enlarged enables the different types of house structure described below to be considered partly as stages in a developmental sequence which parallels the developmental cycle of its occupants. Not every household goes through all the stages in sequence. However, most married couples gradually rebuild and improve their home during the course of their married life, enlarging and reconstructing it as the family increases in size and acquires greater assets. These improvements also reflect the influence of changing fashions: the simplest and smallest houses being generally also the more traditional in style, while the newest and grandest reflect current trends in house design and the increasing influence of urban values in rural life.

The simplest, poorest, and most traditional type of village house is raised on wooden posts (*tiang*) about four feet off the ground. The walls are made of plaited bamboo and the floor of split sections of *nibong* stem, bamboo, or wooden boards, with narrow spaces between them which provide ventilation and are easily cleaned. The roof, *atap*, is thatched and made from *nipah* palm leaves. Such houses have two house ladders (*tangga*): one at the back leads to the open porch (*pelantar*) which leads into the small kitchen (*dapur*); the other leads into the single main room of

6. Group of men move a house to a new site

the house, the 'mother of the house' (*ibu rumah*). The doors are gaps in the walls covered by sliding screens made of the same material as the walls. Windows are similarly square gaps in the wall covered with a wooden shutter.

Most houses in the village are of a larger and more elaborate structure. They consist of a kitchen, *dapur*, and two main rooms: the *ibu rumah* which is used mainly for formal occasions, and the main living area of the house, also known as a *dapur*, which can be regarded as an extension of the cooking *dapur*.

In such houses one part, generally the *ibu rumah*, will show clear signs of having been built later than the rest. The back part, the *dapur*, may have wooden or *nipah* walls and an *atap* roof while the front, the *ibu rumah*, will be constructed from wood and concrete and have a metal roof and glazed windows. The walls and floors are made of wooden boards instead of bamboo, and a corrugated metal roof (*atap zen*) has largely replaced the traditional *atap*. The wooden house posts (*tiang*) have been sunk into concrete plinths which provide protection against ants and termites. The extra room has a third house ladder leading into it. The new part of the house is raised about six feet off the ground so that it is at a slightly higher level than the other rooms.

The third and latest style of house has a *dapur* which reflects urban fashions in house design. It is built at ground level instead of being raised on posts, there is no *pelantar*, the floor is concrete, as is the lower part of the walls. The upper part of the walls is timber, and the roof corrugated iron.

The space under a house may be used for storage of building materials, bicycles, motor bikes, nets, fishing traps, and baskets. There may be a wooden bench underneath for use during the heat of the day which becomes a gathering place for close neighbours. Houses frequently have a wooden chicken coop to one side. At the back, near the kitchen or under the house there may be a shelter for storing cut wood for cooking. Near by there is usually a rice granary (*jelapang padi*) where unhusked rice (*padi*) is stored. These are constructed like miniature houses, raised on stilts and made of wood with *atap* or a corrugated metal roof. Houses never possess more than one granary. Also near the back of the house is a privy with walls of corrugated metal or a fence around it.

Houses occasionally have their own well, either internal in the *dapur* or external, but usually wells are situated outside, and are shared by several houses of one compound. They may be partly surrounded by rough fencing to give some privacy. Bathing takes place here, and women gather to do their laundry during the morning, and draw water for household purposes whenever necessary. The front of the house is often decorated with hanging plants, and each house ladder will have a container of water placed to one side which is used to rinse the feet before entering the house. Windows and doors are normally left open during the daytime except during a major family crisis or dispute with neighbours when communication with other houses is severed.

In spite of the variation in types of houses, the interior division of space conforms to a general pattern. Fig. 1.1 shows a plan which is representative of most village houses. The *pelantar* leads into a small kitchen *dapur* and this leads to a much larger room, the 'living' *dapur*, on a slightly

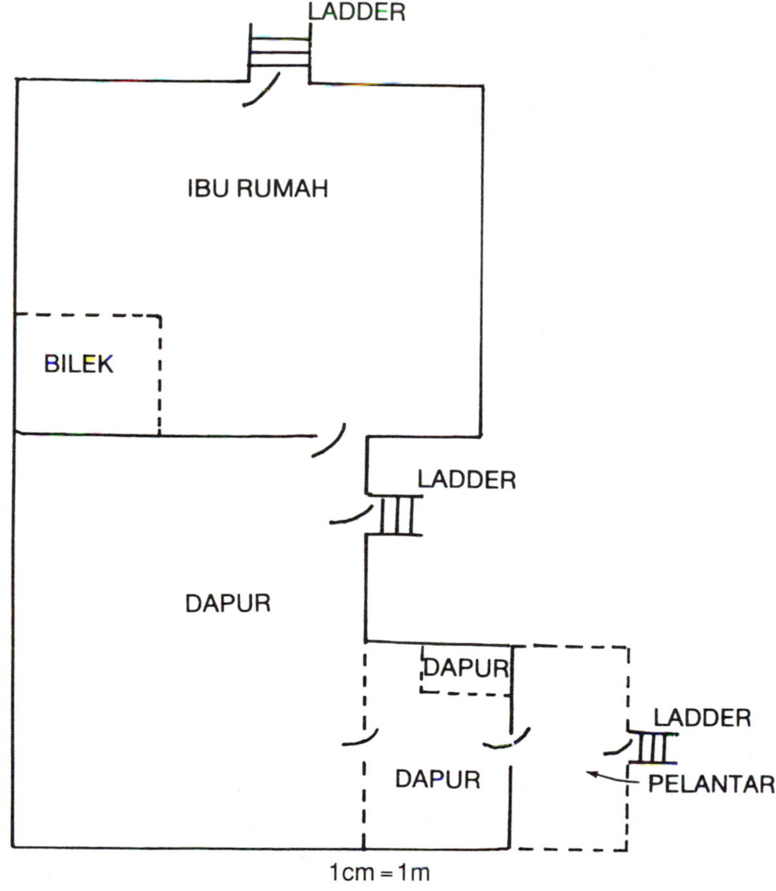

FIG. 1.1. House plan

higher level. This main room in turn leads into the *ibu rumah*, again on a higher level. The house thus consists of two large rooms, a small kitchen, and a *pelantar*, each of the two large rooms having its own house ladder and entrance from the outside. The use of these entrances corresponds to the differing formality of each space and the sex and degree of inclusion to the household of the person entering.

Entering the house from the back, as do all household members and sometimes close neighbours or other frequent visitors to the house, especially women, one comes onto the *pelantar*. Here miscellaneous buckets and basins are kept as well as earthenware jars for storing water and the larger, heavier kitchen utensils. Some kitchen tasks are performed on the *pelantar*: cleaning fish, grinding spices, scraping coconut, washing dishes; household members perform their early morning toilet, and small children are bathed. Water and rubbish drain away through the slatted floor. The wooden door of the *pelantar* leads into the small cooking *dapur*. The stove (*dapur*) has an earth floor which is covered in concrete and a wooden frame; wood and charcoal or coconut husks are used as fuel. Around the stove women keep the kitchen utensils in everyday use: aluminium pans, strainers, kettles, and small quantities of cooking ingredients. Crockery in everyday use, wood for the stove, and oil for lamps are all arranged near by. Women cook, and everyday meals are eaten, in the *dapur* but usually household members do not use it for relaxation.

The 'kitchen' *dapur* leads into the first large room of the house, also known as the *dapur*. This is the main living area for household members. It generally contains little furniture. The wooden floor is partly covered with plaited mats (*tikar*) or pieces of linoleum. On the floor along the walls husked rice in tins and coconut oil for cooking may be stored. There is additional storage space in the rafters for plaited baskets, boxes, agricultural tools, and areca nuts for betel chewing. Home-made kapok-filled mattresses, pillows, and bolsters are spread out at night and rolled up in one corner during the day. Simple shelves or a small cupboard are used for keeping clean clothes in everyday use. If there is a baby or small child in the house a basketwork crib is usually attached to a coiled spring and suspended from the roof. Houses are lit using a combination of fluorescent strip lighting and various types of oil and pressure lamps.

The 'living' *dapur* generally gives a feeling of spaciousness; it is uncluttered, comfortable, and relatively cool. Whatever is kept in it is usually placed along the walls or in the rafters above so that the floor space is empty; windows are small, allowing little light in during the day. Cleaning is easy: dust and rubbish are swept through the gaps in the floorboards.

7. Woman cooking in her *dapur*

8. The 'living *dapur*'

This is the room most used by household members. It is the area where women relax during the day, and where familiar visitors and female strangers are received. Household members and their more intimate visitors may sit or lie on the mats during the day and evening, and a small child can crawl about without causing much damage or getting hurt. The entrance from the outside into this room is often used by neighbours and regular visitors to the house and sometimes by female strangers.

The *ibu rumah* can be reached by going up a few steps from the living *dapur*, and is situated at the front of the house. The house ladder and entrance from the outside into this room is never used by household members or regular visitors but only by strangers, usually male. The front room, as villagers say, is 'for people who have come' (*untuk orang datang*), that is, for receiving and entertaining guests who are strangers. It is the dress that the house shows to the outside world and, increasingly, it is a Westernized and urbanized dress. Provencher (1971: 196) has aptly decribed this room as 'a masterpiece of display'. The household furnishings and prized possessions are set out here. Like a front parlour, it is rarely used by household members; more than any other room in the house it reflects their economic standing.

The contents of this room vary considerably. Some are quite simply furnished with mats and perhaps one cupboard or cabinet, many have patterned linoleum, windows with glass panes and curtains. If the household owns a television this takes pride of place and may have a cloth or crocheted mat draped over it in the daytime. There may be a set of easy chairs and small tables similarly draped, a cupboard where best clothes are stored; framed high school certificates, family photographs, calendars,

9. Display cabinet

verses from the Qur'ān are often hung on the walls. Finally, there may be a glass-fronted display cabinet containing rarely used items of china, pewter, Tupperware, aluminium basins, and glassware.

Sometimes part of this room is partitioned off by screens to form a *bilek*, sleeping area, usually for a young married couple resident with either spouse's parents. They may sleep either on mattresses on the floor or on a wooden bed. The *ibu rumah* generally feels spacious. The room is large and few households own all of the above items. Sometimes an open platform (*beranda*) is built adjoining the *ibu rumah*, and used for receiving guests and as a space where men may sit during the day.

In the simplest and poorest houses, which have only one main room, the *ibu rumah* would generally conform to the description of the 'living' *dapur* given above. At the other end of the spectrum, houses which have recently been rebuilt with the *dapur* at ground level show a significant departure from traditional styles. The *dapur* has plentiful shelf space where kitchen utensils are displayed in a manner that was before reserved for the *ibu rumah*. Similarly, Western-style furniture is beginning to find its place in this room.

According to villagers, houses have three essential parts: the *tiang seri*, the *dapur*, and the *ibu rumah*; the first and the last of these differentiate them from the shelters, *dangau*, built in the fields or vegetable gardens. We have already seen that the *tiang seri* is the abode of the house spirit, who in some sense embodies the house and ensures the well-being of its occupants.

The *dapur* is the second defining feature of the house. Most significantly, a house never has more than one hearth. Villagers were somewhat shocked when I described to them my own house in England where there are two kitchens. They always stress that co-residence necessarily implies the sharing of one hearth. The core meaning of *dapur* is hearth. The actual cooking stove, the room in which it is situated, and the living area which adjoins it in the larger, three-roomed houses, are all termed *dapur*. These two rooms can be seen as extensions of the cooking stove and of each other (see Fig. 1.1). The strong association of this space with women will be discussed in the following section.

The third essential feature of the house is the *ibu rumah*. In the more simple type of village houses this space conforms to the 'living' *dapur* of more elaborate structures, and is then the area where women spend most of their time. This room therefore, like the *dapur*, has an association with women which is revealed in the very meaning of the term *ibu rumah*, 'mother of the house'. The same term is used to refer to the female household head.[5]

I have described how the strong association between women and houses is made evident during their building and in aspects of their structure. This is expressed both as a connection between the building and its female occupants and in ideas about the house as an entity. Informants often simply say, 'houses *are* women' (*rumah—orang perempuan*). The house spirit is not only female, she is also explicitly likened to the mother of the house. One woman told me, 'The house spirit is a woman. That's why we hold the central post, we are going to be the mother of the house' (*Manya rumah—perempuan. Sabit kita pegang tiang seri; kita nak jadi ibu rumah*). 'Men don't stay in the house,' she went on, 'they go out to work, to get food, to get money' (*Orang jantang tak duduk rumah—keluar kerja, cari makan, cari duit*). Another told me, 'The house spirit, that's the mother of the house' (*manya rumah itu ibu rumah*). She went on to explain that was why the spirit had to be wrapped in cloths, like the veil women wear.

A house without a woman is like a house without its spirit. If the mother of the house dies the house is considered empty, *kosong*, and the widower should then look for another wife. Widows, however, can live on their own. While Stephen Headley (1987*a*) has suggested that bodies in Java are metaphorical houses, houses in Langkawi are conceived as persons—female persons who must be appropriately adorned. This is evident in the manner in which houses are conceived, decorated, and furnished.[6]

Women and Men in the House

On entering any house in the village, perhaps the most striking impression for the visitor is the contrast between the overwhelming presence of women and the near-absence of men. Particularly during the day, men are almost entirely missing from the house, engaged in fishing, attending the mosque or coffee-shop, or undertaking errands in the local market town. Those that are present, often old or sick, seem confined to the furthest regions of the house: they sit alone, huddled in a far corner of a room, or, appropriately, they occupy the very margins of the house space: perching

[5] Elsewhere in Malaysia this part of the house is often called the *anjung* or the *rumah tangga* and the term *ibu rumah* refers to the main body of the house (Hilton 1956: 143).

[6] The animated and person-like quality of houses is a phenomenon which occurs regularly in Southeast Asian cultures (see Waterson 1990; Errington 1989: 84) although it is not restricted to this region (see e.g. Carsten and Hugh-Jones 1995; Daniel 1984: 149–53).

on a doorsill or verandah, half in and half out of the house, watching the comings and goings of the neighbourhood.

In contrast, women dominate the house space with their presence. They walk freely to and fro as they go about their tasks: cooking, looking after children, cleaning, or weaving mats. They utilize the central areas of the room and sometimes the margins too; there is no sense of confinement or restraint in their movements or use of space. The sitting positions prescribed by Malay formal etiquette are largely ignored: women may sit cross-legged, with legs stretched out in front of them, or even lie about on the floor.[7]

This lack of restraint in the way they range themselves in space is also reflected in other aspects of women's behaviour within the house, particularly that of older women. Their conversation is neither dull nor subdued. In the absence of men it is likely to be particularly full of lively gossip and jokes spiced with sexual allusions. Laughter is frequent, conversation often bawdy. Nor does it necessarily change in character in the presence of men of the household. Subjects of local interest, feasts, rotating credit societies, marriages, and disputes are all discussed in a lively and opinionated manner.

Young women are modestly, if informally, dressed within the house. Their mothers and grandmothers may simply wear a sarong tied under the arms with no blouse on top, leaving their arms and shoulders and the lower part of their legs exposed as long as no male strangers are present. As if to underline their status and their release from many of the social constraints that govern the behaviour of younger women, they often have mouths stained red from habitual betel-chewing, and they are seasoned smokers of cigars and home-rolled cigarettes.

Although older women are less constrained in their behaviour than young girls, this does not apply to the expression of affection between women. Relaxed physical contact: touching, grooming, an affectionate hold, tickling, are all normal aspects of close female relations, particularly between peers, often between young unmarried girls. Indeed this kind of contact between women provides a very marked contrast to behaviour between women and men.

Even within the house it is rare to see physical contact between adult men and women. These restrictions do not, however, apply to young children, who play together and may be caressed by their parents or parents' siblings of either sex. In other respects men and women of the

[7] See Provencher (1971: 164–7) for a description of formal sitting positions.

same house behave towards each other in a relaxed manner. Women do not modify their movements, sitting positions, or dress when male members of the household are present. Men and women of one house eat together and converse rather freely in each other's presence.

Villagers themselves minimize the association between specific areas of the house and men or women, saying, 'it is not calculated' (*tak kira*); that is, not strictly followed. It is difficult to ascertain whether such segregation is in fact less strictly observed in Langkawi than elsewhere in Malaysia—partly because observers have tended to concentrate on formal contexts where such segregation is always marked (see, for example, Provencher 1971: 165). However, in a village on mainland Kedah I was specifically told that the *beranda* was the men's part of the house whilst in Langkawi people say, 'here we sit together, not on different sides' (*disini duduk sama kali, tak ada duduk sebelah sebelah*). The impression given by Banks (1983: 96) and others, that women are more or less restricted to the back of the house, or otherwise constrained, is thus highly misleading and can be said to apply only to occasions when male strangers are present.

Men of one house tend to be less close than women, and in adulthood relations between closely related male consanguines are often based on avoidance. Nevertheless, within the house affection may be displayed by fathers and grandfathers towards young children and between brothers of all ages. Particular ties may be less close than the corresponding ones between women, but the general atmosphere remains friendly, relaxed, and informal, and this is manifested both in conversation patterns and physical posture.

When male strangers come to the house, segregation by gender becomes more marked. These guests are received by men in the *ibu rumah* (or on the *beranda*), while women of the household remain in the *dapur*. If female strangers come to the house they either enter the 'living' *dapur* directly or they graduate there rather rapidly from the *ibu rumah*. Food is handed by a young woman to a man of the household at the doorway; he then serves the guests. However, such formality is exceptional. Villagers say that the *ibu rumah* is for visitors but by this they do not refer to casual, everyday visits from neighbours, kin, and friends, who usually sit in the *dapur*, but to those of strangers.

Even when male strangers come to the house, the restriction of women to the *dapur* operates mainly in regard to young women. Older women may participate in the entertainment and, if no men are present, will actually receive male guests in the *ibu rumah* until a man of the household arrives. It is clear that sex segregation applies in varying degrees of strictness depending on the formality of the occasion and the degree of familiarity between the visitor and the household. When they are at home men of the household spend most of their time, as do women, in the *dapur*, for it is here that the main activities of family life are performed: eating, sleeping, talking, relaxing. While different areas of the house are loosely associated with women and men, and this separation gains strength by the absence of men from the house for much of the day, villagers' own perception of such segregation is that it is rather weak.

The Sharing of Space and Food

The relative weakness of sex segregation among household members inside the house is one aspect of a more general lack of division of interior house space. Different areas of the house tend not to be strongly associated with particular people. Co-resident nuclear families never have a separate annexe or room built onto the house for their use. Household members do, however, have their customary sleeping space, either in the 'living' *dapur* or the *ibu rumah*, where it may be partitioned off by screens or wooden partitions to form a *bilek*, sleeping room. These are usually constructed when more than one married couple co-reside in one house or for adolescent children. Younger children sleep near their parents, grandparents, or other resident adults, and in general their space is less defined than that of adults. Individual household members do not usually have their own space; even at night means of separation may consist of no more than mosquito netting or a flimsy screen. Household members usually prefer to sleep near to one another even when the size of the house would permit some distancing.

The unity of the household is most clearly expressed in cooking and eating arrangements. I have already referred to the fact that houses only ever have one hearth, *dapur*. It is always asserted that however many members, nuclear families, or generations live within one house, they cook and eat together. On one occasion, when I was emphatically told that even if there are three couples in a house they eat together, I objected that in large houses different members quite often eat separately. I was roundly contradicted: 'They eat separately but there is one hearth' (*makan seorang, tetapi satu dapur*). What is important, then, is not eating at the same time but that the same food be cooked at the same hearth. As it was put to me, 'Sitting together doesn't matter, but cooking together does' (*duduk sekali tak apa, tetapi masak sekali*). Of all activities which unite household members on an everyday basis, the most significant, both in terms of the attention it receives and the symbolism with which it is invested, is this commensality.

Food is prepared in the *dapur* by women. In spite of the length of time and the elaborate preparation necessary to produce a meal (often involving two or three hours of labour), women disclaim their own or their daughters' proficiency, and cooking is normally done by young adult women of the household. Nevertheless, a great deal of creative energy is channelled into the preparation of food and a wide range of dishes is prepared in any single week. Different dishes and ways of preparing them are a constant subject of conversation, and at mealtimes older members of the household frequently comment critically on the quality of the food.

The main constituent of the two main meals of the day is steamed rice (*nasi*). The dishes which are most complex to prepare, however, are those which accompany it, which are called *lauk*, and consist of cooked fish or occasionally meat; for example, a fish curry, fried or grilled fish. Other accompanying dishes may include cooked vegetables (*sayur*), raw vegetables (*ulam*), and a condiment prepared from prawn paste, chilli, and tamarind (*sambal belacan*). However lavish these dishes, the most important part of the meal is the rice, and this is underlined by the fact that the phrase *makan nasi*, literally 'to eat rice', means to eat a meal, or simply to eat.

The manner in which meals are eaten shows clearly that rice is their main focus.[8] Each person has their own plate heaped high with steamed rice and the accompaniments are taken in smaller quantities from centrally placed dishes. Young children especially are discouraged from taking too much of these, for it is the rice that is regarded as being particularly nourishing. Rice is the most important nutritional source, without which villagers say they could not survive. As one woman told me, 'One can eat rice without fish, but not fish without rice.'

Once the food is ready for eating, the meal is set out on the floor by whoever has cooked it. Full plates of plain rice are arranged around the centre dishes in a circle for each person eating. To one side will be placed a jug of cold water, a glass, and a finger bowl with water. Also to the side will be a large plate piled high with extra rice for second helpings. In an informal situation the meal would be laid out on the floor of the 'cooking' *dapur*. When visitors are present the meal is generally eaten in the 'living' *dapur*.

[8] See also Zainal Abidin bin Ahmad (1950: 49–52) for an account of Malay eating etiquette, and Gullick (1987: 193–5) for historical descriptions of Malay meals.

Usually no more than four people eat at any one time (the manner of eating—with dishes placed at the centre of a circle and people reaching to them—makes large numbers impractical). When guests are present, higher-status family members, the main income-earner, and guests eat first, but normally there is no rigidly adhered-to eating order; in a large household it varies from day to day. In informal contexts, men and women eat together but where the number of people exceeds one setting of dishes (*hidang*), and strangers are present, they eat separately. Men always eat from a cross-legged position (*bersila*); in informal contexts this is the way women and children sit too. Food is eaten with all the fingers of the right hand (*makan tangan*). It is important to eat tidily, not to get food all the way up one's hand or to let too much of it fall *en route* from the plate on the floor to the mouth. Children are readily scolded for eating messily or greedily.

The meal begins with each person dipping the fingers of their right hand into the finger bowl. After this they take a small portion of rice from their plate and, raising it to the mouth, pronounce the blessing, 'In the name of Allah the compassionate, the merciful' (*bismillah ar-rahman ar-rahim*), and then eat the first mouthful. People say that this customary blessing keeps away the spirits (*hantu*). After the first mouthful of plain rice, each person takes small portions from the central dishes of *lauk* onto their own plate. This is done in such a way that the left hand is never in direct contact with the food. Each mouthful consists of a small amount of *lauk* eaten with a large wad of rice, never on its own. Only when the *lauk* on a person's plate is finished is more taken from the central dishes.

More rice is taken before all the rice on the plate is finished. It is impolite and unusual not to take at least one additional helping of rice. Other eaters are expected to notice their neighbour's plate running low and hand them the plate from which to take more. It is important to leave no unfinished rice on one's plate. As each person finishes they are handed a glass of water which they pour over the fingers of the right hand onto the plate, cleaning the fingers and rinsing the plate at the same time. At this point water is also drunk; it is not usual to do so during the course of the meal. When they have finished, people move away from the eating area; they are not expected to remain. Children either eat before or together with adults; usually one of the adults present hands them food from the central dishes; they are not allowed to help themselves. In this way their consumption of *lauk* and vegetables is supervised and they are seen to consume a good quantity of rice.

It is polite for a host to finish eating after any guest in order for the latter not to be embarrassed or ashamed (*malu*) about the amount they are eating. Villagers say that it is impolite (*tak sopan*) to eat either too slowly or too fast, the former indicating a reluctance to work and the latter greed. However, the rapidity with which meals are consumed is striking, particularly in view of the long hours spent in their preparation. Generally, a meal is eaten in about ten minutes and conversation is minimal during this time.

The preparation and eating of food, and particularly of rice, is, then, a central aspect of household activity; it takes up much attention and time, and is highly enjoyed. In Chapter 6 we shall see that cooked food is a constant item of exchange which is vital to relations between households, both in the form of dyadic exchanges of cooked dishes and, on a wider scale, in communal feasting. Within the household too, eating together is invested with symbolic significance. Even in informal contexts within the home, meals are rarely taken by one person on their own. When this does happen the person eating will always first invite others present to partake of the meal. If they refuse she will tuck herself away in a corner, out of sight of others, and eat hurriedly and furtively as though performing an embarrassing act.[9]

It is significant that newly married couples avoid eating together on their own. When this occurs and is witnessed by others, the couple are teased and show acute embarrassment. As in many other cultures, Malays make an association between eating and sex; jokes often turn on this point. Neither solitary individuals nor couples who have not yet had children may form their own household. Eating together without others is not only an act which carries sexual connotations, but it expresses the boundaries of a commensal group: that which should be the household. A newly married pair, like the solitary person, cannot form a household. They tend to avoid situations which emphasize either their closeness or separateness.

Eating is a social activity which unites household members who form a single commensal group. This is underlined by the fact that if visitors pass by during a meal they are always invited to eat and, equally consistently, they refuse. The invitation is a gesture of hospitality and inclusion; its refusal emphasizes the boundaries of the household.[10] Eating everyday meals in other people's houses is strongly disapproved of; even children

[9] Jay's (1969: 50) description of meals being taken privately and individually in rural Modjokuto provides a marked contrast. See also Massard (1978: 143), who emphasizes the collective aspect of the domestic meal. Food eaten alone is not considered tasty (1978: 146).

[10] See Douglas (1975: 256 ff.).

are discouraged from doing so. I once asked the mother of a house what she would do if members of her house started eating in other houses. The sharpness of her response was typical: 'Eat in other people's houses, make a separate *dapur*' (*makan rumah orang, buat dapur asing*). The reply shows both the importance of eating in one's own house and how the *dapur* connotes both hearth and house. To make another *dapur* in fact means to build another house.[11]

It is significant that the taking of snacks or drinks in other houses is not so ill-regarded and is indeed a normal part of visiting. (The opposition between meals and snacks will be discussed in Chapter 6.) It is partaking in a full rice meal which unites the household. Separate houses are associated with separate rice; when new houses are built they have their own single rice granary. The importance of the shared consumption of rice within the house is linked to notions of bodily substance and kinship which will be discussed in Chapter 4.

The site of cooking and eating, the *dapur*, is the very heart of the house. Cooking and eating are not only activities performed by household members together, they are also performed in an undivided way. This is what gives force to the prohibition on eating meals in other people's houses. Such dispersal represents a challenge to the integrity of the household. Eating outside the house is also invested with symbolic meaning. But I will argue in later chapters that this is in many ways opposed to the meaning of eating within the house, and this opposition is reflected in the types of food consumed and in the manner of consumption.

Women and Houses; the Halus *and the* Kasar

The notion of the *dapur* as the symbolic focus of the house re-emphasizes the centrality of women to the household. For the *dapur* is the area of the house above all others which is associated with women: the place where much of their labour is performed, where leisure is often taken, and the region retired to in the presence of male strangers. Further,

[11] In Minahasa the concept of the *dapur* is even more elaborated: 'The smallest social unit in Minahasan society was the hearth group, *dapur* (hearth or kitchen). Today the term *dapur* is used along with the term *rumah tangga* (*rumah*—house, *tangga*—stairs), which means family. . . . A *dapur* was defined as a group of people who regularly produced, prepared and consumed food together. Usually the members slept under a single roof, but they always shared a single hearth. They were conceived of as "cooking one pot" or "eating from the same hearth." Indeed, from the act of jointly cooking and eating sprang the organisation ethic of the *dapur*' (Lundstrom-Burghoorn 1981: 72).

we have already seen how informal behaviour predominates within the house.

If I have given the impression up to now that relations between household members tend to be informal and relaxed, irrespective of gender, it should be emphasized that, in spite of this, a strict age-based hierarchy of authority and respect operates between generations, and in a weaker form within one generation when age differences are great. This hierarchy marks all aspects of relations from expressivity to the division of labour, and is particularly evident in the relation between mothers and daughters, who between them share most household labour (see Chapter 2).

Malays in Langkawi, like those elsewhere in Malaysia and Indonesia, make a distinction between behaviour which is 'refined' (*halus*) and that which is 'rough' or 'crude' (*kasar*). This distinction has been widely discussed by anthropologists (see, for example, C. Geertz 1960, Anderson 1990 [1972], Provencher 1971, Wilder 1982). However, these writers have tended to focus on the *halus* side of the dichotomy, and understressed the significance of the *kasar* form and its implications for social relations. In so doing it may be that they are following their informants, who undoubtedly invest all that is *halus* with positive values and, when asked about the *kasar*, express themselves in negative terms.[12]

It is clear that the behaviour and interaction which I have described in this chapter: informal, expressive, relatively unconstrained, associated particularly with women, falls broadly within the *kasar* mode.[13] Although in the wider community *kasar* behaviour may be associated with an ideology of familiarity and equality, within the household its association with

[12] Concentrating on the *prijaji* modes which ideally conform to the *alus* ideals, Geertz makes the point that 'Elaborate linguistic forms, speech levels and status markers, formality of behaviour, dissimulation and masking of true feeling, in short "alusness" implies an indigenous hierarchical ordering of social relations' (Geertz 1960: 334). Similarly, Anderson (1990) has noted that being *halus* is a sign of power, a mark of the constant effort and control necessary to achieve this state. Men of power must give the impression of minimal effort, their 'halusness' is an expression of their authority. See Wikan (1990: 15–16, 125) for a critique of concentrating on 'public', formal, modes of behaviour in the Balinese context.

[13] Provencher (1971) links formal courtesy both to the urban context and to a predominantly male ethos. In the rural context, then, where interaction with strangers occurs infrequently, and the claiming of ascribed status is rarer than in urban communities, it is the *kasar* style which dominates (Provencher 1971: 201–3). Provencher notes that whereas relationships to which the *halus* style is appropriate are defined as being between unequals, and are based on shame, control, and embarrassment, *kasar* behaviour obtains between familiars. More particularly, 'the household and the coarse style of courtesy fit together almost perfectly' (ibid.: 184). In the rural context there is, then, an association between the *kasar* style, familiars, status equals, women, and houses. It is perhaps not surprising that Provencher is led to comment on the relative omission of *kasar* behaviour from the literature:

equality is less straightforward. In spite of this, it remains true to say that behaviour in the house is more *kasar* than *halus*, more expressive than restrained. Everyday behaviour can be glossed as informal and *kasar*. Nevertheless, I would argue that to see this behaviour purely in negative terms is a simplification.

As I argued in the Introduction, everyday behaviour, whether it occurs in 'domestic' or 'public' contexts, carries meanings which have political implications; we cannot assume we know what these are. In Langkawi, the significance of 'kasarness', as of other aspects of the house, is not restricted to internal space. Because the wider community is modelled on the house (see Chapter 6), *kasar* behaviour has a communal and political significance. Its meanings can be positively as well as negatively expressed, as will become clear in Part 2, where interaction in the space beyond the house will be examined.

What I would stress here is the way that in everyday life the *kasar* can become a critique of the *halus*. Such a critique is in evidence when, as often occurs in Langkawi, an old woman gives an uproarious imitation of a visiting dignitary to her friends, having just politely served him with food in the most refined manner. Or when men and women engage in sexual bantering while engaged in communal labour. Villagers know the value of politeness but this does not prevent them from exercising the most barbed wit which simultaneously undermines the whole fragile edifice on which this etiquette is built. They are fiercely proud of their own way of doing things, which they often contrast with the ways of urban higher-class people to the latter's detriment. The *kasar*, I am suggesting, can be seen as an alternative discourse to the *halus*, a kind of continuous and often satirical commentary on it. The play between these two modes is both complex and subtle.

The *kasar* cannnot, then, be defined straightforwardly as the opposite of *halus* and associated with everything which is of little value. For, although this devaluation of the *kasar* may often be articulated by villagers themselves, their attitudes are in fact more complex and ambivalent. As Geertz and Anderson make clear, the negative valuation of the *kasar* is linked to hierarchical relations in the political realm. Village people, in so far as they participate in a hierarchical political system, must and do incorporate these values at least to some degree: the peasant seems to be

'It is a style appropriate to a region rarely intruded upon by a stranger, not only because Malays conceal it to protect the back region of a performance team, but also because strangers allowed social involvement are honored and therefore due a more formal style of interactional behavior' (ibid.: 206).

associated with the rough and the crude by definition. For the most part such valuations appear inescapable even when they are negatively applied to the self. However, we know too that at moments actors step out of such a system and seek to change it. And this of course implies the availability of alternative ways of thinking and behaving.[14]

At a certain level, then, *kasar* behaviour has a positive value (which may be only implicitly and occasionally acknowledged), and this is very closely associated with the house, and particularly with its inner region, the *dapur*; indeed it may be said to constitute one of the house's defining features.[15] But this may have a much wider political significance beyond the house.

I began this chapter by recalling a conversation about how new houses are established. Aisyah's 'recipe' for making a kitchen vividly captures the idea that what is important about houses is their *dapur* and the food that is cooked there. It also captures the positive values which the house, the *dapur*, women, and the food that they cook are imbued with. The heat of the hearth is a source of life. The *dapur* and its food sustain those who live together in one house; they are the source of their unity. Hearths are associated with mothers; when women grow up, marry, and have children, they are eventually ready to establish their own house. A mother should then equip her daughter's new hearth so that it can feed the new household. Just as women generate daughters, so old hearths give rise to new ones. The two processes of reproduction are in fact one.

[14] It might be worth considering some of the limitations of Geertz's (1960) classic study of Javanese religion in the light of these comments. If the *kasar* can constitute an alternative discourse with greater political significance than Geertz implies, it may be possible to gain a better understanding of the links between the religious system he describes and the turbulent political events in Java around the time he was writing. As a source of positive values, however ambivalent, the *kasar* mode might then be seen as an aspect of what James Scott (1985) has called the 'weapons of the weak'.

[15] Provencher (1972: 71–2) has suggested that while *halus* behaviour is appropriate to the front room of the house and men, *kasar* is appropriate to the kitchen and women.

2

The Production of Children: House Cycles and Life Cycles

Villagers consider their houses incomplete unless there is at least one child living there. Houses are 'lonely' and 'quiet' without the noise of children. Adults delight in children's company. In old age, couples whose children have grown up and moved away regularly take a young grandchild or niece or nephew to live with them. Just as houses are incomplete without children, so too are marriages. Relations between husbands and wives focus on their children. A couple whose marriage is childless will either divorce or will foster children.

Children are a prerequisite for the establishment of houses. In this chapter I consider the way houses are established, where couples live after they marry, and who lives together in one house. I discuss the production of children in houses; the way in which children are attached to the house they are born in, and symbolic and practical aspects of their growth and development including their relations with parents. An important aspect of socialization is the way children are taught the positive and negative values of being modest or ashamed (*malu*), of being diligent (*rajin*), and of being stuck-up or proud (*sombong*). These values have different implications for girls and boys, for women and for men, and for the young and the old. I discuss the quality of relations within the house between and within different generations, and between men and women as they develop from youth to old age.

The Birth of Children

The fact that new houses are only founded after the birth of children is one aspect of a very great stress on the production of children in marriage. The early years of marriage are often unstable; infertility may well result in divorce. Children of both sexes are highly desired and it is their birth which stabilizes marriage. Childbirth also marks the attainment of full adult status for both women and men whereas marriage alone does not.

The birth of a first child, which occurs in a woman's mother's house, is associated with a complex of ritual procedures which I shall discuss again in Chapter 4.

What should be stressed here is the way mothers and new-born infants are attached to the house during the period following childbirth. In the forty-four days of ritual prohibitions after the birth of children, the mother and new-born child are particularly closely associated not only with the house to which they are confined, but with its symbolic focus, the *dapur*. Birth itself takes place in the *dapur*. Immediately following it, women have heat applied to their bodies in a number of ways. Post-childbirth prohibitions (*pantang beranak*) involve restrictions which prevent them from eating 'cooling' foods and bathing in cold water at the well—instead they use hot water inside the house. Traditionally, they reclined on a platform (*salaian*) beneath which a *dapur* was constructed to warm the mother. This hearth or fire is itself lit from the cooking hearth, *dapur masak*, of the house by the midwife. Today mothers are no longer heated in this way in Langkawi although many middle-aged women have vivid memories of the experience. However, women do still apply to their stomachs a flat stone (*batu tungku*) which has been 'cooked in the *dapur*' (*masak dalam dapur*) and then wrapped in cloth, every few hours after giving birth.

10. Children at a small *kenduri* to celebrate the birth of a child

The symbolic significance of these prohibitions will be taken up again later. Here I want only to underline the very strong association which is made between the birth of children, houses, and the heat of the hearth. The conclusion of this period of prohibitions is marked by a ritual cleansing of the *dapur* by the midwife after which both the mother and child descend from the house. The mother descends first, followed by the midwife, who carries the baby, letting its feet touch, first, the house ladder, then a stone with money on top placed at the bottom of the ladder, and lastly the ground by the ladder. The baby is helped to take a few 'steps' on the ground before the midwife carries it around the house three times and then carries it back inside. The child is attached to the house, its entrance, and its site. It will in this way remember the house however far off it travels in later life and will be able to return to it.

The Growth of Children

Before children learn to walk it is normal for them to spend most of their time inside the house but as they get older they spend more time outside it. Children play mainly outside the house in groups which, although not strictly segregated, tend to be single-sex. As children get older, their association with houses becomes more focused on eating and sleeping. At nightfall, when malevolent spirits are believed to be most prone to attack, it is particularly important for children to return home. Children do not normally sleep in houses where they are not resident.

Throughout childhood, great stress is laid on eating full rice meals in the house where they reside. The behaviour of children who frequently eat such meals in the houses of others is remarked upon and reflects badly on the reputation of adult members of their own households. Children may, however, accept snacks in other houses. These can be defined as food which does not include steamed rice as its main constituent, and is therefore neither a full meal nor proper food in Malay terms.

In spite of the close tie that children have with the house, this need not necessarily be their natal house. About one-quarter of all children are fostered by non-kin or very distant kin, or live with close kin who are not their birth parents. In these cases villagers always stress the importance of the child's own wishes as a somewhat capricious and unpredictable factor—and they deny that any category of kin have a right to claim a child from its parents. Nevertheless, two categories of kin are particularly important in this regard: grandparents and parents' siblings, particularly mothers' sisters. One of the few stated rules governing residence of children after a divorce allows for a perfectly symmetrical division: boys should go to their mother and girls to their father. In practice, this rule is not followed. The mother is regarded as the most suitable person to look after the children, and female consanguines are better than a stepmother. However, when the mother does not have care of the children, the child is more often brought up by the paternal grandparents than the maternal. I discuss the transfer of children further in Chapter 8.

Children's physical appearance and character are believed to be strongly influenced by the people they reside with. Many children do not live with both their parents. In such cases, they are thought to physically resemble and acquire the moral characteristics of those who bring them up. Living and eating together are essential to the process of physical and emotional development. Those one lives and eats with, as well as the food eaten, have a crucial effect on who one becomes. It is for this reason that children are so strongly enjoined to eat meals in the house in which they reside. The connection between eating together and kinship will be explored further in Chapter 4.

Pre-school children of both sexes are the great favourites of adults and have few restrictions placed on their behaviour. They are indulged by parents and grandparents, given sweets and snacks throughout the day; much attention is lavished on them, and it is rare to see a child of this age disciplined physically or verbally. A child generally ignores any adult admonitions and most adults do not persist, unless some danger to a child's safety is involved.

By the time they start school, both boys and girls have been allowed to go their own way to a considerable extent and, although a girl of this age who plays very roughly may occasionally be reprimanded for being 'like a male' (*macam orang jantang*), there is no really serious effort to curb the behaviour of girls more than boys. Noise and clamour are not avoided but are actively enjoyed by adults—without noise a house becomes quiet and lonely (*sunyi*), a negative attribute.

The attitude of parents to young children can be related at least in part to their religious beliefs. A child who dies before the age of 7 (before beginning school or Qur'ān classes) is assured of a place in paradise; this should be a cause for joy rather than grief. Up to the age of 5 or so children can be described as wild (*buas*). From the age of 7, when they begin religious studies, they may be wicked (*jahat*). They are expected to begin to demonstrate signs of rationality and judgement from this time.

'Indulgence', which has also been commented on by other Southeast Asian ethnographers,[1] can, however, be related to factors other than religion. Rather than setting up an opposition between adults and children (those who are sinful and those who are not), the manner in which young children are treated might be taken to suggest that they are seen in some respects as autonomous beings, equivalent to adults. Just as it is not permissible to upbraid or physically assault another adult, so it is rarely permissible to do so in dealings with children. Their behaviour only becomes more controlled, both internally and externally, when they are old enough to understand. The one exception to this is when the child has a younger sibling. When two children quarrel it is always the youngest that is favoured and whose side is taken by parents or other adults. This generally means that the birth of a sibling brings about a significant change in the life of a young child.

The attitude of children and their behaviour does, however, change once they reach school age. From the age of 7 to 11, children attend a state-run elementary school in the village during the mornings, and in the afternoons they receive instruction in the Qur'ān—usually in small groups in the homes of villagers with some religious learning. From this age upwards play is almost totally sex-segregated.

From the time they begin their religious and secular education, children are expected to behave with far greater respect towards adults, especially teachers, but also older kin and parents. They should be less self-willed and more disciplined and controlled, carrying out small tasks such as the delivery of messages or items of exchange, shopping, and household labour. Relations with parents, particularly between fathers and sons, become less obviously affectionate and more distant. One of the chief means by which this shift is effected is through shaming.

The term *malu* denotes shyness, embarrassment, shame. Around the age of 5 the phrase 'aren't you ashamed (in front) of people' (*tak malu orang?*) begins to be used extensively towards children considered to be behaving inappropriately. Such behaviour may consist of bothering adults, shouting loudly, disrespect, particularly to guests, eating impolitely, or being immodestly dressed. *Malu* is a key concept both in training children to adopt more *halus*, refined, patterns of behaviour and in the more general socialization of young children and adolescents. In early childhood, boys and girls tend to be shamed in quite similar ways,

[1] See e.g. Strange (1981: 61–2); Provencher (1971: 132–3); Rosemary Firth (1966: 107–8); Swift (1965: 106); H. Geertz (1961: 114–18).

but in adolescence its significance is different for young women and men. I discuss the importance of shaming and modesty for adolescent girls in the following section.[2]

Young boys are allowed to go their own way in the village and may often be found in its far-flung corners playing in groups; many have bicycles. Although parents worry if they are absent from home for long periods or do not return towards nightfall, boys are nevertheless left to themselves and discouraged from spending a lot of time at home. They may be sent to the shops on small errands but, in general, they participate only minimally in labour activities until after they leave school. They very rarely take any part in household labour; they do, however, look after younger siblings. Most boys do no more than two or three years secondary school—leaving school at about 14.

Adolescence

In adolescence young men are more mobile than women. Very frequently, they become migrant labourers for several years, either working on fishing trawlers from the mainland coast, or as building labourers. Education beyond secondary school is not available in Langkawi and higher education and secondary schooling may lead to migration from the island. Boys are more frequently sent away to secondary school than girls, and occasionally also go on to tertiary education. Once they have completed tertiary education, it is unlikely that they will return to their native village but will instead take up urban salaried occupations or accept a government posting elsewhere in Malaysia. However, these cases form a small minority; for most less-educated young men who have completed primary school and perhaps a few years of secondary school, temporary migrant work with periodic returns to the village until marriage is the norm. During this period young men make remittances to their parents and save towards the cost of their marriage.

During the same stage, young girls are relatively secluded in their homes. They achieve tertiary education less frequently than young men and only engage in migrant labour if the economic circumstances of their family make it absolutely necessary. Such labour might be in the electronics industry or take the form of domestic labour with an urban family. These occupations tend to be avoided and are taken up more by young

[2] See also H. Geertz (1961: 111, 114–18).

divorced women who are childless, or whose children are cared for by other relatives.

The most obvious fact about young boys from school age until marriage is that they spend progressively less and less time at home. In this their behaviour closely resembles that of older male household members. The years of migrant work associate men very strongly with the outside world. In these years, even when they come home on visits, the fact that they are economically self-sufficient allows them to spend much of their time frequenting coffee-shops or taking joyrides around the island on their own motor cycles with groups of friends and age-mates.[3]

During the years between school and marriage, young men's behaviour is not only orientated to the world outside the home, a world of fishing, coffee-shops, football, and close male friendships; it is also more subject to sexual segregation than at any other time in the male life cycle. Unless they are close kin, young unmarried men and women are kept strictly separated. There are no social occasions on which they may meet. Boys are less subject to constant restrictions and shaming than girls. Amongst themselves, their manner is boisterous and lively, sometimes rough. They speak loudly, and their actions and gestures in familiar contexts are neither demure nor refined; they laugh and joke freely between themselves and with old women, who, in many ways, form a female counterpart to young men in their behaviour. While this behaviour is common with their peers, on their rare appearances at home and in formal public contexts, at feasts or in the presence of strangers, youths may appear as embarrassed as young girls.[4]

The weakness of young men's connection to their natal home is underlined by the fact that not only do they spend very little time during the day there, but they may also lose their customary sleeping space at night. A young man will often sleep in various different parts of the house, depending on who else is visiting, or may eat or sleep in the home of neighbours of the compound. Within the house he often appears ill at ease and no less shy than his sisters of similar age. Parents will speak approvingly of how *malu* their son is, just as they do of a daughter.

Whereas adolescence is a time when most boys experience maximal outward orientation, young girls in their adolescent years are increasingly

[3] The pattern of male migration is familiar elsewhere in the region; see Provencher (1971: 73, 141), who comments that of all categories young men are the 'least involved in Malay communities'. See also Karim (1992: 22).

[4] Karim (1992: 130–1) notes the similarity between the restraints on young women and young men. See also Wilder (1970).

confined and restricted in their activities. Ideally, they should go out of the house as little as possible and, then, always with their head covered and, generally, in the company of other girls or women.[5] It is important to emphasize, however, that these restrictions operate outside the compound rather than the house. (See Chapter 6.) If in these years young men's embarrassment pushes them out of the house and into the company of their peers, so that they assume a kind of free-floating existence, the shyness of young women seems to attach them ever more strongly to the house where they live.

Young girls generally continue their schooling for about the same number of years or slightly fewer than boys. In former times there seems to have been more of a discrepancy in the educational level attained by boys and girls. Villagers say that this is due to the importance of maximizing a man's income-earning capacity. They also say that in the past girls were more strictly secluded. Now they are more free to 'come and go' (*jalan-jalan*). Formerly, I was told, parents were not keen to send young girls to school where they might have unsupervised encounters and pick up skills which it would be difficult for illiterate parents to keep a check on.

This difference still operates today although it is less marked. It is now quite normal for young girls to attend secondary school and I know of no parents who today use the argument of modesty as a reason to keep a girl away from school. It is still, however, true that in poorer families boys receive preference over girls in their education but, provided they can afford to, parents will keep daughters at school for as long as sons.

A young girl between puberty and marriage is an *anak dara*, maiden, virgin, unmarried girl, or bride. The equivalent term for a young man is *anak teruna*, but, whereas the female term is constantly used and carries with it a semantic load which has to do with the required behaviour for young girls, the male term is rarely heard outside the context of marriage ceremonies; that is, it usually means groom, and carries few behavioural connotations. An *anak dara* should at all times behave with great modesty. The central concept here is once again *malu*.

In the context of the behaviour of *anak dara*, *malu* means shy, retiring, obedient, and modest. These are the ideals of female behaviour before marriage. Young girls should spend most of their time indoors and be modestly dressed, especially when outside. In former times, these restric-

[5] See Strange (1981: 65, 134–5); Provencher (1971: 74, 139); Wilder (1970: 220, 229–30, 232).

tions were apparently more strictly adhered to: young girls would retire to the kitchen if unaccustomed visitors came to the house. They would be especially embarrassed to be seen eating by strangers, even if kinsmen. In theory, at least, a young bride did not see her husband till her wedding day. Still today, the contrast between the behaviour of *anak dara* and older women could not be more marked. Young girls almost always behave with great regard for Malay etiquette. In their eating habits, dress, and general manner they are often modest and diffident, even in their own home. Outside the compound, contact with young men is severely restricted. *Anak dara*, in Langkawi, unlike *anak teruna*, are prohibited from attending wedding feasts, the biggest social occasion in the village (see Chapter 6).

Another important attribute for young girls is to be hard-working, diligent (*rajin*). Even before they reach school age they are encouraged to perform small tasks of household labour: wash a few clothes, fetch water, wash dishes. While they are actually studying, they generally do only minimal household work but, during school holidays, and especially once they have left school, young girls are expected to undertake a considerable part of household labour: laundering, cooking, cleaning, looking after younger siblings or resident nieces and nephews. As they get older, they become more proficient in these tasks and, gradually, a daughter relieves her mother of almost all household labour.

Rajin is one of the most frequent and highly valued terms of praise for young girls. When visitors come to the house, young girls are expected to busy themselves in the kitchen. If girls go to the house of relatives, they must also immediately make themselves at home in the kitchen and help with housework as much as possible. To be *rajin* is a quality that is highly prized in a young bride—it is what prospective mothers-in-law look for when they begin to search for a suitable daughter-in-law. Girls are, in fact, sometimes sent to the home of relatives precisely to perform such services—either to earn money as domestic servants in the home of friends or relatives in the city, or locally, when sickness or childbirth renders a female relative incapable of household labour.

Not offering to help implies that a young girl is lazy (*malas*), and proud (*sombong*). The latter is one of the key concepts governing behaviour and relationships in Langkawi, and a common term of disparagement. Those who do not actively participate in communal events, are unfriendly, morose, stuck-up, or do not acknowledge duties of kinship are liable to be labelled *sombong*. A corollary of the modesty incumbent on young girls is that they, more than any others, must not appear *sombong*. An *anak dara*'s participation in the household labour of kin and neighbours proves her humility and her acknowledgement of social ties; further, it expresses these qualities on behalf of the household she represents on these occasions.

The valuation of these attributes applies to young girls of all backgrounds in Langkawi. It is perhaps even more important for an *anak dara* from a relatively privileged family to appear humble and modest than for others—her behaviour is more likely to be construed as arrogant and her obvious humility will be doubly appreciated. If *sombong* has an anti-social meaning at its heart it is not surprising to find that strangers from a different community are particularly severely assessed for their humility. When men from the village who have settled on the mainland bring home their city-bred wives on visits, the behaviour of these young women is subject to the closest scrutiny. If the wife in question is silent and nervous (as often happens), and moreover slow to help with work in the unfamiliar surroundings of her husband's home, she will quickly be dismissed as *sombong*.

Marriage

All adults marry, and marriage is regarded as the normal and desired state of adulthood. In Chapter 3 I discuss how the marital relation is based on a model of the relation between older brother and younger sister. In Chapters 7 and 8 I discuss marriage rituals and relations between affines in detail. Here, I briefly outline the principles which govern where couples live after the rituals are completed. In the penultimate section of this chapter I describe how the relationship between a husband and wife changes as they grow older.

People in Sungai Cantik move house quite frequently, especially in the period immediately after marriage. Residence is diverse, complex, and rather fluid, and villagers almost always deny that it is governed by explicit rules. Instead, they stress the unpredictability of where a couple will live after marrying, denying that either the husband's or the wife's parents have any prior claims. The one rule they do always emphasize is that married siblings should not live together because this will lead to quarrels.[6]

[6] For a more detailed account of household composition see Carsten (1987*a*: 98–142; 451–67).

This rule reflects the importance of household unity. In Chapter 1 I described the expression of this in the spatial arrangements of the house, particularly, in the fact that a house has only one hearth. If houses embody unity, this unity is above all expressed by a group of brothers and sisters. Division between siblings is as far as possible denied, but anxiety about division within the house at the same time focuses on relations between adult brothers and sisters. I explore the meanings of siblingship in detail in Chapter 3. The strong prohibition on married siblings residing together is explicitly an attempt to forestall any conflict of interests that may arise between them through their obligations to their own nuclear families.

Men usually marry around the age of 19 or 20, women at about 15 or 16. Women's age at first marriage has been rising in recent years with the increasing importance of education for girls. This means there may be little age difference between spouses. There are no bachelors or spinsters over the age of 25 in the village, and it is not uncommon for widows and widowers in their sixties and seventies to remarry. The avoidance of bachelorhood and living alone, in spite of divorce or widowhood, is a fundamental principle of adult life. It is also extremely rare for a couple of child-bearing age who do not have children to live together without other relatives. Whatever the generational composition of the household, married siblings and their spouses do not live together in one house.

After marriage, residence is rather mobile and villagers themselves are at pains to stress its unpredictability. 'It cannot be calculated (predicted)' (*tak boleh kira*), they say.[7] The balancing of obligations to each partner's kin is a central aspect of marriage and the relationship between affines.

After the marriage rituals are completed (see Chapter 7), the couple stays for different lengths of time in the houses of both sets of parents. This movement is known as *berulang*, literally, a repeated action, or a kind of oscillating residence. The couple may continue to move in this way until the birth of their first child, but gradually they begin to spend more of their time in one of the houses, still making occasional lengthy visits to the other.

Locality of residence after marriage is regarded as highly uncertain. However, it is influenced by the relative wealth of the couple's parents and

[7] H. Geertz has noted a similar lack of rules in Java (1961: 31). Jay reports that 'all my informants strongly maintained, down to the lowest levels of conception, that neither the bride's nor the groom's family was as a rule favoured in the choice of residence'. This, in spite of 'a clear statistical bias in favour of residence with or near the bride's parents or others of her close relatives' (1969: 40).

availability of space in their respective houses. If there is a married sibling and spouse already living in the parental home, either they will have to move out or the new couple will reside elsewhere.[8] If both spouses are local, large differences of wealth between the two families are rare, and the labour requirements of each household may be a more significant consideration. Although it might be assumed that a young man's labour would be more significant to the parental household than a young woman's, ensuring the household's female labour supply is often the overriding concern. I asked one woman about the forthcoming marriage of a nephew of hers; she told me that their final residence was still uncertain. 'The groom's family have no daughters,' she said, 'just two sons; while the bride's family have only one daughter. The young couple could settle in either home.'

Most frequently, couples live with the wife's parents after the period of oscillation. In part this relates to the importance of young women as a source of household labour. From the point of view of both the young woman and the older, there is a great preference for mothers and daughters to share a house rather than mothers and daughters-in-law. This is a reflection of the strong emotional bond that exists between mothers and daughters (see below). The women who live together cook for the whole household at the same hearth. While mothers and daughters amicably divide work between them, such arrangements may be strained when mothers and their daughters-in-law live together. The tendency towards uxorilocality is strengthened by the fact that a woman should always give birth to her first child in her mother's house. This rule is often extended to include a period of some months before and after the birth.[9]

Only after the couple have one or two children do they establish a new household. The birth of children establishes the adult status of the young couple and the viability of their marriage. Villagers imply that establishing a new house before the birth of children would be somehow improper. One old woman told me, 'in the past people didn't allow a couple to build their own house before they had children'. Most frequently, the new house will be in the same compound, *kampung*, as that of the parents. About two-thirds of all houses are built in the compound of the husband's family and about one-third in that of the wife.

Some couples continue to be rather mobile even after the birth of children, changing their locality four or five times during their marital life.

[8] See also Wilder (1982: 39).

[9] See also Strange (1981: 127); Wilder (1982: 45); Djamour (1965: 80); H. Geertz (1961: 68).

Such changes may involve them in periods of uxorilocality, virilocality, and neolocality. They may also move the house itself as well as its occupants. There are other couples who do not establish an independent household but instead settle permanently in one of the parental households, gradually succeeding the parents and caring for them in their old age.

Husbands are perceived to have the main financial responsibility for a new house. Men are the main earners of cash income and are responsible for the economic support (*sara*) of their wives. This is often seen to extend to the husband's parents. In practice, the couple have the main responsibility themselves but both sets of parents frequently help them if they can. Small amounts of money are generally given freely, but large amounts are regarded as debts (*hutang*) and are repaid. Occasionally, more wealthy siblings may also help with contributions to a house. Providing land and materials for a house may be a way for the parents to ensure the residence of the couple near by. In one case a married woman's parents paid for her house, as she herself said, in order to prevent the couple from going to live in the husband's village, some miles away. They succeeded in doing so in spite of the fact that the husband was an only child and his parents therefore might be thought to have strong claims on him. This couple had lived in the wife's parental home until after the birth of their fourth child and the bond between the wife and her mother was a particularly strong one.

Strained relations, particularly between an in-marrying spouse and his or her affines, may encourage a couple to set up an independent household (see Chapter 8). One woman, discussing the future residence of her son, said, 'It's better to build a separate house, otherwise you get quarrels and divorce.' When, as often happens, the couple are from the same village, availability of land in one or other of the parental compounds, or perhaps that of a grandparent, will be an important inducement to building a house there. If no land is available the couple will 'lodge' (*tumpang*) on land belonging to others.

As a couple's children marry they gradually form new households of their own. Some of these may be in different villages, some in different areas within the village, and some will be in the immediate locality of the parental home. The compound comprises the parental home and that of some of the couple's married children. Over time it will develop into a network of households dominated by ties between adult siblings and later between cousins. At any moment all these relations may be represented. The establishment of an independent household might be considered as the solution to the problem of balancing the obligations due to each partner's parents as well as that of strained relations between affines. However, this is only true in a limited sense when, as in the majority of cases, households are established in parental compounds.

Relations between the different houses of one compound are intense (see Chapter 6), and it is for this reason that whether the household is established in the husband's compound or the wife's is significant. The tendency of couples to live in the husband's compound at this stage can be linked to the fact that it is the husband and his parents who have the greater responsibility for financing the construction of a new house.

The interdependence of houses of one compound makes it difficult to consider the developmental cycle of the household independently of that of the compound. In the past, particularly around the beginning of the century when new areas of village land were cleared from the jungle, it was easier to establish new compounds than today when such land as is available must be bought at high prices and registered before it can be built on. The process of development of compounds, and the importance of ties between the households that comprise them, will be described in Chapter 6. In the same way that the household grows and divides to form a compound, the compound itself is the basis of village formation.

When villagers say that residence cannot be predicted, they are not merely being evasive. This is borne out by the complex and fluid practices I have described. The pattern that does emerge as typical—a period of commuting between two houses, followed by a period in the wife's parental home, in turn succeeded by residence in the husband's family compound—is the product of detailed observation rather than villagers' statements. However, it seems to accord with an unwillingness to attribute a priority of rights to either the wife's or the husband's kin and the desire to preserve a balance between them.

Divorce and Remarriage

About three-quarters of villagers have only married once during their lifetime but a substantial minority experience widowhood or divorce and remarriage. Divorce occurs in about one-quarter of all marriages, most often during the first one or two years of a first marriage. About half of the first marriages which end in divorce do so after less than one year, often in the first month (see Chapters 7 and 8).[10] About one-quarter of all villagers

[10] See also Rosemary Firth (1966: 44); Wilder (1982: 73); Strange (1981: 158); Downs (1967: 144); H. Geertz (1961: 75).

have contracted between two and four marriages. Polygyny occurs very rarely, and is always rapidly succeeded by the divorce of either the first or second wife.[11]

If a couple divorce in the first year or two of marriage, they will probably not yet have established their own independent household. Each partner will then return to, or remain in, their respective parental home. Sometimes, however, a divorcee will go to the home of another close relative, particularly if the two parental homes are close to each other. There are no cases of young divorced people living alone in the village. While before marriage young men are markedly more mobile than young women, this becomes less true after divorce. Young women are seen as being more free both to move about the village, to 'go about' (*jalan-jalan*) after a divorce, and to migrate to urban centres and take up employment there.

The likelihood of either partner leaving the village increases if the divorce has involved a scandal damaging to his or her reputation, or if it has developed into a major dispute in the village. Economic factors are also important. Opportunities for women to earn an income sufficient for their own support are extremely limited in the village. If a woman has no parents or siblings to support her she is more likely to move to an urban centre. Men have greater mobility and can maintain their economic independence more easily. After divorce they have a choice of continuing their income-earning occupation in the village or engaging in the migrant work with which they are already familiar.

If a divorce occurs early in a marriage when there are no children, it is easier for both partners to be reabsorbed into their parental households. Once a couple have children this reintegration becomes more problematic as does urban migration. At this stage in their married life a couple are also likely to have established themselves in an independent household. Which partner it is that leaves the conjugal household will then depend partly on the location of the house.

Since the majority of houses are constructed in the compound of the husband's parents, it is likely to be the wife who leaves, at least initially, for her parental home or that of another close female relative. If the couple's house has been built or acquired after their marriage it is regarded as joint marital property (*benda syarikat*). It may be dismantled or sold after a divorce, with each partner taking half of its cash value or half the building materials. Where one partner continues to live in the marital home, the other should in theory be compensated with half its cash value.

[11] See Rosemary Firth (1966: 48, 203); Kuchiba *et al.* (1979: 171).

Whereas after the death of a spouse, the widowed partner generally continues to live in the marital home, after a divorce and the consequent division of property it is less common for one partner to remain there.

Divorce and widowhood are generally followed by remarriage even in old age. Occasionally, divorced or widowed women living with their children form a household, but there are no cases of divorced or widowed men doing so. It is fundamental to the ethos of the house that adults do not live alone. Just as people need houses, so too do houses need people, particularly women and children. A house without at least one woman in it is not a proper house. But this is not all. People need companionship. Houses are lonely and quiet without the noise and hubbub of children in them. Adults think of themselves as sad and deprived without the company of children about them.

Relations between Parents and Children

The tie between mother and daughter is probably the closest and strongest within the household. During the early years of childhood it is easygoing, affectionate, and tolerant. As a young girl grows older, her behaviour becomes more restricted, especially in the years immediately preceding marriage. The relation gradually changes from the informal and relaxed to the hierarchical and restrictive.

At the very centre of this female hierarchy is the issue of household labour. Young girls effectively release their mothers from this work, while they themselves often seem little more than household servants. The increasing confinement of young girls within the home allows mothers to gradually reorientate themselves towards the outside. Young women, as well as being humble and industrious, must also show obedience. In spite of a steady stream of orders relating to cooking, cleaning, laundering, etc., it would be unthinkable for daughters to oppose their mothers or to refuse to carry out tasks. Although this could be described as more authoritarian than any other close kin relationship, this hierarchical core is somewhat obscured by the way mothers help their daughters with housework when necessary, especially when visitors come to the house.

More important is the extremely close emotional tie that binds mothers and daughters together from the early years of childhood. As young girls get older and become less mobile, the relationship is reinforced by the isolation of women together in the house and the absence of men. In spite of the demands of household labour, there is still time for rest and chat;

often female neighbours drop by, exchanging news and enjoying the relaxation. Over the years, mothers consolidate their ties with their daughters; these are often particularly strong with the eldest, who becomes a repository for her mother's wisdom and knowledge. Women often say that the love between female kin is stronger than that between male or male and female kin. Although the bonds of male kinship are legally 'more powerful' (*lebih kuasa*, *lagi kuat*),[12] for example in inheritance and marriage law, women are 'more dear' (*sayang lebih*), they say. Women also sometimes speak of themselves as united by one blood (*satu darah*), while that on the father's side is a 'little different' (*lain sikit*). They consider that agnatic and male kin are more likely to quarrel than those related through uterine ties. This may be related to one of the sources of power of agnatic kinship: property and inheritance through the male line, which is indeed often at the heart of disputes.

Women say that a mother worries for her daughter more than for her son. This emotional closeness, which has another manifestation in women's preference for uxorilocality, qualifies the hierarchical nature of the relations of domestic labour. All young women would prefer to work in their mother's home rather than in that of their mother-in-law; all older women would prefer to have their daughters at home with them rather than a daughter-in-law. Athough a young girl's relationship with her mother becomes more outwardly formal and obviously hierarchical as she grows older, the emotional closeness and intimacy develops and intensifies until the bond becomes a rich source of understanding and support.

When a woman marries, her inferior status as an *anak dara* begins to change. Although in the years immediately after marrying a woman is likely to be heavily occupied with looking after small children, her status begins to rise, especially after she has children, and gradually she becomes more orientated towards the neighbourhood and the community. Women who marry and divorce while still childless (sometimes after only a few weeks of marriage) are noticeably less restricted and more mobile than *anak dara*. Marriage is a first turning-point in the acquisition of full status for women as well as for men. Even after marriage if a daughter moves elsewhere she continues to make frequent visits to her mother and sisters, who also visit her.

Relations between male kin are, on the whole, more attenuated than those between women. Although fathers participate in the care of their small children and are warm and affectionate with sons and daughters in

[12] See also Djamour (1965: 32).

early childhood, they tend to be less concerned with discipline than mothers since they are so often absent from the home. It is this lack of presence on the part of fathers that above all characterizes their relationships with their children, making these less intense than those with mothers. The father–daughter relationship develops from the spontaneous affection of the early years to a less close relationship as the daughter grows up.

The relation between fathers and sons is a more clear case of generation-based hierarchy. As a boy grows up, the easy affection of childhood is replaced by a distant and authoritarian mode. Young men's relationships with their fathers are based on avoidance; they express acute embarrassment and fear when talking about their fathers. When two young men assisted me with survey work, one in his late teens and the other in his early twenties and a trained teacher, they both refused to ask their own fathers questions concerning marital histories. Neither had any difficulty getting the same information from other households in the village.

Since both youths and older men spend almost all their time outside the home where association of all kinds is largely age-based, fathers and sons have relatively little contact with each other after the years of early childhood. Men prefer to fish in non-kin-based groups and their friendships are generally with age-mates.[13]

In comparison with the father–son relationship, that between mother and son continues to be more intense even after early childhood. Female domination in the household is particularly evident in the attitude of older women to grown children of both sexes. Hierarchy in this case is not accompanied by avoidance except in so far as sons are less present in the household than daughters. Grown sons continue to treat their mothers with respect, and women take an active interest in their sons' concerns, including the selection of a daughter-in-law.

Affinal relations, and the complex and sometimes divisive nature of affinity in general, will be the subject of Chapter 8. Here I will only point out some of the qualitative aspects of particular relations and how these may be problematic when they are found within one household. After sons have married, mothers take a lively interest in their sons' new families. They are often quick to interfere and ready to make their opinions known—usually to their sons—thereby causing friction with daughters-in-law. Tension between mothers and daughters-in-law is expressed in a

[13] See also H. Geertz (1961: 121); Swift (1965: 108); Jay (1969: 103–10); Provencher (1971: 136).

number of ways, but one of the indications of its presence is the constantly reiterated denial by older women that they ever meddle in the concerns of married sons, or would accept financial support from them, or side with them in a marital quarrel.

When a couple live with the husband's parents, there may be considerable strain between the husband's mother and her daughter-in-law. The two women are obliged to spend most of their time together and this means that the younger woman will carry out most of the household labour under the supervision of a possibly critical, and almost certainly domineering, mother-in-law. There is very little positive emotional content to relieve the restraints placed on the younger woman. Hierarchy is unqualified by strong affective ties. Such problems do not arise between women and their fathers-in-law, with whom they generally have friendly but rather distant relations.[14]

When a couple live with the wife's parents, the resident son-in-law is likely to provide a substantial proportion of a family's income; he may in fact be the family's main source of support if his father-in-law is no longer productive. The father-in-law becomes increasingly marginalized as the son-in-law takes over his role as main income-earner. Because of this partial or total economic dependence, which may be combined with an aged couple's wish to continue to have a daughter living with them, every effort will be made to ensure smooth relations with a son-in-law. This generally results in an avoidance relation between father and son-in-law.

Resident sons-in-law have much more direct contact with their mothers-in-law, who tend to dominate the household, administering day-to-day finances and supervising labour. As the younger man gradually supersedes his father-in-law in the role of economic provider, he and his mother-in-law begin to occupy together the dominant positions in the household. Relations between them are generally friendly and relaxed. Young men often joke with their mothers-in-law and coexist on a rather less distant basis than with their own wives, with whom there is often avoidance and a considerable degree of constraint in public.

Parents in Old Age

In old age a married couple may continue to live in the marital home by themselves after all the children have left. This possibility is not generally

[14] See Jay (1969: 145–6).

regarded as ideal. Most villagers prefer to live with more people in the house, especially with children. A house with only one or two people in it is decribed as *sunyi*, lonely, and often aged couples bring up a grandchild to avoid this loneliness.

Villagers usually hope that one married child will settle permanently in the parental home. The young couple will gradually take on the running of the house, contributing their income and labour and caring for the aged couple when necessary. There is a marked preference for a co-resident married daughter. Some villagers also say the youngest child should succeed the parents in this way, and the two principles may be combined so that the youngest daughter stays with her parents. In their later years, it is rare for a couple to change residence, except as a result of death and divorce. The loneliness expressed by aged couples is even more pronounced for divorced and widowed persons. If they do not remarry these usually take up residence with a married child. It is particularly common for widowed mothers to live with married daughters. Old age is a time when the close ties between mothers and daughters receive clear practical expression.

Relations of authority within the household and between spouses change as people grow older. Sometime during their old age, or even in their middle years, fishermen experience a sharp break in their productive capacity. Increasing frailty or poor vision prevents them from going out to sea and they cease to make a significant contribution to the cash income of the household. There are few alternative productive occupations to fishing for men, and those that exist tend to be in the subsistence sphere. While they are still able to, men who have ceased to go out fishing involve themselves in agricultural labour. However, men's contribution to cultivation, whatever their age, tends to be supplementary to that of women, who dominate this sphere. During their most productive years, men engage in such activities only occasionally, at times when they are not out at sea. The fact that their contribution to such forms of labour increases in old age is a mark of their incapacity to engage in the proper sphere of productive activity for men—fishing.

As men get older and their ability to perform even agricultural labour diminishes, they have increasingly more leisure time. However, the spheres of leisure activities open to them diminish parallel to their declining opportunities in the productive process. Previously the family's major source of income, they now become economically dependent. When there is no younger man resident in the household, an aged couple are forced to eke out a living through the sale of small amounts of agricultural produce and the contributions of their adult children. In this situation a wife may become the major income-earner of the household. Women's contribution to the family income, which in previous years was supplementary, now becomes vital to the household economy. Whether the main income-earner is a wife or a son-in-law, old men become economically dependent on the women, who control household finances.

The financial dependence of old men limits the way that they can spend their leisure in that they are restricted in one of the main areas of male interaction: the coffee-shop. Unless they are well-off, their attendance there begins to decline. This may also imply an increasing marginality in the world of politics, in which the coffee-shop constitutes the main forum for discussion. A second main area for male activity is the mosque, and perhaps it is not surprising that, in their old age, men become increasingly observant of their religious duties. Not only do they go to the mosque or the prayer house for the five daily prayers, but they often spend a considerable amount of time chatting to each other in the small seating area just outside. Their behaviour presents a marked contrast to that of younger men, whose attendance at the mosque is often somewhat irregular.

It might seem that old men would be in a position to occupy a more central role in household affairs than in their younger years. In fact, old age only underlines the marginality of men to the household. They still spend as much time as possible out of the house and, even during the times they are at home, they take little direct part in the running of household affairs and decision-making. Nor are they treated with particular respect; rather, their wives and daughters, who have overall charge of the household, often treat them much like children. They are sent on small errands to the shops; if they venture to give their opinion during a family discussion they are often ignored or rebuked. When several older women are grouped together an old man often becomes the butt of their jokes.

Women's role in managing the household economy, their control of cash and active involvement in decision-making does not decline in the same way. On the contrary, women's authority in these matters tends to rise with age. Further, in contrast to men, women do not experience a sharp break in their productive capacity in old age. Household labour consists of numerous tasks which require varying amounts of energy to complete. Even women who are quite old and infirm can continue to take an active part in the lighter household chores and in the supervision of young children. To a lesser extent this is also true of some agricultural tasks. Weeding, planting, and harvesting can be done by quite old women;

they do not require the accurate vision or kind of stamina necessary to withstand long fishing trips in rough weather. Thus, the sexual division of labour has a determining effect on the degree of involvement of men and women in productive tasks in their old age. It is possible for women to remain active at an age when men have long ceased to make any substantial contribution to the household income. Although they do progressively less work, this is a gradual process, not the sharp break that their husbands experience. This contrast is often heightened by an age difference between husband and wife. A woman who is younger than her husband continues to be energetic and fit at a time when her husband is becoming increasingly feeble.

Perhaps even more fundamental is the attitude to household labour itself. While it is a husband's duty, prescribed in Islam, to provide for his family, it is regarded as a woman's (but not necessarily a wife's) to do the household labour. Cooking, washing, and cleaning are generally disliked by women, who prefer instead to engage in agricultural work, or, best of all, not to engage in work at all. I have described the hierarchical relationship that exists between mothers and daughters and how this centres on labour. Older women do the preferred tasks of agricultural labour; these may be extremely strenuous and take place in unpleasant conditions but they are preferred for being outside and undertaken in the company of other women. They also spend a great deal of time visiting friends and neighbours and playing a role in the wider community, particularly visits to the sick, the bereaved, and attendance at marriage feasts.

Women's ability to slough off disagreeable chores on daughters or daughters-in-law is, then, a mark of their increasing authority within the household. Far from being marginalized by younger members of the household, old women are treated with respect and often some fear by their daughters and daughters-in-law. I never saw an old woman being checked or rebuked by her daughter although this frequently happens to old men. It would be unthinkable to send an aged mother off on an errand or give her a demeaning task to do in the summary manner with which this is done to fathers. For as long as they are still mentally alert (physical fitness is not the crucial variable it is for men) women continue to play a major role in household affairs.

Because of women's increased outward orientation, close relationships between those of the same age group have a greater chance of finding expression at this stage in life. Women who are special favourites of one another spend a great deal of time together, both in leisure and in agricultural labour. Outside the immediate neighbourhood, as we shall see in Chapter 7, the tie between two women whose children have married, *bisan*, is often particularly intense. This may be both cause and effect of their children's marriage: women who already have a close relationship may attempt to arrange a marriage between their children. Subsequently, duties towards their grandchildren will bring them together. Older women devote much attention and time to looking after their grandchildren. Often they bring up a grandchild if all their own children have grown up and moved away.

When they are not busy, older women can frequently be found in the houses of their neighbours or on an outside verandah, sitting in groups of two, three, or more. Their chat, gossip, and jokes are often licentious, hours may be passed relating stories, occasionally bantering with men who pass by outside the house and teasing young male nephews or cousins, or old men who are considered a little past it. Men, for the most part, keep away from such goings-on—a strategy well-advised in view of the barbed humour that their appearance may provoke.

On these occasions, and in their own homes, the behaviour of old or middle-aged women is markedly different from that of younger ones and this is reflected in dress, body posture, and conversation (see Chapter 1). Their domineering, bawdy bossiness could not provide a greater contrast to the obedient, shy, meek manner expected of young girls.[15]

Thus, while men seem to lose their authority in old age, women gain it. Men reach a peak of seniority once they have married during their most productive years; after this active phase men's authority slowly declines. Never having been anything but marginal to the household and losing their position in the most important spheres of male activity, fishing and politics, they become 'displaced' in a community where women, meanwhile, gradually gain a place for themselves.

The marginality of men to the house is maximized, then, at two points: in adolescence and old age. At these junctures they seem almost to be excluded from participation in their own households. For a woman the years of greatest dominance are those during which she has adult daughters who, if they co-reside, carry out most of the household labour; at this stage she supervises household affairs. A woman's close links with her grandchildren and with her co-mothers-in-law contribute to her status and are a part of her increasing involvement with other houses of the community.

Once women become mentally unfit they are treated by the younger

[15] This dramatic change has I think been under-appreciated by some commentators who tend to see women as in general restrained and submissive; see Banks (1983). Even when this is not the case, the crucial difference age makes is often insufficiently stressed; see, for example, Jay (1969: 45, 61, 92).

members of the household in much the same way as men. The senile are tolerated and looked after in a manner reminiscent of children. It is revealing that the verb used for bringing up a child, *bela*, is the same one used to express the idea of caring for old people. Respect for the aged is a function of a person's ability to actively participate in the spheres appropriate to their sex. For men this is achieved through marriage, economic success, and participation in village politics. Although female status varies with a woman's individual personality and the position of the family in the community, the authority of women in their old age is more obviously an attribute of their position in the hierarchy of the household than that of men.

Conclusion: Children Make Houses

In more than one way children are necessary to the existence of houses and to the production of new houses. When children grow up and move away old people often take in a grandchild as if to ensure the continued reproductive flow of life through the house.

We have seen how children are symbolically and socially attached to the house they are born and reside in. The heat of the hearth, the focus of the house, nourishes household members; the food eaten together is an important part of their connection to each other. In the rituals of childbirth the heat of the hearth is associated with the production of children itself. The reproduction of houses and the reproduction of those who live in them are symbolically linked. And this was made clear in the conversation with Aisyah which I quoted at the beginning of Chapter 1. When a new house is established, its hearth must be lit so that cooking can begin. It is mothers who provide their daughters with the means for this to occur. As mothers generate daughters, so *dapur* generates *dapur*.

Children are an essential part of marriage and they may be said to 'make' houses. One focus of relations within the house is the intergenerational tie between parents and children which I have discussed here. Relations between parents and their children form a crucial axis of life in the house. And this is particularly true of mothers and their daughters—once again Aisyah's 'recipe' for establishing a new house makes the point vividly. But looking at houses, as it were 'vertically', from one generation to another, is only part of the story.

In a later chapter we will see how children also mediate between houses, facilitating the exchanges that houses of one village engage in with each other. This mediating role connects with another set of ties which, symbolically and practically, seems often to have an even greater significance than those between parents and children. This is the relation between siblings. One aspect of its centrality is that siblingship forms a bridge between the house as an isolated entity and the collectivity of houses that form a village. In the following chapter I suggest that an understanding of the association made between siblingship and the house is crucial to an elucidation of what constitutes the house in Langkawi. It also enables us to move outside the confines of the house to the village community.

3

Bodies within Bodies: The House and the Sibling Group

Brothers and sisters are, at least in theory, born and brought up in one house but, as they establish their own nuclear families, they come to live in different houses. Siblings are strongly attached to their natal house and symbolically associated with it, but siblingship is also the idiom of kinship in general and of relations in the wider community. In this chapter I trace out some of the specific and more general meanings of siblingship in Langkawi. I describe how relations between husbands and wives are modelled on an ideal of siblingship and show how these develop over time. The tensions inherent in sibling group dispersal, specifically over inheritance, are discussed. Finally, I look at the extension of siblingship beyond the house, showing how it comes to encapsulate the most central meanings of kinship morality and of morality that extends beyond kinship. I argue that the evocative power of siblingship is bound up with the association made between the house and the sibling group.

House Spirits and Siblingship

In Chapter 1 I described how the house spirit (*manya rumah* or *semangat rumah*) is thought to live in the central post of the house (*tiang seri*). The *semangat* of the house is in fact conceived as one of seven siblings (*tujuh beradik*). Like the *semangat* of rice, boats, and also people, the house spirit is part of a seven-member sibling set. But the status of the different members of these sets is ambivalent. As one old man told me, 'There are seven siblings, seven members (limbs), seven places. They are as one.[1] They live together. They don't have separate names, but they are seven.'[2]

[1] Literally, 'The one that's used is only one.'

[2] *Tujuh beradik, tujuh anggota, tujuh tempat. Yang pakai, satu sahaja. Duduk sekali. Tak ada nama asing tetapi tujuh.*

What is clear is that the seven members of this set are not separable. It is rather that the one spirit has a sevenfold quality and this is envisioned in terms of siblingship. The same man went on to explain how the seven limbs or parts (*anggota*)—the feet and hands, the head and the knees—are the ones that are washed before prayer. 'There are seven parts, seven siblings, but they are as one, they live together.'[3]

An association is thus made between the spirits and the very essence of a number of different entities: houses, boats, rice, and people. They all have the same quality which is both indivisible and sevenfold. It is conceptualized, first, in terms of siblingship, but also in terms of parts of the body. This suggests that, from the point of view of Malays in Langkawi, siblings are no more separable than are parts of the body.

Another old person further explained this notion of sevenfoldness in terms of the *semangat* of the person: 'When we give birth there are seven siblings, seven people. They are all beautiful but they are shadows. We can't see them unless they want us to.' Once again she drew attention to the parts of the body, which are like seven sibs. She and others also asserted that the origin of all these invisible sibling sets, the *semangat* of houses, boats, rice, and people, is unknown. That is, they are not perceived as the children of particular parents, and their parenthood remains a mystery.

Birth, Siblingship, and the House

The association between a set of siblings and the house in which they originate is made ritually at the time of birth. Each child belongs to a set of 'symbolic siblings' whose existence precedes birth. The child and the placenta (*uri*) are conceptualized as 'two siblings' (*dua beradik*). When a child is born the afterbirth, thought of as the younger sibling because it is 'born' last, is washed by the midwife and placed in a woven basket with a nail, salt, tamarind, a piece of white cloth, and pieces of medicinal roots. The nail prevents the afterbirth turning into a malevolent spirit, while salt and tamarind cause it to shrink; either might cause sickness in the child.

[3] See also Endicott (1970: 38–9, 41, 50, 63) on the fragmented yet unitary nature of the *semangat*, which he does not, however, discuss in terms of siblingship. Barraud (1990: 218, 223) discusses the notion of *mat inya* in Tanebar-Evav in terms strikingly similar to those I employ for the *semangat*. The *mat inya* is a kind of sevenfold essence of things which have social value.

The basket in which the afterbirth is wrapped is tied with pandanus (*menkuang*) leaves if the child is a girl, and with rattan (*rotan*) for a boy. These materials are essential to the house, and are associated with its interior and exterior. *Menkuang* is used to weave baskets and mats, the most essential items of house furnishings; *rotan* is used in house-building, especially for tying the house ladder together, as well as being used extensively in fishing boats. In the past a young man who could not tie a house ladder properly was deemed unready for marriage. The ritual ensures that a girl will grow into a good weaver of mats, and a boy into a skilled house-builder. It associates them from birth with the inside and the outside of the house respectively.

The basket is buried by the father under the house so that the afterbirth sibling 'doesn't go anywhere' (*tak pi ke mana*). The siblings are in this way anchored to the house and its site. The manner of burial recalls that of human corpses buried outside the village in the graveyard. Not to bury the afterbirth is likened to abortion; the mother commits a wrong against her child for which she will be held to account when she dies. Similar beliefs about symbolic sibling sets have been recorded widely elsewhere in Southeast Asia[4] and can be related to a complex cosmology which has been explored by Headley (1983; 1987*a*; 1987*b*). What I would stress here is the way that the sibling set is, in this ritual, physically anchored to the house and to its hearth.

A small fire is built over the burial place of the placenta and lit from the hearth, *dapur masak*, of the house. It is kept alight for one week so that the afterbirth shrinks and dries. Were it to swell and remain wet it would cause sickness to its older sibling, the child. Sickness or health of the younger sibling placenta (*adik uri*) is reflected in a similar state in the child.[5] It is the heat of the hearth which can prevent this sickness.

The child's state and that of its *adik uri* are intimately associated. When a baby laughs people say that the afterbirth is saying pleasant things to it; when it cries it is the afterbirth which is causing it distress.

The notion of siblingship thus asserts itself in the womb and continues to influence a child's fortunes in later life. Indeed the very idea of personhood involves the relation of siblingship since even an only child—highly undesired—has this symbolic sibling. Although an individual may

[4] These are often expanded to include the amniotic fluid and caul. See e.g. H. Geertz (1961: 89); Koentjaraningrat (1957: 21; 1960: 95) for Java; Snouck Hurgronje (1906: 375) and Bowen (1993: 216–26) for Aceh; Hooykaas (1974: 93–128) for Bali.

[5] Laderman (1983: 158) makes this connection even more explicitly. See also C. Geertz (1960: 46). Massard (1985: 76–7) mentions that the father must light a small fire on the tomb to be kept alight for forty days. She likens this to the 'sleeping light' of houses.

lack, or be separated from, human siblings she or he is an inseparable part of a sibling set, integral to the notion of the person, whose other members closely affect his or her well-being.[6] One could put this another way: if personhood necessarily involves siblingship, then siblingship is constitutive of the person. In Langkawi, I was told, the afterbirth and its older sister, the child, 'are like one person' (*macam satu orang*). Personhood involves siblingship; siblingship, like personhood, is indivisible.

The Indivisibility of Siblings

I was often struck by the homophonous personal names given to sets of siblings. Amongst the families I knew well such sets of names included Faridah, Fazil, Farizan; Sharifah, Sharimah, Sharizah; Zuhairi, Zunirah, Zuhaiza, Zuhamizan. When I asked my foster sister the reason for naming siblings in this way, she simply said, 'it's nice to be the same' (*seronok semacam*). Villagers often draw attention to the similarity, unity, and resemblance between siblings. The concept of siblingship as a complete and indivisible set of relations is expressed in terms of address and reference.

The term of address and reference for older brother is *abang*; that for older sister, *kakak*; younger sibling of either sex is *adik*. This set of three terms is constantly used in address and reference. Young babies are assiduously schooled in their use from before they can talk. The terms are also used by cousins (indeed, it is extremely discourteous not to do so) but the relative ages referred to are those of the sibling group from which the cousins are descended and not those of the cousins themselves. This has the effect of conflating cousins with siblings at the same time as emphasizing the unity and importance of the original sibling group.[7]

Another system of naming applied to a group of siblings draws further attention to the importance of birth order and at the same time emphasizes again the notion of the full sibling set. This system of address and reference consists of a series of birth order terms to which prefixes may be added to indicate the gender of the person being addressed and their

[6] McKinley (1981: 371–5) makes this point more elaborately. His premiss that 'siblingship [is] presented as an independent principle' in the Malay system accords perfectly with material from Langkawi. He also states that the elder sibling placenta is the same for any group of natal siblings since it returns to the womb to supervise the birth of younger siblings (p. 371). Once again the unity of a sibling group is emphasized.

[7] See also Waterson (1986: 93); Kemp (1983: 86); Bloch (1971*a*: 81) for the same principle in other Austronesian societies.

kinship status *vis-à-vis* the speaker. Starting from a basic set of three terms, oldest, middle, youngest, others are added so that the set may be extended until it contains nine terms. Villagers often differ slightly in the terms they give for larger sibling sets but for a three-sibling set the terms are:

1st born: *Wa/Lung* (from *sulung*, oldest).
2nd born: *Ngah* (from *setengah*, middle).
Last born: *Cu/Su* (from *bungsu*, youngest).

Some people suggested a nine-sibling version which accords with the evidence of other ethnographers.[8]

McKinley (1981: 367–8) has discussed how there are only four fixed terms in the series—'oldest', 'youngest', 'middle', and 'across' (*sulung*, *bungsu*, *tengah*, *alang*)—all the rest being terms which belong to a pair of opposites. The terms thus represent siblingship 'as a complete logical package' which has a 'basically triadic structure of "first—middle—last" ' and this can be expanded to 'first—middle//blocked—intermediate// last'.

In Langkawi these terms constitute one of the most frequent forms of address for co-villagers and are used in a number of ways: most commonly, in addressing members of ego's ascending generation, using the prefixes *mak* or *pak* for parents' sister and brother, and for classificatory aunt or uncle (i.e. cousins of ascending generations). They are also sometimes used to address the grandparental generation with the prefix *tok*, grandparent, and for classificatory (or occasionally for full) siblings, either with sibling terms as prefixes or with no prefix. Once again the prefix used depends on the birth order of the original sibling group, not on that of the cousins themselves. A young woman I knew called her female first cousin (the child of her mother's elder sister) *Kak* (from *kakak*, older sister) *Su* (youngest of her own sibling set), even though the cousin was younger than herself. The kin term prefix may be replaced by a shortening of the personal name used as suffix, especially in reference, for example *Pak Lang* whose name is *Mat* may also be called *Lang Mat*. When a man or woman marries they will be addressed by either their own or their

[8] Hodgson (1967) notes the fact that many of these terms are antonyms and express an idea of balance and complementarity. Wilder (1982: 79–88) uses the term *gelaran* for them and notes that these terms are so significant as to 'imply a major organising principle—siblingship—in the social structure of this community' (p. 88). Interestingly, he also collected a complete set of 9 terms—as also McKinley (1981: 367) and Mintz (1987: 83–4)—and notes that 9 is a key number in many Southeast Asian cosmologies. See also Banks (1983: 57–9).

spouse's birth order term depending on the context. A husband will tend to be known by his wife's birth order name in his wife's village or neighbourhood and by his wife's close kin, and the reverse will apply in the husband's.

A number of principles can be drawn out from this usage. First, the importance of siblingship as a complete set of relations from which other relations derive. Secondly, birth order is not only important in the generation of the original sibling group but also in succeeding generations. The terms which cousins use to each other emphasize the primacy of the original sibling relationship.

As McKinley (1981: 369) has noted, the fact that these terms are used principally for parents' siblings is highly significant. Kinship is constructed 'out of layers of *past siblingship*' (original emphasis) and these terms are thus 'applied to the very first relationship which reaches out from the nuclear family into the bilateral kindred'. They form, as he puts it, 'a cultural bridge between domestic and wider kindred domains'.[9]

Another principle of the birth order terms is that seniority of age is of more importance than gender distinctions (see Errington 1989: 206). These terms are the same for both sexes and are only distinguishable either when personal names are added, or in ego's own and immediately ascending generation, by a kin term prefix. The same is true for the terms *kakak*, *abang*, and *adik* (older sister, older brother, younger sibling), which only differentiate those siblings older than ego for gender.

Closeness between Siblings

Parents express anxiety about the consequences of separating siblings, and, more generally, of not treating siblings in the same way. Siblings should be brought up in one house together although they quite frequently are not. Widespread fostering arrangements together with marital instability often result in siblings being separated. I will take up the more positive connotations of fostering in a later chapter. Twins are regarded as particularly close, and their separation is avoided if at all possible. One

[9] See also Errington (1989: 214); Banks (1974: 54). But I would disagree with Banks (ibid.: 56) when he argues that 'The importance of *filial links* is illustrated in the prescribed use of parental birth order in establishment of the use of relative age terms for individuals outside of one's immediate sibling group' (emphasis added). In a later discussion Banks notes 'the Malay emphasis upon the sibling bond, which is described as equivalent in strength to that between parents and children' (1983: 57).

older woman told me that if twins must be separated it should be done whilst they are very young, before they are fully conscious of what is happening. Once they have learnt to talk they should be kept together so that they will bear no grudge against their mother for not treating them similarly.[10]

Children of both sexes are encouraged to look after their younger siblings and generally do so with great enthusiasm. In the house I lived in, and others that I often visited, older children, like adults, often showed interest in and affection for younger ones, and it was rare to see extreme jealousy between young siblings (although small fights did occur). Since play after early childhood is usually sex-segregated it is normal for siblings of the same sex to be particularly close. This is especially true of sisters, who in their youth will spend much time at home together, sharing household labour, relaxing and talking to each other. In the households I knew best, young brothers tended to be more dispersed, but sometimes these male bonds are also close. Older children have a protective attitude to younger ones—especially if there is a large age-difference between them.

It is rather hard to discern deferential behaviour between siblings in the daily rough-and-tumble of play and squabbles between young children of one house or even between first cousins in neighbouring houses. Instead, older children are socialized from a quite early age to give way to the desires and caprices of younger siblings. If there is a quarrel between children, and parents intervene, the older sibling is always told to defer to the younger. Youngest children receive preferential treatment, getting choice bits of food and being indulged in many small ways. I was often told that a youngest child is likely to be the most spoilt, and when I was asked about my own position in my natal sibling group—last born—villagers would nod knowingly and say 'ah, the favourite'. I can recall no instance where parents explicitly enjoined a child to show respect towards an older sibling.

As they grow older, children spend more time at school and with their age-mates than with their siblings. Behaviour to older siblings and to adults generally gradually becomes more muted and less boisterous. Parents begin to use the shaming techniques I described in Chapter 2, and attitudes of respect are strongly inculcated in school and religious

[10] Massard (1985: 75–6) reports that when twins are born the placenta is divided in two and buried in separate compounds, and that this is to avoid excessive dependency and intimacy between the children. The closeness of twins is so extreme as to be viewed with ambivalence. This bears out the impression I gained from villagers in Langkawi.

classes. Even in adolescence, however, deferential behaviour is more in evidence to members of other households than to one's own immediate siblings.

Closeness between siblings continues into adult life after marriage and the establishment of new households. In Chapter 2 the fact that older sisters frequently look after their younger siblings if the parents have died was referred to. I knew several women who spoke with pride of having in this way taken on the responsibility of marrying off a younger brother or sister. Siblings often live close together, building new houses on the piece of village land where their parental home stands. It is only when they cease to live together through education, marriage, or work that behaviour of a younger sibling to an older one becomes somewhat more formalized and deferential. This is more likely to occur between brothers, who tend to have less to do with each other than sisters.

Adult brothers and sisters continue to visit each other regularly, and if their homes are distant, such visits may be of several days' duration. This is especially true of sisters. While their parents are still alive, the parental home will tend to be the focal meeting-place of an adult sibling group. One married woman I knew used to spend so much time in her mother's house (where one of her married and two unmarried siblings also lived) that she made jokes about how they might as well really be living together. Thus siblings maintain close ties with each other from childhood into adulthood, and these bonds of kinship receive constant acknowledgement in the form of visits, labour co-operation, loans, and financial support.

A young man who lived in a neighbouring house was extremely religious; he put great pressure on the women in his family to behave with greater modesty, particularly in matters of dress. While he was able to have an influence on his nieces (in their early teens), his constant efforts had no effect at all on an unmarried sister, three years older, on his eldest (married) sister, or on his mother. Behaviour between siblings thus tends to reflect relative age more than sex differentiation. Although boys are legally in a superior position, especially over inheritance, this is not reflected in attitudes or behaviour of sisters to their brothers. I never saw sisters show particular respect for either younger or older brothers. On the contrary, since women (even when relatively young) tend to organize household affairs, it was common to witness a young man being bossed about by his sister. Brothers who are much older will sometimes have a degree of authority over a younger sister, but one who is only slightly older or younger will not. Legally, however, a younger brother can act as his sister's guardian, *wali*, and give her away in marriage.

Eldest daughters are often in a particular position of seniority, drawing close to the parental generation. A senior daughter may have quite hierarchical relations with younger sisters, who may still be unmarried, and are likely to do the greater part of the household labour in the parental home and often help to look after the elder sister's children. Two sisters I knew well were in this kind of relationship, with the younger performing far more household labour than the older. Such situations, involving a large age difference, maximize the authoritarian content of the relationship between sisters. Even in cases like this, however, the hierarchy was masked by close emotional bonds and by the tendency of all women to help each other with household labour. It is, then, degree of difference in age that is crucial to the hierarchical content of the relation between siblings, whatever their gender. When siblings are closer in age the relation becomes more egalitarian and companionable. Sisters tend to remain close and affectionate as adults and fostering of each other's children is one expression of this.[11]

Older brothers are usually affectionate to their younger sisters. In one household I knew, an unmarried adult sister was often brought home treats or taken on outings by her older brothers. I know of no case where an older brother had marked authority over a younger sister. However, I observed many instances of adult older brothers being scolded by younger as well as older sisters. In an unusually heated family argument I once saw a younger sister, in her thirties, strike her older brother.

I was often struck by the behaviour of two adult brothers who were close in age and lived in neighbouring houses. Mat and Tam were obviously affectionate and often visited each other's houses, behaving in a very relaxed way together, but this case was quite unusual. Their closeness was intensified by the fact that they were married to first cousins, brought up in the same compound. The relation between two brothers is usually less close and affectionate, however, than that of sisters or sister and brother. Brothers who are not close in age generally spend little time together. In adulthood they may call on each other for loans or other forms of aid, but the emotional content of the relationship is less intense than when they are close in years.[12] In Chapter 2 we saw that married siblings do not co-reside. This means that in adulthood siblings rarely live together except for brief periods following widowhood or divorce.

[11] See also Peletz (1988: 213–17); Jay (1969: 119, 166); Swift (1965: 112); McKinley (1981: 336–9, 376–80). McKinley notes that 'sororal closeness tends to mediate fraternal antagonisms' (p. 337).

[12] See also Jay (1969: 121–2); McKinley (1981: 336–7); Peletz (1988: 29, 40–1) on antagonism between brothers.

Because of the strong emphasis on the unity and harmony of the sibling group, its disruption is highly threatening. Within a group of siblings there is a general notion that marriage order should follow birth order. If a younger sister marries before an older sister or brother this is referred to as 'to step over the doorsill' (*melangkah bendul*, from *melangkah*, a big step or stride, and *bendul*, the wooden sill at the base of a doorway).

Villagers explained that a younger brother may marry before his older brother because it is the side being asked for in marriage, the bride's side, whose sibling group order is perceived to be disrupted in this way. If a younger sister marries before her older brother the birth order of this group is breached, although people say, 'it's not serious' (*tak payah*). In fact this frequently occurs as a result of the difference in marrying age between men and women. In these cases the husband of the younger sister must make a ritual compensation to his wife's older brother in the form of a suit of clothes. This payment is referred to as *salin baju* (*salin*, to change or bestow clothes, and *baju*, a shirt or clothes generally).

The prohibition, and the ritual compensation for breaching it, underline the unity of the sibling group. By taking a younger sister as a wife before her older brother or sister, the in-marrying male violates the order and unity of a group of siblings. This is most strongly marked between sisters, who in fact never marry out of turn. Sibling groups are strongly associated with their house of origin. By threatening to disrupt the natural order between brothers and sisters, the male affine violates the house itself. This is expressed in the linguistic usage: 'striding across the threshold', which signifies an act of aggression against the house itself.[13]

Cousins who live in adjacent houses and are of similar ages are often on very good terms with each other both in childhood and in adulthood. Significantly, these relations are often more relaxed and companionable than those between siblings; they lack the hierarchical tone of siblings who are widely separated in age. One strong expression of this is that, although cousins should in theory address each other using sibling terms derived from the relative age of the sibling group from which they are descended, these terms are sometimes manipulated to take account of the relative ages

[13] Wilder (1982: 58) reports *langkah bendul* in Pahang, but compensation is only paid by the husband of a younger sister to an older sister. Djamour (1965: 71–2) reports the same as Wilder of Malays in Singapore, where the practice is known as *melangkah batang*, 'to stride across a rod'. However, she notes that the Javanese in Singapore extend the practice to cover an older unmarried brother of the bride. H. Geertz (1961: 60) reports that 'a younger brother or sister should postpone marriage till after the older sibling, especially an older sister is married, but this restriction is often ignored or evaded'. A man is found to go through a mock marriage with the unmarried older sister at the same time as the younger sister marries; this ritual is known as *nlangkahi gunung*, 'stepping over the mountain'.

of the cousins themselves or even to erase such distinctions altogether. Two young women I knew well provide a case in point. When I asked them why they did not address each other in the expected way but instead called each other 'younger sibling' (*adik*) reciprocally, they said it was because they were so fond of each other.

Joking and teasing between cross-sex cousins is common, particularly if they are brought up in the same compound or neighbourhood. In the compound in which I lived I often saw adolescent cousins of opposite sex tease each other or interact in quite relaxed ways which would have been unthinkable between other cross-sex age-mates. It is significant that the conflation of cousins and siblings may mean that marriage between them is thought of as incestuous (see Chapter 7). Ideas about cousins expressed in terminology and behaviour indicate that the household in some respects extends beyond the physical structure of the house to include adjacent houses in which parents' siblings and first cousins (classificatory siblings) reside.[14]

Spouses into Siblings

The idea that husbands and wives can at one level be thought of as siblings is expressed in the marriage ritual itself. The idiom of domestic kinship and of siblingship is invoked through the ritual introduction and attachment of the bride and groom to the house of their spouse (see also Bowen 1993: 225).

When the groom is taken in the marriage procession to the house of the bride, he enters through the door into the *ibu rumah*, greets his affinal kin there, is then served a rice meal together with the bride in a *bilek*, and finally the bride and groom exit from the house via the *dapur*. The groom must be sure to leave the house from the kitchen door (*pintu dapur*). The couple then go in procession to the groom's house where the bride is formally greeted by her mother-in-law. She has her feet washed by her mother-in-law in a tray of water in which a stone with money under it has been placed. Villagers explicitly liken this ritual to the first descent from the house by a baby, only in this case the tray with water and money are placed just inside the house at the top of the ladder, whereas for a new

[14] Wilder (1976: 302–4) has emphasized that the prominence of birth order terms can be seen in this light. These terms express 'in the most exhaustive fashion the smallest kinship unit possible—the sibling group' (p. 304). It is these that provide the metaphor for community growth and expansion.

baby it is at the bottom of the ladder on the ground. While babies are taken out of the house they are born in and introduced to the ground around it, daughters-in-law are taken into the house and introduced to the *dapur*. The couple then proceed to eat together once again. Here too the couple enter through the door into the *ibu rumah* and come out from the *dapur*. People say this is to show the house to the new spouse, so that it 'becomes their own house' (*jadi rumah ke diri*).

The marriage rituals will be discussed in more detail in Chapter 7. Here what I would emphasize is the way the bride and groom are ritually incorporated into the house and hearth of their spouse. And that this is symbolically associated with the attachment of babies to the house they are born into. The strong evocation of the idiom of domestic kinship through the prominence of the hearth and co-feeding suggests that the ritual symbolically transforms the bride and groom into each other's sibling. And this suggestion is strengthened by the kinship terms that husbands and wives should use for each other.

Villagers always state that the correct term of address for wives to use to their husbands is *abang*, older brother; that for husbands to wives is *adik*, younger sibling. These terms carry the strongest connotations of consanguineal relatedness. They also imply hierarchy. In other contexts when sibling terms are extended to non-siblings there is often an avoidance of the term *adik* because of its implication of inferiority of the person addressed. It is significant that throughout fieldwork I never heard a husband address or refer to his wife using this term. Wives sometimes refer to their husbands as *abang* (followed by a personal name) but avoid it in address.[15]

The most commonly used term of reference is a personal name, sometimes accompanied by a kin term appropriate to the listener. Young couples go to elaborate lengths to avoid using any term of address to each other. For example, a young mother who wanted to call her husband, sitting perhaps only in the next room, would tell a child to go and call its father, rather than calling out herself. All terms of address in Malay carry status implications for the relationship between speaker and listener; most

[15] McKinley (1981: 358) has discussed this usage and emphasizes the fact that the terms *abang*, *kak*, *adik* (older brother, older sister, younger sibling) imply *three* status levels, not two; for this reason husbands become older brother but wives do not become older sister. The usage is partly a matter of affection and partly implies a seniority relation between husband and wife (p. 352). However, it also 'smooths' the transition between pure affinal categories and sibling ones. His idea that marriage and affinal relations are built directly on present siblingship in much the same way that cognatic kinship builds on layers of past siblingship is highly suggestive (see Ch. 7).

have connotations of hierarchy. Avoidance of these terms suggests an unwillingness to accept such implications.

Part of the significance of the association between the marital relation and siblingship should be clear. Spouses are unfamiliar with each other when they marry. Referring to the domain which above all connotes closeness and intimacy—the house and domestic kinship—is part of the construction of an ideal in this relation. This ideal is rooted in resemblance (a point which will be developed in Chapter 7). Siblingship is also exceptionally malleable. Phrasing the marital relation in terms of siblingship evokes a complex and powerful source of references for young men and women: closeness, resemblance, harmony, mutuality. Siblingship involves hierarchy that can be transformed into equality or vice versa; it is central to kinship morality and to the house. Marriage ought to be imbued with these same qualities.

Wives and Husbands

One middle-aged man described to me how marriage had meant an end to his youthful freedom, the beginning of a more settled existence and an end to a long period of migrant labour. He ceased to spend as much time (and money) with his close friends of the same age in the coffee-shop and had to become more responsible in attitude. In contrast, young women are released from some of the constraints which govern their existence as *anak dara*. This, however, is a gradual process. Newly-wedded couples often have no knowledge of each other before marrying; they appear painfully shy and inhibited in each other's company in the first phase of their married life. Although some of this shyness gradually wears off, married couples continue to avoid contact with each other on all public occasions and often even in their own homes.

During much of the day, spouses are separated from each other by their labour activities; in public contexts all social occasions are sex-segregated. This avoidance behaviour finds its parallel in the home, where spouses rarely sit together on their own. In general, young couples eat with other household members and not by themselves. Husbands and wives of all ages avoid physical contact in front of even close family members. Usually they do not sit near to each other and do not tease or joke together, especially during the early phase of married life. They rarely talk privately together, and in public they each relate separately to other people present.

As a couple get older, they gradually begin to relax more in each other's presence and often a close, affectionate relationship develops. Although they continue to avoid physical contact in public, and participation in social events remains sex-segregated, their conversation, at least in familiar contexts, becomes freer. Once again terms of address are a relevant indicator: husbands and wives continue to avoid them where possible, but they sometimes use the familiar terms for I and you, *aku* and *hang*, reciprocally to each other, especially in private. This usage strongly indicates that spouses are on familiar, relaxed terms and treat each other equally. They may also use personal names to address each other, with similar implications.

Important decisions in the household (for example, over rebuilding a house or other major expense) are usually arrived at after consultation between husband and wife on an equal basis.[16] Everyday matters in the household are, however, dominated by women. This situation is complicated by factors to do with the developmental cycle of the domestic group. A husband who is no longer productive is not the economic provider, while his son, son-in-law, or sometimes his wife on her own, will take on this role. In such cases, which generally occur late in a couple's marital history, a wife will dominate over her husband and may appear to run the household more in conjunction with her son-in-law, or if no productive man is resident, by herself. Early on in the marriage, when a woman may reside in the house of her mother or mother-in-law, the older woman will have a dominant position over the younger.

The middle years of marital life, then, are the ones in which the status of husband and wife most closely coincides. The early restraint and inhibition are no longer present and both spouses are productive in their own sphere. Women are not as *malu* as in their youth, nor yet as domineering as in old age.

Women have a right to expect sexual gratification from their husbands. Women whose husbands are frequently absent from home for long periods hold this against them even if the husband supports his family economically. A recently married woman who was in this situation spoke of feeling 'hungry' (*lapar*) and 'thirsty' (*dahaga*), that is, sexually

[16] Swift (1963: 279) comments that relations between husbands and wives are 'much more egalitarian than at first sight they appear'. My account differs markedly from that of Banks (1983), who argues that Malay men are seen as superior to their wives: 'In short, the male is the most responsible party in a marriage and is also the head of a household' (1983: 66. See also pp. 97–104).

deprived, and this was mentioned in connection with the possibility of divorce.[17]

Husbands are rarely violent towards their wives. In fact, I was told of more cases of physical force being used by wives against husbands than vice versa. Polygamy, although legal, is extremely rare. Villagers say that it is impossible to find a woman who will agree to such a union. The close ties that a daughter maintains with her natal home, particularly with her mother, even after marriage, give her a recourse in marital disputes. Men have reasons to be reluctant to force cohabitation on wives who want to separate. One old man told me that such a procedure would be hazardous since it is women who cook, and one couldn't know what an angry wife might put in the food. I have argued that food and commensality are a prime focus of domestic harmony. These same symbols have equally strong negative potential. In a dispute, poisoned food is a powerful symbol of domestic strife and division.

Hierarchical relations between wives and husbands are a result of each partner's position in the age/status hierarchy of their own sex and the conjunction of this with that of a spouse, rather than hierarchy between men and women as such. There is a broad complementarity in the different spheres of labour which men and women engage in; villagers stress the importance of both men's and women's work. This equivalence does not, however, extend to the legal domain. In Muslim family law, and particularly with regard to divorce (see Chapter 8) and inheritance, women are clearly in an inferior position; this is constantly reiterated by women and men.

Spouses between Siblings: Inheritance and Disputes

As siblings grow up, marry, and have children and settle in different houses they are inevitably divided. Although marriage is conceived partly in terms of siblingship, it also negates it. The spouses of a group of siblings have the interests of their own nuclear families at heart. The loyalty of siblings towards each other becomes divided after marriage. Their property will eventually be dispersed, and in the process their amity may well turn to enmity.

Notions about siblings and about the house express a strong resistance to division. It is therefore not surprising that both the individual owner-

[17] Nash (1974: 38) describes how men are 'expected to perform at continual high levels in marital sex', and that non-fulfilment of such expectations may lead to divorce.

ship of property within the house, and property division among those who originate from one house, are always a source of tension and ambivalently conceived.

During the first months of fieldwork I was often irritated to find that the shoes which I left outside the house (along with those of other household members) had been taken by my foster brother who had the same size feet as me. The source of irritation was twofold: this felt like a curb on my mobility of the most direct kind, and the fact that my shoes fitted him perfectly reinforced the impression that I was much too big by Malay standards. Eventually, the disappearance of my shoes became a running joke, and my foster mother would regularly intervene on my behalf by hiding them for me. This trivial example illustrates how those who reside in one house tend not to have exclusive rights to property. Household members of the same sex often use each other's clothing and other personal articles and these are simply taken without asking anyone's permission. The same principle also applies between children: within a group of siblings no child has exclusive rights over a particular toy.

To a great extent, then, the individual ownership of property within the household is resisted—both formally, in that the rules governing marital assets mean that the couple is a single property-owning unit, and informally, in that co-residents constantly borrow from each other; they informally share space and property.[18] The partitioning of property, and particularly of land, which is both a valuable asset and often held in common by siblings, is always problematic and potentially disruptive to their harmonious relations. The idea that division and disputes are associated is a powerful one; villagers have an overriding desire to avoid the disruptive effects of both, and this has highly significant implications for patterns of inheritance.[19]

The most valuable forms of heritable property are land (primarily that used for rice cultivation or houses), houses, fruit trees, boats, and jewellery. Villagers are reluctant to discuss the inheritance of all of these, and this can once again be associated with the way that property division often involves disputes. Further, there is a reluctance to actually divide such property. This means that aged couples generally farm land jointly together with their resident adult children without any subdivision. One

[18] In contrast, Rudie (1994: 104, 163–4) emphasizes economic individualization and women's economic independence from their husbands, particularly at the time of the fieldwork she carried out in the 1960s in Kelantan, although this autonomy appears to be in decline. Li (1989) emphasizes economic individualism among Malays in Singapore.

[19] I discuss inheritance practices in more detail (especially on the issues of male and female inheritance and Muslim law and custom, *adat*) in Carsten (1987*a*: 234–54, 468–72; 1990). I draw on this material here.

reason given by villagers for not giving property to children is that landholdings tend to be small and subdivision is impractical.

The resistance to dividing property persists, however, long after the death of the original owner. The fact that wills are never made can perhaps be seen as a further manifestation of the same phenomenon.[20] Verbal agreements are sometimes made, however, between offspring and their aged parents concerning division of property after the death of the latter. Pre-mortem inheritance occurs only rarely; it is highly unusual for land, or any substantial amount of movable property, to be given outright to children at the time of their marriage or on any other occasion during the lifetime of their parents. However, as the parents get older, resident children may take on much of the labour of rice-farming and keep a proportion of the crop.

After a death has occurred, the division of property takes place in two stages. The first is informal and generally only benefits the resident children and spouse of the deceased. In every case that I discussed with villagers, this stage involved sons and daughters getting equal shares in the land of their parents. The proportion of the widowed spouse is variable depending on need, age, and ability to participate in agricultural tasks. Women always emphasized the uncertainty of their portion even at the informal stage (a point which I will return to below). However, I did not come across any case of the informal division of land being carried out in accordance with Muslim laws of inheritance.

The formal, legal division of property is costly and often highly complicated because of the large number of beneficiaries that may be involved. This procedure primarily involves the division of land, of which the most significant part is used for the cultivation of rice. The division is decided at the local District Office, with the assistance of a *kadi* (religious judge), and the property is automatically apportioned according to Muslim law (*hukum Shariʿah*).[21] However, provided all beneficiaries agree, they are

[20] See Strange (1980: 135); Massard (1983*a*: 345). This evidence conflicts with Banks (1976: 578), who states that 'Malays dread intestacy'. It is notable that the resistance to making wills is not described in terms of Islamic doctrine.

[21] According to the religious rules same-sex siblings receive equal portions but sons inherit twice as much as daughters; a widow receives 1/8 of her husband's property and a widower receives 1/4 of his wife's; female grandchildren receive 1/2 of the portion of male grandchildren. In cases in which there is a daughter but no son half the inheritance goes automatically to a state land fund, *baitulmal*. However, female heirs are entitled to buy back land from this fund. Where there are no direct descendants, property is inherited by collaterals of the deceased and their descendants. Malay property is automatically apportioned by the District Offices of the state of Kedah according to the above rules. See also Banks (1976: 573–4, 578).

free to reallocate the inheritance amongst themselves in any way they wish and the final allocation will then be registered by the Land Office.

During the first, informal, phase, the property is still legally registered in the name of the original owner. This situation may persist for as long as sixty years, by which time the children of the original owner and sometimes even their children have died. Thus, it is common to find groups of siblings or first cousins living on, and obtaining rice from, land which they effectively co-own but is legally registered in the name of a parent or grandparent who has been dead for many years.

Not only can such a situation come about through the deferral of formal division, but land titles may sometimes actually be bought in the name of a dead ancestor. In one case in which a father asked his children to divide his property equally, the titles to the village land on which the family's houses were built had not actually been acquired by him. After his death his children bought the land titles in their dead father's name, each contributing an equal share. This was done specifically in order to avoid subdividing the land.

More frequently, however, the legal division of property is simply deferred. In thirty cases of formal, legal division of property (*ambil kuasa*) which I analysed in detail, the mean deferral period which elapsed after the death of the original owner was almost twenty years, that is, within two generations.[22]

This evidence, combined with villagers' statements, in which the division of land was often discussed with much bitterness, suggests that, ideally, close kin (siblings and first cousins) should not divide the property they hold in common. If they coexist harmoniously, the legal division is unnecessary and resisted since it is likely to cause friction and quarrels. Whether such disputes are the result or the cause of property division is a moot point—it would seem that often they are both—disputes lead to property division and this itself sparks off further disputes. One woman related how she and her siblings wanted to divide the property of their grandparents while the parents wanted to keep it united. She insisted that disputes occur *before* the partitioning, but once the division was made there would be no more quarrels.[23]

[22] This evidence was obtained from the files of the District Office at Kuah. It consists of every fourth case adjudicated by the District Office in 1981.

[23] The conclusion of Kuchiba *et al.* that the discussion of inheritance implies disrespect to parents and must therefore be avoided (1979: 52) is not applicable to Langkawi. Rather, priority must be given to the centrality of relations between siblings in explaining this reluctance. See also Peletz (1985; 1988).

The breakdown of relations between siblings may have wider ramifications in the community. This is not only because the community is itself built on a model in which kin (that is, people united through extended siblingship) co-operate with each other and live together in a harmonious manner, but also because of the large numbers of people who may be involved. In one inheritance case which I examined the deferral period was fifty-nine years, by which time thirty-nine people had registered their claims. This would have meant that in order to divide the land in accordance with Muslim law it would first have to be divided into 36,288 equal shares. The land office refused to involve itself in such complexities and, instead, simply divided the property between the five children of the deceased—ignoring the fact that these children were all long since dead. The evidence would suggest that the thirty-nine claimants would have got little satisfaction from this procedure. More significantly, a property division involving thirty-nine people, each supported by their close kin and friends, can be assumed to have a highly disruptive effect on relations in a village community.

Division of property then, is an evil in that it implies disputes and separation. However, it is a necessary evil since it is also a means, the only one available, to the resolution of disputes: as one woman put it to me, 'Once property is separated, relations become easier, there are no more quarrels.' And this would suggest that such division is in the last analysis inevitable. However, the divisions within a once unified kin group are now rigidified and made permanent. This fact, which is recognized by villagers, is at the heart of their ambivalence towards property division.[24]

The tendency to avoid dividing property has other implications apart from maintaining kin unity. The avoidance or deferral of formal inheritance procedure limits the subdivision and alienation of land. That this is a conscious process is revealed both in the comments of villagers on those who sell land, who are sometimes referred to as *orang jahat*, 'bad people', and in strategies for keeping land together. Small plots of land which would be uneconomical to divide are frequently kept in their entirety and farmed in rotation (*bergeliar*) by co-owners who are usually siblings or first cousins. This avoids the alienation of property and its unequal division between siblings.[25]

Women often emphasize the uncertainty of their inheritance, saying that the allocation they receive is dependent on their male co-heirs. I knew

[24] See also Nagata (1976: 401–2); Massard (1983*a*: 353); Banks (1976: 577).
[25] See H. Geertz (1961: 52); Swift (1965: 171–2).

several cases of parents who made their children promise to divide land equally between them and such promises were respected. However, the male heirs must agree in order that an equal partitioning of property can take place. Where there are no male heirs, parents sometimes register the land in the name of a daughter before death. This practice avoids the problem of land going to the *baitulmal* (state land fund) and male collaterals, and having to be bought back. There were also cases where land had been registered in the name of a daughter in spite of the existence of male heirs. Parents described such action as a precaution taken to safeguard the inheritance of daughters, in case their brothers claimed the major share of land.

Villagers perceive two problems in the safeguarding of the inheritance of daughters. The first, where there are no sons, is to prevent land from passing to male collaterals. As one woman (who had three daughters recently followed by a son) put it to me, 'If there is one male child we don't worry, the inheritance can be taken. But if they are all girls, the inheritance goes back to the *waris* [nearest male heir], and that's what's hard for women. You do the work but other people gain—your own children don't benefit.'

The second problem is directly linked to the first. That is, when there is a male heir will he respect the wishes of his parents in relation to his sisters? Even in cases where promises to divide property equally have been made, there is no legal obligation to respect these at the time of the *ambil kuasa*.

Where property has been divided informally and equally between siblings, it is always possible for brothers to initiate legal proceedings and thus gain property from their sisters. As one woman put it to me, 'If the brothers are good at the time of the *ambil kuasa*, they will give the same amount to their sisters.' However, women see such cases as exceptional. They perceive the division of property at this time to be more likely to proceed according to Muslim law than custom, *adat*. And as we have seen, strong constraints against dividing property at all work against a strategy of dividing land before death which might assure the inheritance of daughters. In general, this is only done when there are no male heirs.

Although marriage has a positive economic value for women, divorce and widowhood threaten their economic stability, and precisely for this reason it is regarded as important to safeguard women's inheritance rights.[26] It is very significant that women conceive their brothers' benevo-

[26] See also Stivens (1985: 35–6).

lence to be contingent on the latter's marital status. As one woman put it, 'Before men marry they will share inherited land with their sisters. If they inherit after marriage, they will be less generous.' Such comments reveal an ambivalence towards in-marrying women who have the potential to disrupt the unity of the sibling group.[27]

Siblingship Extended

At the beginning of this chapter I described how the *semangat* of houses, boats, people, and rice is conceived as part of an indivisible seven-member sibling set whose parenthood is undiscussed and remains mysterious. This is in fact a stereotypical form for mythical stories in Langkawi. Spirits are often talked about as one of seven siblings whose origins are unknown. It is also the way the human races are occasionally described: they originate from seven siblings which emerged, like Eve, from Adam's rib. Spirit and mythical siblings are inseparable from each other and they have no known origin. They are 'the beginning' of themselves, and in a sense, of kinship since their parents are unknown. On the more mundane level of ordinary human beings, many people in Langkawi seem to think about things in much the same way. Siblings ideally are indivisible and they represent the core of kinship.

Both as a relationship, and as a concept embodying what it means to be kin, the significance of siblingship in Langkawi has many expressions. They occur in daily life and behaviour, residence patterns, terminology, property relations, disputes, ritual, and in relations which, on the face of it, have nothing to do with siblingship—those between spouses or between unrelated neighbours—which tend to be phrased in terms of siblingship.

The centrality of the sibling relation is underlined by the term for 'relatives' and for kinship in general, *adik-beradik*, which is derived from younger sibling, *adik*.[28] Two other observations further underline the way that siblingship is at the very centre of villagers' ideas about kinship. The first is that when asked to trace out a distant relationship, whether in the same generation or between widely separated ones, villagers invariably trace back to the point where ancestors can be described as two siblings,

[27] Banks (1976: 578) states that men 'suspect males outside of the sibling group will use marriage as a pretext to get wealth and preferment from female members'. They use this to justify giving preference to brothers.

[28] See Wilder (1982: 93); McKinley (1981: 336); Djamour (1965: 24); Jayawardena (1977: 23).

dua beradik. Amidst endless questioning on who was related to whom and how, no one ever came to a halt at the point where a kinsperson could be described as the aunt or uncle of another, or the parent, but always where two kinspersons were siblings. Here, then, is a very clear indication that the root of consanguinity is conceived in sibling bonds (see Errington 1989: 218).

The second observation stems from questions which could be guaranteed to arise within a few minutes of anyone meeting me for the first time: how many siblings did I have, and were my parents still alive? It was clear that, in order to place me, villagers needed to see me as part of a sibling group. In fact the form of the question in Malay: *berapa beradik?*, does not mean 'how many siblings *have* you', but 'how many siblings *are* you'. The answer is given by the number of siblings that make up the complete set, rather than dividing such a set and placing oneself in opposition to the other members. Once again the individual is conceived as constituted by her siblings.[29]

In the wider community, strangers are greeted using kin terms which are either sibling terms (for those near in age) or refer to a more distant sibling set. Strangers who are one generation older than ego are often greeted as *Macik* or *Pacik*, terms usually translated as 'aunt' or 'uncle', but it should be clear that aunts and uncles are very much perceived as 'parents' siblings'. I described how all relations are traced back to a point of siblingship and how terms for cousins refer directly to an original sibling group. Terms of address for known neighbours and kin similarly indicate their position as part of a sibling set, as well as a relation to ego traced to siblingship.

Ideas about 'pre-birth siblings' mean that all individuals are conceived as members of a sibling set. Both ritually and practically, sibling sets are closely associated with the house in which they originate. Siblings remain close throughout their lives and are a prime source of mutual aid and co-operation. Cousins, too, are in many ways perceived and treated in the idiom of siblingship.

Just as ties through women are central to the house across generations, it is ties between sisters which are particularly crucial in uniting sibling groups and mediating tensions between brothers. These, and other ties between women, can potentially unite different households and are fundamental in creating links through marriage and fostering. This will be taken up in later chapters.

[29] See McKinley (1981: 365).

I have also described how the concept of siblingship extends to husbands and wives. This conception of the marriage relation is linked to the potential of siblingship for closeness together with equality, its connotations of resemblance, similarity, and common origin. It has a further significance in that, as will become clear in Chapter 8, the community is perceived as a collection of houses united both through past siblingship *and* through the exchange of spouses.

If siblingship is seen as the 'core relation' of kinship (as opposed to the parent/child bond) many elements of a bilateral kindred structure, such as the importance of cousins, and the way kinship is reckoned horizontally, through layers of siblingship, rather than vertically through ties of filiation, fall into place. This point is made by McKinley (1981), who notes that to see the system in terms of filiation forces

> the conclusion that these peoples must have very flexible notions of descent. But the more important truth of the matter is that they have a very tightly packed notion of siblingship. (p. 340)

We can begin to see how neighbours in the village community are conceived in general terms as an expanded sibling group, or descendants of such a group.[30] Their behaviour towards each other should, ideally, follow the moral precepts for siblings; in other words, be based on notions of resemblance and similarity, as well as mutual support and harmony. Siblingship is unique among close consanguineal bonds in that it can carry connotations of both hierarchy and equality. I would argue that this malleability is one aspect of siblingship that makes it appropriate as a metaphor for good relations in the community at large where implications of difference and of hierarchy tend to be strongly resisted.

The resonance of ideas about siblingship thus gains a further dimension from its potential to express close connectedness and similarity in terms which may also imply equality.[31] Sharp distinctions are not made between the related and the unrelated. Rather, relatedness gradually fades away as one moves from siblings to more distant cousins, and then to those whom one has a vague, unspecified connection with. These ideas make it possible for newcomers to become loosely connected, and for these connections eventually to be reinforced through fostering or marriage. Such notions accord well with a conception of co-villagers as equals.[32] They provide a

[30] See Wilder (1976: 303–4; 1982: 37). Errington (1989) on the Luwu of Sulawesi and Bowen (1991: 37–59; 1993: 211) on the Gayo of Sumatra discuss kinship in similar terms.

[31] Bloch (1981) has discussed Merina siblingship in similar terms.

[32] See also Waterson (1986: 93).

direct contrast with kinship in societies where relatedness is conceived on a vertical axis through ties of descent, and which hinge on more absolute distinctions between superior and inferior and the related and the unrelated.[33] In later chapters I will show how this comes to have great significance in a historical context of demographic mobility and economic hardship.

Throughout this chapter I have stressed the way in which siblings are practically and symbolically attached to the house they are born and brought up in. This attachment is, however, always ambivalent and paradoxical. Siblings may be born in one house but as adults they come to live in several. Their dispersal is inevitable, and their unity is at best temporary. Their attachment both to each other and to their house will in the end be severed or attenuated. Although marriage is conceptualized in the idiom of siblingship this too is ambivalent. It is in fact the marriages of siblings which herald their dispersal into different houses. In later chapters these themes will be taken up again but we can begin to see how marriage is not only transformed into siblingship but also on another level opposed to it in the strongest way.

Finally, I return to the spiritual essence (*semangat*) of rice, people, houses, and boats with which this chapter began. Rice, people, houses, and boats are all either living things or things which are lived in. But perhaps it is precisely this distinction between the container and that which is being contained which is here being blurred. Living in and lived in may be conceived in the same way only where boundaries are thought of as highly permeable, present in some contexts, absent in others; where relationships gradually fade away rather than being based on sharp distinctions.[34]

Rice, the symbol of all food, the body which consumes and therefore contains it, the seven siblings which are the body, and the boat and house which contain these individual bodies and their seven-member sibling sets may be thought of as stacked inside each other like so many Russian dolls. But the analogy is also misleading. In this case the Russian dolls have

[33] It is partly because of this structural importance of siblingship that I would not apply the term 'matrifocal' to this system as some writers have suggested (see H. Geertz 1961: 44–6, 78–81; Tanner 1974).

[34] Endicott, drawing on various souces, mostly published at the beginning of this century, discusses how 'On the conceptual plane, the *sĕmangat* contributes to the object's identity, preventing it being merged into another concept, and this is expressed in physical terms as the function of the *sĕmangat* to guide the actions and preserve the boundaries of the body . . . Each *sĕmangat* is naturally differentiated and defined to the same degree as its body' (1970: 63).

different shapes and we find it surprising that they should fit together at all. Their stacking implies they are entities with clear boundaries between them but these boundaries simultaneously merge.

The shapes of the dolls are different and yet their composition is not. They are made of the same stuff, and this is the stuff of siblingship. It is this likeness of composition which enables houses, boats, rice, and people to be thought of both as things which contain each other and are different, and as things which are of the same order and somehow similar. Siblingship is both about resemblance and identity and about difference. Simultaneously individual and multiple, it is the process by which things start the same, multiple entities unified in one body, but become different and separate: bodies within bodies.

4

The Substance of Kinship and the Heat of the Hearth

> Metabolism [in Graeco-Islamic medicine] was understood as step-wise transformations of aliments into humors through a process analogous to cooking, utilizing the body's innate heat.
>
> Good and DelVecchio Good 1992: 263

At the end of the last chapter I described how the person is both individual and multiple. Each body is the container of a sibling set. The *semangat* of the person is part of a seven-member set which may in fact be likened to the parts of the body. The person also has a symbolic sibling placenta which is buried in the ground at birth. Persons and their bodies have a multiple identity and this is conceived in terms of the relation of siblingship.

This chapter is concerned with relations between bodies and between persons. It is about fertility, conception, birth, growth, and death. Rather than give a full description of life-crisis rituals as such, I abstract some connections from a very rich discourse and many complex practices in order to elucidate the way relatedness is thought about. Underlying many of the themes which I discuss is a discourse about blood (*darah*) in which many of the ideas are derived from Graeco-Islamic humoral theory (see Laderman 1992). Blood is central to vitality itself, and to the connections between kin. Blood may be thought of as a potential child (Endicott 1970: 82). It is also, to a greater or lesser degree, what kin have in common, depending on how closely related they are. The blood of full siblings is thought to be the same. Although one is born with blood and this is a source of connectedness between kin, blood changes through life—as does kinship.

Blood itself is formed in the body from food cooked in the house hearth. It is continuously being formed, and also transformed, depending on which house one lives in, and who one shares food with, on a day-to-day basis. This gives a further significance to the conversation with Aisyah which I recounted at the beginning of Chapter 1. Aisyah underlined how the house only becomes a proper house when its hearth is lit and food is cooked there. The process of cooking and eating in houses is at the heart of creating connectedness between kin. The hearth, and who one eats with, are as important in the formation of blood through life as the blood that one is born with, and which connects a child at birth to its siblings and other kin.

I begin by discussing ideas about milk and incest, showing the connections between blood, food, and kinship. I show how siblingship, houses, and hearths are central to blood and to notions of relatedness. I go on to look at ideas about fertility and conception, circumcision, and death, showing how they are linked by the same underlying logic of ideas in which blood, food, and the hearth are central.

The material presented in this chapter is mainly derived from conversations I had with several middle-aged and older women in the village including one midwife. Unlike the preceding chapters, it deals less with what people *do*, and more with how they *talk* about matters like birth, death, and relatedness. In other words, the material I present is not so much based on particular events which I could observe or participate in (and record here) but on the more abstract speculations of some villagers, which necessarily involves a more abstract discussion. Not everyone agrees about the matters discussed, or even knows much about them, although some people seem to enjoy speculating on these subjects. In places, I have recorded different viewpoints where they seem important. But I have also tried to demonstrate that there is an underlying coherence to ideas about relatedness. This coherence should not be taken to imply an absolute fixity to ideas about kinship. On the contrary, I aim to convey the processual nature and transformative potential of the kinship I describe.

I have taken one further liberty with the material I present. Because of the importance of blood as a source of vitality and fertility, and because of its importance in ideas about bodily substance, as well as connectedness between kin, I have sometimes used the term 'substance', or 'shared substance', when I might, more narrowly and literally, have referred to blood—especially blood which kin have in common. This usage seems to me in keeping with the force of the Malay ideas I describe although it perhaps glosses over some of their complexity. I argue that siblingship, houses, and hearths are central to the way shared substance is conceived.

Feeding and Shared Substance

The feeding of milk to a baby from its mother's breast has powerful connotations.[1] This milk is believed to derive from the mother's blood. 'Blood becomes milk' (*darah jadi susu*). The mother's milk is immensely important to a child's physical and emotional development, and to the child's connection with its mother. Children who are not breastfed become ill; they may also not 'recognize' their mother.

Milk-feeding defines the prime category of incest. Kin who have drunk milk from the breast of the same woman may not marry. If such kin of the opposite sex touch each other after the ritual ablutions which must be performed before prayer, the purificatory effect of these ablutions is not impaired (those concerned can still pray without bathing again). This is not the case when non-kin of the opposite sex come into contact with each other. Non-kin 'abolish the [purifying powers of] prayer water' (*batal air sembahyang*); after physical contact, the ritual ablutions must be performed before prayer. Marriage may only take place between those who 'annul the prayer water' in this way. Parents and children, grandparents and grandchildren, siblings, half-siblings, parents' siblings and their nephews and nieces may not marry: they do not 'annul the prayer water'. The connection between milk, prayer water, and incest is constantly emphasized by villagers. It is reiterated in many expressions and phrases: 'kin who drink the same milk don't annul prayer water' (*adik-beradik, kalau makan sama susu tak batal air sembahyang*).

These associations between milk-feeding, incest, and prayer water are Islamic ones. However, they are given a further significance by the power of local notions of siblingship, and by the frequency of fostering. Those who have drunk milk from the same woman are most often siblings. But many children spend a considerable part of their childhood in houses which are not their maternal ones. Formal and informal fostering arrangements substantially increase the possibility that a child may have drunk the milk of a woman who is not her mother. It is this possibility which gives such a definition of incest its particular fascination and horror. As several women with children made clear to me, it is quite easy to imagine a child being casually put on the breast of a neighbour or distant kinswoman and later marrying her child. This ever-present threat looms

[1] For a discussion of wider anthropological issues raised by some of the material in this chapter see Carsten 1995*a*, and the Conclusion to this book.

large in the minds of villagers, and runs through their discourse on incest. Women often described to me how in the past one might easily give a child a breast to comfort it, but that now this is not done. In such a case, if the children later married, the responsibility for incest would be borne by the feeding mother.

Notions of incest thus refer to several discourses. 'If the prayer water is annulled, marriage is possible' (*kalau batal air sembahyang boleh kahwin*). This is a specifically Islamic prohibition which defines Malays and their notions of relatedness in terms of their Muslim faith. Simultaneously, reference is made to notions of kinship and shared bodily substance. What kin have in common in this context is given by their shared consumption of milk as babies. It is derived from their co-feeding, and this also makes reference to blood since human milk is believed to be produced from blood circulating in the body.

Shared bodily substance is derived through shared feeding on milk. And this interpretation is in accordance with Islam. Further, shared blood is also, less directly, suggested by notions of how milk is produced. In these notions the blood that is shared through consumption of milk is not that of the father but only that of the mother or that of another woman. Shared blood is shared female substance.

I would suggest that the categorization of incestuous relations in this way gains its salience and power precisely through its reference to a number of different themes. It combines a religious discourse, which is at the heart of notions of Malay identity, with ideas about feeding which are central to the house and identity in another way. The possibility of shared feeding actually creating shared blood not only underlines the importance of co-feeding and how this is linked to relatedness. In the context of widespread fostering arrangements of different kinds it implies that, in the absence of any other tie, co-feeding can create shared blood, shared substance, and kinship. People in Langkawi say, 'If you drink the same milk you become kin' (*kalau makan sama susu, jadi adik-beradik*). 'You become one blood, one flesh' (*jadi satu darah, satu daging*).

This discussion about incest has a number of important implications because it also applies to feeding more generally. Blood itself is formed in the body from food. Of paramount importance, and in fact inseparable from food in general, is cooked rice. 'Blood, flesh come from cooked rice' (*darah, daging mari pada nasi*), I was told. Eating rice and eating a meal are synonymous in Malay. Food is rice; rice is the defining component of a proper meal.

Those who have blood in common are by definition kin: mothers and their children share blood in this way. Children are formed from the blood of their mothers. The feeding of milk from the same woman to children who are otherwise unconnected transforms them into kin. Thenceforward they have blood in common. I was told that it is 'because children drink the same milk' that they have 'the same blood' (*pasal anak makan susu sama, darah sama*). The blood in the mother's body divides in two to form milk. Milk is formed from blood which in turn is produced from food; milk also, as food, produces blood after it is consumed. Rice too produces blood. Those who don't eat rice become 'dry' (*kering*). 'All that remains is bones' (*tinggal tulang sahaja*). They have no blood.

The sharing of rice meals cooked in the same hearth thus also implies shared substance if in a weaker sense. We might see a continuum between rice (food), milk, and blood. The sharing of any or all of these connotes having substance in common, being related. Traditionally, after being given the mother's breast a child was ritually fed cooked rice and banana because 'cooked rice becomes blood too' (*nasi jadi darah juga*). A baby's body is cold at birth. Breast milk, like blood, is hot; drinking it the baby is heated and after this it can consume rice.

Just as relatives are described in terms of a continuum—more or less distantly related—rather than being distinguished from the unrelated in a clear-cut way, we find a parallel in terms of substance and feeding. Mothers and their offspring, and full siblings, are most closely related through having blood in common. In fact the blood of siblings is identical.[2] I was also told that when someone is ill and requires a blood transfusion they have to be given the blood of non-relatives rather than the blood of a sibling. In such cases it is necessary to change the blood. The blood of a sibling would have no effect because it is the same as that already in the body. More distant than full siblings but still close enough for marriage to be incestuous are those, like foster siblings, who have drunk the same milk. Those brought up in one house who have shared meals in common could technically marry; in fact they are very unlikely to do so.

I would underline how this axis of relatedness (there are of course others) operates through women. Blood, milk, and rice meals derive from women. All of them denote commonality and similarity.

[2] Banks (1983: 51–70) discusses Malay concepts of relatedness, and notes 'the common, substantial, unity of the sibling group' (1983: 57). In a number of other respects, however, our accounts are markedly different. See also Errington (1989: 221–2) on the shared substance of siblings and its implications for notions of relatedness.

Blood, milk, and food are a source of physical strength but they are more than this. It is because mothers are the source of shared substance that the emotional tie children have with their mother is thought to be particularly strong, and this was often reiterated to me. Shared substance gives emotions and words a special effectivity. Love for one's mother derives from being breastfed: 'Drinking milk from her body, you love a mother more' (*makan susu badan, kasih ke ibu lagi*).[3] If a baby is given away, it should first be given its mother's milk. If it doesn't at least taste this milk it won't recognize its mother. A mother's curse has power, unlike that of a father: 'a mother's curse arrives' (*sumpah mak sampai*). Words and emotions gain power *because* children share blood with their mother.

The mother's milk is thus the source both of shared substance and of the strong emotional bond between mother and child. It enables the child to recognize its mother. It is in this sense the enabling substance of kinship. If a mother dies before giving her child her milk the child should be given water cooked in the house hearth before it leaves the house. Water cooked in the natal hearth is the only possible substitute for the mother's milk. And this of course implies that the hearth too is a source of shared substance, of attachment to the house and its occupants.

If milk and blood are the prime sources of shared substance it would follow that transfusions of blood might be problematic in terms of incest. When I asked about the implications of receiving blood during operations in hospital, villagers seemed rather perplexed and worried. Generally, they referred me to those experts whom they thought might have a solution to this problem. But their own creativity eventually supplied an answer in accord with the logic of local notions of kinship. I was told that blood which is donated does not carry the potentiality of incest because it is not eaten: 'it is not eaten, it is put there, added' (*bukan makan, bubuh, tambuh*). It would only be the *eating* of blood which could render relations potentially incestuous.

These speculations 'at the margins' of normal occurrence—when a mother dies, when blood is given in transfusion—show very clearly that notions of shared substance, to which blood and milk are central, are also very much bound up with ideas about shared consumption, feeding, and the house hearth.

[3] Karim (1992: 152) makes the same observation.

Fertility and Conception

Children are created from the seed (*benih*) of their father and the blood (*darah*) of their mother. Different people have slightly different accounts of how this comes about, and the relative importance of the maternal and paternal contributions. One woman put it to me like this: 'The blood of the mother becomes the child' (*darah ibu jadi anak*). She continued rather dismissively, 'What blood is the father going to become?' (*Pak nak jadi darah apa?*) What she meant was that a father's blood has nothing to do with conception. And this is why most people say that 'A child is loved more by a mother than a father' (*anak sayang lebih pada mak ke pada pak*).

A midwife had a slightly different version: 'the blood of the mother and that of the placenta mix together with the seed' (*darah mak, darah uri bercampur sekali*). 'The seed becomes the blood of the child' (*Benih jadi darah anak*). But more blood comes from the mother. That of the father's seed is 'just at the beginning' (*mula-mula sahaja*). According to her, the child's *bangsa*, 'race' or 'descent',[4] comes from its maternal ancestors because the child 'comes from our contents' (*sebab mari kandungan kita*); 'it comes from the mother' (*mari dari ibu*). Heredity (*baka*), in the sense of that which is inherited, comes from the father. Inheritance rights derive from the *benih*.[5]

Most people agree that *bangsa* is a quality to do with blood: 'it becomes one blood' (*jadi se darah*). Some say that blood and *bangsa* are quite simply the same. And that it is inherited in the maternal line. 'Our flesh and blood are on the side of the mother' (*daging, darah kita sebelah ibu*). But *baka* may be described as inherited either patrilineally or bilaterally. We might understand this as expressing the same ambivalence as those inheritance practices which operate according to both Islamic law, favouring the agnatic line, and *adat*, allowing equal inheritance for men and women.

The father's seed comes from the fluid in the backbone (*air tulang belakan*). It is for this reason that men (and women too) are highly reluctant to receive injections at the base of the spinal cord when they are ill. Injections remove the liquid in the bone and weakness results, endangering their future fertility.

[4] Wilkinson (1959: 81) glosses *bangsa* as '[r]ace; descent; family'.

[5] Banks's (1983: 67–9) account of reproductive processes gives more emphasis to the male contribution. In the version he records blood is divided into two components: the male contribution of *benih*, seed, and *baka*, the female contribution of blood which nourishes the seed.

The seed spends forty days inside the body of the father. The first, 15th, and 30th days of the month are the 'days on which the seed falls' (*hari jatuh benih*). If semen is not ejaculated, men become weak. After ejaculation they regain their strength. The seed then 'descends to the mother' (*turun ke ibu*), where it mixes with the menstrual blood. It only has to mix with the blood of the mother once in order to conceive.

Both sex and conception are associated with heat and with blood. Once women are old, that is, after menopause, they 'have no blood' (*darah tak ada*), and they cannot conceive. I was told by a midwife that male infertility results from a lack of seed, for which there is no cure. It is not alterable. But female infertility has to do with problems of the blood.

During menstruation too 'the body is hot' (*badan hangat*). Afterwards it regains its normal temperature. If a woman's blood does not flow as it should in menstruation the 'blood is unhealthy' (*darah sakit*). It is dangerous for a woman of childbearing age not to get her period unless she is pregnant. The blood remains inside her and she becomes sick. If it flows normally or if it grows into a child then she is in good health.

Ideas about menstrual pollution are not very elaborated in Langkawi. Women may not pray or have sex at this time, and may cause ill-fortune to a fishing trip. Elsewhere in Malaysia, Laderman (1983: 73) also notes that a scanty menstrual flow is not considered healthy, and that while sex during menstruation is religiously prohibited, it is also believed to restore potency to a man (ibid.: 74).[6]

Another middle-aged woman told me that infertility in women can be caused by 'a thing' (*benda*) in the uterus which 'eats the seed' (*makan benih*). It bores a hole in the uterus so that the blood is let out. Since it is the blood which 'grows the child' (*membesar anak*), the child cannot survive in its absence. The boring of this hole causes bad pains just before menstruation. Severe period pains are therefore associated with infertility. But these problems are potentially curable through the consumption of medicine and of proper food.

Menstruation, sex, and pregnancy are times of body heating. For conception to take place the 'body must be hot and healthy' (*badan hangat, sihat*). 'The blood of menstruation becomes the child' (*darah haidh jadi anak*). Menstrual blood is thus a potential child, and a good flow is a sign of fertility. I was told that women may continue to menstruate for several months during pregnancy, or even the whole pregnancy. But usually

[6] Siti Hasmah Ali (1979: 113) describes a concoction of heating spices (*majkun*), consumed post-childbirth in mainland Kedah 'to ensure good health and regular menstrual periods'.

pregnancy is counted to begin one month before periods first stop. Many women say that pregnancy can last between seven and twelve months. Most continue for nine to ten.

These ideas show the centrality of the mother's blood to conception and to the formation of the child. Blood, if it is healthy, is associated with bodily heat and fertility. It may also be associated with infertility and illness but, in such cases, blood can be transformed by consuming appropriate food.

Childbirth

The rituals of childbirth are elaborate and complex. They have also changed considerably during the lifetimes of many of the women I know. In some sense, these changes have involved a reduction in the elaboration of the rituals although, I would argue, their underlying logic has been maintained. The changes are partly a result of an increasing medicalization of childbirth promoted by the government, and also of the adoption of more orthodox Islamic practices which has occurred among Malays throughout Malaysia in response to national and international religious activism. I give only a partial account of childbirth rituals here, which both draws on published sources from elsewhere in Malaysia, and indicates what changes have taken place. Once again, my aim is to make explicit some of the meanings of the ideas and practices I describe.[7]

In the seventh month of pregnancy the services of the village midwife, *bidan*, are secured by the husband's mother, who is responsible for her payment. It is from the seventh month of pregnancy that it is believed that the foetus can sustain life.

During the seventh month of a woman's first pregnancy the midwife performs a ritual 'bathing of the stomach' (*mandi perut*) of the pregnant mother and a small feast (*kenduri*) is held. The *bidan* renders the water for bathing effective by reading verses from the Qur'ān and uttering spells (*jampi*) over it. The pregnant woman, wearing a sarong belonging to her husband, is bathed on the house ladder leading into the *dapur*.[8] The purpose of the ritual, according to the *bidan*, is 'to ensure an easy delivery' (*untuk bagi dia senang beranak*), and to 'ask for safety' (*mintah selamat*). In

[7] See Skeat (1900: 333–48); Laderman (1983: 174–207); Wazir Jahan Karim (1984) for other detailed accounts.

[8] Laderman (1983: 88) refers to the cooling properties of this water. I was told that on parts of the mainland the woman is bathed together with her husband.

the past this was followed by another ritual, the 'cradling of the stomach' (*melanggang perut*), which was not performed in Langkawi during my fieldwork. The purpose of this was to ensure the correct positioning of the foetus and an easy delivery.[9]

The post-partum rituals focus on the mother rather than the child; one aspect of them is particularly striking. This is the continued application of heat in various different ways to the mother after she has given birth, which I referred to in Chapter 2. Immediately after the birth, and for some days following, she bathes in *hot* water *inside* the house (normal bathing is done at the well with cold water).[10] Throughout the 44-day period of post-childbirth prohibitions (*pantang beranak*), she must not consume 'cooling' foods.[11]

Older women told me how in former times, during this period, the mother was heated on a platform (*gerai* or *salaian*), beneath which a fireplace or hearth (*dapur*) was constructed by the midwife. Sand was placed beneath the *gerai* to catch any blood which might fall on the floor. At the beginning of this century, Skeat described how

> The fire (*api saleian*) is always lighted by the Bidan, and must never be allowed to go out for the whole of the 44 days. To light it the Bidan should take a brand from the house-fire (*api dapor*), and when it is once properly kindled, nothing must be cooked at it, or the child will suffer. (1900: 342 n. 2)[12]

This heating is no longer performed in Langkawi although many middle-aged women described to me how it had been done when they gave birth. The *gerai* was built in the kitchen (*dapur*) of the house. The fire underneath it was lit by the midwife from the cooking fire (*dapur masak*). Oil was rubbed into a woman's back and she leaned her back

[9] See Skeat (1900: 332–3); Laderman (1983: 87–90); Karim (1984); Massard (1978) for descriptions of this.

[10] Laderman (1983: 175) refers to 'hot' leaves added to this water.

[11] The categorization of foods according to their intrinsic 'heating' and 'cooling' properties is discussed at length by Laderman (1983: 35–72), and also by Massard (1983*a*: 262–8). Post-partum food restrictions are described in detail by Laderman (ibid.: 183–8). See also Fraser (1960: 194); Massard (1978). On the derivation of Malay ideas from Ayurvedic theories and Greek–Arabic humoralism see Laderman (1992).

[12] Together with Laderman (1983: 181) I would argue that use of the terms 'roasting' and 'roasting bed' (by Skeat, Wilkinson (1959: 1005), and others) for these practices is misleading, and 'heating' more appropriate. What is aimed at is a *regaining* of *lost* heat, through a more gentle warming than 'roasting' implies, i.e. a reassertion of the body's equilibrium not an objective rise in temperature; see also Massard 1978. For descriptions of similar procedures elsewhere in the region see Fraser (1960: 194); Hart, Rajadhon, and Coughlin (1965); Siegel (1969: 156–60).

against the *gerai* so that she became properly heated from behind. Women say their 'body was cooked' (*masak badan*), 'cooked inside' (*masak didalam*).

Today women still apply a stone (*batu tungku*) which has been 'cooked in the hearth' (*masak dalam dapur*), and then wrapped in cloth, to their stomachs during this period.[13] In the past, I was told, this heating was more strongly applied. The stone was used until the skin became blackened; women were more healthy, the prohibitions more strictly observed, hot medicines were used, cold food not eaten at all, the heated stone applied more frequently. According to the midwife, this 'shrinks the blood vessels of the stomach' (*kecut urat perut*), and those 'in the uterus' (*dalam sarung anak*). For the same reason the midwife massages a woman on three successive days after giving birth.[14]

It is evident that the process of heating involved in the post-childbirth rituals is designed to counteract the cooling effect of giving birth. This cooling is particularly associated with excessive bleeding.[15] Blood itself is regarded as 'hot'.[16] Hot blood, lost in childbirth, leaves the body over-cooled so that it is dangerous to eat cooling things. We will see in Chapter 7 that marriage involves a process of heating and this may be counteracted by ritual means.[17] In Langkawi, after a couple have slept together they may be described as 'cooked', whereas before they were 'raw'.

Both the *bidan* and other women expressed their belief that, if the post-partum proscriptions were not observed, the mother would become sick. They feared that women would become afflicted with an illness known as *sakit meroyan*.[18] This disease means that the 'blood is cold' (*darah sejuk*), so that it cannot flow. The consumption of cold foods during the period of post-partum prohibitions leads to various kinds of *sakit meroyan*. These include 'skin disease' (*kudis meroyan*); 'meroyan madness' (*gila meroyan*); 'lockjaw' (*sakit kancing gigi*); 'fever' (*demam*); 'blood poisoning' (*bisa*); a disease in which 'the body goes hard and stiff like a plank,

[13] See Skeat (1900: 343); Laderman (1983: 176); Gimlette (1971: 245).

[14] Karim (1992: 144) discusses how these measures are taken in order to restore a woman's beauty, vitality, and sexual performance.

[15] Laderman (1983: 41) makes the same point.

[16] Laderman (1983: 40).

[17] See also Banks (1983: 87), who mentions that *nafsu*, lust, is associated with heat.

[18] Translated by Gimlette (1971: 167) as 'diseases after childbirth'. He states that *meroyan* is derived from *royan*, 'to run, or discharge, of a sore', particularly used for 'abnormal uterine discharges following childbirth'. He continues, 'the causal agent is referred to as *angin meroyan* (*angin*, wind)' (ibid.: 167). See also Laderman (1983: 98, 201–2).

and you can't talk' (*keras*); 'bleeding'; and 'swelling of the blood vessels'. Although women talk of blood becoming cold, *sakit meroyan* is also sometimes described in terms of the body becoming 'overheated' (*hangat lebih*) through the consumption of cold foods so that the blood vessels swell.

Women in Langkawi also speak of 'wind' entering and 'rising' (*naik angin*) up the body.[19] The 'blood will then rise', *darah naik*. Their principal fear is of bleeding, *darah turun*, and that the 'uterus should swell', *sarong anak kembang*, after childbirth. During pregnancy, women say, the uterus swells; after birth it becomes loose and there is a danger it may prolapse. However, during labour itself it is considered healthy to bleed a lot. If the blood of childbirth does not leave the body it becomes 'septic', 'poisoned' (*bisa*). The blood of childbirth is 'dirty' (*kotor*), and should leave the mother's body so that her body becomes 'light' (*ringan*). The flow should then dry up, and the blood vessels of the uterus and stomach should 'shrink' (*kecut*).

Meroyan, then, is a general sickness following childbirth which takes many forms. The village midwife told me that there are forty-four different kinds of sickness and their origin, in all cases, is from the blood. The 'blood is sick' (*sakit darah*). 'Meroyan comes from blood that isn't good' (*nak jadi meroyan dari darah tak elok*).

Immediately after the birth the mother is fed by the midwife with three small lumps of *nasi meroyan*, rice which the midwife makes a spell over and which has been cooked in the hearth of the house. Instead of eating this, the mother mimics eating and it is thrown away onto the *dapur* of the *gerai*. According to the midwife, the *nasi meroyan* is for the *meroyan*, 'to prevent her coming'. It is thrown away so that she doesn't make the mother ill. Here the *meroyan* is likened to a malevolent spirit, *hantu*: it is 'a kind of spirit' (*jenis hantu*), and also 'a kind of blood' (*jenis darah*). 'Its origin is from a kind of blood' (*asal dia pada jenis darah*). 'We get ill, that blood becomes a spirit' (*kita sakit, jadi hantu darah itu*). This happens when the post-partum prohibitions are not followed. This seems to suggest a kind of internal possession in which the sick blood becomes a malevolent spirit.

The midwife, however, went on to put things somewhat differently: the origin of *meroyan* is from us, from our blood. This blood which is not good 'descends back' (*turun balik*). A *hantu* is different, it is not inside us.

[19] See Laderman (1983: 58–60) on *angin*, glossed as temperament. A build-up of *angin* in the body destroys the balance between the four elements, earth, air, fire, and water, and causes sickness.

Whereas *meroyan* is a 'sickness inside the body' (*sakit dalam badan*), a *hantu* is 'from outside' (*dari luar*).

Metal implements such as scissors, betel nut cutters, or a nail in the hair are taken to the well by women who have recently given birth to guard against spirits prone to attack women at this time. Such spirits want to eat women's blood. They cannot be seen, but after giving birth women are particularly vulnerable to them (see Endicott 1970: 62). Especially feared at this time is a vampire spirit of a woman who died in childbirth, Langsuir. This spirit has a hole in her back and very long hair which covers it. She lives in trees in the jungle and especially likes the blood of women who have just given birth. She can take any form, animal or human, but often appears as a beautiful woman. She may be rendered harmless by plugging the hole in her back with a nail or other metal object; she is then immobilized so that she cannot fly.

We have seen that both sex and pregnancy imply 'overheating'; at marriage and during pregnancy there is an attempt to keep cool. Excessive heating in this state leads to abortion, miscarriage, and infertility, perceived in terms of uncontrolled bleeding. In contrast, childbirth implies 'overcooling'; women have to be reheated and this process is closely associated with the hearth and with cooking fire. Excessive cooling at this stage leads once again to uncontrolled bleeding. It is implied that this too would cause infertility.[20]

The same nexus of ideas has been reported of Malays elsewhere. Massard (1980: 359; 1983*a*: 263) states that the absorption of heating food leads to a surplus of sexual energy. Too much heat, however, is likely to impair fertility and be dangerous to the foetus. Laderman (1983: 74) states that conception occurs when both parents are in a 'cool' state, and that 'hot' medicines can cause abortions and have contraceptive qualities (pp. 78, 79).

> The fetus is considered to be a clot of blood in the early stages, and hot medicine is thought to liquefy the blood, and to make the womb uncongenial for the child. (p. 78)

She states that 'hot' foods are avoided during pregnancy in order to control bleeding (p. 82).[21]

In Langkawi, the various interpretations of what may happen after giving birth suggest that sickness can be generated from within by, for

[20] However, Laderman (1983: 176) states that heat is applied partly to *prevent* pregnancy in the near future.

[21] See also Fraser (1960: 194).

example, bad blood, or being too cold or too hot. It can also be caused by an external agent, for example a spirit, which, of course, penetrates the boundaries of the body in an illicit manner. In *meroyan* sickness it would seem that an overcooling or overheating of the mother, caused by the ingestion of cold foods or by wind entering the body, results either in the retention of bad blood, or in excessive bleeding. That which should not penetrate the boundaries of the body does so, and leads to either too little bleeding or too much: the excessive retention or loss of bodily substance. Both of these effects are equally possible and operate within the same cultural logic. In practice, the two effects are equivalent; as Lévi-Strauss has observed in a South American context, women

> are perpetually threatened—and the whole world with and through them—by the two possibilities . . .: their periodic rhythm could slow down and halt the flow of events, or it could accelerate and plunge the world into chaos. It is equally conceivable that women might cease to menstruate and bear children, or they might bleed continuously and give birth haphazardly. (1978: 506)

As well as threatening the temporal order, both the symptoms of the *meroyan* sickness and its various causes can be read as a subtle speculation on bodily boundaries. The origins of the disease are in fact at once external and internal: childbirth itself; the ingestion of food; wind; blood that 'descends back' and becomes poisoned. The typical symptoms are as suggestive as their causes: lockjaw, skin disease, bleeding, fever: the body's boundaries seem to become either too permeable or too rigid. *Meroyan* sickness can be thought of as both like spirit possession and different from it. It is at once internal and external in causation and effect. Appropriately, after childbirth, when the body's boundaries have been dramatically penetrated to produce another body from within, normal health is restored through the reassertion of these boundaries. Sickness implies this has not been achieved. The body is either too closed or too open: it contains more substance than it should, or it loses too much.

These ideas show once again the importance of 'healthy' blood to fertility and childbirth, and to the continued health of the mother. We have seen how the regulation of the flow of blood, as well as its correct heat, occurs through the *dapur*, which acts as a site and regulator of reproductivity in the house. Childbirth, perhaps not surprisingly, introduces another theme—that of bodily boundaries, and all of these ideas recur in notions about circumcision.

Circumcision

I will not discuss circumcision in detail except to link it with the themes under discussion.[22] Writers on Malay ritual and kinship have, I believe, missed some of the significance of circumcision by comparing it with rites of initiation elsewhere rather than seeing it in its own context. Djamour (1965: 106–7) argued that it was difficult to see Malay male circumcision as a true rite of initiation since there is nothing that boys do after being circumcised that they did not already do before. In Langkawi this is far from being the case, but the manner in which circumcision is performed somewhat obscures its significance.

It is very striking that there is no rigid sex segregation during circumcision and that women are present at every stage of the ritual. Boys are not secluded before the actual operation; after it, they are completely in the hands of older female kin for some days as they are nursed in the *dapur* and given the proper food which will enable them to recover quickly. In this way women strongly assert their control over the proceedings until the wound is healed.

Young boys who have recently been circumcised are frequently rebuked for childish behaviour such as crying. I witnessed how a recently circumcised 9-year-old boy was strongly rebuked for appearing naked in the house after bathing when prior to this it would have met with a milder comment. He was reminded of his circumcision and of his duty to behave as an adult. Once circumcised, boys are particularly liable to shaming if they do not obey the rules of Malay propriety.

Villagers readily explain that circumcision (*masuk Jawi*) is a mark of the Muslim faith and is also carried out for reasons of cleanliness and hygiene. During my fieldwork male circumcision was performed when boys were aged about 10. I was told that in the past it had been carried out much later than this, at around 18. This meant that it very shortly preceded marriage. There are a number of indications from people's comments that circumcision is in fact necessary for young men to marry and, specifically, to have sex with their wives. One old man told me that in the past when it was done at a later age, 'people didn't know shame' (*orang tak tahu malu*). He

[22] I do not discuss female circumcision (clitoridotomy, incision of the clitoris) here. It takes place at the end of the period of post-childbirth taboos, and apparently is carried out with very little ceremony by the midwife, *bidan*. Informants tend to stress its insignificance as compared to male circumcision. I never saw this rite performed. See Laderman (1983: 206).

said that in those days children would walk around naked until the age of 10. Young people were less 'clever' (*cerdik*); they didn't know about men and women. 'Now they already know those things by the time they're 10, so they must be circumcised earlier.'

The implication is clear: sex in an uncircumcised state is unclean, and in this respect circumcision can be seen precisely as a rite of initiation.[23] It is also significant that both today and in the past the performance of the ritual was closely associated with that of marriage. This association is explicit temporally—the occasion of a marriage is frequently also the time when a group of young boys are circumcised, and in this way the feasts occur together.

There is a symbolic association too, in that the form of the circumcision ritual, especially in the past, strongly echoed elements of the marriage ritual. I was told how formerly, the night before the circumcision (and before a marriage), the boys would sit in state together (*bersanding*) in front of onlookers in exactly the same way as is done during the marriage ritual. If the circumcision was taking place at the house of the bride, the *bersanding* would involve the boys and the bride together. If it was at the house of the groom, or there was no wedding associated with the ritual, either one boy, or half of the boys to be circumcised, would be dressed as girls to 'take the place' of the bride. Sometimes the boys would have henna applied to their hands in the same way as a bride and groom. The following day they would be carried on a litter to the river to bathe before returning to be circumcised on a platform adjoining the house (*pelantar* or *balai*). Villagers liken this to the way a bride and groom were similarly transported to each other's houses as part of the wedding ritual. The *bersanding*, being carried on a litter, the application of henna, the boys' apparel, strongly recall for participants the central features of the marriage ritual.[24]

It is very striking that the food taboos imposed on boys after circumcision bear a strong resemblance to post-partum taboos. In both cases there is a restriction on the intake of 'cold' foods,[25] although in this case the restrictions last only until the wound is healed. Cold food would lead to swelling; *angin*, wind, may enter the wound preventing it from healing.

[23] Wilder (1970: 222–8) makes this point even more emphatically; he notes that male adulthood comes with marriage and the birth of children.

[24] Skeat (1900: 361) refers to the boy being dressed 'like a bridegroom'. Wilkinson (1957: 49) describes how boys, like bridegrooms, are stained with henna. And he states (p. 75) that in northern parts of the peninsula, circumcision is a preliminary to marriage.

[25] See also Laderman (1983: 63), Massard (1978: 148) on the same point.

Once again this is linked to a control of bleeding and concern that the wound should heal rapidly. Although several women pointed out that these taboos are less restrictive than the post-partum taboos, and those after childbirth seem to be taken more seriously, they nevertheless made a connection between the two states.[26]

Marriage, circumcision, and childbirth are all symbolically and ritually associated. In both childbirth and circumcision the regulated bleeding of both women and men is linked to their proper fertility and to the reproduction of the house. And in both cases this is assured through the action of women in preparing food and in controlling the heat of the *dapur* in which food is cooked. The *dapur* both equilibrates the heat of the body through the provision of food of appropriate heat, and controls the flow of blood leaving the body after circumcision and birth.[27]

The Substance of Death

If life, blood, and fertility are associated with heat it is not at all surprising to find that death should be associated with coldness. But the apparent obviousness of this connection should not prevent us from trying to understand its meaning as fully as possible. In fact people in Langkawi make this association in an extremely emphatic way which suggests that its meaning is both more central and more complex than might be assumed.

'Death is *really* feeling cold' (*mati, rasa sejuk sunggu*) I was told. 'If there is heat, it's all right there's still life' (*kalau hangat, tak apa ada lagi nyawa*). Death is described as coldness and stiffness. In fact, a feeling of extreme coldness may be interpreted as a sign of imminent death. But there is more to it than this.

[26] Wilkinson (1957: 49) describes a rite performed at circumcision, involving coconuts rolled over the boy, that strongly recalls that undergone by women in the seventh month of pregnancy.

[27] See also Massard (1978: 148). Gimlette (1971: 49, 245) describes how the heat of the *dapur* is applied directly to the *bukang* root in the treatment of male loss of virility. That bodily heat may have political implications is suggested by Zainal Abidin bin Ahmad (1947) and Laderman (1981). The latter describes how the Malay ruler's coolness balances the destructive heat of war, anger, dissent, and nature which threaten the body politic. The sultan embodies coolness which ensures the prosperity of the kingdom. Laderman (1992) discusses how although Greek–Arabic medical theories associate heat with health and fertility, pre-Islamic aboriginal notions placed a positive value on coolness and associated it with health and fertility. Islamic humoralism was radically altered in its adoption by Malays.

At the time of death the body loses all its blood. One older woman described how 'when someone dies, the soul leaves the body and all the blood flows out' (*masa dia mati, cabut nyawa, darah terbit*). The blood leaves the body but humans cannot see this. Only the birds and the chickens see it. 'There is no blood at all in the body' (*tak ada darah langsung dalam badan*). The dead become bones and empty blood vessels without flesh or blood.

I was told that if a person dies in the house the blood from their body flows everywhere and becomes mixed with all the food in the house. 'Everything becomes soaked in blood' (*darah basah apa-apa*). It is for this reason that nothing which is in the house may be eaten. Neither food already cooked, nor raw products such as betel quids or water stored in the house can be consumed at this time. Most important of all, no food may be cooked in the house from the time immediately before a death until burial has taken place. Meals can be prepared on a fire made outside the house or in other houses and they must be consumed elsewhere.

After the corpse has been buried according to Muslim rites, the floor of the house is washed and food can be eaten normally once again. Death, then, negates the life of the house and of its hearth. A house with death in it cannot simultaneously produce food and life. There is no cooking and no feeding. People sometimes make an association between houses and mosques at this time. It is forbidden to eat in a mosque. And this suggests that at death the house becomes more mosque-like, that is, it is removed from life in the world.

Death involves the loss of the substance of life, blood. It negates the life-producing centre of the house, the hearth, which is the source of this substance, the place where the food which becomes blood is cooked. Violent death by accident or intention has other implications. Those who are seriously wounded in accidents and are bleeding copiously should not be given water to drink. Like women after childbirth and circumcised boys, they must not be given cooling drinks. The hot blood becomes hotter still, bleeding becomes more severe, and the body becomes weak. Alternatively, the heat of the blood mixes with the cool of the drink so that the blood clots in the body and the wounded person dies. Blood that falls on the ground should be buried in sand and then burnt. Otherwise it will 'clot' (*beku*), and attract malevolent spirits.

I was told several stories of murder which make plain that the taking of life affects the murderer as dramatically as the victim. A murderer is said to become weak, powerless, and frightened; in this state he is liable to be caught. The only way to prevent this is to drink the blood of his victim, his life substance. By performing the act of a vampire spirit, he becomes 'like a spirit' (*macam hantu*). He thus endows himself with superhuman powers: the ability to appear and disappear at will and to evade his pursuers. In this way the killer becomes 'brave' (*berani*), and 'powerful' (*kuasa*). He has all the attributes of a spirit but he is human, as it were doubly alive, super-substanced.[28]

The murderer, then, is faced with two possibilities: he can be consumed by the victim's substance, or by consuming it, be empowered. But once again the notion of feeding is crucial. It is the act of feeding that confers power. The equation of murderers with vampires makes clear that this feeding is in every way negatively construed. Feeding on blood is the negation of feeding on rice cooked in the house hearth: it is death-dealing rather than life-giving; it negates human ties rather than producing them.[29]

Normal death and violent deaths both negate the blood of life and human ties. There is another kind of death which has more ambivalent associations. The death of the martyr has a special place in Islam. In Langkawi myth the quintessential local martyr is Mahsuri, a woman wrongly executed for adultery. In the version recounted to me, Mahsuri was a great beauty married to a local warrior. Her husband was called away to fight against the Siamese, and in his absence, she became friends with a destitute visiting stranger from Sumatra. Her mother-in-law, who resented her, accused her of adultery. Protesting her innocence, Mahsuri was stabbed to death in the chest with a *keris* (dagger). Before she died she asked God to prove her innocence by making her blood white and preventing it falling on the ground. As white blood gushed from her wounds, Mahsuri uttered a curse on Langkawi for the seven generations succeeding her death.

[28] These notions about the power of blood can be related to Endicott's discussion of the Malay concept of *badi* (Endicott 1970: 66–86). The *badi* can be thought of as a harmful expression of disturbed blood—it arises from the blood—and, in the case of a murdered person it is the *badi* which makes this blood especially potent (1970: 72). The *badi* can eventually become an independent spirit, which in the case of a murdered person is likely to be especially powerful and malicious (1970: 73; 74). In the case of a woman who dies in childbirth, it is the *badi* which reanimates her body as a vampire spirit (1970: 72). Endicott points out that vampires, familiar spirits, and *badi* all share an intimate connection with human blood. I am indebted to Robert McKinley for making these connections.

[29] Once again, I am indebted to Robert McKinley for the suggestion that the female vampire spirit, Langsuir, who attacks women after childbirth and herself died in childbirth, can be thought of as the spirit of 'pure alienated kinship'. Her untimely death cuts off the normal process of feeding and making kinship between mother and child. The sucking of blood from her victims is the inversion of the social feeding that should have occurred had Langsuir not died in childbirth.

This story has become famous throughout Malaysia. Mahsuri's grave is now a local shrine and a tourist attraction. Her death is often invoked in Langkawi to explain Siamese invasions, fire, crop failure, and widespread poverty that have historically occurred on the island. In 1989, with the government encouraging development and tourism, I was told that the seven generations had passed and the island was no longer cursed.

But we can understand the myth in another way. I described above how a mother's milk is produced from blood. It is in fact a kind of blood. There are many varieties of blood, some more dilute than others. Blood alone, pure blood, is a very deep red; but other bloods may be less red. I was told that breast milk is a very dilute form of blood which is white; it has very little red blood in it. Elsewhere in the region, white blood is a sign of nobility and potency.[30] White blood is also the proof of Mahsuri's innocence. It is the sign which vindicates her, and is proof of her potency and nobility. It is perhaps only slightly far-fetched to suggest that metaphorically, Mahsuri's white blood might also be likened to breast milk, symbolic of kinship itself. It is a sign that she herself has not negated her ties of kinship by adultery. The logic of this interpretation would suggest that, in her martyrdom, she has produced this substance of kinship and this is an incredibly potent force. Her white blood is so powerful it can destroy fertility and prosperity for seven generations. It gives her curse its potency, just as it is the mother's milk that renders a curse on her children effective. The substance of Mahsuri is super-charged: it is the curse on future kinship throughout the island.

Hearths, Feeding, and Substance: The Process of Becoming

Over the last four chapters I have described what goes on in houses in various different ways. I have analysed the physical structure of the house and shown how it is 'female', but that it also 'contains' the notion of siblingship. I have described the house as an expanded hearth and examined the most important activities that are engaged in there, particularly cooking and eating. The relationships that houses contain have been discussed: once again women and siblingship have been shown to be at the core of what houses are about.

[30] Skeat (1900: 37) mentions that sultans are supposed to have white blood. In South Sulawesi white blood characterizes nobles, and is thought to be especially spiritually potent (Errington 1989: 19). It is also the invisible and potent blood of spirits (ibid.: 51).

The present chapter has been an extended discussion of notions of substance. These notions are both subtle and complex. At their heart are ideas about blood. Kin have blood in common. But the degree to which this is true varies. The most closely related are siblings and mothers and their children. These relations involve a high degree of shared substance. Other kin have blood in common too but to a lesser extent. The sharing of substance is not only a physical attribute. It has emotional qualities. And this is why the affective ties between a mother and her children and between siblings are held to be particularly strong.

Ideas about blood, however, do not imply that substance is given at birth and remains ever after constant. In fact, substance, like blood, has a fluid quality. It is to a great extent acquired and changeable. Blood itself is not just something one is born with. It is continuously produced from food which is eaten. Of particular importance in this regard are maternal milk and rice meals.

Milk itself is produced from blood and is a kind of blood. As a bodily substance it has a particular significance. First, it increases the degree of shared substance and the strength of emotions between mothers and their children and between siblings. But it does more than this. The consumption of the same milk can actually create shared substance between otherwise unrelated people. This would also be true of the consumption of blood. But the consumption of blood has highly negative connotations. It is performed only by vampires and murderers who thereby illicitly acquire the physical strength, the substance, of their victims, ensuring the latter's demise.

Milk, then, may be understood as the enabling substance of kinship: a source of emotional and physical connectedness. But once again this is not the end of the story. To a lesser degree, food cooked on the natal hearth has the same qualities. A tiny infant may be given water cooked in the *dapur* as a substitute for its mother's milk. Food becomes blood. And through the day-to-day sharing of meals cooked in the same hearth, those who live together in one house come to have substance in common. Eating meals in other houses has negative implications. As we saw in Chapter 1, children are strongly discouraged from doing so.

These ideas have a particular salience when people do in fact often move to different houses. Divorce, and temporary or more permanent fostering, lend an enormous force to the idea that living and eating together is one way of coming to have substance in common. Thus the idea that milk-feeding creates the potential for incest is a very real threat in the minds of people in Langkawi. But it has a further significance in the historical context of great demographic mobility which I will describe in Chapter 9. Feeding is one way in which strangers and outsiders can become incorporated into a village community. Being fed, such strangers become, in a weak way, related. More permanent fostering arrangements and marriage are stronger modes of incorporation. All these are ways in which unrelated people may come to share substance.

There are other important implications to the notions I have described. The long process of becoming, acquiring substance, is one that to a very great degree occurs through the actions and bodies of women. Children are produced from the blood of their mothers; their mothers' milk may activate or create kinship. The food cooked in the hearth by women not only nourishes physically, it is central to the process of becoming related. Houses and their hearths are the sites of the production of kinship, women are the major producers.

Substance is both given and acquired; women are essential to this process. Aisyah's instruction for the establishment of a new house, with which I began Chapter 1, now takes on a fuller meaning. In that conversation, Aisyah underlined how a new house is only established when its hearth is lit and food is cooked there, and that mothers provide their daughters with the means to do this. The processes that are set in motion in this way are in every way life-giving. They give life both to the house and to the people that live there; each reproduces the other. The *dapur* is the place where food is cooked. It is also the heat of the *dapur* which regulates more directly the heat of women's bodies at childbirth, and to a lesser extent those of men after circumcision, ensuring their future fertility.[31] The heat of the hearth symbolically controls the reproduction of humans and houses. It is also, of course, the place where raw food is transformed into edible substance which later becomes bodily substance. The *dapur* produces blood and regulates its flow, thereby ensuring reproduction.

In the second part of this book I show that the transformative process which occurs in the hearth has a wider symbolic significance. Things which come into the house from the outside and which are symbolically opposed to houses may be converted there, and rendered edible. The *dapur* is the transforming centre of the house; it produces life.

[31] It may be significant that soot from the house hearth is used to protect children on excursions away from their own home. Women often dab soot from the *dapur* onto the forehead of a small baby or child when taking them out of the house to visit other villagers.

Houses, Bodies, and Boundaries

These chapters have had another theme: the notion of boundary. In Chapter 1 I described how the house can be seen as a *dapur* within a *dapur* within a *dapur*. The cooking stove, kitchen, and living area of the house are all given by the same term: houses are expanded hearths. The house spirit, who may be said to embody the house, is herself one of seven siblings, although only one of these is active, and the degree to which these siblings have separate identities is ambiguous.

These same ideas are echoed in notions of the person. Each person is part of a sibling set. And these ties are conceived as being more or less unbreakable. The identity of an individual is always bound up with that of their siblings. This is underlined in notions of symbolic siblingship. The younger sibling placenta reflects and influences the fate of the older sibling child.

The *semangat*, 'soul', or 'vital force', of the person, like that of the house, is one of seven siblings. Once again the exact status of the different members of this set is unclear. The set is both one and seven. One might say that persons and houses are simultaneously individual and multiple. They always contain the possibility of being either. And in just the same way a human sibling set has both a single and a multiple identity. Growing up in one house, it will eventually come to be embodied in different houses.

These ideas suggest a very subtle and complex speculation on ideas about boundaries. Where does one house end and another begin? Where does one person end and another begin? We are confronted with the possibility of boundedness only to see it recede before us.

Sickness and health reveal the same concerns. Disease may have internal or external causation. In fact it may itself reveal a fascination with notions of internality and externality and their interrelationship. After childbirth, when one body has literally produced another from within, these ideas become explicit. The permeability of the body's surfaces at this time is especially problematic. The mother's body has opened up to let out that of the child inside. In order to restore her to her normal medium state of semi-permeability her boundaries must be reasserted. There is always the danger that she remain too open and lose her bodily substance, or become too closed, retaining too much substance and becoming poisoned.

Bodies are simultaneously bounded and porous. It is hard to say where one person stops and another begins. The person contains within herself the core of relatedness which is siblingship. What is true for persons is also true for houses and in exactly the same way. In Chapter 1 we saw that the house is envisaged as a body. It is also clear that the body is in another way a house, containing other bodies.[32]

Like bodies, houses are simultaneously bounded and porous. They have a single and multiple identity which again is envisaged in terms of siblingship. In the second part of this book I show why the boundaries of the house are always problematic. And how it is that the village can be seen simultaneously as an expanded house and as a collection of different houses.

One way of thinking about these ideas is in terms of boundaries. But in another way they also express a concern with notions of similarity and difference: where one thing stops being the same and becomes something else. It is in terms of an endless speculation on similarity and difference that local perceptions of kinship are worked out. But to understand the significance of difference we have to step out of the house and deal with the outside world.

[32] This idea has been explored by Headley for Java. He describes how the Javanese treat their bodies and their kingdoms as houses, and how the body 'physically houses siblings during gestation' (1987*a*: 143).

PART 2

Outside the House

5

The World Outside

The first part of this book was concerned with life inside houses. Some of the symbolic aspects of that life might be summarized as being about the production of similarity. Notions of kinship and shared substance tend to emphasize being the same rather than being different. The second part of the book attempts to explain why people in Langkawi put such a strong emphasis on being the same. It shows that the house and the actions of women have a significance in Langkawi that goes beyond what in anthropology is often (and misleadingly) called the 'domestic domain'. The present chapter is a rather rapid sketch of the world beyond the house. This is a world which contrasts in every way with what houses are about. Its essential qualities are division and difference, and the principal actors in it are men.

In the chapters which follow this one I discuss how these two worlds can come together in the space just beyond the house: the compound, the neighbourhood, and the village. I show how the outside world can be incorporated symbolically into the house by a number of different means but how this world is also simultaneously held at a distance. In this process the actions of women come to have a wider 'political' significance.

The outside world which I briefly describe here is a complex one. People in Langkawi are confronted in their daily lives by the state, national politics, a world religion, and aspects of the national and international economy. To say 'confronted', however, gives a misleadingly passive impression of their involvement in these institutions. In fact, they are fishermen and rice cultivators for an export economy, as well as consumers. They are deeply concerned with local politics: they vote and hold political meetings and informal discussions. They watch television, and talk and think about what they see. Many regularly attend the mosque and are deeply religious; those who are less observant must also constantly consider the place of Islam in their lives. All these are very active issues and involvements.

Economy, politics, religion might each merit a monograph in their own right.[1] Here I consign them to a short chapter. This should in no way be taken as indicating a valuation of these concerns. The issues they raise are complex, nor can they be thought to be in any way peripheral to the lives I describe here. But one cannot tell all the stories at once. The one I have chosen to tell, for a variety of reasons, is a different one. It is told, as it were, from inside the house. Political, religious, and economic aspects of life are described in this chapter as part of this story, not independently of it. The view on them which I present might, then, be glossed as that from inside the house.

I describe how the world of women and that of men are separated. Women are involved in subsistence rice production, vegetable gardens, and in various aspects of labour in the house. Men engage in fishing, formal political and religious activity, and social intercourse which takes place outside the house in the commercial area of the village, the coffee-shop, and the mosque. The world in which men engage is intrinsically divided along political and religious lines. It is a competitive world of achievement. In contrast, the house, in which women dominate, is a space where difference and competition are negated, and where what is stressed is unity and similarity. In this chapter I not only describe the contrast between these worlds, and how the outside world is kept at a distance from the house. I also begin to show how these two worlds interact with each other. Women are engaged in a constant act of transformation in which they 'process' the world outside, converting the products of commercial activity and political division, as they enter and pass through the house, into the unity and similarity that constitute kinship.

Women and Men

The village of Sungai Cantik is made up of several named hamlets (*kampung*) over which a single elected Village Development Council (*Jawatankuasa Kemajuan Kampung*, JKKK), headed by a village leader (*Ketua Kampung*), has jurisdiction. The council is responsible to the leader (*Penghulu*) in the local district (*mukim*). The most important functions of the JKKK are the administration of government subsidies and loans, and other local matters, excluding the religious. This is the lowest

[1] There have been a number of important studies of class antagonisms and rural politics in a context of rapid socio-economic transformation in Malaysia (see Syed Husin Ali 1975; Rogers 1977, 1993; Scott 1985; Shamsul 1986; Wan Hashim 1978). For studies which focus on religious radicalism see Kessler (1978); Nagata (1984); Chandra Muzaffar (1987).

tier in the hierarchy of government and the only one in which officers are elected rather than appointed. However, in practice, the powers of the JKKK are severely limited by the *Penghulu* and the District Office which oversees the whole administrative area (*daerah*) of Langkawi. As we shall see, the activities of the JKKK are one source of division in the village.

The administrative unit partly coincides with the *kariah*, the community of people who pray together at one mosque every Friday and on religious festivals. Islam is central to villagers' perceptions and their sense of identity as Malays. In terms of belonging to one community this religious unit has at least as much significance as the administrative one. In many respects, the mosque forms the focus for a community made up of several hamlets, or neighbourhoods, which may be situated so close together that they effectively merge. Islam is, in the most general sense, a force for unity among Malays; however, because political differences in Malaysia are often played out in a religious idiom, it is also a source of the most bitter divisions.

The economy of the village is based primarily on fishing, and secondarily on rice cultivation. Many households grow enough rice to meet their subsistence needs, either wholly or in part, although some own no rice land at all. There are no big landowners in the village and very few people own enough land to sell surplus rice. Rice is closely associated with the house and with the values of close kinship. This is apparent in its cultivation as well as its consumption. The cultivation of rice is dominated by women, and relies heavily on co-operation between kin.

Technological changes in the 1970s and 1980s meant that rice-growing became less profitable and significant as an income-earning activity, whereas fishing became more so. This was a result of the advent of inboard motors (with which the great majority of boats are equipped), government subsidies and loans, which aimed to lessen the dependence of Malay fishermen on Chinese middlemen, and ice-making facilities which helped establish a large export market for fresh fish. This economic shift was highlighted by villagers' statements that in former times well-off people in the village would sell rice and buy fish, and that this was no longer the case. In the early 1980s the majority of fishermen still sold their fish to Chinese middlemen based in the village, although their dependence on the latter was probably less complete than in the past. Fishing is an exclusively male activity; it is competitive and commercial, and involves men in relations with non-kin in preference to kin.

The commercial area of the village is separate from the hamlets in which most Malay villagers have their houses, and is situated on the coast of the fishing bay. It is dominated by men, and by a mixture of Malay and Chinese retailers. Fronting the shore are the homes and business premises of the Chinese middlemen who buy most of the produce of the village fishermen. Along the shore and stretching some way inland are several sundry shops, coffee-shops, and a barber's. Fishermen pass through this area as they go to and from the boats and often stop in the coffee-shops. At all times of the day groups of men can be found chatting in the coffee-shops or around the barber's. Women and children come on shopping errands but usually return home quickly.

The export market in fish means that the village economy is closely linked to the wider economy of Malaysia and is extensively monetized. Villagers receive government subsidies and loans for housing, fertilizers, and fishing equipment. They often have reason to make trips to the main town of Langkawi, Kuah. Negotiation of government loans, visits to the hospital, division or sale of landholdings, purchase of commodities, drawing pensions or cheques, or, simply, pleasure take both men and women to Kuah, but in the main transactions are performed by men. Villagers also often go to the head village of the *mukim*, which has a greater selection of shops, a large mosque, high school, government clinic, and a small daily fish market. Once again, it is men more than women who make such trips.

The activities in which women and men engage are thus to a considerable degree segregated, and this is reflected in the physical space occupied by each sex. Women perform all household labour; only men fish. Agricultural labour is to a great extent shared but women and men perform different tasks, and women usually dominate its organization. Men tend to avoid sitting in houses during the daytime. When they are not fishing they spend their time on maintenance work on boats and nets, on errands in the local town, at the mosque, or, most frequently, at the coffee-shop. Women pass much of the day either in their own houses or visiting female neighbours, friends, and kin in those near by.

In terms of a sexual division of space, houses might be opposed to boats, mosque, and coffee-shop. The division not only reflects the segregation of labour but also of activities. The coffee-shop is the main forum for informal political discussion. Women very rarely go to coffee-shops, nor do they participate more than minimally in formal political activity in the village. They rarely attend meetings; when they do so, they do not engage in public discussion. Behaviour too in the coffee-shop can be contrasted to that in the house: it is louder, rougher, and less refined. Men compete with each other through their voices and gestures as well as their ability to pay for what is consumed there.

The coffee-shop can be considered as a kind of men's house. But the rules that apply in it are in every way different to those of houses. Ordinarily, full rice meals are not taken in the coffee-shop but in the house. Snacks and drinks are consumed in the coffee-shop. Food is of course paid for; and payment tends to take either individualistic or hierarchical forms: very often it is the captain of a boat who treats his crew.

Different rules of commensality further underline the distinction between coffee-shop and house. Those who consume together in the coffee-shop are friends, political associates, fishing crews, unmarried men who associate as a 'gang'. They are not usually close kin. It is particularly notable that fathers and sons avoid each other. One young man described rather vividly to me how if a son was about to enter a coffee-shop and saw his father already seated there he would go on to a different one, or at least sit at a different table. Several other men agreed with this, saying the sons in such a situation are 'embarrassed' (*malu*), and go elsewhere out of 'respect' (*hormat*).

The coffee-shop is men's space as houses are women's. It is also a region in which a set of names applies which gives a clue to the nature of gender division in Langkawi. In general, women can only be addressed and referred to through the use of a combination of personal name and kin terms. These also apply to men. But men have another set of names which emphasizes their individuality and personal achievements: they have nicknames, *gelaran*. These are given to men by their friends, usually in the years before marriage, when coffee-shop attendance becomes established. The names are inspired by a man's personal attributes. Physical appearance, character, a special liking for a particular food, or a notable and often comical event in someone's life may be commemorated in a name.

Typically, the names have a concise wit: abbreviations may obscure their meaning or even their existence to outsiders. Tok Din Udang acquired his name from a remarkable taste for prawns (*udang*); his son, Ali, is known as Ali Belacan, from the prawn paste used as a condiment in every meal because, after all, *belacan* is derived from prawns. Wi T'ang got his name from a protestation he made when caught gambling by the police. He said he was *tumpang sahaja*, 'just squatting', a phrase usually used to refer to living arrangements. These nicknames epitomize men's individual and personal life histories. Villagers explain them by saying it's hard to distinguish between people when the same personal names are given so frequently. There may be twenty Mats in any small neighbourhood.

This of course is equally true for women as for men. Personal names belong to a rather restricted set. In this sense they are not 'personal' but apply to large numbers of people. But it is significant that this matters more for men than for women. Men can be more individual than women. Their achievements are more important to their status. In fact the world they participate in is highly competitive and divisive. Their achievements matter, and this is reflected in naming systems.

This discussion has implications for concepts of the person and their link with gender in Langkawi. Analysing notions of person, time, and conduct in Bali, Geertz (1973) has stated that personal names there are 'arbitrarily coined nonsense syllables' (p. 369). In Langkawi kin terms, personal names, and nicknames often turn out to have very well-packed meanings but these are thoroughly obscured by abbreviation. This may be significant in view of the well-known argument that Geertz based on this ethnography: that the Balinese have a 'depersonalising conception of personhood' (p. 391). Evidence from Langkawi leads me to suspect that the Balinese may have rather more complex notions of personhood than he suggests.[2] In Langkawi at least, 'personhood' is not constant for age, gender, and context. One can have more or less individuality depending on 'who' one is, and in what situation.

Men's status can be measured in political and social life, in their economic success, and, as they get older, in the religious sphere. Loosely, it corresponds to three different spaces: the coffee-shop, the boat, and the mosque. The coffee-shop is the region where much political discussion is carried out, discussion which also occurs in formal political meetings which are public, or behind closed doors in private. The political world is both divided and hierarchical. The Village Development Council, JKKK, is the lowest level in an administrative hierarchy reaching up through the state. The council members have considerable control over the payment of government grants and subsidies.

These grants are a considerable source of division in the village. Competition occurs between more and less loyal political allies, closer and more distant associates and kin, those to whom favours are owed and those who are in debt, and the more and the less poor. There is another division, played out in more absolute terms. This is a political divide between followers of the ruling UMNO (United Malay Nationalists' Organization) and those of PAS (Partai Islam), the fundamentalist Islamic party. PAS constitutes the most significant Malay opposition to the government in Kedah. In the recent past it has won state elections in Kedah.

[2] See Howe (1984); Hobart (1986); Wikan (1990) for critiques of Geertz's theory of personhood in Bali.

At the village level, those who support PAS are generally excluded from most benefits which accrue to loyal government supporters. But the divisions are more than economic and political. Partly because they are played out in a religious idiom—with each side accusing the other in terms of their faith and observance, in effect, their morality—the repercussions reach far into the social life of the community. Visiting pattern, marriages, disputes, economic associations, which mosque is attended for Friday prayer, are all affected. At election time especially, the divide between UMNO and PAS supporters goes to the heart of village life. Disputes are rife and bitter.

The fact that political differences are articulated in a religious idiom limits the extent to which Islam itself is a unifying force in the village. At one level Islam is central to villagers' identity. They continuously emphasize that they are 'Malay people, Muslim people' (*orang Melayu, orang Islam*). The fact that national, ethnic, and religious identity are conflated in these perceptions underlines the importance of Islam to this discourse.

From school age upwards, all male members of the *kariah* should attend the main religious service of the week at midday on Friday. Fines are levied on fishermen who go out to sea before this service. The fact that this is perceived as both a religious rite and as one of community is underlined by many villagers' comments that these fines distinguish Sungai Cantik from all other villages.

But Islam is also universal: it links together not only all Malays, but also people of widely different origins and cultures around the world, who may even at times go to war with each other, as people in Langkawi are quite aware. While Islam provides a sense of community with other Islamic people at a very general level, it is also a source of division.

At the local level too, political disputes between PAS and UMNO supporters have led to mosques which are built with government money being declared *haram* (forbidden by Islam) by the more religiously orthodox. Villages become divided along lines of allegiance to different mosques. This may result in men participating in Friday prayer in a different *kariah* from the one in which they live. But because the Friday service is both a communal and a religious rite this is ill-regarded. One woman emphasized to me how important it is to go to the mosque in one's own *kariah*: 'Praying elsewhere doesn't count; it's not rewarded' (*tak berkira; tak pahala*). The Muslim community is in this sense a divided one, and the divisions are simultaneously political, local, religious, and even moral.

Even when disputes are not played out in an overtly political or religious idiom, it is not clear that Islam, the institution of the mosque, or the person of the imam, can bring divided villagers together. In Chapter 8 I describe a long-running dispute in the village. During this dispute, many villagers expressed their regret that the imam was unable to play a peace-making role, because he himself was closely related to some of the participants, and was thus unable to mediate between them. In other words, the imam is merely a fellow-villager; he is a participant in village events like anyone else, and not above them. This of course relates to the fundamental egalitarianism of Islamic notions which (together with the mildnesss of his personality) limited the potential power of the imam to draw people together.

Although Islam is central to the identity of both women and men, the extent to which the mosque constitutes a religious and communal centre is further limited by gender divisions. Women generally conduct their daily prayers in their own homes and they do not attend the weekly service at midday on Fridays. Men who are not fishing often congregate outside the mosque in a seating area especially favoured by older men for conversation. Women normally only attend the mosque on the most important religious festivals, and occasionally for evening prayer. Both women and men actively participate in religious life—there are, for example, several female Qur'ān teachers in the village who give lessons in their houses—but the locus for this activity tends not to be the same.

Men, then, dominate formal politics and religion. Women's strong association with the house, with relations between kin, and with subsistence production should not, however, simply be thought of as a result of exclusion from the 'public' domain. The house and women do not simply, and by definition, constitute a residual domain of the 'private'. During the run-up to elections, in particular, women often expressed their rejection of political activity to me in terms which suggested that this is, at least in part, a positive moral choice.

Women may speak contemptuously of male political activity which they see as divisive, and linked to the pervasiveness of disputes in the village. They are particularly scathing about the way such disputes divide neighbours and kin and may even affect the selection of marriage partners. One old woman, Aminah, told me how women ought not to engage in political activity. 'They haven't studied', she said. 'And they don't understand the exact differences between political parties.' She stressed the stupidity of villagers: 'While the party leaders eat from one tray (*satu hidang*), those below quarrel.' When her grandparents were still alive, she went on, there were no political parties. 'Why should we need them now?

They just lead to quarrels between kin.' She emphasized that political difference was no bar to marriage. 'Those that claim otherwise are stupid. We are all Muslims.'

Aminah's own family was divided along PAS/UMNO lines. She was speaking from the heart about how political activity goes against what she sees as traditional values and destroys the harmony which should unite kin. In this light, women's very marked lack of enthusiasm for attending and speaking at political meetings can be seen as expressing a conflict between the political world and its activities, and kin ties. Many women perceive their role as being to maintain good relations between houses and between kin. They are also aware that this often places them in conflict with things which men do. Men too, of course, regret the divisions created by politics—at the same time as being highly involved in them.

It is of course significant that Aminah expressed her opinions about political division in an idiom of commensality. Political leaders of opposing sides eat together while their followers quarrel. The image is resonant: the kinship of party leaders is suggested by their co-feeding. Their duplicity is clear to all but the ignorant.

It is ironic that on the same day as this conversation with Aminah I came across a young kinsman of hers, compiling a list of PAS members to send to the local District Officer so that none of them would receive the subsidies for which fishermen are eligible for their boats, engines, and

11. Men vote at a village meeting

nets. Such subsidies, which are supposed to go to those most in need, are also available for housing. The young man told me with great pride that such lists had been kept for the previous four years with the approval of the leaders of the JKKK. Aminah's family would have been on this list.

Men and Fishing

While it is possible to avoid political and religious controversy to some extent, men must engage in economic activity to gain their livelihood. Here too men's way of doing things can be contrasted with women's. In this section I will summarize some of the basic principles involved in fishing: ownership of boats, division of earnings, and recruitment to fishing crews, before looking at the way rice cultivation is organized in order to show how in this sphere of activity too, men's world is divisive and competitive and contrasts with women's.

Men and women believe that menstruating women may bring misfortune to a fishing trip through their presence on the boat or by touching the net. All women are therefore excluded from marine fishing trips.[3] Men begin to fish after leaving school when they engage in migrant work on the mainland. Most young men leave the village and work on the big fishing trawlers that operate from the mainland Kedah coast. Young men from the locality work and live together. While these young men physically leave the community they remain part of it. Not only do they work in groups together, but they also return together on visits to the village every few weeks. This phase of productivity is a prelude to marriage and the assumption of full adult status in the village. The young men's earnings, which are crucial to this process, are sometimes remitted to parents and are defrayed against the expenses of marriage. The greater part of these earnings is spent on rebuilding or extending the parental home at this time.

After marriage, men reside and work in the village. They fish in local waters in smaller boats, most but not all of which have inboard engines. Some of the fish caught are sold and consumed locally, but the majority are bought by Chinese middlemen and exported to Penang and Singapore. Fishing is thus highly commercialized and is not a subsistence occupation.

Most fishing crews consist of two to four men (depending on the

[3] Raymond Firth (1966: 105) also reports that 'no women go to sea' on the east coast.

12. Fishermen going out to sea at dawn

operation), aged between their early twenties and late forties. Once they are in their fifties, men begin to go to sea less frequently. The majority of boats in the village are owned individually by single owner-users. Joint ownership is rare but a significant minority of boats are 'owned' by Majuikan, the government fishing development agency, which puts up the money for the boat which the fisherman then repays in monthly instalments, eventually becoming the owner. The third type of boat ownership involves boats owned by Chinese middlemen (*towkay*), who usually take 50 per cent of the earnings of the boat, or buy the catch at half price, with the rest divided between the crew.

Boats, engines, and nets represent a substantial investment of capital, well beyond the reach of most fishermen. This heavy investment is generally financed by loans—either from the government or from Chinese *towkay*. The single owner-users include many fishermen who are repaying loans to Chinese *towkay*. My foster brother and other fishermen in this category explained to me how payments are made with fish, rather than money, and the amounts vary in accordance with the catch. Such fishermen regard this system of repayment as being more flexible than government loans. Thus my foster brother described how in an unproductive month inability to pay the fixed instalment would necessitate a round of letter-writing and/or interviews to negotiate a deferment. He argued that from the fisherman's point of view, a more flexible, open arrangement with a *towkay* seemed more attractive, especially as the latter loan is 'interest free' in contrast to the former.

Fishermen who are repaying loans to Chinese *towkay* are involved in a long-term contractual relationship. They sell all their catch to the *towkay* at a fixed price which is usually 5 to 10 per cent less than the market price. The fisherman is described as 'tied' or 'bound' (*terikat*) to the *towkay*, who in return distributes various 'favours'. One fisherman described how the *towkay* had in the past agreed to defer a repayment during a poor fishing period, used his connections to negotiate a good price on new equipment, given further loans for repairs to the boat and engine, and loaned his own boat when that of the fisherman had broken down.

It is clear that such 'favours' in fact serve to perpetuate the relationship between *towkay* and fisherman, until the latter is bound in a web of debts and obligations to the former. This fact is clearly perceived by the fishermen themselves. The relationship may even be passed from father to son. When my foster brother began fishing on his own as a young man, the *towkay* of his father, with whom there was already an established relationship, seemed the most likely person to look to for a loan to finance new capital.[4]

The distribution of earnings between crew members (*anak awak*), the captain (*tuan bot*), and the boat owner, if different from the latter, varies according to the kind of fishing and the particular crew.[5] However, in all cases one basic principle applies: apart from each person's earnings, a separate share is calculated 'for the boat', the *syir bot*. This share accrues to the boat owner. From it he pays for fuel, the cost of maintenance of the boat, and, in many cases, repayments on loans. As much as possible of the boat share is saved separately against future expenses on fishing equipment. Fishermen always reiterate that it is not used for general household expenses.

The usual practice is for earnings to be divided in half. One half is the boat share and the other is divided equally between crew members, including the captain.[6] Apart from their cash earnings, fishermen also divide up a small proportion of the day's catch between them. In contrast to their money earnings, however, the shares of fish are precisely calculated so that

[4] See Raymond Firth's references to the *daganang* system (1966: 60–2, 377–84).

[5] See Raymond Firth (1966: 235–57, 318–29) on the complexities of the distribution of earnings and the difficulties of obtaining such data. I did not conduct detailed research into this area and include the information only as a rough guide to the practice.

[6] While the principles of dividing earnings were often described in these rather simple terms, more detailed questioning often revealed a more complex division, with variations depending on the type of fishing and the particular crew.

each member of the crew, including the captain, takes an exactly equal portion of the catch home with him.

While participants state that the particular division of cash is fixed for each fishing crew and type of operation, it is in fact subject to substantial variation depending on the size of the catch. Almost all owners reduce the boat share when the catch is small. I was told that if earnings were very low—as often happens—they would be equally divided so that the income of the owner was the same as that of the other crew members. Thus, periods of successful fishing would maximize income differences between the two categories of fishermen, while periods of low productivity would be associated with greater equality of income. Reductions in the boat share are particularly likely when the captain is also the owner and when he and the crew members are closely related, generally through kin ties. The tendency to reduce the boat share reveals very clearly the tension involved in purely commercial relations with Malay co-villagers, especially when they are close kin.[7]

Fishermen say that in recruiting to fishing crews there is a strong preference for non-kin. The relationship between crew members is temporary, flexible, and mobile—there is a rather rapid turnover in the personnel of fishing crews, with people frequently participating for a matter of months or weeks. This mobility, coupled with the highly commercial nature of the relationship, is ill adapted to the kind of behaviour associated with close kin—relations with whom are built above all on notions of permanence and reciprocity.[8]

Fishermen frequently speak of the dangers which result from having kinsmen as crew members: any disputes arising from the commercial activity of fishing have severe repercussions on harmonious relations between kin. The manner in which this subject is discussed is reminiscent of the way fears are expressed on the subject of marriage between kin. In the latter case, the potential for disputes between the married couple having a wider significance for relations between kin is seen as an important factor working against kin endogamy (see Chapter 7). In much the same way it seems that the highly commercialized relationship between crew members

[7] In contrast, Raymond Firth states that 'the kinship ties of these fishermen do not inhibit their economic calculation, though they may soften its intensity . . . economic competition between kin may be keen' (1966: 348).

[8] Raymond Firth too reports a great fluidity of personnel in fishing crews (1966: 114–15). In contrast, Fraser (1960: 134) remarks on the durability of fishing groups and how they provide the basis for other forms of co-operation, e.g. house-building groups (p. 141), in southern Thailand. However, kin are nevertheless called on more for co-operation in rice cultivation than in fishing (p. 137).

13. On a fishing boat

is unsuitable amongst kinsmen—there is simply too great a risk of disruption through disputes.[9]

Out of 22 boat crews consisting of more than one person whose composition I recorded in 1981, 12 were made up entirely of unrelated men, and another two of a mixture of kin and non-kin. Five crews were made up of a father and his son(s), and five contained brothers. A relatively low proportion of kin in fishing crews, which is also documented for Malays elsewhere,[10] relates to another aspect of relations between crew members which makes them problematic for some categories of close kin. The relationship between the *tuan bot* and his crew is a strictly hierarchical one. Not only does the *tuan bot* take a share of the earnings, which is at times substantially higher than that of his crew, but his behaviour during fishing trips clearly reveals his superior status. The *tuan bot* continually gives orders to the crew and supervises the work of its members. He is responsible for the route the boat takes, the timing of the casting of the nets, and for all the other aspects of the labour process, as well as the division of the earnings at the end of the day. He is in many ways in the position of boss.

The strongly egalitarian nature of social relations in Langkawi, the attempt to cast all relations as far as possible in a non-hierarchical mode is very marked. This is particularly true of relations within the same generation where there is a narrow age difference and no overriding difference of status. It is therefore significant that where fishermen do fish with their kin the most frequent ties are between father and son or between brothers. The former relation is always a hierarchical one, and the latter tends to take this form when there is a large age difference between the brothers. In other words, although fishing together is best done with those who are completely unrelated, the relation between captain and crew members is compatible with hierarchical kin ties such as those between father and son or older and younger brother, separated by a wide difference in age. It is highly problematic in a relation of amicable equality such as that between first cousins, or between affines. These relations are very rarely found in fishing crews.

[9] See also Nagata (1976: 402) on how fragility of kin ties is used to justify lack of economic co-operation. McKinley (1975: 34–5) and Li (1989: 83–8) comment on the problematic nature of economic calculation between kin for Malays.

[10] See Carsten 1987*a*: 203–13 for more detailed information on the composition of fishing crews and division of earnings. Raymond Firth (1966: 106) cites a ratio of kinsmen to non-kinsmen of about 1/4. Firth explicitly states that 'the Malay fishing unit is not primarily dependent upon kinship as the tie of association' (1966: 105). See also Fraser (1960: 33–4) on how Malay fishing crews are not based on kinship in southern Thailand.

As in other spheres, avoidance of disputes, especially between affines, is one of the most important factors in determining recruitment to fishing crews. Relations within the crew are preferably with those with whom a dispute would be least disruptive—non-kin, or with categories of close kin where there is a relatively great ability to avoid such disputes because of an 'in-built' tolerance of hierarchy and where the closeness itself inhibits the possibility of relations breaking.

Not only do crews preferably consist of non-kin, but these characteristics of fishing are categorically opposed to ideals of behaviour between kin. In a community in which people see themselves as united by ties of kinship, and in which there is, moreover, a concern to conduct relations on an egalitarian basis, fishing might be said to be in many senses 'anti-community' as well as 'anti-kinship'. It is therefore perhaps unsurprising that there has traditionally been a tendency to enter relationships in this sphere with the Chinese, who remain outside the social and moral community of the Malays.

Women and Rice Cultivation

The different tasks of rice cultivation, associated with different phases in the crop's growth, are generally performed by either men or women but not by both together. The division of labour is flexible enough, however, for it not to be unusual to see exceptions to this rule. The organization, and most of the labour itself, are dominated by women, particularly by those in middle age who are no longer tied to the house by young children. Work in the rice fields (*kerja bendang*) is generally preferred to housework (*kerja rumah*). Although older women sometimes claim that their daughters remain at home because they enjoy housework, this is usually strenuously denied in private by young women themselves.

The fact that rice production is predominantly female is partly a concomitant of men's involvement with fishing. In this respect, women often reiterated to me how they perceive a difference between themselves as the wives of fishermen, and women in inland communities, who are seen as being more confined within the home. Women's dominance in the sphere of rice cultivation is not, however, merely of practical significance. The centrality of rice in Southeast Asian cultures is well documented. For Malays, not only is rice the basic staple and the most important constituent of meals, it also plays a role in almost every ritual and, in the recent past, *padi* was itself the subject of a major set of rituals. The vital role of

14. Woman planting rice seedlings

women in the cultivation of this economically crucial crop with its rich symbolic load provides one indicator of the authority of women in Langkawi, and this authority begins to rise at precisely the age when women are most active in this work.[11]

The rice seed is sown in nurseries by women. This work is generally done individually; however, women who are not planting a large area frequently use the same nursery. A charge may be levied but when those concerned are close kin and neighbours, as is usually the case, this is generally not paid.

Clearing and ploughing the fields is men's work and is done with the aid of Japanese mini tractors which are hired out along with the labourers to use them. Once the land has been cleared, ploughed, fertilized, and flooded, all tasks performed by men, it is ready for the seedlings. Preparation of the fields, then, the only phase of rice cultivation undertaken exclusively by men, has been almost completely commercialized, utilizing hired labour and machinery.

Transplanting (*bertanam*) the seedlings from the nurseries to the *padi* fields is exclusively female labour. The work is occasionally done indi-

[11] Maznah Mohamed (1984: 117) has described how women with high status are those actively involved in production in a community on mainland Kedah. She emphasizes (p. 121) an age hierarchy governing control over production. However, she argues that their age limits women's socio-economic power since it makes them dependent on male relatives (p. 107). In Langkawi, I would argue that this is not the case.

vidually, but generally women prefer to work in groups. After transplanting, the rice plots must be kept free of weeds and the water levels checked. This maintenance is usually performed by men or women individually.

The final stage of the rice cycle is the harvesting. Reaping is done by women using a short sickle-shaped knife (*pengiau*). Bundles of cut *padi* are left on the stubble by women and picked up, usually by men, who beat them over a short ladder placed across the inside of a large tub, *tong*. While reaping is done exclusively by women, threshing is undertaken mainly, but not exclusively, by men.

Harvesting and threshing of small plots are sometimes done by members of a single household working together, but in general larger labour groups of up to twenty-five people, many from different households, are preferred. Harvesting, even more than transplanting, is a time of co-operative labour. I participated in many such co-operative work sessions, which formed some of the most enjoyable moments of fieldwork, and was always struck by the festivity of these occasions and their unconstrained atmosphere. The midday meal and break are minor informal celebrations where news and stories are exchanged. Children may be present, food is plentiful and good; it is eaten with particular relish; behaviour is highly informal; women and men tease each other and act without the restraint that is normal in more formal contexts within the house. Women may dress up in each other's clothes, exchange jokes (often heavy with sexual innuendo) with each other and with men, and they laugh freely. It is no wonder, then, that women say they prefer to work in groups, that it is faster, pleasanter, less lonely that way.

People in Langkawi distinguish several ways of recruiting the collective labour that is used in transplanting and harvesting, and it is significant that both transplanting and harvesting are dominated by women. Of these different categories one of the most widely used is a form of co-operation referred to as *tolong-menolong*, 'to help'. This is unpaid help given to kin, neighbours, and friends on a single occasion, for example one day of harvesting, for which no short-term reciprocation is required. In practice, labour reciprocation, though not precisely calculated, is often made within one planting and harvesting season. Those who are called upon to help are usually close kin, neighbours, or affines. Often these categories overlap, and, in general, those involved are close associates with whom exchanges of visits, food, and services are frequent. There is a noticeably high proportion of affinal kin in such groups.

A second important category of co-operative labour is *berderau*. Under this system a team (usually between two and thirty) work together for one season of planting and harvesting. They all transplant or harvest each member's crop in turn, exchanging labour on an equal basis on each person's land in rotation. Reciprocation always occurs therefore in the short term, and is rather precisely calculated. The composition of these groups does not necessarily present a great contrast with those of *tolong-menolong*. Once again close consanguines and affines, are well represented. But in the larger groups unrelated neighbours or more distant relatives are included, categories that would not normally be found in *tolong-menolong* groups.

Many villagers told me that in the past the *berderau* system was used more extensively than it is today. They linked this change with changes in the method of threshing *padi*. Until about the mid-1970s paddy was threshed by trampling, *irek*. Now that it is done by beating, the work progresses more quickly and people prefer not to *berderau*.[12] Correspondingly, they say, there has been an increase in the use of wage labour. Several women pointed out to me that the *berderau* system has the disadvantage that each person in the team has to continue working until the last person's rice is brought in. If wage labour is used, each household is only responsible for its own crop, and therefore the work is carried out over a shorter period.

Whether or not *berderau* exchange was used more extensively in the past, it does appear that the role of wage labour is increasing. As we have seen, it is particularly prevalent in the preparation of the fields for planting, the only exclusively male task of the rice cycle. Where hired labour is used for transplanting and harvesting, that is, female tasks, it is often used together with the unpaid or partly paid labour of close kin.

Between reciprocated labour exchange and wage labour there is another category of co-operation, *upah pinjam*, literally 'borrowed wages', whereby a proportion of the going wage rate is paid, usually to distant kin or affines. Generally, those recruited in this way live outside the immediate neighbourhood of those recruiting them, and are not involved in the intense exchange relationships that are characteristic between neighbours of one compound or between close kin or affines.

Although *upah pinjam* is, strictly speaking, wage labour, it actually occupies an intermediate space between relations which are so close as to

[12] This change in technology also relates to beliefs about the rice spirit (*semangat padi*). The introduction of threshing by beating is believed to have angered or upset the rice spirit, which has since fled to Thailand (where threshing is still carried out by trampling). The rituals for taking in the rice soul or rice baby were abandoned at the same time. See Endicott (1970: 23–4, 146–53); Skeat (1900: 225–8, 235–49) for a description of these.

be quite incompatible with financial reimbursement for labour, and those which are distant enough to tolerate a pure commercial content. Such intermediate relations are typically with distant kin and affines. In other words, they are with co-villagers. Wages paid for rice production are thus always qualified by kinship and community ties. Labour recruitment through *upah pinjam* and other arrangements which have a commercial element but are yet not fully commercialized and which rely heavily on the moral content of such ties show this very clearly.[13]

Rice cultivation is almost exclusively for household consumption. Female-dominated production, then, involves family members, their closest kin and affines, and co-members of the community in subsistence production for consumption in the house as an undivided unit. While some aspects of production are partially commercialized, in particular those in which men predominate, the degree of commercialization is limited by the moral precepts of kinship and community.

It is clear that fishing, carried out exclusively by men, is conducted on an entirely different basis from rice production, which is female-dominated. Whereas rice is grown almost entirely as a subsistence crop for household consumption, fishing is the most important means of acquiring cash and is a highly commercialized activity. While rice production involves co-operation with close kin, as well as more distant relatives and co-villagers, fishing is carried out either individually or, ideally, with unrelated men. Co-operation between women in rice production for cash, when undertaken, typically involves equal sharing of earnings, whereas income from fishing is highly differentiated and the labour process itself is one in which orders are given and taken.[14]

The overriding commercial nature of fishing relations is underlined not only by the precise calculation of earnings and the temporary nature of crews, but also in the way that fishermen eat together on the boat. Or rather, in the way that they eat separately: each fisherman brings his own individual portion of rice and takes his meal separately and without sharing. Eating rice together is a potent symbol of house and kin unity; this does not occur on a fishing boat. Fishermen, it seems, are neither of one house, nor even in this sense of one boat. After a successful day's fishing,

[13] Nagata (1976: 405) has also commented on a reluctance to pay *upah* to kin because this affirms social distance.

[14] Similarly, Bailey (1983: 81, 187–90) has emphasized a contrast between co-operation in rice-farming and the tensions and conflict involved in individualistic and commercialized fishing.

the captain may treat the crew in the coffee-shop but this food consists of drinks and snacks, not a full rice meal. It is eaten in neither the boat nor the house; nor does it replace food eaten in the house. Even the most substantial of snacks will be followed by a full rice meal eaten at home at the appropriate time. Above all, snacks are not cooked in the house but bought. If they are paid for by the *tuan*, this further underlines the hierarchical and commercial nature of the relationship.

It is worth contrasting these commensal patterns with those which occur for co-operative work parties in rice cultivation, which I described above. In the latter case, when kin and neighbours work together they eat a full rice meal together in the most festive and informal atmosphere.

If fishing can be seen as in some way 'anti-house' and this is symbolized by the non-commensal relations of men of one boat, rice cultivation, by contrast, can be seen as precisely embodying the values of the house and of community in at least some of its aspects. Indeed, the consumption of rice sustains these very entities. It is in a sense the substance of the connections between their members. And this is neatly summed up by the fact that co-operative labour groups always eat a full rice meal (*makan nasi*) together—indeed this is the high point of the working day.

We can now begin to understand why it is that women are completely excluded from fishing—an activity which embodies a negation of all the values with which they are most closely associated. Perhaps even more significantly, we can also see why it is that men are not explicitly excluded from rice cultivation, why they must be included in this activity. For the contrast between male economic relations and those which underlie predominantly female co-operation in rice cultivation is highly significant when we consider ideas about community. It is out of the kind of co-operation which women engage in that at least one notion of community can be seen to derive. And yet, as I will argue, the fact that this notion is 'female' is often problematic. Men's inclusion or reintegration into this community is always finally necessary.

Women and Money

The contrast I have drawn between the world of women and that of men is encapsulated in women's and men's different relations to money. Both women and men are closely involved with money, handling it in their normal, day-to-day activities, but their relation to money is entirely different. And here I summarize an argument I have made elsewhere (Carsten 1989).

First, as should already be clear, almost all cash is earned by men from fishing. Women sometimes earn small amounts of money by making and selling rice cakes, selling fruit and vegetables, or from collecting bivalves from the rocks on the sea-shore. But usually this kind of produce is consumed at home as a special treat; in any case, the cash generated by such activities is usually occasional, and insufficient to support a household. It is notable that women often send men or children out to engage in direct sales of this kind of produce for them rather than go themselves. Women are not involved in either the processing or the marketing of fish as they are elsewhere in Malaysia.[15]

Secondly, although men earn money, at the end of each day they hand it over to women, who control daily household expenditure. At the same time as giving their wives money, men usually hand over to women a few fish to be cooked for the evening meal. Men keep for themselves a small amount of 'coffee money' (*duit kopi*).

Income earned by either spouse is regarded as 'joint property' (*benda syarikat*). Husbands and wives do not maintain separate funds or save separately. While women administer daily expenditure, income is regarded as belonging to both spouses equally. Although major items of expenditure are decided upon after a process of joint discussion, all day-to-day expenses are controlled by women. However, once again, women often send men or children out to do the actual buying.[16]

Households may maintain more than one fund, depending on how many economically active and self-sufficient couples live in one house. A husband and wife who are co-resident with their married daughter or son would save separately if both couples were still economically active. And this is explicitly a way of avoiding conflicts of interest, and facilitating separation of co-resident couples should disputes occur. Once the older couple cease to earn enough to support themselves, these separate funds are no longer maintained.

The individuation of earnings, and the partial separation of funds within the house, is, however, denied in the way daily expenses are met. Whatever the living arrangements within one house, and however many

[15] See Strange 1980; Rosemary Firth 1966; Raymond Firth 1966.

[16] The administration of household finances by women is a common feature of Malay life (see Rosemary Firth 1966; Rudie 1993; 1994). Rudie reports that men are increasingly running household finances as men's earnings become more significant than women's in the community she studied in Kelantan.

couples live there, the precise division of daily household expenses, 'kitchen expenses' (*belanja dapur*), is left uncalculated. While it was quite easy to obtain detailed accounts of household expediture, it was almost impossible to get accurate information on how much had been spent by which person and on what. Instead, I was simply told, 'Whoever has money spends.' 'Whoever has money goes to buy.' There is one *dapur* in the house, and all its expenses are met, at least in theory, by all household members collectively.[17] In this way, women neutralize the individuating effects of divided earnings. In its passage through the house, the values of money are transformed from the divisive, commercial, and competitive associations of the way it is earned. Instead, it becomes imbued with the values of kinship and unity associated with the house, and above all with the *dapur*.

Although consumption and saving emphasize the unity and undifferentiation of the house, there is one form of saving that involves co-operation between houses. This is the rotating credit association (*kut*).[18] These organizations are run by and for women; typically, they involve about ten to twenty members. Each member contributes a fixed sum of money every week, and this is collected by the 'head of the *kut*' (*kepala kut*). Each week, one member receives the total collection—the order in which they do so being fixed in advance by drawing lots, or by mutual agreement, at the beginning of the cycle. The *kut* may be terminated after one cycle, or may begin again. Some *kut* survive for many months.

What is notable about these associations is that they involve women very closely with money but they do so in rather a special way. First, when I enquired from several women who organized these associations how they chose the other members, I was told that they tried to find members they could 'trust' (*cahaya*); they look for 'close people' (*orang dekat*). This notion of closeness conflates kin, neighbours, and affines; it is the same notion that governs marital choices (see Chapter 7). In fact, the great majority of members of one *kut* are close kin: cousins, aunts, nieces,

[17] In contrast, Rosemary Firth (1966: 17) comments on the ease of separate cooking and budgeting arrangements within one house on the east coast. See also Rudie (1994: 90–1, 101–18) for a more recent study of these arrangements in Kelantan. In Langkawi, while separate saving and budgeting do occur to a limited extent, unlike on the east coast, this division is negated in cooking and eating arrangements. See also Li (1989), who emphasizes the economic individualism of Malays in Singapore.

[18] *Kut* is an abbreviation for *kutipan duit*, literally, a collection (or subscription) of money. For material on similar institutions elsewhere see C. Geertz 1962; Ardener 1964; Lundstrom-Burghoorn 1981.

mothers, daughters, sisters. Affines tend to be chosen more rarely because relations between them are often somewhat strained. The relations between members of a *kut*, then, are quite unlike fishing relations between men; they are, above all, based on kinship and trust, and they have a strong moral content. Relations between members of a fishing crew, by contrast, are temporary, commercial, and hierarchical—they are much better suited to non-kin.

Secondly, although the *kut* might seem to be about cash, the money is always either used for the purpose of buying household items, or these items (such as aluminium saucepans, sets of Tupperware bowls, trays, glasses, crockery) are directly purchased by the *kepala kut*. In fact, the goods acquired are almost always directly associated with cooking and eating, and with the *dapur*. Rather than collect the contributions themselves, women often send a child to do so for them, as if to mitigate their association with money. The *kut* is thus aimed less at the accumulation of money, than at the creation of a chain of generalized consumption between houses, and between their *dapur*. Houses or hearths are linked together in a chain of equal and shared consumption of the same articles.[19]

In this way, there is an avoidance of an association between the house and the accumulation of money, in other words, of values which would negate the house. Just as in budgeting and day-to-day expenditure the divisive and individuating effects of money are avoided, the same process occurs in the way money is saved. Once again, money is removed by women from the context in which it is earned by men; and its associations are transformed from the individualism and competition of commercial relations, to the sharing, mutuality, and reciprocity of kinship. In the process, money itself has been transformed from an article of exchange to one of consumption.[20]

[19] See C. Geertz (1962); Jay (1969); Lundstrom-Burghoorn (1981) for descriptions of similar organizations in Java and Minahasa.

[20] Rudie (1993; 1994) has taken issue with my interpretation of women's relation to money (Carsten 1989), which she finds inapplicable in the Kelantanese case. Much of this seems to me no more than a basic ethnographic difference between Langkawi and the east coast of Malaysia, rather than a matter of 'analysis' as Rudie (1993: 111) suggests. Unlike east coast women, women in Langkawi in the early 1980s did not engage in trade to any significant degree (Carsten 1989: 129). I would not necessarily expect this avoidance to persist under present conditions in Langkawi. Rudie (1993: 111; 1994: 111) also implies that I suggest women convert money from a 'commodity' to a 'gift'. I have avoided phrasing the argument in these terms partly because in Langkawi the boundaries between these categories are quite unclear. It is central to the argument of this book (and my earlier article) that division and exchange are always potentially convertible into unity and sharing.

Women thus imbue money with the values of kinship and morality, the values of the house, with which they themselves are closely associated. Just as they cook the fish which men bring home for the household meal in the *dapur*, women transform the equivalent of fish, which is money, in the *dapur*. Money is transformed from a means of exchange to a consumption good whose function is to reproduce the house. And here once again we see the centrality of the functioning hearth not just to the processes of kinship, but also to 'domesticating' what is external to the house. When Aisyah told me that the establishment of a new house involves a mother enabling her daughter to light the house hearth, and to cook a meal there, she might be said to have been referring to all these processes.

In order to be able to transform what is external to the house, women must isolate themselves from the commercial relations of fishing, and from the competitive relations of trade and the market. Thus, by handing money over to women, men avoid the divisive dangers of the commercial relations in which they engage. Women transform the effects of these relations into the sharing, unity, and similarity that characterize relations within the house.

Transforming Difference

In spite of the economic, social, religious, and political differences between villagers which I have described in this chapter, there is a very real sense in Langkawi that such differences are irrelevant or erased. All villagers perceive themselves as 'village people' (*orang kampung*). They often say, 'we are all poor people' (*kami semua orang susah*), and contrast themselves with 'urban people' (*orang pekan*), particularly with those who earn regular wages or salaries (*orang makan gaji*). In comparison to this latter category they feel themselves to be badly off, not only in terms of relative wealth, but because of the great irregularity of income and lack of security that fishing involves. Villagers refer to the élite and professional groups of Malaysia as 'people of rank' (*orang pangkat*), or 'high rank' (*pangkat tinggi*). They perceive themselves as 'people of low status' (*orang bawah, orang rendah*), 'peasants' (*ra'ayat*).

Although Langkawi forms part of the mainland state of Kedah, islanders frequently speak of 'going to Kedah' when they make trips to the mainland. In other contexts too, they refer to Kedah in a manner which indicates that they perceive Langkawi as being distinct from the mainland state rather than an integral part of it. It is these contrasts which inform villagers' self-perceptions, fostering a sense of unity and a 'spirit of equality' which pervades their daily dealings with each other. There is a strong emphasis on conformity which extends to etiquette and aesthetics. Co-villagers tend to be treated in a broadly similar manner, informal codes of behaviour are adopted as quickly as possible, and status distinctions tend to be ignored.

The conceptualization of their society as different from the mainland and as one in which similarity and equality are more important than difference and hierarchy can be related to aspects of social organization in Langkawi. The dominance of fishing, in contrast to irrigated rice agriculture, and the fact that land is a less significant resource than on mainland Kedah, has meant that inequalities based on the differential ownership and control of land and its inheritance have been less marked than on the mainland. While ownership of boats and nets certainly leads to wealth differentials, it could be argued that these tend to be less permanent and entrenched than those associated with a land-owning élite. Until recently, the greater part of fishing capital was controlled by Chinese middlemen and this may have further fostered a sense of unity among Malay villagers.

These ideas are reflected in the perceptions of many villagers. They often draw attention to a difference between themselves and rice cultivators, emphasizing the uncertainty of income gained through fishing. Profits from agriculture are seen as more certain and predictable. But when the fishing is good, they say, then fishermen give fish away to their kin. Such fish are not sold, they are given as alms (*sedekah*). These are 'given without calculation' (*bagi, tak kira*). Thus local people see the very uncertainty of their predicament as a source of a special generosity, an unwillingness to engage in close calculation of profits. And this idea of their own special position is reflected at a communal level, for example in the pride in the proscription on fishing after a resident of the parish (*kariah*) has died.

An ideology of similarity can, then, be seen as a concomitant of villagers' own perception of their position in the social and class structure of present-day Malaysia. For most villagers the differences separating these classes have, at least until recently, had more significance than minor differences of rank or wealth which distinguish members of one class from each other.[21] It remains to be seen, however, whether such an ideology will persist in the future in the context of the growing wealth differentials that have arisen as a result of inflation in land values and the development of

[21] Such ideologies have, however, also been reported on the mainland. See, for example, Syed Husin Ali (1964: 47, 58, 59); and, in a more ambivalent form, Nash (1974: 41).

tourism on the island. In Chapter 9 I will examine the significance of egalitarian perceptions in a historical context. We will see what historical circumstances might be associated with an ideology which puts an enormous emphasis on similarity and closeness.[22]

It is clear, however, that these perceptions constitute, at least in part, a denial of the division and difference which fragments the world outside the house. We have seen that local notions of gender separate to a considerable degree the world of women and that of men. And that these same conceptions associate men very strongly with this fragmented and fragmenting outside world. Through their labour, their politics, their religion, and their sociability, men are irrevocably linked to the sources of division. Indeed, men's very personhood, embodied in nicknames, is constituted by individual, competitive achievement.

Women, by contrast, are associated with a different set of values: with the house and with relations between kin. That kinship is conceived as a sharing of substance which may be as much acquired as given at birth has highly significant implications when we consider the relation between the world inside the house and that outside. We have already begun to see how women transform what is produced outside the house into something imbued with the values of kinship and the house. In the following chapters, we will see how other aspects of this outside world can, through the actions of women, be simultaneously kept at a distance and incorporated into the house and thereby transformed. It is because kinship is always 'in process', being acquired, that the possibility of transformation is there, and that difference can be erased.

[22] Scott (1976) has emphasized that such tendencies should not be over-romanticized. His own important study (1985) shows well the effects of increasing economic polarization on social relations and perceptions in a community on mainland Kedah in which land is the most important productive resource.

6

Between Houses: Visiting, Eating, and Feasting

The last chapter described how Langkawi villagers' experience of the state, and of national and local political, religious, and economic institutions, is both fragmented and fragmenting. In this chapter and those that follow I show how an opposition between the house and the similarity of substance that unites those within it, and the divisive world that lies beyond the house is overcome.[1]

The problem is how to pass from the inside to the outside, how to have daily dealings in the world beyond the house, as villagers must, without getting engulfed by it. The divisions that I have described always threaten to disrupt villagers' inner space, and they must be kept at bay. In fact, what I will show is how, by various symbolic and practical actions, the space that the house occupies can, in symbolic terms, be almost infinitely extended to include the world beyond.

Another way of phrasing this problem is in terms of boundaries. For the point at which the house and the outside world meet is of course particularly crucial. And it is therefore necessary to understand how boundaries are conceived and what their salience is. In one way the perceptions I describe might be said to be precisely about the art of not drawing boundaries. But this is an over-simplification. The significance of notions of boundary is all the greater where they can be both created and, simultaneously, made to disappear.

We have, of course, already met this problem in another guise when we looked at notions of siblingship and of the body. There we saw how there is always a great ambiguity over the point at which one thing ends and another begins. And that the person might be said to be simultaneously individual and multiple. We also saw how, because the house is so strongly associated with siblingship, this same ambiguity applies to the house. The house embodies siblingship, can likewise be individual or multiple. It can incorporate other houses.

[1] Some of the material in this chapter is discussed in Carsten 1987*b*; 1995*b*.

Siblingship, we saw too, is about both similarity and difference. Phrased in the idiom of being the same, having the same origin, it contains the seeds of its own division into difference. And once again these notions are pertinent when we consider the relation between different houses. It is on the boundary of the very subtle distinction between being the same and being different that life in the world beyond the house is played out.

From the House to the Village

When walking through the village, I was often struck by how difficult it was to see where one landholding ended and another began. Boundaries between compounds, neighbourhoods, and villages are difficult to discern. The ambiguity of boundaries is captured in the very term for a village community: *kampung*.

The word *kampung* has a wide range of meanings. First, it refers to a whole village. This is its primary referent: a villager who is asked what *kampung* she is from will generally reply giving the name of her village. Secondly, it can be a small sub-village or hamlet that forms part of a larger village and has its own prayer house, *surau*, and is distinguished by a name and boundary. Thirdly, *kampung* is used to refer to a group of houses situated on a piece of land which has not been legally divided. The land is registered in the name of one owner (or a group of owners) who may be either alive or dead—in the latter case it is utilized by descendants of the original owner. The number of houses in such a group varies but it is usually between one and six. This third meaning of the term *kampung*, then, corresponds to the English *compound*. Fourthly, *kampung* or *tanah kampung*, 'kampung land', may be used to mean land which has been cleared for the purpose of house-building, whether or not houses have yet been actually built. In this sense the land is differentiated by its use from other types of land—for example, jungle (*hutan*), paddy land (*sawah*), etc. Here *kampung* refers to land used or intended for habitation. There are thus four meanings of *kampung*: village, sub-village, compound, and land used, or intended, for residence.

Kampung also carries with it a more vague sense which explains its wide-ranging reference. This sense includes a notion of community: people who are located in a specific area of social as well as geographic space, who, ideally at least, are all kin—although the precise relationship they have to each other is undefined. There is a substantial degree of village endogamy in Langkawi (see Chapter 7) which enables people to think of the community as one made up of people who are related to one another; this is frequently expressed in such phrases as, 'we are all kin here, there are no strangers' (*kita semua adik-beradik di sini, orang lain tak ada*).

In practice a *kampung* may constitute a large village of several thousand residents—a political and administrative unit—or it may simply be a compound with anything from one occupant to fifty. It may be made up of one house or several hundred. The residents should, ideally, be related to each other, but the way in which they are is left vague and undefined. They may be close consanguines or distantly connected affines—on the whole, people prefer not to distinguish between these categories because to do so would be divisive in a context where endogamy plays a major role in binding people together. The term *kampung* expresses through its generality an unwillingness to differentiate people from each other and it thereby stresses the unity of the community.[2]

Most significantly, *kampung* includes as its referents both the house and the community. And between these units there is another, the compound, which is also expressed by the same term. There is thus a continuum between the individual house, the compound, and the community at large.

The Compound

I was often struck by the marked informality of visiting patterns within the compound. These visits stand in marked contrast to all other forms of visiting. They take place frequently—often the same person may drop in several times in one day—and at all times of the day. Visitors are treated and behave in a similar way to house residents. They enter through the entrance to the house that leads into the cooking *dapur*—the one most commonly used by those who live together. Women, in particular, behave with an extreme lack of formality: they sit or lie in positions normally only permissible within their own home. Older visitors treat children of the house they are visiting in much the same way as their own children: they send them on errands, give them chores, and do not show the same indulgence and tolerance displayed to the children of strangers. The manner of conducting these visits provides a clue to the way compounds are thought of.

[2] Swift (1965: 144) has also commented on the range of meanings of the term *kampung*. His argument that in the past the use of this term must have been less ambiguous because of lower population density seems somewhat tenuous. See also Kuchiba *et al.* (1979: xi–xii) and Fraser (1960: 101–4).

Compounds, *kampung*, are landholdings that have one or more houses on them and are registered as single holdings with single or multiple owners (who are either dead or alive).[3] Land is generally registered in the name of the person who first cleared it. It is then inherited by the original owner's children. Some children may take up residence in other areas where their spouse may have access to land.

When married children move to a different neighbourhood they retain rights to the house land of their parents, and they or their children may later move back to the parental locality. It is not uncommon for grandchildren to activate land rights in the compound of their grandparents after marriage. If the grandparents are dead, this pattern may not reveal itself in the co-residence of grandparents and grandchildren but in the high frequency of first-cousin ties. Land rights may be consolidated through marriage between cousins. Since inheritance is in both the male and the female line, and locality of residence after marriage is uncertain, grandchildren of either sex may take up residence in the locality of grandparents on either side in this way.

The compound is, then, a collection of houses of closely related consanguines. Frequently the residents of different houses or their parents have at one time shared a common house. Different houses are commonly occupied by parents and their married children, or members of an adult sibling group who originate from a common house. When houses are occupied by non-kin these are generally landless people and their occupancy is temporary. By a similar process to the expansion of houses, compounds also grow and divide. As compound land is subdivided, consanguines come to occupy adjacent compounds. A criss-crossing web of relationships and interconnections will thus characterize any neighbourhood.

The nature of this process means that the compound can be viewed as an extension of the house. And this is revealed in the terminology for neighbours. Neighbours within the compound are referred to as 'neighbours of one house ladder' (*jiran se tangga*). Compounds are conceptualized as having their origins in one house.

This notion is demonstrated in behaviour, visits, and exchanges within the compound. Visits within the compound are not scrupulously returned and may indeed show great imbalance if it is easier for one person to visit

[3] e.g. in one *kampung* with a total of 28 houses in 8 compounds there were 14 sibling links between houses in the same compound; 8 parent/child ties; 5 first-cousin links; 2 grandparent/grandchild ties; 3 households not consanguineally related; and 1 more distant consanguineal link.

than another. Refreshment does not have to be provided for these visitors (although snacks are frequently consumed), whereas it is always produced for those from further afield. Visits may be short or long in duration and often have no purpose except conviviality. Co-residents of one compound tend to meet and talk inside houses rather than outside them or on their thresholds (although these kinds of meetings do also take place).

Although male compound residents do visit each other, the most frequent visitors are female. During the day, when most men are out fishing, women spend most of their leisure hours with others of the same compound, either within the house or underneath it in the shade. It is notable that, whereas women always cover their heads and often put on better clothing when going outside the compound, when circulating within it they do not change their dress in any way. This is one of the most obvious markers of the fact that behaviour within the compound is almost undifferentiated from behaviour within the house. Further, it is notable that the relative seclusion of young girls (*anak dara*) occurs not within the house, as villagers often claim, but within the compound. *Anak dara* are active participants in informal visits to their compound neighbours.

In the long-running dispute which I describe in Chapter 8, the oldest women of the houses involved had an enormous say in how the other members of their own houses and neighbouring ones behaved. These older women would hold forth at length (both to each other and to younger men and women) on what should and should not be done and the moral codes involved. On several occasions, an older woman ordered the windows and doors of her own house to be closed to cut off exchange with neighbours the household was disputing with. But women dominate social relations in the compound as they do in the house in a more positive spirit too. It is women who perform most of the visits and exchanges which are a part of daily life. Just as a woman's authority within the house increases with age, so within the compound senior women attempt to exercise moral authority over the actions of younger residents and this is especially clear during disputes.

There is frequent exchange of goods and services between houses of one compound; in particular, raw and cooked food is often given. Newly collected fruit, freshly caught fish, or some special cooked dish or delicacy may be taken by children from one house to another. Once again women dominate these exchanges. The informal gift of a dish of cooked food (for example, a fish curry, fried noodles, special cakes, or a snack) is common within the compound but rarely occurs outside it. Such gifts are characteristically not immediately or directly reciprocated.

Co-members of a compound frequently exchange agricultural labour, and this tends to be unformalized, and expressed as 'just helping' (*tolong sahaja*), rather than the more formal arrangements for reciprocal labour exchanges. When Halimah contributed her labour to her brother and sister-in-law (and next-door neighbours) she joined a harvesting group which they had organized on an *upah pinjam* basis. The other members of this group were resident further away or quite distantly related to the organizers. Halimah alone refused payment, saying she was 'just helping'. Residents of one compound will give each other aid in the form of labour on other occasions too: house-building, house-lifting, at feasts or the preparation of a special meal to mark an occasion, at times of illness or childbirth. Such aid does not require short-term reciprocation, although in the long run it is probably balanced.

The frequent and 'unaccounted' rendering of assistance in the form of labour, food, or loans is, then, a central part of what it means to be of one compound. To an extent these relations are governed by what Sahlins (1972) has called 'generalized reciprocity'. Sahlins characterizes such reciprocity as that where

> the expectation of a direct material return is unseemly. At best it is implicit. The material side of the transaction is repressed by the social: reckoning of debts outstanding cannot be overt and is typically left out of account . . . the counter is not stipulated by time, quantity or quality: the expectation of reciprocity is indefinite . . . The requital thus may be very soon, but then again it may be never. (Sahlins 1972: 194)

The appropriateness of this formulation was brought home to me when, at a certain point in a series of mutual provocations between two households engaged in a dispute, one sibling called up a loan which had been made to the neighbouring household some months previously. This act was regarded as highly provocative, inappropriate between such closely related households. It aroused anger and itself provoked a further round of negative exchanges. There seems little doubt that this is reciprocity in which 'a direct material return is unseemly' and where 'reckoning of debts outstanding cannot be overt' without disrupting the relationship.

I described in Chapter 3 the resistance to dividing property. A consequence of this is that rice land as well as compound land is often co-owned by houses of one compound. Another resource that houses of one compound use together is water. Each compound has one well where female residents do household laundry each day, draw water for household use, and where women and men bathe several times a day. Thus land, water, and, to a lesser degree, labour and food may be used in common by households of a single compound.

It would seem then that there is a considerable degree of *sharing* of resources within the compound. Gibson (1986: 220–1) has criticized Sahlins's use of reciprocity, arguing that sharing among the Buid constitutes an actual denial of reciprocity. For the Buid, sharing involves an obligation to give, but none to receive or to repay the giver. According to this formulation, 'sharing' seems to fit the relation between houses of one compound in Langkawi more closely than Sahlins's generalized reciprocity.[4] In Langkawi the sharing characteristic of houses of one compound is contingent upon a notion that these houses originate from one house within which division of all kinds of property is greatly resisted and consumption is shared. To varying degrees, resources within the compound are co-owned and there is a strong idea that things which are not owned in common should be given freely without expectation of a direct material return.

The significance of frequent gifts of cooked food is clear. If the kinship of those who live in one house is to a large extent predicated on the fact that they eat from one hearth, the giving of cooked food within the compound can be seen as the construction of a limited form of commensality in this unit. This, however, is always circumscribed: it does not extend to eating full rice meals together.[5]

The concept of the compound as an extension of the house receives another expression in the kin terms used within it. Compounds consist of different houses established by the children of an original couple. In succeeding generations, different houses are linked by ties of siblingship and between cousins. In Chapter 3 I described how cousins use sibling terms when addressing or referring to each other. These are derived not from the relative age of the cousins themselves but from the birth order of the sibling group from whom the cousins are descended, as though cousins from different houses are transformed into siblings whose origins are from the same house.

The concept of incest in Langkawi reflects the notion of the compound as an expanded house in another way. I once heard women discussing the

[4] Gibson's use of 'sharing' implies that everyone has equal rights to what is being shared. It is also clear that the animals which are killed are closely associated with particular households (ibid.: 43). But everyone in the community is entitled to a share of the meat, indeed sharing is largely what defines these communities (pp. 119–20, 218).

[5] Massard (1983*a*: 363) makes a similar suggestion and notes how the sending of children on such errands (who need not be formally invited inside to eat) excludes the possibility of eating with co-villagers.

propriety of an impending marriage between cousins in a manner which made clear that this was on the edge of what was acceptable. Eventually, they agreed it was all right because the cousins had been brought up far apart. Although first-cousin marriage is strictly permissible, it occurs infrequently (see Chapter 7). Because first cousins have a 'quasi-sibling' relationship with each other, such marriage carries connotations of incest. It is only allowed if the cousins live far away from each other. Cousins from the same compound are so close as to be almost siblings, for whom marriage would be incestuous.

Visits and Exchanges within the Neighbourhood

Within the neighbourhood which extends beyond the immediate compound, relations take a slightly different form. Labour exchanges within a locality tend to be balanced and short-term; they are typically organized through arrangements which emphasize balance and immediate exchange, such as 'rotating co-operative labour' (*berderau*) or 'borrowed wages' (*upah pinjam*) described in Chapter 5. People within such a neighbourhood do not normally give long-term unaccounted help as they do within a compound.

Similarly, cooked food is not given in the frequent and casual way that it is within the compound. During the month of Ramadan more formalized food exchanges occur: cakes are sent at nightfall in a container, which is emptied and refilled with ones of a different variety before being sent back. Once again children are the means of effecting these exchanges. This practice, known as 'to return the container' (*membalas bekas*), occurs between houses of one compound but is especially characteristic between houses of friends and kin in the wider neighbourhood. Here relations are characterized by a more direct and immediate reciprocity, a stress on balance and equality. *Membalas bekas* epitomizes this immediate and direct exchange. When by chance two exchanging households have made the same cakes they will swap the exactly identical article—made in different houses. Exchanges of cakes during Ramadan are in an idiom (food-sharing) resonant of the mutuality of those who share one hearth but their form stresses immediate and like return.[6]

Outside the compound, another kind of informal visiting occurs within

[6] Jay, observing very similar kinds of symmetrical exchanges in Java (1969: 176–7, 227–82, 250–3), has noted the fact that they express an ideal of social equality within the community, 'a community of peers' (p. 228). This image of a community of like houses engaged in symmetrical and balanced exchanges is highly pertinent to Langkawi.

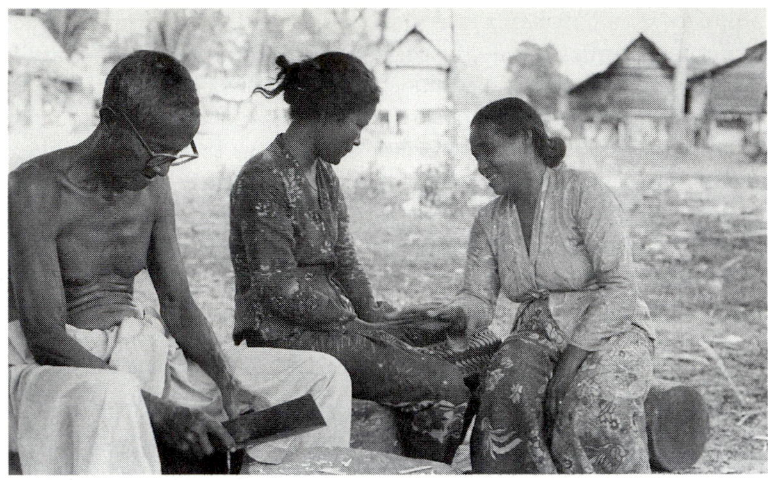

15. Meeting between houses

the immediate neighbourhood, once again dominated by women.[7] These visits are for pleasure and relaxation in the company of others. Women normally cover their heads when leaving the compound but do not alter their clothing in any other way for these kind of visits. This form of sociability commonly occurs on the periphery of a house: on the outside verandah, underneath the house, or under a tree between a group of houses. Visitors on familiar terms are often invited into the house, but once there would have to accept more formal hospitality including light refreshment (coffee, a sweet or snack). Often they refuse the invitation and instead will stand or sit outside the house and carry on a conversation there. Local visitors who do enter the house will accept a snack and they may also be offered a full rice meal, especially if it is being eaten at the time by members of the household. I described in Chapter 1 how such offers, however pressing, are always refused.

The tendency to carry on a conversation under a house or at its margins can be related to the degree of formality of the relationships involved. Entering the house marks either a more formal and distant relationship, that of strangers or distant kin, or an extremely close and familiar one. In all cases the degree of formality is unavoidably expressed by the entrance one uses (members of the house and their very close kin or neighbours use

[7] Women's dominance in inter-household visiting has been reported elsewhere in Malaysia, see Wilson (1967: 122, 50–1) and Provencher (1971: 139).

the kitchen door; strangers use the most formal entrance). Within the slightly wider neighbourhood, relationships fall between these two categories and are conducted on the periphery of the house with as little formality as possible, as though not to draw too rigid a distinction between those who have a constant right of access and are treated as house residents, and those who do not have this right and would therefore have to be treated with formality if they did enter.

Residents in such a locality are often related although they may have difficulty in tracing this out precisely. In fact, because of the degree of endogamy, there may be several ties linking co-residents of one neighbourhood. Villagers do not make a distinction between affinal and consanguineal ties on a general level, or when tracing out relationships. They recognize the network of interconnecting ties, saying, 'We are all kin' (*kami semua adik-beradik*). In general, there is an avoidance of distinguishing or drawing boundaries between different groups of people.

Villagers prefer to see a continuum of relatedness from close kin (*adik-beradik dekat*) to distant (*adik-beradik jauh*), and even those who are completely unrelated may be described as being 'a little connected' (*sangkut sikit-sikit*), in an imprecise way.[8] Differentiating between kin and non-kin, or between kin and affines is associated only with disputes. Both formal and informal visiting are a way of publicly declaring the harmoniousness of social relations; when these break, communications are cut. All visits and other forms of exchange come to a halt. It is for this reason that visiting, and women's role in maintaining relations of this kind, is significant beyond the level of dyadic relations between houses.

The reluctance to draw distinctions is expressed spatially in the absence of fences in the village. These are generally only erected as a result of disputes. Similarly, boundaries between different sub-villages with different names are often difficult to distinguish.[9]

Informal visiting takes place between three main categories of people: people of one neighbourhood; those who are friends (*kawan*); and affines. People who reside in the same locality, or within a short distance of each other, may develop an especially close tie. They may be consanguineally or affinally related but the intensity of exchanges between them surpasses that which is normal for this category of relationship. These friendships

[8] See also Bloch (1978) on avoidance of tracing complex genealogical links among the Merina; Firth (1974: 46–7).

[9] This reluctance to draw boundaries is also noted in Kuchiba *et al.* (1979: 206) for a village in Kelantan and by Provencher (1971: 185). Outside Malaysia see Fraser (1966: 32) and Jay (1969: 229–30).

occur between age and sex peers during years of greatest leisure. They are common between unmarried youths, unmarried girls, and between older women.

Friendships between young women spring from ties formed at school or in the neighbourhood. Young women often form close, intimate relations with their peers but the ties tend to be dyadic, personal ones without the wider implications of female friendships formed in later life.

Older women often have special friends with whom they interact more intensively than with other categories of female peers—exchanging frequent visits, helping each other with labour, performing co-operative agricultural labour, and confiding their personal problems in each other. My foster mother had a particular friend in the neighbourhood whom she often saw in this way several times a day. These two women were on especially intimate terms, and joking and humour were a very important ingredient in their friendship—the two of them enjoyed many hilarious moments together when other members of their families were not present. Because of the dominant position of older women in the house, relationships like this one often link houses in a close way, with labour exchange occurring regularly, and other members of the house becoming friends. Female friends of this kind may try to arrange a marriage between their children. In the case of my foster mother such a marriage had occurred between her daughter and her friend's sister's son.

In contrast, male friendships tend to focus away from the house—meetings take place in coffee-shops in the village or the local town, and may in fact be opposed to the house as a social unit. They are associated with an institution: the coffee-shop, and sometimes with activities—gambling, drinking, spending money freely—which men and women regard as potentially threatening to household harmony. These activities may limit consumption within the house, and negate kinship itself. I mentioned in Chapter 3 how one man described to me how, when he married, the chief change in his lifestyle was that he had virtually ceased to socialize with his friends. He regarded his responsibilities as a married man as incompatible with the free and easy lifestyle of his young peers and, in particular, with their spending habits. In this sense, male consumption negates the house, while female organized consumption is constitutive of it. Women's friendships, far from being potentially disruptive of houses, foster relations of all kinds between them. They are part of the close ties within any neighbourhood, creating a sense of community which centres on the house.

The final category of informal visiting involves affines. The relationship between affines will be discussed in detail in the following two chapters. Here I will only discuss the importance of frequent visiting as a means of confirming a relationship which is always potentially unstable. A failure to comply with obligations to visit may be interpreted as either the cause or the effect of a dispute. There are two categories of affines who are particularly constrained to visit each other frequently—one is female co-parents-in-law (*bisan*) and the other a non-resident female daughter-in-law and her mother-in-law.

The degree of formality of these visits varies partly according to distances involved: when the two houses are in close proximity the visits are likely to be frequent with the minimum of formality. In these cases women generally dress up but behaviour is not formalized. A young woman will participate in the household labour of her mother-in-law, who meanwhile occupies herself with her grandchildren. Affines who live further away will visit each other more rarely and their visits are likely to be more formal.

Affinal visits in fact show a rather tense combination of formality with informality. It is important to go to an affinal house in good clothes. But it is also important, particularly for a young and recently married woman, to participate in household labour in a manner which shows she is not proud (*sombong*). I witnessed several young women visiting the house of their mother-in-law in best 'going out' clothes who, within a few minutes, had entered the *dapur* and were helping with the preparation of whatever meal was being cooked there in a manner that was almost ostentatiously humble. It is significant that affinal visits frequently involve eating a full meal together with house members *as well as* a snack. Indeed, I was often struck by the almost aggressive manner in which this might be insisted upon by the mother-in-law. Close affines (particularly *bisan* and daughters-in-law) even from quite near by will participate in the house meal in direct contrast to other co-villagers. In this respect there is a clear attempt to include visiting affines in the house, and also to prolong their visit as much as possible.

Affinal visits fall between informal neighbourly visits and formal ones which mark an occasion. The ideal is that affines should visit each other frequently: non-visiting is interpreted as an insult and may eventually jeopardize affinal links. These ideals are not very different from those which govern visiting between kin but because of their fragility and instability affinal ties require more constant confirmation. All forms of exchange, not only visiting, are much stressed.

Although male affines participate in these exchanges, it is women who dominate them. Certain aspects of these visits—the fact that they occur inside the house, that female affines assist with labour, the consumption of full meals, etc.—indicate an attempt to assimilate affines to close kin or household members which conforms with the informal aspects of the visits. However, this seems to be contradicted by their 'display' component: the manner in which women dress up for them—a daughter-in-law visiting her mother-in-law may take several small children with her, all in their best clothes. Their procession through the village to the affinal household is thus a public statement of their recognition of these links.

Affinal visits can thus be seen as a more regularly activated and, in some respects, a more formal version of the informal visits between neighbours and close kin. The informality is a corollary of the fact that affines should not, ideally, be distinguished from kin, but the necessity for their regular occurrence belies this fact. These visits show a tension not present in other forms of visiting. In fact their informality has a coercive quality which is revealed in the way daughters-in-law in best clothes *must* participate in household labour in the *dapur*, and in the almost enforced consumption of a meal which in other contexts is restricted to household members.

Although women participate more than men in all forms of informal inter-household exchange, it is notable that, as the degree of formality (and often the geographic distance) involved increases, so too does male participation. Kinswomen who reside at some distance do not usually come on a rare visit unaccompanied by their husbands. Usually such visits are undertaken by couples and may have a particular purpose in view, for example an invitation to a marriage feast, or a request for help with co-operative labour. During school holidays there is a high frequency of visits between the more distant villages of Langkawi and even from kin resident on the mainland. On such occasions husbands and wives generally arrive together, dressed in best attire, and accompanied by one or more of their children. Even in these visits sex-segregation is not strict. Usually men and women sit together and drink coffee and eat a small snack. Children receive a great deal of attention and are usually given a large portion of refreshment and sometimes pocket money too.

Formal Visiting in the Kampung

Visits to the sick (*tengok orang sakit*) and visits to the dead (*tengok orang mati*) epitomize the principles of formal exchange in the wider community. Kin and co-villagers are strictly enjoined to perform these visits; the sicker a person is, the more important to carry out this duty. Once a person has died co-villagers are strictly enjoined to pay a visit to the bereaved house in which the dead person is laid out. In fact this is the strongest obligation that members of one community have towards one another. It may also be the occasion that marks the end of a long-running dispute, and the only means of achieving this.

Both men and women perform such visits but, in general, husbands and wives do not go together: rather a group of women from the houses of one compound, and possibly some adjoining houses, make the journey together while the men go separately, either in groups or alone. Each household sends a man and a woman (usually the oldest married couple in the house) but they go as male and female representatives of that house. Usually children are not taken, and this clearly distinguishes these occasions from informal ones at which children are always welcome. Both men and women dress formally when visiting the sick or the dead.

As only happens on the most formal occasions, the house is divided into a men's and a women's part. Men and women do not use the same entrance or sit together. After they have entered, visitors take a seat on the floor in the appropriate area, sometimes first taking a look at the condition of the sick person. They do not remain on their feet but sit wherever they can find room. Sometimes there are well over a hundred people inside a small house; conditions are hot, cramped, and uncomfortable, yet it is important to make a prolonged stay. Talk is conducted in low voices; men sit cross-legged (*bersila*) and women sit with legs folded to one side of their bodies (*bertimpoh*). These are the prescribed formal postures for men and women. Everyone sits facing the sick person. Verses from the Qur'ān may be read by male kin or someone religiously learned. Visitors leave unobtrusively, bowing low as they pass in front of those still seated.

Visitors should not display their grief by weeping; their behaviour is quiet and respectful. Many of the male visitors stay inside only briefly; once they have looked at the sick person or corpse they pass outside and congregate with other men below the house. Refreshments are not generally served during these visits although occasionally snacks are offered.

The importance of men's involvement in these rites is indicative of their communal nature. Each house must send its male and female representatives but the fact that they neither make the journey together (unless they travel a long distance), nor sit together, can be seen as a denial of close individual bonds of kinship while emphasizing the asexual ties that unite co-villagers. The proscription on the presence of young children can be seen in the same light. Children in the company of their parents would represent close consanguineal kinship—precisely what is negated in a ritual which minimizes all forms of exchange. Food, conversation, individual expression of emotion are all controlled. Instead, there is a focus on the ingathering of the whole community, especially the religious *kariah*, made up of those who pray together at one mosque, with representatives from as many houses as possible. Many of these same themes are played out at the most elaborate communal ritual, the feast (*kenduri*).

The Kenduri

Kenduri are held to mark a great variety of occasions: after a death; before going on the Haj or a long journey; to celebrate the passing of exams; at the mosque to mark the end of the month of pilgrimage on *Hari Raya Haji*; even to celebrate the victory of the local football team. Feasts vary in scale from those with only about ten guests to those with several hundred. A basic principle of them all is that meat is eaten—a small *kenduri* will usually have chicken, duck, or goat meat; for large ones a water buffalo is killed. The most frequent and the largest *kenduri* are held for marriages at both the house of the groom and that of the bride. It is these that I describe here.[10]

The *kenduri* is effectively organized not by the hosts (who pay for it), but by the community. Some days before the *kenduri*, arrangements for the labour and preparation are made. The most important principle is that those who hold the feast do almost none of the work themselves. Each *kariah* has a number of male and female 'feast leaders' (*ketua kenduri*), who are responsible for different aspects of the work for every marriage *kenduri* held there. The stress on these communal officers distinguishes the *kenduri* in Langkawi from other areas in the region.[11]

The *ketua* are chosen as people who are not proud (*sombong*) or quarrelsome (*sompak*). The use of the communal officers is a sign of the hosts' generosity and that they trust (*cahaya*) the community in general to take on this function. The converse may also be true: food cooked by the

[10] Others are similar in form but generally smaller and the communal aspects are less prominent.

[11] Massard (1983*a*: 241) describes how 'specialists' (*tukang*) are chosen by and from the host family. They are thus different for each *kenduri*. Strange (1981: 121) briefly mentions the existence of similar but less elaborated offices in Terengganu. See also Jay (1969: 297) for rural Java, where a major *slametan* may be organized either by a resident official or through individual exchanges between households.

community may be eaten without fear of poisoning or witchcraft. It is in any case considered unfitting for those holding the event to do the work themselves. People say that at the *kenduri* 'the house is surrendered' (*serah rumah*) to the *ketua* who take over its running for the occasion.

A few days before the *kenduri*, the *ketua* come to discuss the arrangements with the host couple. The number and choice of guests rests with the hosts. In fact the choice of who will be invited depends largely on the scale of the *kenduri*. If the size is to be limited, then neighbours of the immediate locality and close kin from elsewhere will be asked; if it is on a bigger scale the whole *kariah* and relatives from distant villages and even from the mainland are invited.

Villagers emphasize that these decisions are taken together by the husband and wife. Invitations, 'calling people to eat a feast' (*panggil orang makan kenduri*), should be delivered verbally by the host couple. They inform each household to be invited a few days before the occasion (today written invitations are sometimes sent). It is important for both the husband and wife to go because it is the man's responsibility to invite male guests and the woman's to invite female ones. In fact, much of the inviting is done by the hosts' kin, thereby avoiding some embarrassment over the selection of guests.[12]

Invitations are always politely accepted, although I was told that obligations to attend are not as strong as they are at deaths. It is important for attendance at different feasts to be reciprocated (*membalas*). As with the exchange of visits, labour, and of cakes during the fasting month, it is considered ill-mannered not to return what has previously been given. At the *kenduri* it is also important not to go straight home after eating, but to stay and help with the labour. If all takes place in the appropriate way with the help of the *ketua kenduri*, and the work is 'not done individually' (*tak seorang-seorang*), then people say they 'look after the village community' (*jaga masyarakat kampung*).[13]

Serious labour begins one or two days before the *kenduri*. Most of the guests who live within walking distance, and close kin from elsewhere, begin to congregate towards midday in order to help with the preparations. Sex-segregation is marked: women arrive separately from men, usually in groups. They wear formal dress with their heads covered. Men

[12] Fraser (1966: 36), commenting on the same phenomenon, notes that a refusal to attend is an affront to the intermediary rather than the host.

[13] Scott (1985: 177) has described a decline in feast-giving as a concomitant of increasing socio-economic polarization in an area of mainland Kedah. Invitations express divisions rather than solidarity (pp. 238–9).

arrive singly or in the company of others; they busy themselves constructing the special eating area for the men, a 'meeting place' (*balai*), and a raised external extension to the *dapur* (the *pelantar*). Women meanwhile pound spices and make the ground fried coconut used in curries (*kerisek*). All the necessary equipment: cauldrons, pounding vessels, crockery, wood for the *balai*, belongs to a co-operative (*syarikat*) to which the majority of villagers contribute.

Although there may be as many as a hundred people of each sex present, usually only about twenty work at any one time. The atmosphere is relaxed and friendly, there is much joking and recounting of news, and a marked informality to the proceedings. Usually it is older women who take part—those not responsible for looking after small children (although they may bring a grandchild with them). The men are of more mixed ages, although older men predominate.

The slaying of water buffalo and chickens usually takes place on the afternoon of the day prior to the feast. This is men's work; women watch but they stand some distance away. Meanwhile men and young boys look on or participate in catching chickens and tying up the water buffalo, which is then slaughtered by cutting the throat according to the Muslim rites. The meat is cut into large hunks from which it is taken off the bone by men.

The night before the *kenduri*, the hosts and many of the guests who help with the labour get little or no sleep. After the evening meal, many of the same people who constructed the *balai* and made *kerisek* return to the house of the *kenduri* to give their help again. Under the direction of the *ketua*, the men cut the meat into pieces and scald it, in preparation for cooking the following day. Meanwhile, women husk more coconuts and thinly slice ginger, onions, and garlic in large quantities. Women also cut up fruit and vegetables for the curries and arrange large numbers of betel trays. Most of the female work takes place on the *pelantar*, while the men cook on fires made on the ground outside the house. The labour takes many hours; although many women take their turn, only a small proportion of them are actually working at any one time. The atmosphere is again friendly and relaxed, stories are told, there is bantering with the men, and the house is crowded with people, inside and out. Many relatives will stay the night, while those from close by return home around two or three in the morning to get some sleep.

The following morning work begins early: from about nine o'clock onwards, people arrive to help. By this time the cooking should already be under way: under the directions of the *ketua*, huge cauldrons of rice

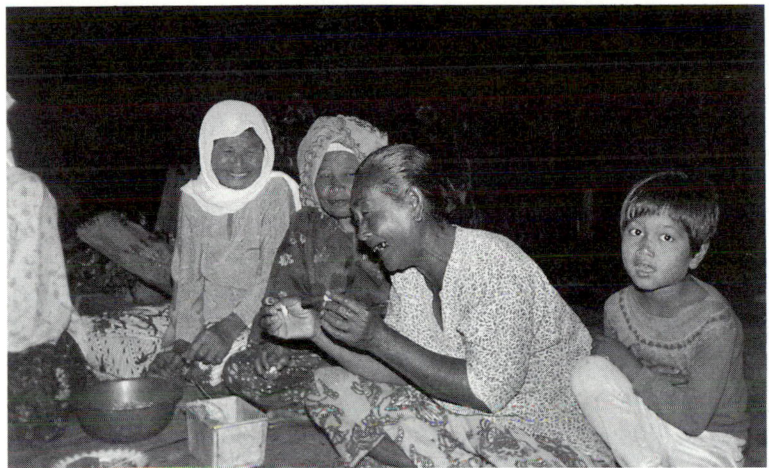

16. Women participating in labour the night before a feast (*kenduri*)

cooked in coconut oil and spices (*nasi minyak*) are prepared, as well as the curries and a pickled fruit relish (*acar*). Cooking is done outside the house, and although women do much of the preparation (particularly the slicing and cutting of the ingredients), *kenduri* cooking is always described as men's work.[14]

As the morning wears on, more and more people arrive; men and women come separately, each dressed in best clothes. Women wear good sarongs and blouses or matching suits composed of a long skirt with a tunic top (*baju kurung*); they have their heads covered with a veil (*kain telekung*). Men wear sarongs or trousers, shirt, and a prayer hat (*songkok*). Most people remain outside the house: women squat on the ground, men stand around the cooking area. Before the feasting begins, it is usual for women to give all the small children (who are often the grandchildren of the adult guests) food so that they eat together. Around the same time, some of the men go inside the house, and sitting cross-legged on the floor (in the *ibu rumah*) they chant verses from the Qur'ān in unison (*meratib*).[15]

[14] In contrast, Rosemary Firth (1966: 152, 156) and Rudie (1994: 180) note that women cook at *kenduri* in Kelantan (see also Strange 1980: 143), as also in Modjokuto (C. Geertz 1960: 12).

[15] The religious aspect of the marriage *kenduri* was not particularly prominent at the time I conducted fieldwork in the early 1980s. See Bowen (1993: 229–50) for a detailed discussion of the *kenduri* in Aceh, where participants view them as 'events of transaction and communication with spiritual entities' (1993: 229).

17. Men cooking for a feast (*kenduri*)

18. Children are served food at a feast (*kenduri*)

Meanwhile, on the *pelantar*, women arrange the dishes which accompany the rice (*lauk*) on trays ready for eating. Inside the house, other women in the *dapur* arrange cooked rice on plates. Those women not working remain sitting, either outside the house or in the *dapur*, chewing betel and talking to each other.

Behaviour inside the house is much more formal than outside. Women sit in the prescribed positions: legs folded to the right side of the body (*bertimpoh*) when eating. They keep their heads covered at all times, and there is none of the joking and banter which characterizes the preparations outside. Men eat before women; once the food has been set out on trays on the *pelantar* by women, men carry them to the *balai* and the *ibu rumah* where the men eat. They are not served by the women. Groups of three eat together from one tray (*hidang*) of the shared dishes which accompany the rice while sitting cross-legged on the floor.

Eating is completed with great rapidity.[16] Men carry their trays back to the *pelantar*, where women clear the plates and begin the washing-up. Many women help in the work of lifting stacks of dishes up and down, putting away unused food, and washing the dishes. Those who are quite old and would never wash dishes in their own homes, distant and wealthy relatives expensively decked out, as well as the more humbly dressed, assist in the general clearing. To avoid doing so would be regarded as 'lazy' (*malas*) and 'proud' (*sombong*). It reveals a wish to keep aloof from the general goings-on which is much disapproved of. The actual eating at a feast takes only a few minutes while the labour takes many hours. Those who go home immediately after they have eaten are antisocial; they are not solicitous of the 'community spirit' (*masyarakat kampung*). No one is excused from participation in these tasks, and it is notable that dish-washing and clearing, which are the lowest-status forms of household labour, are the special focus of co-operative effort.[17]

Once the men's dishes have been cleared, women put food out on trays for the women to eat. There is a great reluctance to be among the first (not everyone can eat at the same time) and a general air of embarrassment. Women eat inside the house in the *ibu rumah* and *dapur*. Women often complain of still being hungry after a *kenduri*, and this is partly a matter of constraint. But it also expresses something else. *Kenduri* food is standardized. It includes rice cooked in oil (*nasi minyak*); one or two different meat curries with or without vegetables; a sweet fruit relish (*acar*); fish; and a sweet fruit dish made with coconut milk. The most striking characteristic of this food is its richness; in contrast to everyday food it has a high meat, fat, and sugar content. Both meat and fat are regarded as 'heating' foods.

[16] C. Geertz (1960: 13) makes a similar observation for Modjokuto, where, in contrast to Pulau Langkawi, most of the food is uneaten and taken home.

[17] See Scott (1985: 196–8) for the relevance of being perceived *sombong* in a stratified community in mainland Kedah. Wikan (1990: 63–73) discusses the importance of not appearing arrogant in Bali.

In contrast, steamed rice and many kinds of fish, the main constituents of everyday food, are thought of as neutral, while many vegetables are 'cooling' (see Laderman 1983: 45–8).

Both men and women hinted that, in spite of the richness of the food, it is not really satisfying. They say the food is 'hot' (*hangat*); they don't get 'full' (*keniang*); and that the food isn't 'tasty' (*sedap*). It is for this reason that they often eat another full rice meal on returning home to get properly full. This of course suggests a resistance to the idea that food cooked by the community is as nourishing and good as that cooked in the house.[18]

The work of washing dishes and clearing continues for some hours and none should leave before participating in a good part of this. Women take leave of each other in the formal Malay manner, individually greeting all the women around them before exiting, usually in the company of those they came with.

The *kenduri* represents a heavy outlay of expenses for the hosts which can vary from a few hundred dollars to about two thousand. Many people get severely into debt at the time their children marry. They do not expect to recoup more than about half of their initial expenditure on the *kenduri*. The lower the expenditure is, the higher the proportion that will be recouped. At one small *kenduri* for which the expenses were very low a profit was made. However, this was an unusual occurrence, and the occasion itself had aroused some disapproval—partly because the *ketua* had not been used, and the desire to save money was obvious. Generally, people expect to lose heavily—especially at the weddings of sons.[19]

Help may be gained with these expenses from gifts and loans from kin. Often a system of contributions in the form of loans from kin, neighbours, and friends, known as 'to plant' (*bertanam*), is used.[20] Under this system contributions, such as about sixteen pounds of rice, or fifty cakes, are requested by the hosts from co-villagers. Those who 'plant' in this way expect to reap at a later date: the loans are repaid in kind when the creditors later hold their own *kenduri*. It follows that people are only

[18] Provencher (1979: 48) has stated that Malay feasts are 'arenas in which symbolic relationships between food and society are acted out most explicitly'. However, he also suggests that Malay preoccupation with food 'represents an oral fixation of libido'.

[19] In contrast, Rosemary Firth (1966: 156) and Fraser (1960: 143) report that on the east coast and in southern Thailand profits are expected from feasts.

[20] It is said that whereas in the past kin would have given, nowadays they *tanam* and that the *bertanam* system was only used by non-kin in the past; it is difficult to verify such assertions. In other contexts I was told that the *bertanam* system was *not* as widely used today in Langkawi as in the past.

willing to involve themselves in this form of exchange when they have a child who is nearing marriageable age and they can expect to recoup their outlay in the not too distant future.

There are other smaller-scale exchanges in more extensive operation at *kenduri*. When guests arrive they make some form of contribution. Women usually take with them a food container with uncooked rice in it. This is emptied out by women in the *dapur* when they arrive, and before they leave it is refilled with portions of cooked meat dishes (*lauk*) with which they return home. These are intended for members of the household who did not come themselves. Those women who do not bring rice, and all men, make a small contribution of money ($1 or $2) which is handed to the host or hostess. Guests who give money receive a hard-boiled egg in return.

There has been an increasing monetization of these exchanges: I was told that men used to take sugar, and women took rice or cakes where today they often both take money.[21] In spite of these changes, the associations which were described in the previous chapter—between women and domestic consumption in the *dapur*, and men and money—are once again in evidence at feasts. Rice is associated with women, the house, and the *dapur*, as are the cakes which women make there. Sugar is a 'raw product' which must be bought commercially in exchange for money. Exchange of raw food for cooked, of credit and debt, labour, news and conversation, are all important aspects of the *kenduri*. The events that I have described here celebrate marriages, perhaps the most symbolically important of all exchanges.[22]

Men and women are separated during the preparations for the *kenduri* and even more strictly at the event itself. They are also associated with different contributions, different ingredients, different spatial zones, and different labour. Women bring uncooked rice; men cook it; it is then arranged by women for both men and women to eat. Men cook the food outside the house, whereas in everyday circumstances women cook inside the house. Women exchange uncooked rice (grown mainly by women) for food cooked by men. Men exchange money (obtained through the exclusively male activity of fishing) for eggs—which are cooked and wrapped by women. These aspects of the exchanges and contributions of men and women emphasize their complementarity.

[21] Exactly the same association between women and rice, and men and cash was observed by Rosemary Firth (1966: 154). By 1963 both men and women gave cash.

[22] See also Massard (1983*a*: 369–71) on how *kenduri* exchanges link a chain of households.

Sex-segregation is clearly one of the distinguishing features of the *kenduri* from the time that invitations are first issued. Both men and women attend but, as at visits at deaths and sickness, they attend separately, each household sending at least one male and one female representative. While unmarried young men frequent the *kenduri*, unmarried young women (*anak dara*) may not. It is not a meeting place for unmarried young men and women. This is one of the many ways in which individual sexual ties (or potential ties) are denied on these occasions. Although children attend (unlike at visits to the dead), they do not remain together with their grandparents or parents but are encouraged to play and eat with their age-mates—as if to form a 'community of children' by themselves. An image of a community of shared children, or grandchildren, is created.

Although women actively participate in the *kenduri*, and the roles of men and women are in many ways complementary, it is clear that men's contribution is more stressed, and this is expressed in the assertion that the cooking is done by men. The community is projected in an image of commensality—that which is normally the province of domestic kinship. However, the normal practices of eating in the house are inverted: *men* cook *outside*, men and women eat separately; even the vessels used are not household ones but communal. Further, the food consumed is different and in some ways superior to everyday food: it contains meat, fat, and sugar, acquired with cash through the labour of men. Women bring uncooked rice, their own subsistence produce, but take back to the house this superior nourishment. There is a denial of the house and the bonds within it in the most explicit way. Men and women contribute as men and women separately and equivalently but not as whole houses or as married couples.

The celebration of the community made up of men, women, and children and the denial of difference, individual houses, and individual marital and parental bonds, can be related to a notion of an endogamous community. Drawing attention to the existence of bounded groups would be divisive. Ideally at least, everyone is related to everyone else and is essentially similar. Male participation and the role of men is particularly stressed because, although the *kenduri* is an occasion at which men and women come together, it is associated with activities in which women normally dominate (cooking, food, kin ties). Although the specific union of two individuals in marriage is underplayed, it is particularly appropriate that the most lavish and elaborate of rituals of community is associated with this rite—for it is at marriage that the notion of communal endogamy is acted out and becomes a reality in everyday life.

House and Community; Private and Public

While women dominate in everyday exchanges between houses, both men and women actively participate at feasts. Behaviour within the compound is, I have argued, almost indistinguishable from that within the individual house; in many contexts it can be said to be based on an idea of mutuality and sharing. And this has its roots in the undivided unity represented by the single house from which compounds arise.

Compounds can be seen on the one hand as miniature communities—like the wider village they are called *kampung*—but also as extended houses. If the compound operates as an extended domestic group, it follows that the model of community is one that is also based on the domestic group and the house. In other words, there is a continuity between the concept of the individual house, the compound, and the wider community. This continuity is expressed both terminologically and physically in the reluctance to draw boundaries around these units.

The same continuity is expressed in the symbolism of food-sharing. The house is the place where close consanguines cook and eat full meals together. During visits and at the coffee-shop snacks are eaten but almost never full meals. At the *kenduri*, where the community takes over from the house, a full meal—or rather, a particularly lavish and 'heating' full meal—is eaten. The community represents itself at the *kenduri* in the idiom of the house, but also as something stronger and more powerful than this unit. Villagers explicitly say that the house 'surrenders' to the community, which then takes over its function of food-sharing. This representation is accomplished by a reversal of the normal rules which operate within the house.[23]

The notion of community is, then, based on the individual house. These houses are constantly engaged in balanced and symmetrical exchanges. And once again the exchange of food plays a symbolically important role in these. Houses in the wider neighbourhood exchange incomplete meals, snacks. The fact that these houses are conceptualized as being essentially alike is encapsulated in the fact that such exchanges tend to be short-term, and that what is exchanged is always similar. Indeed, during Ramadan, houses of a neighbourhood may in one moment exchange the exactly identical gift of cakes.

A marked formalization of behaviour, in both dress and manner, distin-

[23] I would therefore modify Massard's (1983*a*: 98) interpretation that cooking and eating outside represent an extension of private, domestic space. It is also the public which is extended into the domestic.

guishes the *kenduri* from everyday occasions. The fact that this is more pronounced inside the house than outside can be related to the surrendering, *serah*, of the individual house and its occupants to the community as a whole. The function of host and hostess is reduced to the minimal one of greeting most of the guests. In fact, neither the term 'hosts' nor 'guests' is used on these occasions—to do so would force a distinction that is actually being elided: it is the 'guests', in the form of the community as a whole, who take on the responsibilities of the 'hosts'.[24]

The *kenduri* is in fact the most prominent locus of refined, formal (*halus*) behaviour in the village; indeed such behaviour is markedly absent in most other contexts, and particularly absent from the house in everyday contexts (see Chapter 1). At the *kenduri* the emphasis is on control and restraint: body posture, speech, laughter, manner of eating, are all highly circumscribed. People frequently speak of feeling 'embarrassed' (*malu*) at a *kenduri*. In Chapter 1 I discussed how *halus* behaviour has hierarchical implications. In Langkawi, however, what is stressed is conformity and *mutual* respect rather than hierarchy and unilateral respect. Participants behave in the most controlled manner while at the same time displaying their humility and sameness by taking part in labour. Difference is to a great extent erased.

This extreme emphasis on conformity is manifested in many contexts of life in Langkawi. It is, for example, evident in women's attitudes to dress, especially for formal purposes. Colour, style, fabric, choice of garments and accessories are all highly predictable. And, as I myself experienced when I attempted to dress in the proper way in Langkawi, deviations are much disapproved of, and women are quick to express their negative opinions.[25]

At the *kenduri* the stress on controlled behaviour and conformity is more marked than on any other occasion. Clifford Geertz (1960) aptly summed up the effects of such behaviour (which, however, he interpreted in terms of psychological goals) at similar occasions in Modjokuto:

> At a *slametan* everyone is treated the same. The result is that no one feels any different from anyone else, no one feels lower than anyone else, and so no one has a wish to split off from the other person. (1960: 14)

[24] In Java, Jay (1969: 212) notes that every married couple should be invited and that ritual prominence is given to the notion of the house. However, from Geertz's description it seems that women cook (1960: 12) and only male guests attend (see also Jay 1969: 208). This is entirely different from Pulau Langkawi.

[25] Similarly, Kuchiba *et al.* (1979: 258–88) note the stress on similarity and conformity within the Malay community and an association between the feeling of shame, embarrassment, *malu*, and being different. To be different is improper and rough or crude (*kasar*).

The marriage *kenduri* is an absolutely standardized occasion with only very minor variations to distinguish one from another. The aim is not so much to outdo neighbours through originality or lavish display, but to do exactly the same and thereby become indistinguishable from them. It is not the individual occasion that is celebrated, there is no room for individual expression: the *kenduri* is a communal feast—it is this that is being expressed in the notion of the surrender of the house to officers of the community, in the residual role that the hosts play, in its standardization, and in the notion that to come and to participate in labour is a way of fostering the 'community spirit'.

I have argued that one image of community projected at *kenduri* is that of similar houses exchanging with each other. The idea of the community as a collection of similar houses without clear-cut boundaries has been referred to in earlier ethnographies of the region. However, generally this has been seen as a negative attribute, a factor which somehow 'inhibits' social organization, rather than being part of it to be analysed and explained. Thus Clifford Geertz observed of Java:

> There is no organic religious community, strictly speaking, among the *abangans* . . . There is only a set of separate households geared into one another like so many windowless monads. (1960: 128)

In Malaysia, Wilson (1967: 45) linked this household orientation to a 'lack of sociological unity' of villages in which

> social life . . . revolves around the individual and small clusters of individuals, such as households . . . [R]elations within the village are more incidental than structured. (1967: 145)[26]

What I emphasize here is how an understanding of what 'houses' are about, and of their complex associations, is essential to an understanding of 'community'. The two categories constantly refer to each other. However, it makes no more sense to consider houses as external to the community than it does to view individuals as beyond the social. The village community encompasses houses and individuals, but the meaning of these categories is determined in relation to each other, and in indigenous terms. These meanings cannot be assumed in advance.

[26] Jay (1969: 229–30, 238, 240, 261, 281), however, has used similar ethnographic material to argue that a tendency to resist drawing boundaries within or around neighbourhoods, and to construct an image of random dyadic and equal exchanges carried on between households, fits well with an ideological stress on egalitarianism, an image of a community of peers.

In a similar spirit, we need to be careful when constructing oppositions between private and public, female and male, domestic and political, and mapping them onto each other. Wilson described how the functioning of neighbourhoods 'as social aggregates depends almost entirely on the women, for it is they who activate potential relationships' (1967: 122–3). Such clusters of households were 'purely social in import and quite irrelevant to any sort of political alignment' (ibid.: 124). Wilson here drew a distinction between the 'social' and 'political' based, seemingly, purely on formal political activity. Household clusters were 'almost exclusively domestically oriented' (ibid.: 124) and hence by definition non-political. However, I argue that the significance of these relations to harmony in the wider community can be seen as a 'political' as much as a 'social' fact. Wilson's distinction between the 'domestic' and 'political' which 'concerns only men' (ibid.: 141) both minimizes the significance of women's involvement in inter-house relations, and over-simplifies the relationship between male and female domains.

Similarly, the division between men's and women's worlds can be associated once again with that between *halus* and *kasar* behaviour. However, it is important not to over-simplify the gendered associations of these two modes of behaviour. I have shown how the *kenduri* is associated with *halus* behaviour as the house is with *kasar*. But although *halus* behaviour may dominate in the public context and *kasar* in the private, both the house and the community may be associated with behaviour which is either. (For example, *kasar* behaviour in the coffee-shop, or at agricultural work parties; *halus* style with strangers in the house.) In other words, *kasar* can be associated with the house *and* the community in their 'private' aspect; and *halus* with the 'public' aspects of both these units. The association that has been made between *kasar* and women, and *halus* and men (Wilson 1967: 143; Provencher 1971: 140, 184, 206) is, then, less straightforward than first appears.

Divisions between women and men, private and public, *kasar* and *halus*, must be understood as part of an indigenous system of classification and ideology of gender relations, rather than as constituting analytic categories. Following Rosaldo (1974), Reiter (1975), Harris (1981), and Yanagisako (1987), I would emphasize that while it may be possible to separate the 'domestic' and the 'public' or 'political' at the level of indigenous categories, the house must be analysed in terms of *both* its public *and* its private aspects, just as the community should be examined as a 'public' 'political' unit and as one made up of 'private' houses connected through ties of kinship. The concept of community in Langkawi, as denoted by the term *kampung*, precisely involves an interweaving of the private and domestic with the public and political.

Analysing the same theme, Unni Wikan (1990: 41–62) shows how while from a Western point of view the private may be assumed to be associated with relaxed behaviour between intimates in their own kitchens or living rooms, and the public with formal, polite restraint suitable for the street or market, in the Balinese case these associations do not hold. For the Balinese, it is precisely the visits of intimates and close neighbours into the 'private' world of the house that are most fraught with danger and for that reason demand politeness and restraint:

> 'Most dangerous are the neighbors,' say Balinese, 'for they come all the time.' And where do they come? Into one's sitting room and kitchen. Do you then relax, secure in the warmth and safety that inhere in such places? On the contrary, you try to make your face look bright and clear and be as respectful as you can. (Wikan 1990: 56)[27]

The significance of the house in Langkawi lies in the way its different aspects can be adapted to fit either a 'public' or a 'private' image. Women's visiting between houses has both private and domestic as well as political or public implications. There is, then, more than one way of looking at the community. While it can be seen as a formal, political unit, dominated by men who form associations which have little basis in kinship, but are characterized by mobility and flexibility, it can also be seen as a collection of houses, tied to a specific locality and connected to each other through kinship links, primarily through women. In this sense it seems that since the house is female-dominated, so is the notion of community. But by taking over from women their normal role in the house at the most central rite of community, men assert their integral role in this aspect of community.

The image of the community as an expanded house is simultaneously elaborated and denied through an assertion of something more powerful than the individual domestic house. However, this in itself gives rise to further problems: the paradox that superior *kenduri* food leaves those who partake hungry and unsatisfied may be remembered. One might be tempted to suggest that the richness of the food cannot compensate for the insubstantiality of a community in which kinship has been systematically denied.

[27] See also Errington, who writes of Luwu in Sulawesi, 'it would be a mistake to equate "front guest area" and "back family area" to "public" and "private" spaces. Both are social spaces, and in that sense both are "public"' (1989: 71–2).

Similarity through Difference; Difference through Similarity

A notion of the community phrased in a house idiom raises another problem. The wider community contains potential affines—in direct contrast to the house. There is thus an inherent contradiction in relations with the wider community: they are based on a model of domestic kinship—close kin with whom sexual relations would be incestuous—but, potentially at least, relations in the community at large are affinal. Behaviour between affines which shows a greater formality than that between close consanguines, and a closer observance of the rules of reciprocity, reveals this tension very clearly. Nor is it surprising that young unmarried girls are excluded from the *kenduri*. If the community is represented in the idiom of the house, but also as something greater at such feasts, then the possibility of new affinal links, which are links between houses, being formed must be excluded. At the *kenduri* unmarried men and women cannot meet and married couples are separated. The concept of the community can be seen as being rooted in affinity as well as in domestic kinship, but this representation is always ambiguous. The ambiguity has to do with the nature of affinity in Malay culture, which, as will be explored in the following chapters, is itself subsumed under kinship.

Once again the symbolism of food-sharing is relevant here. For it is worth noting that affinal visitors, even from close by, may be pressed to consume a full meal together with household members, and this distinguishes them from other co-villagers. The fact that they may consume either snacks or full meals neatly captures the ambiguous nature of affinity: partly based on a model of exchange relations between equal partners to which incomplete meals are appropriate, and partly subsumed to domestic kinship, the province of the house, the *dapur*, and the full rice meal.

In this chapter I have described a continuum which runs from the house to the compound to the village, and which is paralleled in the way relatedness is conceived as gradually fading from the very close to the distant. These same ideas are reflected in idioms of consumption. The full rice meal eaten in the house by those who are closely related fades into more attenuated forms of commensality. Distantly connected people offer each other incomplete meals in the form of snacks, usually coffee and sweetmeats. Resources which are shared in the house, and to a lesser extent in the compound, are more immediately and directly reciprocated in the wider community.

In one way this suggests a very strong resistance to drawing precise distinctions or to putting up physical boundaries between social categories. But in the last chapter it was also suggested that there was a strong opposition between the house and the wider world beyond it. The world of men—political division, competitive economic activity, the coffee-shop, and male friendships—always threatens the shared consumption, the kinship, that is continuously produced in the house. We can also see how kin and non-kin, rice meals and snacks, sharing and exchange, can be opposed to each other in symbolic and practical terms.

There is, then, considerable ambiguity about the relation between such categories: it is *both* contrastive and continuous. In certain contexts the 'distant relative' is redefined as someone unrelated, or as Malays literally put it, 'just a person' (*orang sahaja*), that is, a stranger. Snacks may be so substantial as to become meal-like. Close affines are more or less coerced into eating both snacks and meals. The immediate exchange of the very same cakes at Ramadan effectively blurs the distinction between exchange and sharing.

It is in this sense that constructing a set of oppositions seems misleading; equally, the continuity of categories is always open to reformulation and challenge. Neither of these images is completely wrong. But always they must be seen in terms of the other. The imposition of boundaries, the assertion of difference, gains its salience precisely from a context in which they can always be denied. Similarly, the resistance to drawing boundaries, the assertion of similarity, only makes sense when seen through the filter of distinctions and differences which are perceived to exist in the world out there.

In the space between the world out there and the inner sanctuary of the house there is always a tension. In one sense the house is infinitely extendable, as the opposition with the world beyond is symbolically erased. But in order to achieve this, the house must continuously absorb and incorporate the difference and division that exists outside it. This process of absorption involves a series of symbolic transformations of those things which are brought inside. Perhaps the most important of these transformations is that involved in marriage. We shall see in the following chapter that marriage precisely encapsulates the tension between the outside and the inside, that which is different and that which is the same.

7

The Incorporation of Difference: Marriage

In the last chapter I argued that houses may be symbolically expanded in order to negate the division that exists in the world outside, and which always threatens to destroy the inner harmony of the house. The compound and the neighbourhood can be viewed as expanded houses. And this is clear in the way visits are conducted and in patterns of commensality. At communal feasts, the whole village seems to be envisaged as an enlarged domestic group. Such feasts are held, above all, to celebrate marriages.

The marriage rituals themselves are long and complex, and feasts are just one aspect of them. In this chapter I describe wedding rituals in some detail, beginning with the matching of a bride and groom. These rituals may be viewed as a long process which is itself 'about' the incorporation, or denial, of difference. The process involves transforming the bride and groom from affines into kin. In other words, it converts them from those who are different into those who are similar.

The marriage rituals have many aspects. One of these is the elaborate exchanges between the bride's side and the groom's. What is emphasized in these exchanges is the equal status of the two sides—that of the bride and groom, their respective parents, and their houses. The image of a community made up of equally exchanging units is one we have met before. It recalls the way visits, snacks, and labour are exchanged in the wider community. However, such exchanges often have a rather tense and competitive edge. And this is certainly the case for the exchanges which are part of the wedding rituals. Here it seems that the achievement of equality, or similarity, can only come about through a rather intense and often precarious competition. The tension involved is signalled by the way the main parties avoid each other throughout these rituals, and by the prominence of intermediaries.

The tension of the marriage rituals can also be related to notions of affinity. Affines are, by definition, different. One way of viewing the rituals is as a process in which this difference is denied, or incorporated into the house. The in-marrying affine becomes incorporated into the house and *dapur* of her or his spouse. We saw in Chapter 3 how a married couple is thought of in an idiom of siblingship. But notions of affinity are more complex than this. There is also a sense in which affines should already be kin prior to marriage. Marriage is thought of as endogamous. But notions of endogamy conflate genealogy, geographic proximity, status, and general similarity. As though not to draw rigid boundaries between people according to any particular criteria, marriage should simply occur between those who are 'close' in a rather unspecific way.

Once again this idea of closeness is not straightforward. Too much closeness between spouses carries connotations of incest and, in the event of marital disputes, may also lead to quarrels between kin. Affinity, then, is always a precarious balance between too much and too little closeness. One recurrent image from the marriage rituals is that of affines as potentially malevolent outsiders—and here the fear of witchcraft is prominent. Another—and more domesticated—image is of affines becoming incorporated into the house and into the *dapur* of their spouse. In the rituals themselves both images figure prominently. Affinal relations always involve a very great tension between their two aspects. On the one hand affines are indistinguishable from kin, on the other they are different. But a successful marriage is one in which the 'domestic' image of affinity has overcome the image of affines as divisive and threatening outsiders. In the long term, married couples should have children, and affines should become kin.

One reason for devoting a whole chapter to wedding rituals is the immense amount of attention which villagers give them. Weddings are the most elaborated and important of life crisis rituals. They occur very frequently, and they represent a very heavy outlay of expenses. Weddings absorb more money than any other event, except perhaps house-building. But major house improvements are often actually encompassed by the preparations for a marriage. Weddings involve the whole village and, especially when the bride and groom come from different villages, often more than that. The feasts which celebrate these events involve hundreds of people, as I described in the last chapter. The processions between the house of the bride and the groom may also involve hundreds of people. The rituals are communal events in another sense too. Just as at the *kenduri* the house 'surrenders' to the community, so the wedding is taken over by intermediaries and by ritual specialists who act for the whole community. The couple and their parents sometimes seem to have rather minor roles in this extravaganza.

In order to make the description of these rituals easier to follow, I list below the various stages which take place over several weeks or months. The order between some of these stages may not be strictly adhered to, and some stages may be amalgamated or omitted. The main participants at the rituals are the *anak dara*, bride, the *anak teruna*, groom, and their respective *tukang bersanding*, 'enthronement specialists', who prepare them for the rituals.

Stages of Wedding Rituals

1. *Minta*—informal 'asking' for the bride by the groom's side.
2. *Tetap belanja*—'settling (or fixing) the expenses'. Meeting held at bride's house to agree the amount of the 'marriage expenses' (*belanja kahwin*) which are given by the groom's side to the bride's.
3. *Tanda jadi*—'creating the sign'. Small amount of money, betel-nut tray, and (sometimes) ring sent to bride's side by the groom's.
4. *Meminang*—'to ask in marriage', 'betroth'. Large part of *belanja* sent to bride's family. This can be done together with (2) and (3); the term *meminang* can also be used synonymously with (3).
5. *Bertunang*—'to betroth'. Exchange of gifts between groom's side and bride's. Can be synonymous with (4).
6. *Akhad nikah*—Muslim marriage ceremony.
7. *Malam berhinai*—'henna night'. Bride and groom have their hands and feet stained with henna separately in their respective houses.
8. *Kenduri*—feast; and *bersanding*—enthronement of bride and groom, at house of bride.
9. *Kenduri*—feast; and *bersanding*—enthronement of bride and groom, at house of groom.
10. *Tunggu dara*—'watch over bride'. The bride spends her first night at the groom's house, accompanied by her female relatives. The couple sleep separately.
11. *Mandi berlimau*—'lime bathing'. Ritual bathing of couple outside groom's house.
12. *Sambut-menyambut*—'exchange visits' between house of bride and house of groom. The couple alternate in prescribed order and duration between the two houses, beginning at house of bride.

The Matching of a Bride and Groom

In Chapter 2 I attributed the absence of post-marital rules of residence and the reluctance to predict where a couple will live to an attempt at avoiding any imputation of superiority to either side. The comment of the woman who noted with approval that her grandparents on both sides were migrants (*bangsat sama bangsat*) is representative of countless comments on the suitability of a match which hinges always on the similarity of the attributes of the bride and groom.

The idea of the compatibility of two partners in marriage is encapsulated in the concept of *raksi*. Wilkinson gives the following definition of *raksi*: 'born under similar stars and likely therefore to live together in perfect harmony' (1959: 938). The astrological compatibility of a young couple is assessed by a *bomoh*, traditional healer, diviner, before the marriage. As Wilkinson notes, the concept of *raksi* hinges on similarity.[1] But this similarity is not restricted to the astrological realm. A well-matched bride and groom are alike in all their attributes. Rather than blending complementary characteristics in order to achieve a balanced whole, the aim is to match those who are suited to each other by virtue of their similarity.

This similarity should be revealed in their physical appearance: a couple are described as *raksi* when they are of similar height, skin colour, and build. Before weddings, people will comment with approval if this is so. The couple should be approximately the same age, of similar personalities, and their backgrounds should be similar in wealth and status. I even heard approval expressed at the fact that the names of a couple, being homophonous, were *raksi*. In the next chapter it will become clear how important it is for the two sets of parents of the couple to be *raksi*. The ideal of compatibility being achieved through resemblance is neatly captured by the Malay saying which describes the ideal match as being 'like an areca nut split in two' (*seperti buah pinang dibelah dua*).[2]

When the parents of a young man begin to look for a wife for him they will, apart from the criteria already discussed, have in mind that she should be pretty, hard-working (*rajin*), a good cook (*pandai masak*), and that she should not 'run around' (*jalan-jalan*), in other words, she has been properly secluded. One woman told me that when her sons married she looked carefully at the reputations of the mothers of her sons' prospec-

[1] Astrological compatibility is also important in Java; see H. Geertz (1961: 60, 142); Jay (1969: 37, 40, 161); C. Geertz (1960: 30–1, 34) on the *petungan* system. As in Langkawi, this system refers to fitting well together. Fraser (1960: 180–1; 1966: 64) also refers to the concept of *raksi* and divination used in choosing marriage partners among Malays in southern Thailand.

[2] Similarity of status and other attributes as a basis for compatibility in marriage is likewise stressed by Strange (1981: 106, 110, 114); Nash (1974: 36); Banks (1983: 152); and by Syed Husin Ali (1975: 95) in other areas of Malaysia; and by H. Geertz (1961: 57) and Jay (1969: 129) in Modjokuto.

tive wives. She wanted to make sure that they didn't 'get mixed up with other people's husbands' (*kacau suami orang lain*), and that they set a good example to their daughters. If a girl had 'good descent' (*keturunan baik*)—referring to the maternal side—this augured well for the daughter. As she put it, 'One can't read people's hearts so the best way to tell about a daughter is by the behaviour of her mother.'

Both men and women prefer to take previously unwed spouses when they marry for the first time. Ideally, a first wedding is between a virgin or young girl (*anak dara*) and a previously unwed man (*anak teruna*). Villagers state that it is impossible to persuade a woman into a polygamous union. Polygamy does occasionally occur for a brief period when a husband tricks a woman into believing that he is unmarried, but it is normally rapidly followed by the divorce of one or other wife because no woman will tolerate such a situation.[3] While there is a greater stress laid on female seclusion and virginity than male, the existence of reciprocal terms, the preference for previously unwed grooms, and the refusal to countenance polygamy, reveal some symmetry in marriage preferences and attitudes to previous sexual experience in men and women.

Who Marries Whom

In Chapter 4 I discussed notions of shared substance. We saw how co-feeding creates the possibility of incest. Those who drink milk from the same mother are thought of as being so much of the same substance that they may not marry. This is most true of siblings. Another common way of describing relations which are incestuous is in terms of whether or not physical contact 'annuls the effect of prayer water'. People wash before prayer in order to purify themselves. Contact with persons of the opposite sex destroys this purifying effect, except in the case of close kin. Parents, full siblings (and half- or step-siblings if they have drunk milk from the same mother), offspring, nieces and nephews, aunts and uncles, grandparents, grandchildren, and spouse's parents do not destroy the effect of these ablutions. Villagers say that it is these latter categories of kin that may not marry: 'If the prayer water is annulled they may marry'.

Marriage between first cousins does occur but it is at the limit of

[3] A similarly negative attitude to polygamy is widely reported among Malays elsewhere. See Fraser (1960: 210); Rosemary Firth (1966: 56, 203); Strange (1981: 141, 142, 146); Kuchiba *et al.* (1979: 36, 170–1); Djamour (1965: 82–7).

closeness which is acceptable. Discussing a forthcoming marriage between first cousins, a group of women referred to it as 'marriage of two siblings' (*kahwin dua beradik*). It was clear that the marriage was viewed with some concern, but also, finally, that it was acceptable when one of them pointed out that the partners were from different localities.

Even when they are of similar ages, if the bride and groom are cousins, but of different generations (*pangkat lain*), this is not particularly approved of, although it occurs quite often. People from different generations are, in some sense, not equivalent, and this makes it difficult to regard them as having the equal status which is the ideal.[4] Similarly, marriage between a woman and her patrilateral male consanguines also carries connotations of inequality and thus creates a slight anxiety. A man in this relation can act as a woman's *wali*, guardian, and give her away in marriage. Marriages between a woman and a patrilateral male cousin 'break the *wali*' (*patah wali*)—the male consanguine cannot act as *wali* after the betrothal.[5]

Marriage between affines occurs rather frequently and is thought of in positive terms. One case of two brothers who had married first cousins and next-door neighbours was often pointed out to me as a particularly good example of such marriage. Marriage between step-siblings (*anak tiri kahwin anak tiri*) can also occur provided they have not drunk milk from the same mother. The term used for such marriages refers primarily to the couple's parents. Co-parents-in-law are reciprocally known as *bisan*, and the relation between them is very important (see Chapter 8). Marriage between step-siblings is known as 'co-parents-in-law of one pillow' (*bisan sa bantal*). While the term *bisan sa bantal* is used to point out the close relationship, its use does not seem to be pejorative. In '*bisan* of one pillow' marriage, it is the repeated affinity which is stressed, not the siblingship of the couple.[6] It is as though attention is drawn to the closeness and similarity in the background of the young couple. If the matching and compat-

[4] Djamour similarly notes a theoretical ban on intergenerational marriages between close kin but states that in fact it is more serious if a man marries a woman in a senior generation (1965: 69–70).

[5] Hildred Geertz (1961: 59) and Jay (1969: 27) report a *prohibition* on this form of marriage. See also Djamour (1965: 14); Wilder (1982: 57).

[6] Wilder (1982: 56–7) refers to the same expression being used when the *bisan* marry *after* their children. In Langkawi this is known as *bisan se bantal balik*. *Balik*, back or return, because it is the parents who are following the children. Banks (1983: 154) states that such marriages have negative connotations. See Waterson (1986: 104) on how at marriage the Torajans cease to emphasize siblingship and redefine the couple as potential affines. Once they have married, consanguineal ties are again stressed.

ibility of one marriage can be successfully repeated, there is a kind of redoubled effect of harmony, suitability, and similarity.[7]

In spite of these positive effects of marrying affines, the concern about marriage between close relatives is often expressed in more general terms which encompass virtually all categories of kin. Villagers invariably say that they like to marry their kin but, if subsequently relatives quarrel, then things become very difficult. One woman, closely involved in a dispute with cousins and neighbours over the broken marriage of her niece, said 'We like to marry relatives, but if they quarrel it's finished, everything goes sour.'

The potential dangers of entering into affinal relations with close kin is very clear at the time of negotiating a match. To refuse an offer of marriage is a highly delicate matter. There is a great chance that those who are refused will feel slighted and people take considerable care to avoid this. When those requesting are kin the risk of giving offence is even higher. People say that it is more difficult to refuse kin than non-kin. Marriage between kin represents an ideal provided it works. It then underlines the harmony that should exist between relatives. However, if the marriage is not a success the opposite is true. Disputes between kin and neighbours then become rife, dividing the village.[8]

Where divorce is always a possibility, the effect of marriages between kin breaking down will be highly disruptive for relations between wider kin (see Chapter 8). In selecting marriage partners, villagers tend to perceive the potential disadvantages of marrying kin as looming larger than the actual advantages. The endless ramifications of marital disputes and divorce bear out their perception.

More than two-thirds of all marriages in 57 households of the village which I included in a household survey in 1981–2 were between unrelated spouses. About one-fifth of marriages were within second-cousin range, and these marriages made up nearly two-thirds of all kin marriages. In general then, villagers' statements voicing concern over marrying kin are borne out in their practice. There is no evidence either from people's statements, or from tracing marital histories, of specific categories of kin being preferred—beyond a general tendency to marry first and second cousins.

In apparent contradiction with these attitudes, however, people often

[7] The significance of multiple affinity is also stressed by Wilder (1982: 63–5).

[8] A similarly ambivalent attitude to marriage between kin has been noted by ethnographers in Java. See H. Geertz (1961: 59–60); Jay (1969: 130). And elsewhere in Malaysia, Kuchiba *et al.* (1979: 159–60); Downs (1967: 139); Strange (1981: 109).

assert that they like to marry 'close relatives' (*adik-beradik dekat*). By this they mean those living close by. Locality is in fact one of the most important criteria for choosing a spouse. That the category *adik-beradik dekat* conflates kinship with neighbourhood is clear from countless conversations with people in Sungai Cantik. For example, one woman, discussing the impending marriage of her son, said that people liked to marry 'close' because then both sets of parents-in-law could easily help look after the grandchildren. 'Those who live close by become kin', she said. 'Those who live far off become strangers.'

We have seen how locality is a fundamental criterion for inclusion in rotating credit societies and labour groups, and for inviting people to a *kenduri*. It is locality that to a large extent determines the recognition of kinship. Marriage within a small locality is highly significant. In more than one-third of all marriages in the household survey I conducted both spouses were from the same hamlet. And more than two-thirds of marriages involved partners from neighbouring hamlets or villages within a radius of two to three miles.[9]

The desire to maintain rights over a couple's residence means that parents do not seek to maximize the wealth or status of their child's spouse's family. When I asked one woman, then looking for a bride for her son, whether she would seek a wealthy bride, she said no, because in that case it would be unlikely that the couple would stay in her home after the marriage. In another case involving a young man who had achieved university education and worked as a civil servant on the mainland, his parents wanted him to take a village bride who lived close by. If he married someone from far off, it was explained, his mother would have to go and stay with them whenever her daughter-in-law gave birth. When there are differences of wealth or status the couple are expected to reside with the wealthier family.

However, while the residence of the couple is a critical factor when arranging a marriage, it is itself a contingent element in a more general ideology governing marital choices: that like marries like. It is this ideology of marriage between those who are similar that gives meaning to the preference for local endogamy. For it is the people who live in the same place, neighbours and co-villagers, who are above all thought of in this way.

[9] The statistical significance of local endogamy has been noted by many others writing on the area; see Syed Husin Ali (1975: 48); Wilder (1982: 60); Kuchiba *et al.* (1979: 2, 159–60); Jay (1969: 131). The Langkawi figures fall broadly within and towards the upper end of this range.

Betrothal

Marriage proceedings are initiated by the groom's side. When a young man wants to marry he asks his mother to look around for a suitable bride or tells her that he has someone in mind. At this stage the proceedings are informal and variable.[10] One young married woman described to me how her mother-in-law had watched through a chink in the house wall as she performed household labour to make sure that she was diligent (*rajin*). A visit to the house may be arranged in order for the young man to get a quick glimpse of his future bride. Although they will not meet properly, she may be sent on an errand and he will have a chance to observe her and give his approval. In general, however, there is no direct contact between the pair, either at this stage or later in the marital negotiations, until the actual ceremony itself.

Once a young woman has been selected, the attitude of her parents to the match, particularly her mother, will be sounded out informally. Sometimes the young man's mother will go directly to see the prospective bride's mother. One woman described how her son-in-law's mother had come to her house and looked at her daughter. She had phrased her proposal as a joke: 'come let us two become *bisan* (co-parents-in-law)' (*mari kita bisan kedua*). In the next chapter the significance of this formulation, which indicates the importance attached to the relation between *bisan*, will become clearer. When the two mothers know each other less well, the young man's mother will send an intermediary to sound out the opinion of the mother of the prospective bride. At this stage it is women who have the prime responsibility in initiating proceedings.

Villagers assert that young men and women should follow their parents' wishes over the choice of spouse. However, they also claim that nowadays parents' wishes are less strictly adhered to than in the past: the man may make a choice himself and ask his parents to set the negotiations in motion; the woman may register her unwillingness to enter into a match and parents are unlikely to enforce their will on her. An *anak dara* should not refuse her parents' choice. However, even when her opinion is disregarded, we shall see that a young woman does have a chance to assert her wishes after the marriage ceremonies have taken place.

[10] In contrast, see Kuchiba *et al.* (1979: 30), where a young man's *father* is reported as selecting the bride, and Fraser (1960: 205), who describes marriage as being initiated by the groom's father. But Strange (1981: 46, 104) notes the important role of mothers in selecting a child's spouse. Swift, similarly, reports that women of the groom's side initiate marriage proceedings (1965: 114).

If the parents of a young girl are reluctant to accept the proposal they will try to phrase a refusal as delicately as possible at this stage. They may say their daughter is still too young, or that she doesn't want to marry yet. The refusal will attempt to minimize any insult the groom's side may feel. The fact that such refusals are usually conveyed through intermediaries lessens their direct impact.[11]

Once the young woman has been 'asked' (*minta*) in marriage and her parents' approval of the match has been obtained, the formal proceedings are got under way.[12] There are various stages to these and sometimes some of them occur simultaneously or are omitted altogether. One basic principle is, however, always adhered to: from the time of the *minta* onwards, the betrothed couple and their parents avoid direct contact almost totally and the negotiations and exchanges are conducted through intermediaries.

Sometimes the bride's family calls together their relatives, the imam, and the elders of the village to see if everyone 'agrees' (*setuju*) to the match, and an answer is then sent to the groom's family via a cousin or other relative of the bride. In other cases, after the *minta* the next stage is the formal negotiation of the bride price (*belanja kahwin*, literally 'wedding expenses'). This negotiation is known as 'settling the expenses' (*tetap belanja*), or sometimes 'the accounting' (*berkira*).

'Settling the expenses' always takes place in the house of the bride. It always involves relatives 'on the side of the groom' (*belah anak teruna*) and 'on the side of the bride' (*belah anak dara*), elders of the village, and the imam. Although both men and women attend this occasion, it is men who do the actual bargaining, but this occurs within rather narrow limits. Although the parents of the couple to be betrothed may be present at the accounting, they never participate directly in the bargaining.

At the time of settling the expenses, the other donations of the groom's family apart from the cash for the wedding expenses are also agreed. These generally include a suit of clothes and a ring, which are not given until later. On the same occasion a small amount of money, a betel-nut tray (*bekas pinang*), and sometimes the ring are presented to the bride's side by that of the groom. This is known as 'making the sign' (*tanda jadi*). This is the first prestation made in the marital negotiations; it is a sign of the agreement between the two families, and once it has been given, the

[11] Djamour (1965: 74) discusses the delicacy with which a refusal must be phrased in order to avoid insult to the groom's family and their revenge in the form of witchcraft.

[12] The following rituals of betrothal are described in some detail but with different emphasis by Djamour (1965: 73–5).

couple are considered betrothed. If the engagement is now broken off by the bride's side the sum is returned, if by the groom's the money is forfeited.

The next stage is for the groom's family to send a substantial part of the expenses (usually half) to the bride's family. This is the 'betrothal', or 'asking in marriage' (*meminang*, to ask in marriage, from *pinang*, the betel-nut formally presented on this occasion). This prestation should be accompanied by others: a ring, a suit of clothes, make-up, shoes, and a betel tray. However, in Langkawi usually only the 'expenses' (*duit belanja*) and the ring are sent. People frequently point out that poor people can't manage all the expenses of this part of the ritual, contrasting their customs with those of wealthier urban people. Drawing attention to the fact that people in Langkawi marry within a small locality, they also say that the betrothal is only done properly when a couple live far apart.

Villagers' descriptions of these exchanges vary considerably, both in terms of the items actually sent and the timing of the events. Some accounts place the 'asking in marriage' together with the 'settling of the expenses' and 'making the sign', while in others it takes place afterwards or may be omitted altogether. In the latter case usually only the money and the betel tray are sent but not the accompanying gifts. In all cases, however, some part of the expenses is given in advance and is used by the bride's family to defray the costs of the marriage. In yet other accounts the actual terms *tanda jadi* and *meminang* are used synonymously to refer to the event which legitimizes the betrothal of the couple. This is then followed by a visit to the bride's house by the groom's intermediaries to 'fix the day of the wedding feast' (*tetap hari kenduri*). This date is always decided by the bride's mother.

Once the day of the *kenduri* has been fixed, the bride's side send a collection of cooked food—cakes, cooked rice, chicken curry—to the groom's house. The groom's family send back various bought gifts, including a suit of clothes or material, shoes, make-up, and uncooked food—flour and sugar—in return. This series of exchanges is not always carried out; it is referred to as 'to betroth' (*bertunang*). Once again intermediaries, not the couple or their parents, actually take the gifts. The terms *bertunang* and *meminang* can thus be used more or less interchangeably to refer to the exchange of gifts that takes place after the expenses have been settled and, more broadly, to mean betrothal.

All the events so far described occur within a fairly short period of time, usually no more than a few months or weeks. Certain themes stand out in people's accounts of betrothals. First, there is the avoidance behaviour of the couple and of their parents. Villagers say they would be 'embarrassed', 'ashamed' (*malu*) to interact directly with their prospective co-parents-in-law and that therefore they 'get their relatives to go' (*bagi adik-beradik p'i*).[13] It is during the negotiations that imputations of superiority or inferiority on one side or the other are most difficult to avoid. By using intermediaries, however, their impact may be mitigated and the ideal of equality in marriage preserved. Secondly, by calling on the village elders and the imam to give their agreement to a match, and to witness the agreement of the expenses, marriage is taken out of an individual context and becomes a matter for the whole community.

The same process of 'deindividualization' occurs in the way people talk about the exchanges which are part of betrothal: these are always expressed as taking place between two *sides*, that of the man (*belah jantang*) and that of the woman (*belah perempuan*). This rather structural perspective suggests that marriage is viewed very much as an exchange, and that the units exchanging are not named individuals nor even bounded houses but all the relatives of each spouse. If in the end these 'sides' are likely to overlap, and on another level they may be said to dissolve, this is a paradox which will be explored further in the following chapters.

The fact that all the initiative during the early stages of marital negotiation lies on the side of the groom's family would seem to contradict the assertion of equality between those who intermarry. Further, the flow of prestations is rather heavily weighted in one direction: it is the bride's family which receives not only a substantial payment, but also gifts and visits from the groom and/or his relatives. And it seems that villagers find the idea of the betrothed woman or her parents visiting the house of her future husband even more disturbing than visits in the opposite direction. However, in the subsequent stages of the marriage ritual the idea of balance between the partners and their families is very clearly present.

Marriage payments during my fieldwork in the early 1980s were in the region of 1,200–1,400 Malaysian ringgit. As is clear from the term 'wedding expenses', this money is intended to meet the expenses of the wedding on the bride's side. It is immediately, and almost literally, consumed. The main items of expense are clothes, gold jewellery, bedding, and the wedding feast.

The 'expenses' (*belanja*) are sent from the groom's to the bride's par-

[13] Avoidance between the two sets of parents and the use of intermediaries during the marriage negotiations are widely reported (although little commented on) in the area. See Swift (1965: 117); Fraser (1966: 29); Djamour (1965: 73–4); Syed Husin Ali (1975: 103–4); Jay (1969: 137).

ents, and are regarded as belonging to them and not to the bride herself. The bride receives no cash and it is her parents who decide how the money will be spent. However, the gold jewellery bought does become her property and may subsequently provide a basis of economic security. The *belanja* is usually met out of the combined savings of the groom and his parents. Generally, the former makes a substantial contribution out of his earnings as a migrant worker. Villagers expect to spend a substantial sum of money on the wedding of a son, and a much smaller one on that of a daughter,[14] calculating in both cases that they will recoup about half of the expenses of the feast from the contributions of the guests. However, in recent marriages of men from the village who had become urban wage-earners and had married women who were similarly employed it was regarded as quite normal for the *belanja* to be split and for the bride herself to put up half the amount.

On the day of the wedding ceremony itself the whole sum is still sent to the bride's parents as if it were actually being given in full on that day. People say that it is given in this way 'just to let people see it' (*untuk bagi orang tengok sahaja*).

While the *belanja* is not strictly regarded as the wife's property, there is one part of it which does belong to her. This is the *mahr*, the sum settled on the bride according to Muslim law, which is usually called *mas kahwin*, 'marriage gold', or 'contents of the marriage', *isi kahwin*, in Langkawi. This sum is calculated as part of the *belanja* but belongs exclusively to the bride. In some states of Malaysia the amount of the *mahr* is fixed by the state religious authorities but this is not the case in Kedah. This means that the proportion of the *belanja* that is made up of the *mahr* is a matter of negotiation. If the bride's side break off the engagement the sum of the *tanda jadi* must be returned. In fact, villagers say that twice this sum ought to be forfeited but that this is never done because they cannot afford to. Similarly, after the marriage ritual, if the wife seeks a divorce before the marriage has been consummated, they maintain that twice the amount of the *belanja* ought in theory to be returned to the groom's side, but this does not happen. The part of the *belanja* that is the *mahr* is never returned and remains the property of the bride.

The *mahr* is thus significant in two ways: first, it belongs to the bride herself and is non-returnable. Villagers assert that while in some states it is fixed at 12 Malaysian ringgit, the fact that in Kedah it is negotiable

[14] A son's wedding may cost as much as 6,000 Malaysian ringgit, including the feast, the 'expenses', and improvements to a house. A daughter's might come to about one-quarter of this.

means that astute parents may nowadays try to force up the amount of a daughter's *mahr* relative to the total *belanja*. The second important point about the *mahr* is that it may in fact not be paid at the time of the marriage ceremony but simply registered as 'owing' (*hutang*). If this is the case then it should be paid at the time of a divorce although sometimes a woman seeking a divorce from a reluctant husband may 'remit', or renounce her claim to the debt (*halalkan hutang*).[15]

One effect of local 'variations' to the ritual is that the exchanges between bride and groom become less unequal. The groom does not send all the gifts which normally accompany the *belanja* to the bride, only the *belanja* itself. And the purpose of this, it is always stressed, is simply to cover the wedding expenses, in other words it is consumed directly. Further, when a boy from the village marries an urban girl who is economically independent it is fully expected that the pair should share the marital expenses between them. It was also noted that both partners lose exactly the same amount if they break off the engagement. In the following section we will see how the idea of a 'balanced exchange' is expressed in the marriage ritual itself.

The Marriage Rituals

There is no fixed rule for how quickly betrothal is followed by the Muslim marriage ceremony, the *akhad nikah*. Usually it is a matter of some weeks or a few months. During this interval the couple should not see each other and are kept strictly separated.

The *nikah* takes place in the house of the bride, if possible on a Thursday evening, *malam Jumaat*.[16] During the afternoon, relatives and neighbours gather at the house of the groom where coffee and cakes or a sweet gruel may be served. The groom is sent off to the house of the bride accompanied by large numbers of relatives and friends. This is the 'sending to the wedding' (*hantar nikah*). Today it usually takes the form of a motor-cycle cavalcade; groups of men and women travel separately. The groom is not accompanied by his parents.

Together with the groom are sent the 'marriage prestations' (*hantaran*

[15] See Wilkinson (1959: 389), who translates *halalkan hutang* as to remit a debt. This practice is also followed by Malays in Singapore, see Djamour (1965: 132–3).

[16] The most complete accounts of the rituals of marriage in recent times are those of Djamour (1965: 75–8); Swift (1965: 112–20); Strange (1981: 117–27); and Rudie (1994: 181–6). For fuller but less recent accounts of more elaborate versions of the rituals see Skeat (1900: 364–96) and Winstedt (1982: 115–23).

nikah). These consist of various decorated dishes of fruit and sometimes cakes, a betel tray containing betel-nut, gambier, lime, tobacco, leaves of the betel-vine, cloves, and 20 Malaysian ringgit (exactly half the registration fee for the marriage paid to the imam, the other half being paid by the bride's side), the ring, and—the centrepiece, which is always highly decorated—the money of the *belanja kahwin*. These are borne to the house of the bride by female relatives of the groom.

The groom wears traditional Malay costume, consisting of an embroidered cloth worn over prayer clothes (*kain songket*) and Muslim prayer hat (*songkok*). At the bride's house men and women, relatives of both the bride and groom, sit separately in the formal area of the house (*ibu rumah*). The prestations are placed on the floor near the imam, who makes a note of the amount of the *belanja* and the *isi kahwin* and the value of the ring. At this time the bride is kept in seclusion, usually in a small screened-off room in another part of the house. She too has been dressed in traditional clothing which may match in colour and cloth that of the groom.

In the absence of the bride herself, but before her father or legal guardian (*wali*) and three witnesses (*saksi*) who are 'officers of the mosque' (*pegawai masjid*) and the assembled relatives of the bride and groom, the imam reads the Muslim marriage service and the groom makes his marriage vows. The groom and the bride's guardian state that they are agreed to the match and they, the imam, and the witnesses all sign the marriage contract. After this, the groom is taken to meet the bride. Until recently, I was told, this first meeting occurred not after the *nikah*, but at the 'enthronement' (*bersanding*, see below). The change seems to be part of a more general shift of focus towards the more Islamic part of the ritual. If the ring has not been sent at the time of the betrothal, the groom places it on the bride's finger.

This meeting is generally very tense and both partners show extreme embarrassment. The bride wears a veil and frequently the groom wears dark glasses so that in both cases their faces are partly covered. The bride's isolation from any close female relative, particularly from her mother, is striking. She is likely to be overcome with embarrassment and nervousness. More than once I saw a bride burst into tears at this time, and this is considered quite normal. Nor are young girls given any comfort or support by their female kin. Women say that the bride's mother would be 'embarrassed' to look after her, and that she has guests to see to.

After the *nikah*, coffee and cakes or sweet gruel are served before the visitors on the groom's side, including the groom himself, return home. Prestations (*hantaran*) from the bride's family are sent with the groom and his relatives which are once again borne away by women. These usually consist of a number of decorated trays of cakes or biscuits and fruit. It is considered proper for the number of trays to slightly exceed the number sent by the groom's family. On this occasion, as on others during these rituals, the gifts sent by the groom's side consist of money or things bought with money, and of 'raw produce' (*benda mentah*), while those sent by the bride are mainly 'cooked things' (*benda masak*), and not bought goods.[17] Villagers say that in the past they didn't send *hantaran*, because they were too poor. The *nikah* is usually followed either immediately or the next day by the feast and *bersanding*, the ritual enthronement of the bride and groom in front of the wedding guests which takes place first at the bride's house.

Until recently, on the night before the feast, called 'the night of the small watch' (*malam jaga kecil*), while the cooking preparations for the feast were being made by neighbours and kin, the bride and groom would have henna applied to their hands and feet in their respective houses. For this reason the night is also referred to as the 'henna night' (*malam berhinai*).[18] Today it is rare for the groom to be hennaed; I was told that it is a Hindu, not a Muslim, custom. They would then be enthroned (*bersanding*) separately in the two houses. I never saw this done; the preparations of the bride and groom which I witnessed were carried out on the day of the feast held at the bride's house.

Two ritual specialists (*tukang bersanding*) take responsibility for the bride and groom throughout the marriage rituals. There is one male *tukang* and one female in the community; they take responsibility for the groom and bride respectively at all marriages in the locality.[19] These two specialists who ritually prepare the bride and groom for marriage are a further example of the use of intermediaries in marriage. Just as the

[17] Jayawardena (1977: 27) observes that in Aceh the groom's side send goods obtained in the market, and the bride's cooked food prepared by women in the kitchen.

[18] Djamour (1965: 75–6) refers to *two* nights of henna staining, both occasions occurring in the bride's house. See also Skeat (1900: 375–7); Winstedt (1982: 118); Wilkinson (1957: 56).

[19] Skeat in this context refers to 'staid duennas, who are called *Tukang Andam* (i.e. "coiffeurs"), and a personal attendant or nurse, called *Ma'inang* (*Mak Inang*), who appears to act as a sort of Mistress of the Ceremonies' (1900: 375). But Skeat makes no reference to an equivalent role being played for the groom. Winstedt (1982: 117) refers to a 'magician . . . to protect the groom, and a matron to protect the bride'. Clifford Geertz (1960: 57) mentions the bride and groom being dressed by their respective *tukang paras* in Modjokuto. Strange (1981: 118) refers to a female *tukang bersanding* who, among other duties, counts the bridewealth and supervises the *bersanding* (pp. 123–4). Massard (1983*a*: 243, 271) refers to the *mak andam* of the bride. The term *Mak* (or *Pak*) *Andam* is also known in Langkawi.

kenduri is taken over by officers of the community, the role of *tukang* further emphasizes that marriages are a communal concern. It is significant that villagers frequently say that they prefer the two *tukang* to come from close by one another, otherwise they are likely to compete with each other to see who is 'more skilled' (*lebih pandai*). These skills refer to witchcraft and supernatural dangers faced by the bride and groom.

The threat which outsiders represent is thus made explicit and it is perceived in terms of divisive competition between those involved. Outsiders in this context are those from another locality rather than non-kin. The potential threat may in fact come from supernatural beings, outsiders, co-villagers, and even from the *tukang* or the bride and groom themselves. It is partly by restricting the main actors involved in marriage to an immediate locality that such dangers are minimized.

Each side chooses its own *tukang* in an attempt to insure themselves against any potential danger to the bride or groom, but it is the responsibility of the groom's side to pay for the services of their own *tukang* as well as that of the bride. The ritual preparation is essentially the same for the bride and the groom. They are each prepared in their own house in the relative seclusion of a screened room (*bilek*) with only the *tukang* present.[20]

The primary stated purpose of the ritual is to make the two partners look 'beautiful' (*cantik*, *elok*) and this is always emphasized by those involved. The preparation involves shaving all facial hair, uttering various spells, and bathing the bride and groom in specially treated water before they are dressed in their wedding clothes. For the groom, these clothes include an outer sarong (*sampin*) worn over trousers and made of embroidered cloth, a prayer hat (*songkok*), dark glasses, and a Malay dagger (*keris*). The bride should be dressed in an outfit which matches that of the *anak teruna*. Her hair is put up and dressed in elaborate style, she is heavily made up, and is adorned with as much gold jewellery as possible. The bride's mother avoids the room where she is being prepared and takes no part in the proceedings.

The ritual preparation is not, however, simply a matter of beautification. As one *tukang* told me after I had watched him prepare a young man for marriage, its purpose is to keep away evil spirits and the devil. This is done by ritually securing the entrances of the body so that spirits and sickness cannot enter. He said there were many devils (*iblis*) and evil

[20] For a fuller account see Carsten 1987*a*: 361–81. Skeat (1900: 352–5) has an account of 'the rite of tonsure (*berchukor*)' which he describes as taking place before marriage only when this has been postponed from childhood. See also Massard (1983*a*: 243, 271); Winstedt (1982: 117).

spirits (*jembalang*) and that the ritual sets up a barrier at the entrances to the body (for example, the big toes and thumbs) so that these cannot enter. He went on to explain that this was a time of special danger to the groom when different ritual healers, magicians (*bomoh*), try their strength against each other. The danger also emanates from other people: those who are jealous of the bridegroom, those who have been refused by the bride's side before he was accepted, and others 'who have familiars' (*orang hak bela iblis*) may attack him.

These dangers are manifested through various different agents. First, spirits, and here the *tukang* mentioned *jembalang*, *jin*, and *iblis*. Wilkinson (1959: 417) translates *iblis* as 'satan' but also as 'any demon'. *Jin*, according to Wilkinson (ibid.: 471–2), is a 'polite equivalent for *hantu* (evil spirit)'. Wilkinson translates *jembalang* as 'the spirits to whom offerings are made when the soil is disturbed for planting or to provide foundations of a house; and ill-luck about a house or building is put down to them . . .' (ibid.: 458). The *jembalang*, then, are associated with the earth, particularly in its uncultivated form, and with fertility. I was told there are many different kinds of *jembalang*: those which live in the ground threaten cultivation; those which live in the house threaten the house; those which live in the body may cause sickness. *Jembalang* in the body have a direct effect on fertility. In the past couples who had a number of children who died in childbirth were put through a special ceremony to get rid of *jembalang*.

In the ritual preparations for marriage the association of *jembalang* with the feet and the area below the body is clear. As the body is cleansed they are passed *downwards* and must be prevented from rising up again. Finally, the bodily hair is buried in the earth from where the *jembalang* come. The *jembalang* may be regarded as potentially threatening to the fertility of the soil, the house, and its occupants. As marriage constitutes new fertility, the couple and the house they will live in after the rituals may be particularly vulnerable to attack from *jembalang*.[21]

It is through the extremities of the body, particularly the toes and thumbs, that these spirits may enter. The ritual focuses on these extremities and on the outside of the body in general. It is the outside of the body that is shaved and cleansed with protective water. The internal is safeguarded and this is explicitly expressed in one of the spells incanted in my

[21] See also Laderman (1983: 125), who refers to 'the spirits of the earth' who, being 'attracted by the sweet blood of parturition dripping through the floorboards to the ground below', may attack women in childbirth. Wilkinson (1957: 61) mentions propitiation of the 'earth spirits' when foundations of a new house are laid.

presence where reference was made to the closed 'heart' (*hati*).[22] It is the *hati*, liver or heart, that is regarded as the seat of emotions, the essence of the internal.[23] Thus a kind of barrier is erected during the ritual between the outside of the body and the internal. It may be significant here that it is to the hands and feet that henna is applied before marriage.[24]

The dangers to the bride and groom are also manifested through human agents. These may include involuntary attacks from spirit familiars associated with a particular human individual. They may also be threatened by magic from *bomoh* or *tukang* competing with each other, and this can be best guarded against by choosing two *tukang* from within one vicinity. There is a threat from those who bear grudges, are 'sick at heart' (*sakit hati*), as one *tukang* phrased it. Here jealousy, especially on the part of rejected suitors of the bride, is particularly potent.[25]

It is thus fellow villagers, as well as malevolent spirits and external agents, who pose a threat to the bride and groom. And this accords well with the ambivalent attitude to co-villagers: kin and affines; those with whom marriage is incestuous, but also with whom it is prescribed; those with whom harmonious relations are enjoined, but also with whom disputes occur.

The Bersanding

The *kenduri* at the bride's house is held on the same day as, or the day before, the *kenduri* at the groom's house. The parents of the bride do not

[22] The spell was: '*Sireh*' (the leaf of the betel-vine), 'enfold suspicion, enfold suspicion, danger. Stay away evil eye. Be near closed heart, love me.' (*Hai sireh sangka lipat, lipat sangka mara. Beri jauh marah mata. Sampai dekat tertutup hati, kasih sayang kepada aku.*) The *tukang* told me that the spell was for 'safety against danger' (*selamatkan bahaya*); to keep away the 'devil' (*iblis*).

[23] See Wazir Jahan Karim (1990) for a detailed examination of emotionality during the betrothal period. She discusses the role of the *hati* as the source of emotions and passion (1990: 26–8).

[24] I am grateful to Maria Phylactou for this suggestion, which is given further weight by Endicott, who argues that the form of the henna-staining ceremony 'suggests that at one time spirits were believed to attend this ceremony, though the purpose of the visit is not clear . . . Possibly the marginal state of the people involved exposes them to spirit contact, and the magic is merely intended to protect them in this inevitable association. On the other hand, it may be that spirit helpers are called in to protect the couple from other spirits which have gained access to them because of their position between clear social categories' (1970: 171).

[25] See Wazir Jahan Karim (1990: 40–7) for a discussion of vulnerability to witchcraft in the courtship period. Djamour (1965: 74) also mentions the danger of witchcraft from previously rejected suitors. See also Wilkinson (1957: 52) on the danger of feuds after broken engagements.

attend the *kenduri* held at the groom's house, and the groom's parents do not attend that at the bride's. The guests are chosen on grounds of kinship and locality (see Chapter 6), and often number several hundred. The enthronement of the couple (*bersanding*) occurs at the same time as the *kenduri*. It is always done first at the house of the bride, and then at that of the groom.

When the bride and groom are ready, the groom is taken by his relatives and his *tukang* to the bride's house accompanied by some of the bride's relatives. This may occur at the same time as the Muslim marriage ceremony (*nikah*) but is usually one or two days later. In the past the groom was carried on a decorated litter (*berusung*) made by the groom's side in the shape of a boat, but this is no longer done.

Other observers have described the groom's side as forcing an entry into the bride's house before the *nikah* or the *bersanding* and a mock fight taking place with women on the bride's side obstructing their way and the payment of a ritual fine by the groom's party.[26] I was told that such a fine was levied in the past in Langkawi: the groom's people could only gain entry to the bride's house by 'redeeming the bridal seat' (*tebus pelamin*) on which she sat. The groom's side had to enter the house on the opposite side from this seat. But I was told there was no mock fight to gain entry because the '*tukang* is there to take them in'. This emphasizes the protective and mediatory role of the *tukang*. The people of the bride's house 'surrender to the *tukang*' (*serah ke tok tukang*). The groom and his party enter the house through the formal entry of the house (the *ibu rumah*).

The high point of the marriage rituals now occurs: the enthronement (*bersanding*) of the bride and groom on decorated seats in front of the wedding guests who are attending the *kenduri*, the idea being that the couple are like king and queen. This is done first inside the house in front of the women and children, and then outside in front of the male guests.

The bride and groom are exceedingly nervous and uncomfortable. The latter frequently wears dark glasses in order to hide his face; the former is veiled; both should appear *malu*. If the bride smiles it is said that she is under the influence of the groom's *tukang*; she is aggressive and encouraging. The *bersanding*, then, is something of an ordeal for the principal participants. This aspect is heightened by the fact that, far from being an occasion of deep seriousness for the spectators, considerable sport is made of the event. Repeated attempts are made to get the bride and groom to smile or laugh, to persuade the groom to touch the bride for the benefit of

[26] See Skeat (1900: 381–2); Winstedt (1982: 118–19); Strange (1981: 123); Swift (1965: 116–17). Wilkinson (1957: 57) describes ritual humiliation of the groom's party.

19. Bride and groom sit in state (*bersanding*)

the photographer (the taking of photographs is central to the *bersanding*). They are made to sit and stand together in countless different poses, always exactly matching each other. On one occasion I saw a bride break down under the strain. The spectators meanwhile laugh, talk, and joke freely, as if to test whether the bride and groom are under any malevolent influences.[27]

Once again the bride and groom receive no comfort or support from their close relatives. The groom's parents do not attend the *kenduri* or *bersanding* at the bride's house. The bride's parents keep well away from the *bersanding* in their own house.[28] The couple have their respective *tukang* in attendance and these appear in many of the wedding photographs in poses reminiscent of parents in photos taken at Western weddings.

There is a sense, then, in which the *bersanding* seems almost an anticlimax. The ritual for which such elaborate preparations are made lasts for only a few minutes, and is performed primarily inside the house to an audience of women and children who often ignore or giggle at it. Often the couple do not *bersanding* outside the house for the men at all. The degree to which women take over and dominate the house on these occasions is

[27] Strange (1981: 123) describes how the groom's friends shout ribald comments at the *bersanding* and Swift (1965: 116) comments on the casualness of this ceremony.

[28] The parents' avoidance of the ceremonies held in each other's house is also noted by Strange (1981: 121); Swift (1965: 117); and by Jay (1969: 134, 137) for rural Modjokuto.

20. Bride and groom *bersanding* outside with their respective *tok tukang*

striking. This central part of the marriage ritual focuses on the house and women.[29]

In the past there were various forms of entertainment during the *bersanding* at the bride's house, including *silat* (Malay martial art) performed by male relatives of the groom, and music.[30] Having paid to enter the house of the bride, the groom's side entertained that of the bride. Traditionally, at this point the bride and groom and their *tukang* were then served coffee and cakes. Nowadays the bride and groom may eat a rice meal together in a *bilek* under the supervision of the *tukang*.[31] After this both the bride and groom take leave of the bride's relatives. It is particularly important that the groom should leave the bride's house from the *dapur*. In this way his incorporation into the bride's house is emphasized.

[29] The mutual feeding of rice by the bride and groom at the *bersanding* reported by Djamour (1965: 76); Skeat (1900: 383); Fraser (1960: 207); Wilkinson (1957: 58) does not take place in Langkawi. However, its symbolism accords well with the analysis presented here: the couple represent a potential domestic unit defined by its co-eating. Their kinship is created by this shared consumption.

[30] A brief description of such entertainment which features ludicrous dancing and singing on the part of women is given in Djamour (1965: 76). Strange (1981: 120–1) describes something similar taking place after the *nikah* in which there is a display of aggressive sexuality on the part of young men, and women behave in a sexually provocative manner.

[31] In the past they would only eat such a meal in the house of the bride after the *kenduri* and *bersanding* in the groom's house.

The groom and his relatives then return to his house. There is then a *kenduri* and *bersanding* at the house of the groom. This may be held on the same day or the following one. If the two occasions are temporally separated, the groom and his male and female relatives go in procession to the house of the bride to take her back with them to the groom's house. The groom greets the father and mother of the bride and her male and female relatives. The groom's party are served coffee and biscuits while the bride and groom sit near one another with their *tukang* in attendance. After the refreshments have been consumed, the bride and groom take formal leave of the bride's parents and the other relatives in the house and are taken back to the house of the groom by the latter's relatives. The bride is accompanied by her *tukang* and three or four older female relatives but not by her mother.

In former times they would have both been carried on a litter; today they are likely to travel by motor cycle or even car. On arrival at the groom's house *beras* (raw husked rice) and *padi* (raw unhusked rice) are thrown over the bride. I was told that the throwing of rice at this time over 'outsiders' (*orang luar*) is to 'banish evil spirits' (*buang hantu*). The bride then formally greets her mother-in-law. In the past, the bride would have her feet washed by her mother-in-law in a tray of water, in which a stone with money under it has been placed, before entering the house. In Chapter 3 I described how villagers link this ceremony to the way newborn babies are attached to their natal house.

The reception of the bridal party at the groom's once again expresses the idea of affines as outsiders and potentially harmful to the household they are entering. But the foot-washing ritual, and the fact that there is no fine levied at the house of the groom nor any entertainment laid on by the bride's side, as well as the reception given the groom at the bride's house, suggest the bride's side is of higher status than the groom's. I was told that in the past it was said that the bride's side was of higher status; now, however, people 'don't take account' (*tak kira*). Undoubtedly, there are elements of ritually expressed inequality present in spite of the strong emphasis on the similarity of the bride and groom.

Once inside the groom's house, the bride is taken to a *bilek* (screened-off room) where she is re-dressed and made up by her *tukang* and some of the female relatives of the groom. This re-dressing is more than a simple costume change. She has already been lavishly adorned in her own house and in order to be re-dressed she must therefore first be partially *undressed*. Apart from her clothes, her hair and make-up are redone, and her female affines also bedeck her with plenty of their own gold jewellery. (I once counted 5 heavy chains, 15 bangles, earrings, and 5 rings, all gold, on a bride being prepared by her affines.) There is a strong attempt on the part of the bride's affines to take control of her and make her theirs which seems almost like an assault, and this is reinforced by the bride's isolation from her own kin. When both the bride and groom are ready, they once again *bersanding* in the manner already described.

After the *bersanding*, the bride and groom and their *tukang* eat a rice meal. The bride does not return home but spends one night in the groom's house. The bride and groom sleep separately (the groom may go to a different house) and the bride is 'watched over' (*tunggu*) by her *tukang* and two relatives.

In the recent past, another ceremony was performed early the next morning: the 'lime bathing' (*mandi berlimau*). The bride and groom sat on a raised platform adjoining the house, erected for the *kenduri*, and were liberally doused with water by the spectators.[32] This bathing clearly has purificatory associations. It might be suggested that while the bathing of the bride's feet represents purification and incorporation at the individual and house level, the bathing of the couple by all the spectators is a similar act of purification and incorporation at the level of community, and a further expression of the way marriage is taken over by the community at large. While Skeat (1900: 386) refers to 'holy water' being used in this ritual, Swift (1965: 116) describes the couple being taken to a well or stream. Both sources of water are of course instrumental in the cleansing and purification of the whole community. It may also be significant that incest pollution is described in terms of a nullification of the purificatory effects of prayer water.

Lime, which is referred to in the name of this ritual in Langkawi, is regarded as cooling.[33] I would suggest that its use, like that of similarly 'cooling' elements which are applied in the preparation of the bride and groom during the ritual preparations before the *bersanding*—in particular, 'cooling powder' (*bedak sejuk*) and their repeated bathing in cool water—implies that, among other dangers, marriage may involve a process of 'overheating' just as childbirth is dangerous for its 'overcooling' effects. Consummation is explicitly regarded as a 'cooking' process (see below) and women who are particularly passionate may be described as 'hot' (*hangat*).

After the bathing, the couple are fetched by the bride's relatives and

[32] See Skeat (1900: 386–7); Wilkinson (1957: 58); Winstedt (1982: 120–1); Djamour (1965: 76–7); Swift (1965: 116); Banks (1983: 149–50) for descriptions of this event.

[33] See Gimlette and Thomson (1971: 149).

taken back to her house. There they are given a proper rice meal to eat in each other's company. They stay there for two nights, sleeping together for the first time on the second night in a specially prepared *bilek*. After two nights they are again fetched back by the groom's relatives to his house, where they stay for another two nights. This process is repeated twice more: the couple are fetched from the groom's house by the bride's relatives. This time they stay in the bride's house for three nights. They are then fetched back to the groom's house for a further three nights.

This movement back and forth is known as 'exchange visits' (*sambut-menyambut*). The bride and groom are fetched three times by each side and taken to their affinal household, once singly and twice as a couple.[34] The first three times they are received in this way are known as *sambut mentah* (*mentah*, raw, unripe). After this the bride and groom sleep together in the bride's house and the next three exchange visits are known as *sambut masak* (*masak*, cooked).

The implication is clear: after the marriage has been consummated it is cooked; before, it is raw. It is notable that during the wedding rituals the couple progress from taking a snack in the company of witnesses to eating a rice meal alone together. They progressively share consumption to a greater degree as they become married. The rituals may be said to transform them from co-villagers for whom snacks are appropriate to people of the same house with substance in common. Marriage may be seen as a process of 'cooking' which begins with consummation and culminates with the birth of children. In fact, consummation is generally deferred for some days after the couple begin to sleep together. It is sleeping together, and the sexual act it implies, which can be said to initiate the 'cooking' which eventually produces children.

The deferral of consummation is expected by women, who frequently told me how frightened they had been when they first married. The groom is expected to wait until the bride is ready; she should invite him to sleep with her. In fact a bride's refusal to consummate a marriage is an accepted way of obtaining a divorce, and provides her with an alternative to refusing a match beforehand, which is generally unacceptable.[35] I knew of a number of instances of divorce before consummation.

[34] Kuchiba *et al.* (1979: 31–2) refer to such a ritual shuttling to and fro in mainland Kedah and also in Malacca (1979: 239); see also Swift (1965: 116–17); Fraser (1960: 208); Rudie (1994: 186).

[35] Deferral of consummation for some days is also reported by Strange (1981: 124); Djamour (1965: 77); Fraser (1960: 208–9; 1966: 72); Winstedt (1982: 120); Swift (1965: 123); H. Geertz (1961: 75); Wilkinson (1957: 59). Divorce of the couple before consummation has occurred is referred to by Fraser (1960: 209) and by Djamour (1965: 77), who also describes how a bride may take this means in order to refuse a match arranged by her parents.

The deferral of consummation can be seen as one aspect of a more general pattern of avoidance behaviour between bride and groom. Many women described to me their extreme embarrassment and shyness during the first days they spent in their parents-in-law's house. They described how they went veiled in the house and hardly looked at, or spoke to, their husbands. Newly married women are supposed to behave with humility; they should perform household labour with diligence and generally appear *malu*. Young men too expressed their embarrassment and feelings of isolation on first going to the house of their wife's parents. However, old people often complain that young people nowadays are not sufficiently *malu*: they go about together when betrothed, young brides go bareheaded in the house of their parents-in-law, where, they say, far from retiring to the *dapur*, they will, likely as not, serve the coffee to guests.

It is hard to conceive of any ritual expressing more clearly the idea of marriage as a balanced exchange than the *sambut-menyambut*. The visits are balanced in the order that they take place and in duration; the pattern is fixed and symmetrical. In 1989 I was present in the village when a marriage took place at which the order of these visits was disrupted. When the groom's party went to fetch the bride to take her back to his house for a *bersanding* there, her family wouldn't give her up. He returned without her, highly embarrassed and ashamed. The bride's side thought that the groom should first sleep at the bride's house, and only then would the couple sleep at the groom's. They were highly offended because in their view the groom should have come to sleep at the bride's house on the previous day. This would have been both inconceivable and highly embarrassing to the groom's party because the feast at the groom's house had not yet been held and the couple were therefore at this point not properly married. The problem, it was explained to me, was that the bride's family were from the north of Langkawi where the custom (*adat*) derives from Thai Malays and is slightly different.

This example shows very clearly how important is the idea of balance in the exchanges between the two sides, and also its potential precariousness. Marriage involves a feast and *bersanding* in both houses and there are suggestions of competition between them. This is clear in the prestations which are sent to each side by the other (the cooked gifts sent by the bride's side should just slightly exceed the number of gifts sent by the groom's side). It is also clear when the bride is re-dressed by her affines, and when the groom's party attempts to gain entry to the bride's house. The hints of resistance and aggressiveness at these junctures indicate how the equal status of the two sides is achieved through a competitive struggle. In 1989 I was specifically told that the wedding rituals can be done in two ways. The first involves both houses in a *bersanding* and *kenduri* in the manner I have described. This is explicitly described as 'to compete' (*berlawan*). The second way, which I have never known done, is for the *bersanding* and *kenduri* to be held at only one house. This is always the bride's house. But this of course would involve a very strong admission of poverty and inferiority by the groom's side which would be more or less unthinkable in Langkawi. It would also involve parents favouring daughters over sons so that the principle of equality among siblings would not be upheld.

Once the *sambut-menyambut* is over, the bride and groom should visit their relatives on both sides, ideally staying for short periods with some of them. They then begin a period of more flexible but still mobile residence when they 'alternate' (*berulang*) between the two parental households.

From Difference to Similarity

I have argued that marriage in Langkawi operates according to an ideology of balanced and competitive exchange. This ideology is expressed in many different aspects of marriage, perhaps most significantly in the high level of local endogamy. It is above all by marrying neighbours and co-villagers that the notion of a community made up of similar houses exchanging on an equal basis is lived out.

Throughout the rituals of marriage the idea of like marrying like is constantly emphasized. It is evident in the notions of compatibility, and in the exchange of marriage gifts. While the principal prestation, the *belanja kahwin*, is given in one direction only, it is always emphasized that this is only to cover the expenses of the wedding. It is neither a payment in exchange for a bride nor is it money to be saved and put towards the cost of a new house. It is cash immediately consumed by the wedding itself; much of it is actually eaten by the community. And where brides are financially independent, these expenses are shared by the bride and groom. Other gifts which accompany the *belanja* tend to be carefully balanced in the returns made by the bride's side.

The equal status of the two sides involved in a marriage is so central a principle that there is almost total avoidance between the bride and groom, and between their respective parents, from the moment the marriage has been proposed until the completion of the rituals. A concomitant of this avoidance is the dominant role of intermediaries, who have a kind of distancing and 'neutralizing' effect, throughout the period of betrothal and the marriage rituals. At every wedding ritual the same ritual specialists (*tukang*) are involved. The great prominence given to these ritual specialists, who play the same role in every marriage within the community, is instrumental in the construction of an image of marriage as a communal event. This image receives further emphasis in the arrangements at marriage feasts which were discussed in the last chapter.

It is clear that local endogamy is a major factor in the construction of this image of marriage and that endogamy plays a major role in binding people of one locality together. This effect has been stressed by Clifford and Hildred Geertz for Bali. They also emphasize, however, that 'if endogamy makes for intragroup solidarity it also makes for intergroup conflict' (1975: 103). Tensions in affinal relations reveal that endogamy can act as both a divisive and a cohesive force in the community.

Returning to the notion of marriage as an equal exchange, I described how the clearest expression of this occurs in the last phase of the ritual. The precisely balanced toing and froing between the two affinal households neatly captures (and attempts to resolve) the problem of unequal status implied by staying put in one particular house.[36] So far I have stressed those aspects of marriage which conform to the ideology of equal exchange within a close community. However, this view of marriage is not entirely straightforward. There are elements of the marriage ritual, including the prestations, the reception of the groom's party at the bride's house, and that of the bride at the groom's, which seem to contradict this image. We have also seen a pull towards another image in which the bride's side has superior status.

There is no doubt that affinal relations always reveal a particular tension and this may be linked with the problem of constructing equality between the two sides. Indeed this equality can only be 'constructed' through competition. In this respect it may be recalled that men's attitude to fishing with their kin was phrased very similarly to the ambivalence expressed over marriage between kin. Fishing, like marriage, may be said to be competitive and divisive. However, whereas in fishing the consequences of disrupted relations are as far as possible minimized, this is generally more difficult in marriage.

Villagers' attitude to kin marriage expresses this problem very clearly. However, they themselves often elide the difference between kin and neighbour, substituting the category of 'closeness' which can refer to

[36] Bloch (1978) discusses how the Merina attempt to resolve a very similar problem posed by marriage through an articulation of practice and ritual. The role of intermediaries is also very prominent in Merina marriage.

either. In Chapter 3 I described how the relation between husband and wife is itself conceived in terms of siblingship, emphasizing the shared substance of husband and wife.

While the notion of marriage between people who are similar is very dominant, another view of affines is also projected in the ritual: affines as outsiders, potentially harmful and dangerous. This is especially clear in the preparation of the bride and groom for marriage, and in the reception of the affinal party at the house of the spouse. Here the categories of evil spirit, outsider, co-villager, neighbour, and affine are all potentially dangerous and are, on one level, merged.

The image of affines as outsiders, intruders, who disrupt the integrity of the house is one we have encountered before. In Chapter 3 I described how the marriages of a group of siblings should ideally follow their birth order. If it does not, the in-marrying affine incurs a ritual fine and is said to 'stride over the threshold'. I also showed that, to a great extent, affinal relatives are excluded from the household, and may be said to be in opposition to it.

It might be suggested, then, that the very strong emphasis on similarity and closeness, the phrasing of marriage in the idiom of siblingship, the ritual feeding, and the very strongly asserted incorporation of the new affine into the *dapur* of his or her spouse are all part of a ritual construction of sameness and domestic kinship in marriage. For, as I have argued, what actually exists in the world outside the house is not similarity at all but endless difference. And of course it is highly significant that the marriage rituals may also be 'read' as an elaborate speculation on notions of insideness and outsideness. The boundaries of the body and of the house become peculiarly signified. They are continuously defended and then breached. One might say their existence is asserted in order to be denied.

In this context it is significant that a refusal of an offer of marriage may lead to accusations of witchcraft. A refusal indicates an unwillingness to be incorporated; it asserts boundaries. This causes offence and jealousy which result in witchcraft, expressed as the illicit breaching of the boundaries of the body or the house. It is this that is guarded against in the protective rituals which the bride and groom undergo.

Looked at in one way we have the assertion of two contradictory images in marriage: similarity and difference. But if we take a longer view, we can also see the marriage rituals as the beginning of a long process of incorporation, of creating similar substance, which is finally realized in childbirth.[37] Marriage begins the process of becoming the same. And in this respect it helps to start out as near that ideal as possible.

The process of incorporation is conceived in the idiom of houses, hearths, cooking, and feeding. Marriage is a 'heating' process, as is sex. Incorporated into the affinal hearth, through feeding and sex, affines may be turned into siblings, and once located there they will in turn give birth to new siblings. The cooking of new and different ingredients produces more of the same substance. Houses reproduce themselves through marriage.

But affines always remain a little different. They can never quite *be* siblings. And it is this that gives affinity its edge. Beyond the house, as well as within it, affinal relations have an inherent tension and fragility. In the following chapter we will look at some of the wider consequences of this.

[37] See also Errington (1989: 252) on the incorporative aspects of marriage.

8

Producing Similarity: Affinity and the Sharing of Grandchildren

Marriage in Langkawi is a process of incorporation. The rituals begin the transformation of affines into consanguines. Childbirth marks the achievement of this transformation. New sibling sets, by definition, signal the incorporation and blending of the different substances of their parents. Out of difference has come similarity.

This chapter explores some of the implications of these ideas. It also shifts from the discussion of abstract principles to the tensions and difficulties of everyday life. The first half of the chapter concerns a dispute, which highlights by default the subject of the second half, the ties that bind affinal (and other) houses together.

The ideal of sameness in marriage involves very great tensions in relations between affines. Straining to achieve likeness and similarity, affines may find their differences come between them. Marriages founder, and with them relations between houses in the wider community. In this fragile scenario the relation between the two sets of parents of a married couple has a particular practical and symbolic importance. And this is especially true once they have common grandchildren. It is co-parents-in-law, *bisan*, who in more than one way make a marriage. It is their shared grandchildren who mark the successful reproduction of the houses of their grandparents and, more generally, of the community at large. In the second half of the chapter, I return to the more abstract level to show how grandparents and grandchildren embody the principles of unity and exchange which are threatened in disputes.

Affinity as a Category

There is a paradox at the centre of notions of affinity. On one level affines should be indistinguishable from consanguineal kin, on another they always remain distinctly affines. Both these images occur simultaneously:

affines are both constituted as a category and denied. The assertion of something called 'affinity' and its simultaneous denial is expressed in various different ways.

Affines may be referred to by use of a suffix after an appropriate consanguineal term: *mentua* for a parent-in-law, *ipar* for a sibling-in-law, *menantu* for a child's spouse. Thus mother and father-in-law are *mak* and *pak mentua* respectively; elder sister-in-law is *kakak ipar*, older brother-in-law *abang ipar*, etc. It is possible to refer to affines collectively by the term *adik-beradik ipar*, 'kin-in-law', but this rarely occurs.[1]

What is, in fact, most striking about these terms is how infrequently they are heard even in reference; in address only consanguineal terms are used. Thus, mothers-in-law are addressed simply as mother, older sibling-in-law as older sibling. It is highly impolite to address or refer to these affines in any other way in their presence. Even in their absence, the appropriate consanguineal terms are usually used. In Chapter 3 I noted that this conflation of affines with consanguines occurs even between husbands and wives, who should address each other as younger sister/older brother, although in fact they experience quite a lot of uneasiness with these terms.

When talking to or about one's affines, then, although affinity is to an extent acknowledged and is usually distinguishable from consanguinity, there is at the same time a strong attempt to transform affinal relations into consanguineal ones. This paradox in many ways forms the central problem of the present chapter. It results in a tension in relations between all affines.

Affinal relations tend to take stereotypical forms: avoidance behaviour is common between brothers-in-law and between sons-in-law and their fathers-in-law. Joking behaviour often occurs between cross-sex affinal siblings and between a son-in-law and his mother-in-law. Female affines may interact more intensively than male ones because of household labour requirements. The relation between a daughter-in-law and her mother-in-law is frequently a very tense one. A husband's mother is often implicated in the divorce of her son (see below).

In Chapter 2 I suggested that affinal relations could in some way be seen as standing in opposition to principles of household unity. Villagers talk of their concern to have no more than one married couple in any generation

[1] McKinley comments on affinal terminology and on the fact that it is *ipar* that is used rather than *mentua* or *menantu*: 'marriage and affinal relations are built directly on *present siblingship* in much the same way that cognatic kinship builds on layers of *past siblingship*' (1981: 354, original emphasis).

living together, and they explain this as an attempt to minimize tension between affines. If marital exchange is premised on equality and symmetry, then we might expect these tensions to be heightened where two families, who have exchanged a son and daughter in marriage, come to be related on an unequal basis. The fragility of affinal relations in such a context was clearly expressed in a long-running dispute which occurred during my fieldwork.

Difference between Affines

The dispute in question began over a marriage and involved two households, but escalated in such a fashion that eventually most of the village was divided over it. Many of the themes which have been discussed in earlier chapters are touched on in these events. Although this account 'begins' at a certain point, the longer I lived in the village the more I became aware of the extent to which everyone possessed potentially harmful knowledge about others. Such knowledge might take the form of personal grudges, concern episodes from the past that others would wish forgotten, or it could relate to old disputes. Sometimes it would be activated, much of the time it was not. However, it was always a potential resource when people quarrelled. The history of any dispute thus always 'begins' in the middle.

Because of the nature of the events I describe, and the tendency for the dispute to escalate, it was difficult to remain aloof from what was happening. I was a frequent and welcome visitor in several of the houses centrally involved. Throughout, I tried to maintain this neutrality, and on the whole people sympathized with my wish to do so. But inevitably, there were many upsetting incidents as visits and exchanges between the disputing houses became more and more strained.

A diagram showing the kinship links between the households centrally concerned is shown in Fig. 8.1. Minah and Bunga in households A and B are *bisan* to each other. Minah's son, Din, is the resident son-in-law of Bunga in house B, married to Bunga's daughter, Mariah. Minah is also *bisan* to Rohana in house C. Minah's second son, Mat (younger brother of Din), is married to Rohana's daughter, Faridah, and the couple live with Rohana in house C. Bunga and Rohana's sister-in-law, Yah, her husband, Man, and their son, Non, live in house D. Houses B, C, and D are all situated in the same compound and are united by ties of siblingship in the senior generation. Minah lives in a different area of the village in house A.

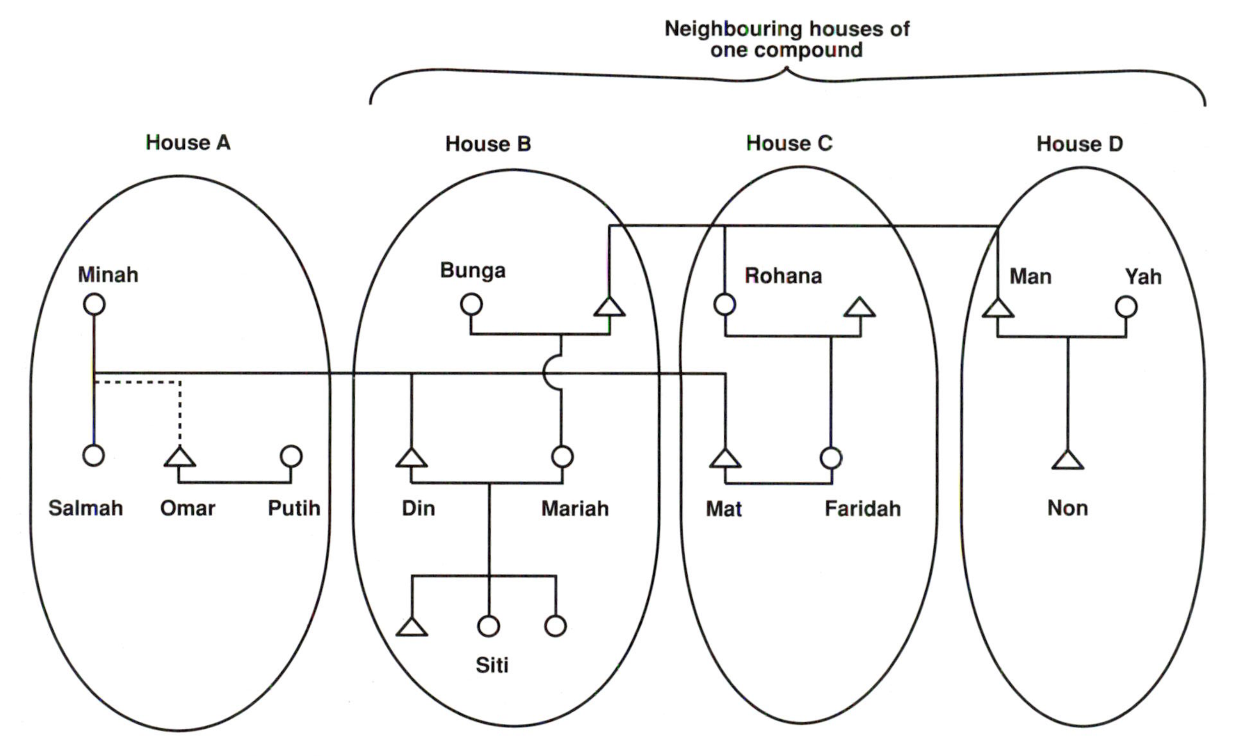

FIG. 8.1. Diagram to show kinship relations of principal participants in dispute

The history of this dispute is one of relations between various sets of affines and, appropriately enough, the story begins with a marriage. Minah's second son, Mat, worked on the fishing trawlers off the mainland coast. There he had a friend, Omar, originally from the east coast, whom he brought home on several visits. Mat's mother, Minah, considered this young man as her foster son, *anak angkat*. The fact that she did so is one indication of the flexibility of notions of fostering, for Omar never spent more than a total of a few weeks in her house. However, Minah arranged a marriage between him and a girl in a nearby house, Putih. The marriage took place shortly after I began my fieldwork.

Minah's son Mat is a pivotal character in the story. He worked as a sighter of fish, *taikong*, on the trawlers, a rare, highly skilled, and, by village standards, very highly paid occupation. He was also unusual in that he continued to work on the mainland after marrying. Before his marriage his parents received the greater part of his earnings and this made a very substantial contribution to their income, which had rapidly risen considerably higher than that of their neighbours and co-villagers.

Shortly before I began my fieldwork, Mat had married into household C situated in the same compound as B. Mat's wife, Faridah, was in fact the first cousin (FSD) of his elder brother Din's wife, Mariah. Thus the younger brother had repeated the alliance made by the older, and this is generally an approved strategy which consolidates a previous alliance between two families. After marrying, much of Mat's income went to his wife's family with whom he was then residing. Generally, once sons have married they do not continue to support their parents unless the latter are incapable of doing so themselves. However, because Mat's income was so large, he continued to be able to remit substantial sums every month to his parents so that they remained relatively wealthy by village standards.

Mat's older brother, Din, had meanwhile been living uxorilocally in household B since his marriage about ten years previously. He and his wife had three children, the second child being a daughter, Siti. Din's wife's father no longer went out fishing and the family depended almost exclusively on Din for their income. While at the time of Din's marriage his parents and those of his wife were of approximately equal wealth, the intervening years had radically altered their relative positions. The contributions of his brother Mat's income had substantially increased the wealth of their parents, while Din's wife's parents had suffered a decline. The maintenance of the latter's position was absolutely dependent on the continued residence and financial contribution of their son-in-law.

During January and February of 1982 it became clear that relations between households A and B were becoming strained. In the middle of the rice-harvesting season, a time when all available labour is utilized to the full, Din went on what was essentially a pleasure trip to the mainland. His mother-in-law, Bunga, who was responsible for organizing the household's harvest, was highly put out by the timing of his absence. She felt that it was inconsiderate of him to leave at this time. While she thought it inappropriate to try to impose her own authority on him—indeed she said that she was afraid to do so—she felt that his own mother, Minah, should have told him not to go and blamed the latter for taking no action, saying she was 'sweet of mouth only' (*manis mulut sahaja*); that is, hypocritical.

Some weeks later, Bunga complained that her *bisan*, Minah, had stopped coming to the house, although now she was visiting again. She said that she didn't go to visit Minah much but that this was different because Minah ought to come to see their grandchildren. Bunga also complained that her own son, Hussin, who lived and worked on the mainland, was not sending her any money. She said this was embarrassing in view of their relation with Din's family.

Around the same time it became clear that the marriage of Omar and Putih was not prospering. Minah's daughter, Salmah, told me that Putih was angry because her husband was working on the fishing trawlers on the mainland and had not returned for two months. Salmah described how Putih and Omar had quarrelled in Minah's house and Putih had thrown a rice pot at him; he had cried and now Putih wouldn't talk to any of them and wanted a divorce. During this conversation Salmah cast various aspersions on Putih's character, including that she was prone to 'run around' (*jalan-jalan*), that she mistreated her own mother, and that she was only interested in her husband's money.

Putih was the niece of Yah, who lived in house D in the same compound as B and C. All these three households contained siblings in the senior generation. Of these siblings, Yah's husband, Man, was the youngest.

When Putih's marriage seemed precarious the members of household D took her side. Her aunt, Yah, said, ironically, that Minah was the best of mothers-in-law, she had complained in turn about each of her daughters-in-law, first Mariah, then Faridah, and now Putih. Yah said Minah was rich but not happy, and that she used other people's poverty. Yah also said that she herself often scolded her own children but never her children-in-law.

At this point the situation began to deteriorate rapidly. There was an open confontation between Minah and Yah which took place in house D.

After Minah had left, the talk immediately turned to money. $2,000 of Din's money had been used to rebuild house B; Mat had lent $900 for Hussin's wedding. This latter sum was to be returned that day. Minah enjoyed quarrelling, they said, now that she had money; before it was different.

Households B and D, neighbours of one compound and close kin, thus allied themselves against A, the affines of B. However, even at this point the impossibility of the situation was perceived by those in house D. They told me that Din would have to side with his mother and that his wife Mariah was stuck in between. Mariah herself spoke against her mother-in-law at this stage, claiming that she meddled in the borrowing of money when it was none of her business since it belonged to her son, Mat.

The following day, Yah said that Minah wanted Omar to divorce Putih and that he didn't want to. She contrasted Putih's parents' poverty with Minah's wealth and said it was difficult for the former to keep Omar. She then suggested that Minah was knowledgeable in the art of witchcraft (*ilmu sihir*), and that this took the form of putting things in food, causing those who ate it to stay at home and forget their obligations. Yah was particularly bitter about the way Minah was informing the whole village about what was going on.

I was then absent from the village for some days and during this period Omar and Putih were divorced. The divorce was initiated by Omar and none of the marriage payments were returned. By the time I returned to the village, a fundamental—but perhaps predictable—shift in the alliances between the households concerned had taken place. This was clear on the night of my return when events reached a kind of climax of hysteria.

Late at night, the neighbourhood was alerted by screams and cries coming from house D where Putih was then staying. She was lying on the floor in some kind of fit while her aunt Yah was weeping, as were her two adult sons, one of whom was being kept away from Putih by his older sister. The latter was scolding both of her brothers, telling them they were shameful, and at one point she physically attacked one of them, some years older than herself.

Given the general uproar, it was difficult to get much sense of what was going on. However, what was clear was that the members of this household believed that Putih was under the influence of witchcraft: as they put it, 'people doing her' (*orang buat dia*). Bunga, who had come running from house B, suggested that Din and Mat should both go to the mosque and take an oath, *sumpah*, to swear their innocence. And it transpired that two sons from house D had tried to attack Din and Mat as they returned to their houses from the shop. Din and Mat were accused of buying articles to be used in witchcraft by their sister Salmah. While the men of households B and D were fairly well out of control by this time, the women were making a strong effort to keep the situation as far as possible in hand.

In the ensuing days all communication between the neighbouring houses B and D ceased: both sides kept the shutters closed on the windows facing each other's houses. Members of each house gave their opinions on what was happening and the air was thick with recriminations and bitterness. In house B I was told that it was sinful (*berdosa*) to quarrel with people so close; attention was drawn to the religious piety of people in house D, how much they prayed, implying they were hypocritical. Members of house D described how in the past Minah had quarrelled with Bunga, accusing her of making advances to her husband who had himself threatened Minah with divorce. She 'liked to quarrel' (*suka bergaduh*), they said, while Bunga and her daughter Mariah were both 'good people' (*orang baik*).

In other nearby houses people ranged themselves on one side or the other according to their kin connections or other allegiances. Always this involved bringing up events from the past to demonstrate the quarrelsome aspects of someone's character. And often women implied that jealousy over men on the part of other women was a reason for such disputes. Many people regretted the fact that the imam was necessarily involved in the quarrel since he was Mat's wife's uncle. Normally, he might be expected to take a peace-making role by calling all the participants to his house and mediating between them.

The most disturbing aspect of the dispute was now the fact that relations between three neighbouring houses—B, C, and D—containing siblings in the senior generation, were severed. The importance of siblingship as an ideal for proper relations between kin has been stressed, as well as the normally close interaction between households of one compound. The fact that this ideal harmony had been shattered was highly distressing for those concerned. If the imam could not repair relations, it was thought to be the duty of Man, the youngest brother in the senior generation of these houses, who lived in house D, to initiate a peace-making process.

As the main festival of the year, Hari Raya Puasa, which marks the end of the fasting month, approached, the level of general anxiety increased. On that day younger kin ritually ask for pardon (*minta ma'af*) from their elders for any wrongs they have committed. Pardon should be requested and granted with sincerity so that old grudges are erased or forgotten and harmony confirmed. With relations between house D and houses B and C quite disrupted this was clearly impossible.

On the morning of Hari Raya Puasa, the youngest son of Yah in house D, Non, went to house C to *minta ma'af*, first from his aunt, Rohana, who was also the mother-in-law of Mat. She proceeded to give him a moral lecture on the wrongs he had committed. Meanwhile Mat, his wife, and mother, Minah, who was visiting the house, retreated to the *dapur* at the back of the house. Although Rohana tried repeatedly to call her son-in-law, Mat, to come and take part in the pardoning, he was himself reluctant to do so and was, furthermore, being dissuaded by his mother, Minah. Meanwhile, Non became offended and tried to leave the house; he was restrained by Rohana, who kept telling Mat to come, which, finally, he did. They asked each other's pardon under the most strained circumstances and a discussion ensued. Then Minah intervened with further recriminations and Non abruptly left without asking pardon of either her or Bunga, who had meanwhile arrived from house B. From this point on, relations were truly broken and interaction between the various houses ceased.

In their comments on all these events, villagers often drew a distinction between kin and affine. Thus, one woman told me that it is particularly difficult to live with one's mother-in-law because it is sinful (*berdosa*) to contradict or get angry with her, more so than with one's own mother, because a mother-in-law is 'unrelated' (*orang lain*).

Din himself, in a frank conversation which took place about three months after Hari Raya Puasa, regretted how things had turned out. He recalled how different life had been before when he would regularly go to the neighbours in house D to borrow money or give fish. It is significant that in the view of members of house B one of the most provocative acts in the dispute had been the recalling of a loan to them by house D. Now things were 'unpleasant' (*tak seronok*), Din went on, no one wanted to continue but it 'had happened' (*terjadi*), and there was nothing to be done. Sooner or later there would be peace again because they were kin and also because they were neighbours. As soon as someone became ill, or in the event of a death in one house of the compound, the others would have to visit. He said that it was up to Man, the youngest brother in the senior generation in house D, to call everyone together and make the peace; that he hadn't done so showed that he was proud (*sombong*).

Kin that quarrelled were like dogs, Din continued. He recalled how a daughter from house D had harangued his wife Mariah, saying that he,

Din, should not have entered into the dispute because he was only married here and should go back to his own *kampung*. He was ready to, but they were one family. He and Yah in house D were related. As a boy he had come here all the time, and had he returned to his own neighbourhood, Mariah's parents would have followed. He had looked after his parents-in-law for eight years while their own son studied. In fact, the son-in-law from house D shouldn't have interfered because he was 'unrelated' (*orang lain*) and could return to his own neighbourhood (*kampung*) in a dispute.

While kin and affine are thus conflated ideally and when relations are harmonious, the potential for separating these categories remains and is often realized during disputes. Boundaries may be reasserted when relations have been disrupted.

Another theme which emerged strongly was the role that *bisan* should ideally play in such disputes. I was constantly told how important it was for *bisan* to be on good terms with each other, how they should never enter into any marital dispute on the side of their own child but always take the part of his or her spouse. While disputes between a married couple were to be expected during the early phase of a marriage, if the relation between *bisan* was harmonious nothing serious would come of them. However, if the *bisan* entered into a quarrel and, particularly if they supported their own child, divorce would be a likely outcome.

One of the daughters from house D told me how her older brother had in the past quarrelled with his wife, and had even been physically assaulted by her, but when he had come home their mother 'wouldn't let him enter the house' (*tak bagi dia naik rumah*), and sent him straight back. When she herself had been living in her natal home after her marriage, if she wanted to quarrel with her husband she had had to do so very quietly in order not to incur her mother's anger. Minah, however, always entered into disputes. For example, she had been angry with her son Din for buying furniture and for financing the rebuilding of his parents-in-law's house; furthermore, she was sexually jealous of her *bisan*, Bunga.

Such comments were not confined to this particular dispute. Frequently, I was told how important it was for *bisan* to be on good terms in order to safeguard a marriage; it was up to the *bisan* to make the marriage work. The role of *bisan* in preventing disputes is clearly regarded as crucial and people frequently alluded to the tension caused by differences of wealth between two families related by marriage. Observers often singled out Minah's wealth as a factor which influenced her behaviour or caused problems in her relation with her *bisan*.

Disputes also clearly express ideas about antisocial behaviour. Being proud (*sombong*)—the denial of which figures prominently in behaviour at a *kenduri*—is an accusation made in quarrels when people do not show the reciprocity expected of kin. They are perceived as putting themselves above others whom they are close to. Those who 'like to quarrel' (*suka bergaduh*) are regarded as antisocial and divisive. Disputes involve the negation of ideal codes of behaviour and finally of relations themselves. This is often expressed in the calling-up of loans at these times, an action regarded as particularly provocative. Similarly, other forms of exchange cease: of food, of words, of gifts, and even of sight—as when houses cut off their aspect onto each other.

Antisocial behaviour, however, is above all thought to be displayed by those who are knowledgeable in witchcraft (*ilmu sihir*). And it is highly significant that such people typically apply their art to food to be consumed by their subjects. This of course implies that they are women. We shall see below how those versed in witchcraft form part of a wider category of poisoners relevant to the discussion of divorce.[2]

Divorce

Villagers think of marriages as involving two crucial relations apart from that between husband and wife. One is the relation between *bisan*, and the other that between mother-in-law and daughter-in-law. In spite of the crucial role of sons-in-law in the dispute I have described, it is the relations between women (between female *bisan*, and mother-in-law and daughter-in-law) which are seen as responsible either for exacerbating tensions, or for smoothing them over. To a great extent, these two relations form a complementary pair, reinforcing each other when they are harmonious, and acting negatively on each other when they are not. Being a good mother-in-law involves not being over-critical of one's daughter-in-law. The ideal parent-in-law scolds her own child and not the child's spouse.

It is widely recognized that the relation between mother-in-law and daughter-in-law is likely to be difficult, particularly where the two women co-reside. In their accounts of experiences of divorce, women very fre-

[2] See Parry (1985: 614) on witchcraft expressed as the threat of being fed something by a person who bears ill will in North India. He suggests that the potency of this threat is particularly strong because of the resonance of food as a symbol of nurture and kinship. In mainland Kedah, Scott (1985: 187) has discussed how the verb 'to eat', *makan*, can express exploitation, as in 'he wants to eat us', *dia mahu makan kita*.

quently spoke of bad relations with their ex-mother-in-law as the main cause of a marriage breaking down.[3] During the dispute I have described, the relationship between Minah and her daughters-in-law was often pointed out as being particularly difficult. Minah was regarded as interfering, and this was seen as causing tensions in her sons', and her adopted son's, marriages. When I asked women about the reasons for a divorce I was often simply told that they had been disliked by their husband's mother and that the latter had 'ordered him to divorce' (*suruh dia cerai*). One woman, Aminah, related how her mother-in-law had disliked her and hadn't allowed her out of the house. She had tried to prevent Aminah from visiting her mother or her aunt, but when the latter had fallen ill, Aminah had gone to see her, despite her mother-in-law's objections. When she returned she found her husband had packed up her belongings, and she returned to the house of her mother.

When a couple live with the husband's parents, and the bride's parents live far away, a woman's desire to visit her mother or other kin may lead to disputes and finally to divorce.[4] In Chapter 2 the very close emotional bond between mothers and daughters was described. It provides an absolute contrast to the relation with a mother-in-law, which is usually spoken of in terms of fear, *takut*, and embarrassment or shame, *malu*. When marriages break down women usually return to (or remain with) their mothers. There is thus a potential conflict between a woman's allegiance to her husband and mother-in-law and her emotional attachment to her mother. It is clear that conflict will be especially intense when the couple reside virilocally (as in the above example) and a young woman is placed under the direct authority of her mother-in-law. But to some extent this tension is always present in the first months of marriage because of the way the couple move between the two houses. Tension between Putih and Minah, her husband's adoptive mother, was clearly one problem in the marriage of Putih and Omar.

After the initial period of shifting residence, it is in fact usual for couples to reside uxorilocally until the birth of at least one child. Locality of residence is decided by discussions between female *bisan* after a marriage has taken place. Given that residence in either parental household has inherent tensions, establishing a new house is likely to provide the best insurance against divorce. That this solution is an imperfect one is clear from the close relations within compounds described in Chapter 6. Residence in either the wife's or the husband's natal *compound*, rather than

3 See also Djamour (1965: 119); Jay (1969: 146).
4 Djamour (1965: 118–19) makes the same observation.

house, may lessen the imbalance of loyalty and affiliation, but it cannot altogether remove it.

The first months of marriage are recognized as being particularly unstable. Thus the divorce of Putih and Omar, which occurred in the first weeks of marriage, was by no means unusual. In Chapter 7 I described the refusal of a newly-wedded woman to consummate a marriage as one means for her to register her objection to a match. A similar course is sometimes taken by young men. I knew several men who had been married for many years to their present wives but who related how their parents had arranged a first match, often to a relative, which they had agreed to rather unwillingly. They had gone through with the wedding but the couple had separated after a few days. Often the aim was to marry a woman of their own choice and the divorce was rapidly followed by a second and stable marriage.[5]

This initial instability may take a less radical form when a couple quarrel and divorce (*cerai*) but this is later revoked (*rojok*) by the husband. Under Muslim marriage laws a husband may divorce his wife by pronouncing the divorce formula (*talak*), which is then registered with the imam or *kadi* (religious judge).[6] The repudiation (*talak*) may be pronounced up to three times, either in succession or on separate occasions. The first two times the divorce may be revoked, but after the third *talak* this is not possible. In the course of marital rows such 'divorces' and revocations are not uncommon. Minah, who was generally regarded as being a difficult character, had been divorced in this way by her rather mild-mannered husband. Her daughter, Salmah, told me how six days after her own marriage her husband had divorced her and returned to the house of his parents because he wanted to marry someone else. His parents had told him to go back to his wife and threatened to beat him. When parents-in-law do not side with their own child in this way, their intervention is regarded as particularly good and likely to cement the marriage. Salmah's husband had revoked the divorce but she had insisted that a condition (*ta'alik*) be put in the marriage contract under which if he took a second wife he would 'pronounce one *talak*' (*jatu satu talak*); that is, they would then be divorced for the second time and in the event of one more such pronouncement the divorce would be final.

A *ta'alik* is quite frequently added to marriage contracts in this way,[7]

[5] See Ch. 2. This is also noted by Downs (1967: 144).

[6] Legal and other aspects of divorce among Malays in Singapore are discussed in detail by Djamour (1966; 1965: 110–40).

[7] See Djamour (1965: 111, 114; 1966: 38–76) on this practice among Malays in Singapore.

for example to enforce abstinence from gambling. This procedure is one of a number of ways in which women actively control their marital histories despite the relatively disadvantageous position imposed by Muslim marriage codes. In this example Salmah portrayed her husband in an utterly ineffectual light. His parents chose his wife against his will and his one attempt to assert himself failed. Salmah related these events in the presence of her husband, who appeared extremely embarrassed throughout, but made no intervention of his own. Salmah, on the other hand, appeared to be enjoying herself immensely, and even pointed out her husband's evident discomfort to me before he made a hasty escape.

This example also underlines women's rejection of polygamy. It was in order to safeguard herself against her husband taking a second wife that Salmah imposed a *ta'alik*. Women never consent to marry a man who already has a wife. Men must therefore resort to deception in order to achieve such a union. When this is discovered, one of the wives will immediately force the husband to divorce either the other or herself. There had been several such cases in the village. In one, a young woman had married a man from the mainland who claimed that the woman who was in fact his first wife was his sister. The second wife subsequently ran away from him and returned to her natal home in the village.

In cases where a woman wishes to obtain a divorce she has a number of resources, formal and informal. One is to obtain a 'divorce by redemption' (*tebus talak*); this involves the wife returning the marriage payment to her husband. This form of divorce cannot be revoked. If she is divorcing during or immediately after the wedding rituals, she has to return the 'wedding expenses' (*belanja kahwin*). Later on in the marriage, she would return her own portion, the *mas kahwin*, or, where it is still 'owing' (*hutang*), she would 'renounce' (*minta halal*) her claim to it.[8] In fact this form of divorce occurs rather rarely because of women's lack of independent financial resources. However, I knew of one case in which the whole *belanja* had been returned immediately after a marriage because the wife had wanted to marry someone else. In cases where a husband has deserted his wife and not maintained her over a number of years a judicial decree of divorce (*pasah*) may be pronounced. I knew of only one such case in the village, which involved a woman who at the time in question had been living on the mainland. Interestingly, one of the accusations made by Putih about her husband Omar was that he had gone away for two months. The idea that husbands should not simply go off for months on

[8] See also Djamour (1965: 124, 133).

end, and should support their wives, is a powerful one. Women's grudges against husbands who do not comply with these norms are regarded as legitimate.

More often than returning the marriage payments, a woman may persuade her husband simply to pronounce a *talak*. While a husband is not legally obliged to comply with his wife's wishes, it is generally accepted that women are in a position to make life so intolerable for their husbands that eventually they will concede. Usually sufficient quarrels will achieve this but there are other more potent threats available. One old man told me how, after six years of marital quarrels, he had finally granted his wife a divorce in this way (against his own wishes) because it was women that did the cooking, and he didn't know what she would put in the food if he continued to refuse her request: he feared that she would poison him. It was clear from conversations with other men that this belief is widely held and that a number of different substances are thought to be used as poisons (*racun*). Both Minah and her daughter Salmah were thought to be causing quarrels and sickness through the use of poisons and witchcraft.[9]

It may be significant that while I only once heard of a case of a husband physically assaulting his wife, I was often told of marital quarrels in which a wife had shown violence to her husband. Thus it was not unusual that Putih had thrown a rice pot at Omar; or that Salmah's husband had been threatened with a beating when he tried to leave his wife. Women's active participation in controlling the course of their marriages is recognized by men. The latter's perception of women as knowledgeable in witchcraft and as potential poisoners is one clear expression of this.

Quarrels, childlessness, jealousy, prolonged absence on the part of a husband, may all result in the breakdown of a marriage. Women also feel entitled to sexual satisfaction in marriage and this may become a source of grievance—and a subject of humour. (This was another implication of Salmah telling me about Putih's complaint that her husband had gone away for two months. By telling me this, Salmah was also hinting at Putih's sexual rapaciousness.) Women directly and, more frequently, indirectly initiate divorce procedure. I also knew women who had refused to be persuaded to accept a revocation of a divorce and others who had refused to cohabit with a husband when the latter was unwilling to grant a divorce. However, women themselves are quick to emphasize their relative powerlessness compared to men under Muslim law.

[9] Provencher (1979: 48) describes the prevalence of beliefs about poisoning in Kuala Lumpur. Significantly, poison here is revealed by 'cool' food being 'hot', and 'hot' food being 'cool'. See also Massard (1983*a*: 268).

Relations between Bisan*; the Birth of Grandchildren*

In Chapter 7 I discussed ideas about mutual compatibility of spouses; to a great extent these centre on the matching of a bride and groom through similarity of their attributes. However, when the parents of a groom select a spouse for him, their choice is to a large extent governed not by the qualities of his bride-to-be but by those of her parents, their potential *bisan*.[10] This became clear to me after I had spent a considerable time trying to elicit information on the ideal qualities sought in a young bride. Villagers' statements on this subject always seemed remarkably unrevealing. The young girl should be beautiful, I was told, and hard-working (*rajin*). At this point the conversation usually came to an inconclusive halt.

However, when I asked people what qualities they looked for in their *bisan*, their answers were altogether different in tone and more revealing.[11] The most important attribute of *bisan* is that they should be 'good people' (*orang baik*). In this context *orang baik* are people who are not quarrelsome, do not gossip, and are not proud (*sombong*). We have already seen that these attributes have to do with the essential role that *bisan* are expected to play in maintaining and harmonizing the marriage of their children. In the dispute surrounding Omar and Putih's divorce, this was continuously emphasized—particularly with regard to Minah's behaviour.

In the context of spouse selection we saw how the concept of *raksi* is significant in stressing resemblance as an ideal in marriage. However, this applies as much to the parents of a couple, the *bisan*, as to the bride and groom. People say they 'go by the *bisan*' (*kira bisan*) rather than their children. I was often told that as long as the *bisan* are *raksi*, even if the couple are not, a marital dispute will not be serious. As one woman put it, 'If the old people are all right, then if the young people are a bit less so it doesn't matter.' When ritual specialists divine the course of a marriage before the wedding, they always make sure that both the couple and their parents are *raksi*. People say that *bisan* should be of the same wealth and the same rank (*pangkat*). However, they also emphasize that marriage within the community generally conforms to this ideal since there are no big wealth or status differentials locally.

[10] Some of the material used in this section is also discussed in Carsten 1991; 1992. The standard Malay spelling is *besan* (Iskandar 1970). Here I use the spelling which accords with pronunciation in Langkawi.

[11] Strange (1981: 110) also notes the importance of co-parents-in-law when parents choose a match for a child.

In the last chapter I discussed the avoidance between the parents of a betrothed couple prior to their children's marriage. All the marital negotiations are conducted through intermediaries. Neither the bride's parents nor the groom's attend the marriage feast or the *bersanding* that is held in the house of their *bisan*. After the marriage, the relationship between *bisan* is gradually transformed into a close and seemingly friendly one. This shift from avoidance to close interaction mirrors the change in the relation between husband and wife, which gradually becomes relaxed and intimate. It can also be linked to the ideal of marriage taking place between equals. It is particularly during the delicate negotiations for a marriage that any direct interaction might lead to imputations of inequality between the two sets of parents. This is also expressed in the marriage rituals: the *bersanding* and the *kenduri* are held in both the house of the bride and that of the groom; it is even more clear in the ritual shuttling between the two houses which follows this.

Gradually, however, the couple begin to spend more time in one house or the other and usually the first period of married life is spent mainly in the wife's natal home. It might be expected that some attempt would be made to redress the inequality of the couple's affiliation to a particular household. It is in this light that the intense exchanges that characterize the relation between *bisan* may be viewed.

The relation between *bisan* receives continual emphasis in everyday life. *Bisan* constantly visit each other's houses and are engaged in a complex web of exchanges involving food, labour, services, and loans. Although men play a part in these exchanges, it is women who are the most active participants and this has partly to do with their dominant role in household affairs.

These exchanges do not in fact necessarily take place between the actual *bisan* but they are usually described as if they did. For example, it is very common for female *bisan* to send each other dishes of cooked food such as special curries or rice cakes. However, since it is young women that normally cook, the gift might more accurately be described as passing from daughter-in-law to her non-resident mother-in-law. Similarly, when assistance is required for agricultural labour *bisan* are frequently called upon. Rather than go herself, however, a younger member of the household may be sent. The way in which people single out the *bisan* as leading actors indicates the special significance of this relationship.

Bisan are frequently called upon during rice-harvesting, for work in the vegetable gardens, house-building, for loans of cash or equipment. They send each other gifts, especially of cooked food and of raw produce. They are often the most frequent visitors in each other's houses apart from immediate neighbours. A high value is placed on reciprocity in these exchanges. Neglect of obligations to give assistance is a frequent source of bitterness, and such grudges may be brought up much later in a dispute. In the early stages of the dispute described in the first part of the chapter, Bunga complained about her *bisan*, Minah, not visiting the house frequently enough; it was particularly important that Minah should come and see their shared grandchildren.

In one way, of course, the mutual assistance supplied by *bisan* is of the same kind as that given to close kin or immediate neighbours but there is a qualitative difference. First, this has to do with the emphasis on reciprocity already mentioned. In the case of kin and neighbours there is a greater tolerance of imbalance in the short term. Secondly, and following from this, the exchanges between *bisan* not only occur with great frequency, but they are also particularly marked. They receive constant attention—while those between close kin and neighbours tend to be taken for granted. Nor is there any other affinal relation that receives this kind of stress. On one level, then, it is as if an attempt were being made to assimilate a bond of affinity into the realm of consanguineal kinship. On another, this attempt is belied by the very emphasis it receives, by the intensity of the exchanges and the importance of reciprocity.

The paradoxical nature of the stress on affinity which '*bisan*ship' represents is even more obvious when terms of address and reference are considered. When *bisan* address each other they generally use an appropriate kin term. If, as is often the case, they were related before the marriage of their children, they may continue to use the same terms of address. Sibling terms and personal names are often used. The term *bisan* is principally used in reference, and as such it occurs constantly in conversation. Villagers rarely refer to their *bisan* in any other way.

As a term, *bisan* is almost unique in Malay kinship terminology in that it is perfectly reciprocal. It makes no distinction of age, sex, rank, or generation. Terms for every consanguineal relation within the same generation differentiate according to at least one of these principles and this differentiation carries clear implications of hierarchy. The terminology clearly expresses the notion of similarity on which the relation is founded.[12] Further, the term *bisan* does not distinguish those who were

[12] See Wilder's discussion of such 'self-reciprocal' (1976: 301) terms. He compares them with birth order terms used in Pahang, Penan death names as described by Needham (1954; 1959), and teknonymy in Bali. Wilder associates birth order terms with a centrifugal society, the establishment of new sub-groups, and an image of 'assured expansion'

related before the marriage of their children from those who were not. It could be said to be a 'purely affinal' term. The only other affinal term which is similarly symmetrical is that for co-siblings-in-law (*biras*), which is never normally used in Langkawi.[13] However, in marked contrast to the *bisan* tie, the relation between *biras* is not elaborated in any way in Langkawi. Indeed the only time I actually heard the term used was in direct response to my own questioning. In contrast, the relation between *bisan* appears to be less important elsewhere in the region.[14]

Although affines normally use consanguineal kinship terms to address each other, *bisan* are exceptional in that they may actually address each other using the term *bisan*. They often call each other 'grandparent *bisan*' (*tok bisan*). By using this form of address they draw attention to one of the most important constituents of their relation: their common grandchildren.

Responsibilities towards grandchildren are an important aspect of grandparents' lives, and it is once again significant that many of these are thought of in terms of the link between *bisan* rather than through an adult child to a grandchild. These responsibilities begin with a first pregnancy. In the seventh month of pregnancy the services of the village midwife, *bidan*, are secured by the husband's mother, who is responsible for payment of the midwife. The affiliation of the couple and the unborn child to the home of the wife's mother at this time is balanced by the responsibilities undertaken by the husband's mother from the seventh month of pregnancy onwards.

Villagers refer to the pregnant woman's mother's 'surrender' (*serah*) to the *bidan* at this time.[15] This recalls the surrender of the house to communal officers at the *kenduri*, as well as the role of the *tukang* in marriage. It suggests that birth, like marriage, is deindividualized, and is taken over by the community. Further, the relation is one between the potential grandmother, rather than the mother, and the *bidan*. In other words, the com-

(p. 304). Self-reciprocal terms provide a means of incorporating people without forming exclusive groups.

[13] *Biras* is a reciprocal term of reference applied to the wives of two brothers, the husbands of two sisters, or the husband and wife of a brother and sister. However, Djamour (1965: 29) refers to it being used only for the husbands of two sisters; and Wilder (1982: 89) for a WZH and HBW. As such this term clearly forms a logical pair with that for co-parents-in-law, *bisan*.

[14] In general this relation has received little attention in the literature, which suggests that its significance in Langkawi may be exceptional. H. Geertz (1961: 30); Jay (1969: 149–50); Djamour (1965: 73) all refer to avoidance and formality between *bisan*.

[15] See also Karim (1984) for a mainland Kedah community.

munity takes responsibility for the child not through the parents but through the grandparents. At the births which I witnessed the pregnant woman was not looked after or comforted by her mother, mother-in-law, or other close kin.

As the pregnancy advances, the husband's mother begins to buy articles of clothing and other necessaries for her grandchild. At the time of the birth itself, the *bidan* officiates again; not only does the husband's mother continue to pay for the midwife's services, but she is expected to go to the house of her *bisan* and often stays there for some days.[16]

The obligations performed during pregnancy and at the birth of a child are perceived in terms of the relation between *bisan*. Women say that these duties are a 'responsibility between *bisan*' (*tanggungan antara bisan*). They continue after the birth of a child. The husband's mother pays for the *kenduri* and services of the *bidan* at the ritual first shaving of the child (*cukor anak*) seven days after birth. At these times women speak of going to see their *bisan*, or of sending gifts to *bisan*, and worry about causing offence to them if they do not fulfil such obligations. Thus when Bunga's daughter, Mariah, gave birth to a child, Mariah's mother-in-law, Minah, came to stay in the house. But her presence, and her financial contributions, were always expressed in terms of the *bisan* relation between Bunga and Minah. The link between *bisan* continues to focus on the welfare of their common grandchildren throughout their childhood. Especially during the children's early years, it is important for the female *bisan* to make protracted visits to the home of her counterpart, in which the young couple reside, whenever a grandchild is sick or for any social occasion concerning them.[17] A quarrel between *bisan* is feared precisely because it is perceived as likely to cause the separation of a set of grandchildren; they will be 'split up' (*pecah*).

These obligations, then, do not constitute a balanced set. If, as is normally the case, the couple reside with the wife's parents, the main burden of visiting falls to the husband's mother. She is expected to actively participate in looking after her grandchildren and to contribute her labour during any crisis. Not only are grandparents expected to visit their grandchildren, but the latter must also visit the former at frequent intervals and often stay the night there. Once again, where the children

[16] Wilkinson (1957: 41) states that 'The honour of the first introduction . . . [the *bidan*] gives to the child's grandmothers.' Jayawardena (1977: 28) describes how the husband's mother gives gifts, clothes, and linen for the baby at its birth in Aceh.

[17] H. Geertz (1961: 28) mentions the importance of the husband's mother sending gifts to her grandchildren.

and their parents are normally resident with one set of grandparents it is particularly important that they make visits to the other set. As we have seen, failure to do so is likely to lead to grudges between *bisan*.

Grandparents also frequently bring up one or more of their grandchildren. In fact, they do so more often than any other category of kin apart from parents. This means that in old age couples often do not have to live alone. It has a further significance in that very often couples bring up a grandchild in this way when their *bisan* reside with, or in the same compound as, the young couple and the rest of their children. Once again this can be seen as a way of balancing the affiliation of the couple and their children to the two sets of grandparents.

This became clear to me during the dispute which I described earlier. Bunga and the members of her household (B) faced a conflict between their allegiance to Minah (Bunga's *bisan*) on the one hand, and to the household of a sibling and next-door neighbour (house D) on the other. If they continued to maintain their close relations with their neighbours, they risked offending Minah. This would have very serious consequences. It would put at risk the continued residence of Mariah, Bunga's daughter, and her husband (Minah's son) in Bunga's house, and would even jeopardize Mariah's marriage. It was highly significant that Mariah's husband, Din, was the sole income-earner of the family. Finally, this household had no choice but to completely break off relations with their neighbours: all interaction between houses B and D ceased.

At the same time, and as if to reinforce their allegiance to Minah, the second child of Mariah and Din—Siti—was transferred to Din's parents. At the time, members of both Minah's and Bunga's households told me that this was done because Siti herself wanted to stay at her paternal grandparents' house. In general, when children are fostered adults emphasize the decisive role of the child's own wishes. However, Siti herself did not seem completely happy with the arrangement, and often expressed a wish to go back home. When I returned to the village in 1988, Siti was once again living with her parents, Mariah and Din, and Mariah's parents. I was told that houses B and D had repaired their relations with each other sometime previously, on the occasion of a death in house D. Shortly after this Siti had apparently been fetched back from Minah's by Mariah's father.

Forced to ally themselves with either their close neighbours and kin or the parents of their son-in-law, Bunga and her husband had no choice but to break their relations with the former in order to secure both the livelihood of the whole family and their daughter's marriage. The transfer of a child at a time when all relations had reached a crisis point was an extreme expression of this allegiance. The 'gift of a child' can be seen as the 'supreme gift' to use a term Lévi-Strauss (1969: 65) has adopted in a different context.[18] It is this gift which in the last analysis can correct the imbalance created by affiliation to one grandparental home.[19]

Similarly, it is possible to understand why it is that villagers vigorously deny that either set of grandparents has rights to a grandchild, in a manner which recalls their denial of rules of post-marital residence. I was frequently told that there was no obligation to give a child to any category of kin living without children. Neither grandparents nor any other kin can demand a child. After a divorce children should, ideally, be shared, boys going to their mother and girls to their father. The importance of a child's own wishes in deciding their residence is always emphasized. And this is a way of stating that no one has a prior claim to the child. When asked why a child lived with her grandparents, the invariable answer was because she wanted to: 'she follows her own wishes' (*ikut suka dia*). However, in several cases known to me, it was not absolutely clear that this was the case.

The sharing of common grandchildren is, then, a crucial element in the relation between *bisan*. People in Langkawi often stress the particular closeness of *bisan* and say that it is having grandchildren in common that makes them so. Villagers say that once they have grandchildren, *bisan* become kin. Conversely, if one partner dies before a couple has children and the remaining partner remarries, the '*bisan*ship' of the original couple's parents lapses. This is not the case if there are grandchildren: the *bisan* then maintain their relation. It is not surprising that one of the terms of address *bisan* use, *tok bisan*, emphasizes their role as co-grandparents. It is through shared grandchildren that the relation between *bisan*—a relation of affinity—is actually transformed into one of consanguinity.

This also explains why it is that the birth of a first child is particularly emphasized in rituals of childbirth. For not only does the first child

[18] See also Massard (1983*a*), who emphasizes women's role in these exchanges, which she sees as an alternative to marriage. In this community in Pahang it is girls that are exchanged between women at adoption, and men that circulate at marriage.

[19] Cunningham (1964*a*) describes how the loaning of children to parents among the Atoni reaffirms a fragile tie. I would disagree with Maeda (1975), who sees the frequent bringing up of grandchildren by grandparents among Malays in terms of a dyadic tie between them. See also Barraud (1979: 187–203) on the need to understand adoption in the same context as other exchanges, particularly marriage. In this Moluccan society marriage involves the circulation of women, and adoption the circulation of men. Adoption involves the relation between houses: it assures their continuity when marriage fails to do so.

21. Women preparing leaves for rice cakes (the three older women in the foreground are co-mothers-in-law (*bisan*))

establish the consanguineal principle in a new nuclear family (and couples never establish a new household until they have at least one child). But it is also the first child that actually creates the kinship link between co-grandparents.

However, the stress on '*bisan*ship' must also be seen as a stress on affinity. It is an expression of the kind of relations that should ideally exist between affines. And in this context what is particularly emphasized is the balance and symmetry that should characterize these relations. '*Bisan*ship' embodies these qualities in a way that is not achieved in any other relation of affinity. And its constantly reasserted equality contrasts even more strongly with close consanguineal relations.

Further, the relation between *bisan* is one between the two senior couples in two houses. These couples are the joint heads of the houses they occupy. The many different kinds of exchanges which take place between *bisan* are in essence exchanges between houses. To put it another way, exchanges between houses are thought of as exchanges between *bisan*, and this is clear from the way these exchanges are conducted and described by the participants. In other words, relations between houses are based on an idea of symmetrical exchange occurring between equals.

In the preceding chapter I referred to a named category of marriage—

that between stepchildren—which is known as '*bisan* of one pillow' (*bisan se bantal*). The term refers to a peculiarity of this kind of marriage: the *bisan* are so close as to be married to each other and occupy one house (or bed). Whereas the partners to a marriage normally occupy different houses before marriage and one house afterwards, in this case they already occupy one house before they marry as do their parents. The marriage in some sense fulfils a phantasmagoric ideal of closeness, but it is also premised on a non-ideal—divorce or death must have ended the previous marriage of each partner's parents.

If relations between houses are essentially thought of as relations between *bisan*, grandchildren are often the means by which these links are activated and their frequent focus. Children are often used as messengers between houses. They may carry words, food, gifts, loans, and money. When relations are tense this role becomes particularly important: they interact when adults have difficulty in doing so. In the dispute I have described in this chapter, it was notable that children could move between the various houses when relations between their respective parents had become quite strained. But when relations broke down completely, even very young children were prevented by adults from paying visits. And this partly related to fears of witchcraft. Under these conditions, children ceased to exercise their mediatory role.[20]

Hildred and Clifford Geertz (1964) have discussed how teknonymy in Bali can be seen as part of a 'downward-looking' kinship system in which the stress is on future generations. I discuss the more general regional significance of this insight in the following chapter. In Langkawi, I would argue that the emphasis on the production of children in marriage can equally be seen as an emphasis on the production of shared grandchildren of *bisan*, and this process is itself intimately bound up with the reproduction of the community at large. When Siti was transferred from the house of her maternal grandparents to that of her paternal ones, one could say that she was living out such an image of community. However, the unhappy circumstances which surrounded this transfer make it clear that relations between houses and between *bisan* are often less than ideal, and only maintained at great cost.

In spite of such strains, it is shared grandchildren that in many ways constitute the practical reality of links between houses.[21] And it is not surprising that the term *tok*, 'grandparent', constitutes the most common

[20] See also Cunningham (1964*a*).

[21] See Waterson (1986: 106–7), who also links a close relation between *baisen* among the Toraja to teknonymy and a downward-looking attitude to descent.

prefix for addressing or referring to older members of the community.[22] But the image of a community of shared children moving between houses is realized in other ways too, most notably in more general transfers of children.

Fostering

The fostering of children covers a number of different arrangements, which villagers do not always distinguish from each other. I have discussed these arrangements in an earlier article (Carsten 1991), which I draw on here. The simultaneous possibility of making or erasing distinctions between children who are genealogically related, and different kinds of foster children, recalls the way affinal relatives can be both conflated with, and distinguished from, consanguineal ones.[23] Such distinctions are sometimes made, but they are often blurred or ignored.

A foster child (*anak angkat*)[24] may have lived from birth to the age of 17 with her foster parents, or have spent a few years with them; the term may cover a university student who stays with a family for two weeks, or (as I myself experienced) an anthropologist who arrives for two years. Nor do different terms exist to distinguish a foster child who has no rights of inheritance from his or her foster parents from one who has been formally adopted.[25] Ideally, there is a sense in which different kinds of foster children should not be distinguished from each other; likewise, there is a strong idea that an *anak angkat* should not be distinguished from a child who is genealogically related although, in fact, such distinctions can be significant.

The majority of children live with their parents from birth until they

[22] It can be used with a name or a title: e.g. the imam may be referred to as *Tok Imam*.

[23] Earlier (Carsten 1991), I used the term 'conception-parents' for the parents responsible for the conception of a child, and the term 'conception-child' for the child produced by the parents' act of conception. This was to avoid any imputations of our own notions of folk biology in terms such as 'biological parents' or 'genealogical relatedness'. While I have not used the same terms here, I would still emphasize the necessity of suspending our own notions of what constitutes 'biological relatedness' when interpreting the present material.

[24] The term literally means 'raised' or 'lifted' child in the sense of having been taken up and put down elsewhere; see McKinley (1975: 61). He translates this as 'transferred child' to convey the broad scope of the Malay term.

[25] Formal adoption (involving legal proceedings, and the acquisition of inheritance rights) is prohibited in Islam, and is very rare among Malays. Djamour (1965: 31, 34–5) notes the same lack of distinction made among Malays in Singapore. See also McKinley (1975: 62–3), who links the ambiguity of terms to the conditionality and tentative quality of all forms of parent–child ties in Malay culture—in contrast to the categorical nature of siblingship.

have completed their education. Many continue to reside in the parental home until after they have married. At the time of my fieldwork, out of a total of 143 children and young people under the age of 23 who were still unmarried, 111 (77.6 per cent) were living with both parents; 32 children (22.4 per cent) were not living with both their birth parents.

It is possible, for analytic purposes, to divide children not living with both their birth parents into two categories: first, those living with a divorced or widowed parent. There were 15 such children in the village (10.5 per cent of the total 143). In 7 of these cases (the children of 3 sets of parents) the parent they were living with had subsequently remarried. The second category is those children being brought up by neither of their birth parents. There were 17 children (11.9 per cent of the total) in this category.[26]

In this second category villagers themselves often make a further distinction between fostering a child and bringing up the child of a close relative. Not infrequently, children reside more or less permanently in the house of a close relative. Such residence varies in duration: it may endure for most of a childhood, for a few months, or for some years; it may begin when the child is a baby or when he or she is already an adolescent. It may or may not involve visits of varying duration and frequency to the parental household. When a couple bring up their grandchild, or a younger sibling, they usually do not refer to the child as a foster child (*anak angkat*) but say they are 'caring for', or 'bringing up' (*bela*) the child, and specify the kin relation involved. In these cases the child uses appropriate kin terms for these relatives, whereas an *anak angkat* always uses parental terms of address and reference for her foster parents.

In fact, an *anak angkat* is not necessarily unrelated to her foster parents although the connection in these cases tends to be rather distant. In the great majority of cases, if there is a distant kin connection it is through the foster mother.

The considerable blurring between these categories is expressed emotionally. Indeed, a distant or non-existent genetic link may be 'compensated' by a strong affective one. It is considered normal for a transferred child to love those who bring it up more than its genetic parents. Such children are also considered the obvious favourites of their adoptive parents. This was often pointed out to me by friends in the village when we

[26] See Goody's distinction between 'crisis' and 'voluntary' fostering (1982: 23). Rosemary Firth (1966: 105) has given the following statistics for Kelantan, which are surprisingly similar to those for Pulau Langkawi: 25 per cent not living with both parents; 11 per cent living with adults other than parents; 14 per cent living with a divorced or widowed parent.

were talking about the warm and affectionate relation between my foster mother and myself. But it is not only affection that is acquired through living together. Children transferred from a young age are presumed to take on the physical attributes of their adoptive parents, coming to look like them in the same way as children one has given birth to. They also acquire the character traits of the people who bring them up. Once again, changes to my own physical appearance while I lived in the village were always viewed in these terms, and were a great source of interest and approval.

The causes which precipitate fostering by distant kin or non-relatives are almost always the death of one or both parents or their divorce. From the point of view of the foster parents, bringing up another person's child confers merit and prestige. Those to whom children are given in this way are, by definition, 'good people' (*orang baik*). One woman, Yah, would sometimes tell me about several foster children she had cared for in the past, as a way of telling me how trusted and well regarded she was by her fellow villagers. Fostering is also a way of avoiding divorce when a marriage is infertile. An old couple I knew, Man and Tih, had both brought up the child of the wife's sister, and that of a non-relative, but had never conceived children themselves. The husband, Man, had had a previous childless marriage which ended in divorce. Fostering can also correct an imbalance in the sex ratio of children in accordance with the ideal of having roughly equal numbers of boys and girls in the house.

In the case of divorce or the death of one parent, a child may be brought up by the other parent, but the father never has sole care of the child. He can only continue to look after his children if he lives with at least one female relative or if he remarries. By contrast, widowed or divorced women sometimes bring up their children alone, although this is financially difficult. There is a general reluctance to put children under the care of a stepmother, who is regarded as potentially malevolent.

The categories of kin that most frequently bring up children are, in order of preference, grandparents, older sisters, and sisters of either the mother or father of the child. Roughly equal numbers of female and male children are brought up by their close kin.[27] Although children are often cared for by grandparents, older sisters, or aunts and uncles, villagers

[27] This fact accords with villagers' oft-repeated assertion that they value male and female children equally. Nevertheless, there is a slight imbalance in favour of girls, which is more pronounced in the case of grandchildren being raised by their grandparents. The imbalance is even more marked in Massard's material. She stresses (1983*a*: 104, 111) how fostering involves the transfer of female children between women.

always emphatically deny that these kin have absolute rights to a child even if they are childless. Nevertheless, the grandparents on either side, and a mother's sister, are regarded as having particularly strong claims to a child if they themselves have no young children. Grandmothers and the mother's sister are thought likely to be particularly affectionate to the child, and thus be suitable for this role.

The reasons for a child being cared for by close kin are often practical, as when a couple have a large number of children or when they are so close in age that their mother is overburdened with work. This is particularly likely if these kin have no young children of their own. In such cases, when a baby is born it is generally an older sibling who goes to the home of relatives. However, villagers say they are embarrassed, ashamed (*malu*) to give a child away, that they should have an excuse for doing so. If a child is given to close relatives the shame involved is obviated.

It is always clear that children are much wanted and loved, and that one only gives a child away with great reluctance. It is equally true that those people who have no children in the house miss having them, and would always like to foster. In general, villagers speak in terms of the voluntary and emotional aspects of fostering rather than rights or duties. The desire of parents to keep their own children takes priority over the claims of other relatives. It is only once a couple have three or four children that the desire of one partner's parents for a grandchild to live with them, or of a married sister who is childless, would be taken seriously into account.

Villagers do not formally acknowledge that either the husband's or the wife's kin have prior rights, but ties through women are regarded as being emotionally stronger and closer. Thus after grandparents, it is the child's mother's sister that people most frequently say they would be most happy to give a child to.[28] This, as McKinley (1975; 1981) has forcefully argued, can be seen as reflecting the emphasis on closeness between siblings—in Langkawi this is especially true between sisters. The distinction villagers make between looking after the children of close relatives, and fostering

[28] H. Geertz (1961: 40–1) cites a preference for giving a child to a female relative and especially the parents' siblings, particularly the mother's sister. Djamour (1965: 93) observes that grandparents frequently bring up children. Jay (1969: 72) states that in Java siblings have rights to a person's children. In Negeri Sembilan, Swift reports that women have rights to their sister's children (1965: 12), and Peletz (1988: 230) also emphasizes ties between sisters in adoption. McKinley (1975: 103–6) shows how transfers of children between siblings are the most frequent, followed by those transferred to their grandparents. Massard (1983*a*: 103) states that children are most frequently fostered by their mother's sister. Throughout this area, then, the rights of grandparents and of the mother's sister to children seem to be particularly strong.

non-relatives or distant kin, is a way of stressing the enormous importance of siblings and grandparents—the categories of close kin who usually care for a child in this way.

The emotional closeness which derives from ties through women, and which is expressed by women's residence in their maternal household when they give birth to their first child, is thus further emphasized in fostering arrangements. A child's emotional tie to its foster mother is expressed in co-residence. And people always talk about the reasons for a child living with foster parents in terms of the affection between the child and her foster mother. If, as I have suggested, the co-substantiality of kinship is largely created through shared consumption, then women play a decisive role in this creative process through cooking and feeding.

We saw in Chapter 4 how the acquisition of substance after conception begins with feeding in the uterus, as the child acquires blood from its mother. The process continues with the provision of breast milk and cooked food, but these may not be acquired from the birth mother. In constituting themselves as foster kin who, ideally, are undifferentiated from the genealogical kin, women actually create kinship. They provide the locus for this shared consumption to take place as well as furnishing its material and emotional content.[29]

The residence of children is often talked about by villagers in terms reminiscent of post-marital residence. Often, when children were living with their grandparents I was told that their residence was 'not fixed', or certain (*tak tentu*), and that the child was alternating between the parental home and that of the grandparents. This alternation is described using the same term, *berulang*, as that used for the alternation between the two parental homes in the first phase of married life. And people always talk about where a child lives in terms of the child's own emotions and desires. I was frequently told that there was no reason for a child to be living with grandparents, she or he simply preferred to do so, or was 'following her own wishes' (*ikut suka dia*).

Following the individual wishes of a child is, of course, another way of stressing the uncertainty of residence, since such desires are seen as intrinsically unpredictable. In this way the voluntary and contingent as-

[29] McKinley (1975: 62, 180) reports how transferred children say that their adoptive parents are their real parents because these were the ones to feed them. It might be suggested that in view of women's crucial role in the creation of kinship, Langkawi kinship could be labelled 'matrifocal', as, for example, Hildred Geertz (1961) has proposed for Java. While fully acknowledging the importance of women's creative role in constituting relations, I hesitate to use this term, which seems misleading in view of the enormous significance of siblingship.

pects of a child's residence are emphasized. However, we saw earlier how the amount of attention paid to the wishes of a child may be greater in theory than in practice. Siti's transfer to her paternal grandparents' house was a response not to her desire to move, but to a need to reaffirm relations between her two sets of grandparents. And this relates to the crucial role which I have already described children playing as mediators between affines, particularly as the shared grandchildren of *bisan*. The gift of a child to one spouse's parents provides a means of balancing the duties performed to the parents of the other spouse.

Two Models of Community

In this chapter I have described villagers' ideas about affinal relations and their practical expression. The dispute I described made clear how affinal relations are supposed to conform to an ideal of symmetry and equality, but how these ideals lead to strains and difficulties in everyday life. The divorce between Putih and Omar was not simply an expression of their own incompatibility. It revealed other tensions between affines in different houses. And these tensions are inherent in local notions of affinity.

On one level 'affinity' appears to be accorded an explicit existence, and can be opposed to ideas about consanguinity. This is expressed in a number of ways, most strongly in the relations between *bisan*, which are based on symmetry, exchange, and equality, while those of consanguinity are based on hierarchy and unity. The household and affinal relations seem in many ways to be opposed to each other.

But, on another level, affinity appears to merge with consanguinity and, paradoxically enough, this too is captured by the relation between *bisan*, in particular by the emphasis on their common grandchildren. If links between houses in the community are on the one hand conceived as links between *bisan* (mediated by their shared grandchildren) they are at the same time seen as links between siblings, as was described in Chapters 2 and 3.

It is clear that children capture a central ambivalence in notions of kinship. They embody both the close consanguineal unity of the house and the exchange relations between houses, relations which often seem to be disruptive of, and opposed to, the unity of the household. Both marital relations and the commercial ties of fishing are highly unstable and are thought liable to cause disputes between close kin.

We can begin to see that it is possible to draw out two models of community in Langkawi, and these appear to be opposed to one another. In sketching out these models I would stress that they constitute polar images, neither of which can ever be wholly satisfactory because each implies a rigidity and fixity that is in fact absent. It is always possible to move between the two and to transform one into the other, and this possibility is an essential part of the creative dynamic of the kinship I have described.

The first model is based on the house and on siblingship. Persons united through these ties should ideally hold property in common; they are conceived as an undivided group who share consumption. During the course of the domestic developmental cycle new houses are established as the siblings, having grown up and married, have children. Frequently, these houses are on the same compound land as either the husband's or the wife's parents. Eventually, neighbouring houses of one compound come to be occupied by adult siblings, or by the descendants of a sibling group. To a considerable degree compound members share resources, particularly land. As compounds themselves expand they are subdivided, and new ones are formed in the vicinity. Neighbourhoods come into existence in which houses are connected to each other through ties that can be traced back to siblingship. The village community is formed through the process of house expansion.

This continuity between the house and the community is expressed in the term *kampung*, which can refer to a compound, a small hamlet, or a large administrative and religious unit consisting of several small hamlets. The compound itself may have one house or ten houses built on it. In other words, the house and the wider community are linked through the term *kampung*: the latter, at least in some contexts, is conceived as the former writ large.

Similarly, the community is conceived as being united through ties of siblingship. Sibling terms, or derivatives of these, constitute some of the most common forms of address and reference for co-villagers. When two people are asked to trace out a kin connection, however distant, they always begin or end at a point where two ascendants can be named as siblings. When villagers emphasize their connectedness to each other in a general way they say, 'We are all kin here, there are no strangers' (*kita semua adik-beradik disini, orang lain tak ada*). The term for kin (*adik-beradik*) is itself derived from that for younger sibling (*adik*).

The notion of the community as an expanded house is expressed at communal feasts at which the most powerful domestic symbolism is used to evoke a sense of community. Such feasts involve members of the community consuming one extravagant meal together. Yet at the same time, as I have already shown, such feasts constitute in another way a direct negation of the house. Domestic ties are denied, domestic rules of cooking and eating are inverted.

This ambivalence can be related to the second image of the community: that which is based on exchange. Houses engage in a series of reciprocal and equal exchanges of visits, gifts, and labour with each other. The commercial transactions of the fishing economy and the tense equality of marital exchanges are explicitly seen as potentially threatening to domestic harmony and unity—particularly among siblings.

Inasmuch as houses represent sibling groups which share resources and consume together, with different houses eventually coming to contain different members of sibling sets, they also represent *bisan* exchanging on an equal basis. If siblings share consumption to a degree that renders marriage between them incestuous, *bisan* are those who, by definition, exchange sons and daughters in marriage. Both *bisan* and sibling sets are intimately linked to the conceptualization of the house. How can this tension be resolved? In the following section I suggest that it is children who provide a solution to this problem.

Children as Agents of Transformation

In Langkawi notions of relatedness are founded on shared consumption in one house. Siblings share consumption more fully than all other categories of kin. They are normally brought up in the same house and share food from birth on. It is feeding that creates blood, and human milk is seen as a form of blood. The prime category of incest is between those who have drunk milk of the same mother, in other words siblings. Siblings are thought to share consumption to a degree which would negate the exchange that is marriage, and to a greater degree than all other categories of kin.

I described in Chapter 3 how children, in so far as they are part of a sibling set, embody houses, and are anchored to them. It is now clear that this association is so strong as to overcome the fact that children may not genetically belong to such a set, just as it may overcome the actual division of a sibling group into different houses. Residence and co-consumption in a house can confer membership in the sibling group associated with that house, even for a child who is fostered there.

Children also mediate between houses. They seem almost to embody exchange as they take words, gifts, and money from house to house. And this role is most fully captured when they themselves take up residence in another house through the various forms of fostering that occur in Langkawi.

The different aspects of fostering reflect children's capacity to participate in the two images of community which I have outlined. In so far as they are brought up by their older siblings, or by parents' siblings, they may be seen as demonstrating the unity of the sibling group and the extensive sharing that occurs within it, as McKinley has argued. They are living out the notion of the village community as an expanded house. But, when they move to the houses of distantly related or unrelated co-villagers, they are involving themselves intimately in the exchanges that occur between different houses of the community.

This idea is also present when they reside with their grandparents, as they frequently do. Residence with grandparents, as we have seen, reflects, and may compensate for, the imbalance caused by post-marital residence in the context of an ideological stress on marriage between equals. In this light it must be considered as an aspect of marital exchange itself. It is also clear, however, that the birth of grandchildren signals the formation of new sets of siblings and the establishment of new houses. Sets of grandchildren represent both undivided domestic consanguinity *and* affinal links between houses. In fact their birth transforms the latter into the former: once *bisan* have common grandchildren they are, in local conceptions, united by a consanguineal tie.[30]

This, then, is at the heart of the ambivalence which children embody. It is because they themselves have a dual aspect—representing the point of transformation of two opposed images—that they can perform in their daily lives a constant mediation between these images. As products of their parents, children divide houses from each other, and emphasize their exclusivity. Through the mobility of their parents, the possibility of fostering, and as products of their grandparents, they unite different houses.

If grandchildren can take up residence in the house of either set of grandparents then it follows that these two houses can actually come to contain siblings. The circle is completed as two houses are linked by both an affinal tie and one of siblingship. The fostering of children can utilize pre-existing ties of siblingship and reinforce them; it can also actually create such ties.

[30] Errington (1989: 254) uses the term 'apical children' for those who link previously unrelated affines. She notes how a child's birth implies a reconfiguration of the border between kin and non-kin.

The movement of children can always be interpreted in a number of different ways, from sharing to exchange. In fact, the movement of children blurs the distinction between sharing and exchange in that it may be interpreted either as exchange between discrete units or as sharing within an expanded unit. Sharing, in that from one point of view it breaks down the boundaries between houses and is constitutive of the image of community as an enlarged house; exchange in that, from another point of view, it is part of a series of reciprocities between discrete and bounded household units. And in the last analysis it is this ambiguity which lends it force.

The ambiguity surrounding children's movement can now be linked to the considerable blurring between different fostering arrangements which I described above. Distinctions may be made at one level only to be elided at another, just as affines may be distinguished from consanguines only to merge with them at another level. It is this ambiguity which potentially allows the rapid absorption of newcomers to the village through their transformation into affines and foster kin (as in the case of Omar), and eventually, the transformation of these categories into consanguines.

Children have this capacity to both unite and divide houses to a particularly heightened degree because they are not yet fully formed. It is their 'unformedness' or 'incompleteness' which lends them their ability to move, seemingly unaffected, between houses. This unformedness might be considered to some extent an inherent quality of childhood. Physically, children as they grow are acquiring substance and form more obviously than adults. Young children, in particular, are not considered to be fully in control of their desires. If two children quarrel it is always the youngest who is favoured when elders settle the dispute. The younger child is thought to be less capable of understanding particular rights and wrongs through rational consideration.

The incompleteness of children can be related to the fact that they have not yet married or had sex.[31] They have not directly participated in, or incorporated, the division which affinity introduces into the unity of the sibling group. In this sense we can understand why it is that they have the capacity to involve themselves in exchange without being affected by it, why the actual separation of young siblings does not appear to raise major problems. Because their association with their own sibling group has been untainted by the divisive dangers of affinity, it is strong enough to

[31] Ariès (1962: 103–4) has discussed how children were in some sense immune to sexuality in 16th-cent. Europe. It is clear that the association he makes between children and irrationalism (1962: 116), and which he sees as belonging to 20th-cent. Western history, may occur in other contexts.

overcome partition. In this respect we may recall children's 'non-individuality', which I discussed in an earlier chapter: conceptually, they are not fully separated from other members of their sibling group; practically, they are ideally placed to be thus separated and to involve themselves in both sharing and exchange between houses.

It is having children that confers adult status; conversely, childlessness is the mark of childhood. Incomplete themselves, children, who constitute one half of a house, have the capacity to complete the other half—the married couple without children. Likewise, children must eventually be themselves completed by marrying and having children. The child becomes a completed adult through having children and then grandchildren. Children's substance is not given ready-made at birth. Rather, both their substance and their sociality can complete, but must also be completed by, that of others.[32]

In Langkawi the stress on the production of children in marriage can equally be seen as a stress on the production of shared grandchildren of *bisan*, and this process is itself intimately bound up with the reproduction and expansion of the community at large. It is through the production of children and grandchildren that consanguineal ties are created from affinal ones, and new sibling groups come into being which will in the future intermarry. In this way, links between households are reproduced through grandchildren. The community is envisaged as one of shared grandchildren. This image, which we saw projected at communal feasts, is realized in the widespread sharing and exchange of children that occurs in fostering. Grandchildren resolve the opposition between siblingship and marriage, between sharing and exchange, and between unity and division. They constitute the practical reality and the full complexity of links between houses. Their growth and their movement embody the process that is kinship.

This processual aspect of kinship is one I wish to stress. The two images of community which I have described negate each other if we see them as still photographs coexisting in time. As moving pictures in a sequence they do not. The assimilation of affines into consanguineal kin is a continuously ongoing process. Potential marriage partners, who may be consanguineally related, become betrothed and so constitute themselves as affines. The ritual avoidance that they and their parents undergo during the marriage proceedings asserts their difference from consanguineal kin.

[32] I am indebted to Marilyn Strathern for suggesting the ideas expressed in this paragraph.

But the rituals also begin a long process by which these same affines are incorporated into the hearths and houses of their spouse. Finally, when children and grandchildren have been produced at these hearths, consanguinity has been produced from affinity, and different blood has been made the same.

9

Coercive Incorporation: The Historical Construction of Community

This chapter may be read as an experiment in scale. The analysis shifts away from the contemporary reproduction of the house and community in Langkawi to their historical construction. I begin by recapitulating some of the themes already encountered, linking the reproduction of individual houses to the reproduction of the community at large.

The second section evokes a different time-frame. It summarizes some aspects of the historical forces affecting Kedah and Langkawi and suggests how these might have impinged on the lives of rural people. In the third section this history is linked to the experiences and memories of present-day villagers. Warfare, land shortages, and poverty in the region have meant that the village population has been extremely mobile during the nineteenth and twentieth centuries. I argue that the symbolic and practical features of kinship described in earlier chapters gain another level of significance when placed in this historical context. These features of kinship have allowed villagers in Langkawi to make their homes and their communities, to assert control over their own lives, in the face of powerful external constraints.

In the fourth section I link the way people in Sungai Cantik remember their past to contemporary features of kinship. I suggest that population mobility coupled with an emphasis on siblingship may provide some clues to the broader understanding of bilateral kinship in Southeast Asia.

In the final section I show how the individual experience of the anthropologist can be analysed in the same way as the lives of the people she studies. It can be examined in an anthropological spirit rather than a self-analytic one. I argue that my own experiences constitute a condensed form of the historical processes at work in the wider society.

The process of kinship that I have described so far is one that has meaning for individual persons, for couples, and for families. The good life involves marrying, having children, seeing them marry and have children in turn, and thus becoming a respected grandparent. So, at the end of life, one does not merely look back on one's achievements, but since these are always being projected forward in time, one also looks forward at what is being produced and what will be produced in the future.

But, as I have emphasized, these are not simply images of domestic reproduction. The same processes are at the heart of the creation and reproduction of the village community in Langkawi. This community is one which sees itself as made up of kin, people who are all alike. It is one in which there is a continuum of relatedness from the close to the distant which operates in an idiom of siblingship. Strangers, affines, distant kin, spouses, siblings are different points along this continuum. In principle, those who are strangers, affines, and distant kin now, can be transformed into spouses and siblings in the future. The process at this level too is one which negates difference and produces similarity. And the symbolic site of the transformation of difference into similarity is the house, the energy for it provided by the hearth. As Aisyah impressed upon me in the conversation I recounted in Chapter 1, the reproduction of the community is premised upon that of the domestic hearth. Shared grandchildren encapsulate both sides of the duality between house and community. They are at once the embodiment of domestic reproduction and of a more diffuse process of creating kinship in the wider community.

Although I have emphasized the processual aspects of these notions of kinship, so far the time-frame has been a contemporary one. The image of reproduction I have described is orientated to the future—as it is for people in Langkawi. However, from the point of view of the analysis of kinship I would argue that the significance of these ideas emerges in the context of a specific history.

Langkawi in Regional History

In Southeast Asia the traditional state (*negeri*) was defined by its centre not by its boundaries (Anderson 1990; Tambiah 1976; C. Geertz 1980; Wolters 1982; Errington 1989).[1] Gullick (1983: 56) has described how the boundaries of mid-nineteenth-century Kedah were not clearly defined; the state was made up of a central core zone and an imprecise outer zone. Indeed, the ruler might not even know where the boundaries of the state were (Gullick 1987: 28). Power was concentrated at the centre of the *negeri*; at the outer margins the power of a ruler faded imperceptibly away

[1] Parts of the following argument appear in Carsten (1995*c*).

and merged with that of a neighbouring sovereign. The geographic extent of the kingdom was always in flux (Anderson 1990: 41). In fact, the power of a ruler was revealed not so much by the extent of his kingdom, but in the number of people he controlled. High status implied a large following (Gullick 1987: 48). Victorious rulers might augment their power during periods of dynastic conflict by moving large numbers of people to the centre (Anderson 1990: 43). Thus the sociology of power hinged on ties of fealty between persons, not on the unambiguous mapping out of space.[2]

Those who lived at the periphery of the kingdom were least subject to the control of the sovereign. This is very clear in the case of the hill tribes, whether they were swidden cultivators or hunters and gatherers. The history of groups like the Kachin of highland Burma (Leach 1954) or the Buid of Mindoro (Gibson 1986) is one of continual attempts to avoid domination by the lowland states. To a lesser extent the same processes seem to have characterized relations between rulers and their peasant subjects in the lowlands.[3]

Adas (1981) has discussed the tendency of peasant tenants or labourers in pre-colonial and colonial Southeast Asia to transfer their allegiance to alternative rulers, or simply to move further from the centre, when the burdens of taxation and corvée labour became too great (see also Tambiah 1976: 120–3). Focusing on Burma and Java, Adas characterizes these wholesale migrations as a form of 'avoidance protest' (1981: 217). He stresses the importance of low population density and the existence of refuge zones of unoccupied lands (1981: 219). Adas describes how peasant rebellions in Java and Burma increased when colonial powers imposed the bureaucratic measures associated with a modern nation state. These included the replacement of permeable border zones by fixed frontiers, and consequent restrictions on peasant mobility. Kratoska (1985) and Gullick (1987: 100–9) have argued that peasants in late nineteenth-century Malaya were not particularly attached to their land and frequently abandoned it if they could move elsewhere, and if their livelihood was uncertain (see also Karim 1992: 75–6, 85).

In a context where power was measured by control over people rather

[2] Karim (1992: 82) discusses how British rule in Malaya institutionalized the boundaries of the state as well as those of the districts (*daerah*) into which states were divided. Eventually the boundaries of villages, which had been undefined because of competition between village chiefs (*penghulu*), were also formalized under the British.

[3] Atkinson (1989: 258); Errington (1989: 29–30); and Wolters (1982), amongst others, have cogently argued that the hill tribes and the Indic states of Southeast Asia have, historically, been politically integrated and should not be considered in isolation from each other.

than land, where administrative structures were weak, where population densities were low, and land on the periphery readily available, it seems that the ability of peasant cultivators to simply move to pioneer areas on the periphery exerted a serious limit to the control of rulers.

Many of these factors characterized late nineteenth-century Kedah, the Malay state on the fringe of which Langkawi is situated. As Sharom Ahmat (1970*a*; 1970*b*) has shown, at this time the economy of Kedah was essentially based on rice cultivation. The power of the sultan depended on control of economic resources through taxation. But Sharom has emphasized how, in contrast to other Malay states, the political and economic structure in Kedah was highly centralized. The limited resources and small population of Kedah meant that an elaborate administrative apparatus was unnecessary; members of the royal family held most of the important political posts.

Sharom argues that these factors encouraged political stability in Kedah at this time (see also Gullick 1983: 69). The revenue of the state depended on the ability of the *raayat* ('the masses') to cultivate rice without major upheaval. Kedah's rice was largely exported to Penang, which was dependent on it for its food supply. It was thus in British interests too to maintain political stability. Sharom's argument is particularly relevant, because a point which emerges clearly from it is the importance to the state of rice cultivation proceeding without disruption:

> Both the sultan and other members of the ruling class were aware that their interests dictated that the masses should not be exploited, for in such an event they could either adopt a policy of non-cooperation or in the last resort, migrate. (1970*b*: 121)

A British administrator's contemporary comments make this point even more forcefully:

> In a Malay state, the exaction of personal service from the rai'yat is limited only by the powers of endurance of the latter. The superior authority is obliged, from self-interest, to stop short of the point at which oppression will compel the cultivator to abandon his land and emigrate. (Maxwell 1884: 104)[4]

Sharom emphasizes the efforts made to minimize this exploitation and shows that where local leaders (*penghulu*) were the subject of complaints from peasants to the sultan for their corruption or excessive use of forced labour, they might well be replaced (Sharom 1970*b*: 121).

[4] See also Gullick (1987: 107) on the complaints of British administrators at the end of the 19th cent. about 'people wandering from place to place'.

Although it appears that during this period there was minimal migration, the seriousness with which this problem was taken by the sultan demonstrates very clearly the strength of the threat and its disruptive potential.[5] In spite of Sharom's description of the 'stable demographic pattern in Kedah' (1970*b*: 122) at this time, it seems that this pattern was not wholly consistent. He cites two cases of groups of villagers migrating in the 1880s causing 'considerable alarm among the ruling classes' (1970*b*: 121). These resulted in the administration taking measures to prevent the recurrence of such movement.[6]

Discussing the same themes, Banks (1983: 9–44) has emphasized that Malaya can be seen as a 'frontier society'. He suggests that nineteenth-century Kedah was characterized by two styles of life. One, on the plain, near to the royal court, was highly stratified. Peasants were subject to heavy demands of forced labour, military service, and taxation. This, together with the fragmentation of landholdings, led to migration to the fringes of this society. The isolated areas to which these peasants migrated were characterized by relative freedom from the exactions of the sultans, lower agricultural yields, less marked wealth differentials, and a more egalitarian social order. In these distant areas of refuge, however, they 'had to put up with lawlessness and periodic oppression by outlaw bands' (Banks 1983: 19).[7] Banks's discussion refers to Sik, a hill district of northern Kedah. But this characterization might also apply to Langkawi, which in 1850 was characterized by a British observer as 'inhabited by a race of Malays, who are, in general, thieves, and commit frequent acts of piracy' (Topping 1850: 42).

This historical outline suggests that in the nineteenth century economic and political upheaval on the mainland, as well as a shortage of land and the demands of labour and taxation, had a profound effect on the local population, and that migration may have been the best means of avoiding

[5] It was for this reason that the sultan relaxed the obligations of the *raayat* to perform forced labour (*kerah*) (Sharom 1970*b*: 121). However, Gullick (1983: 66) links a heavy *kerah* burden in mid-19th-cent. Kedah to the low population. See also Gullick (1985: 116; 1987: 98–100, 111–12).

[6] One case involved a group of 60 families who intended to migrate to the Dindings in Perak, and the other a group of peasants from Yen who moved to a neighbouring district. See Scott (1985: 245–6) for a discussion of flight as a means of resisting oppression on mainland Kedah. Syed Hussein Alatas (1968: 584–5) has described how this means of avoidance rather than defiance conformed with peasant values.

[7] See Cheah Boon Kheng (1981: 112) for a description of the 'endemic' banditry and outlawry in the northern border areas of Kedah at the end of the 19th cent. Gullick (1985: 117) describes disorder and gang raids on the border between Kedah and Province Wellesley.

their full impact. The experiences and memories of villagers in Langkawi which I describe in the next section bear out this hypothesis.

I also suggest that Langkawi must be considered in the regional context of Southeast Asian maritime kingdoms. In this region a history of trade and the movement of people have been associated for thousands of years (see Coedès 1968; Wolters 1982; Reid 1988). It is notable that Kedah was an important trading centre in the pre-colonial era, and the history of the state can be read as a continuing interplay between attempts by rival external powers to wrest control over trade from Kedah's indigenous rulers, and the latter's struggle to maintain their political and economic independence (see Bonney 1971). Kedah's border location, its role as an entrepôt for land routes to other areas of the peninsula, and the mobility of people and commodities were all highly significant in shaping the history of the colonial and pre-colonial state. Langkawi was by no means marginal to this trading history. For example, in the seventeenth century Langkawi, then known as 'Pulau Lada' (Pepper Island), was a major centre of pepper cultivation for export.[8]

So far, I have focused on the historical conditions which made population mobility a significant aspect of social life in the Southeast Asian *negeri*. It is also clear that this mobility persists today in the rather different conditions of the modern nation state. In so far as this mobility is confined within the borders of the Malaysian state, it raises no particular bureaucratic problems. Indeed, from the Malaysian government's point of view it is to be encouraged since it lends a considerable flexibility to employment patterns which is highly advantageous in the context of rapid economic development. However, where migration is transnational the situation is somewhat different.

Many of the villagers I know have kin in southern Thailand. Life histories which I collected indicate that this has been an important area for migration to Langkawi. As economic conditions in Malaysia become significantly better than in Thailand for peasants and fishermen, controls over the flow of people crossing the Malaysian–Thai border have been imposed more stringently. However, villagers' perceptions and practices with regard to the movement of people and merchandise indicate that they still regard southern Thailand as very much part of their social world. It is common for villagers to visit their kin on the other side of the border, particularly to attend marriages and funerals. Kinship ties across the

[8] By 1850 pepper was no longer an important export commodity (see Bonney 1971: 6; Sharom 1970*b*: 124) and was not grown in Langkawi (Hill 1977: 50).

border are constantly re-established. In the early 1980s it was not considered unusual for marriage or fostering to result in a young person from southern Thailand coming to live in Langkawi. But villagers were of course aware of the bureaucratic complications that might ensue.

A Village of Migrants

What traces has the regional history which I have outlined left in the lives and relationships of people in the village of Sungai Cantik? I begin with paradox. It is central to my argument that kinship in Langkawi is focused on the future rather than the past and is encapsulated in the process of producing grandchildren. In such a context memory has a peculiar significance. During the period between December 1988 and March 1989 when I conducted research on the history of migration in Sungai Cantik, I was again and again struck by the different attitudes which villagers of Sungai Cantik held to present relations compared to past ones. It is not simply that the villagers I talked to are not greatly interested in their origins, although that is certainly the case. Some villagers had great difficulty remembering where their parents had been born, let alone their grandparents. Very few people knew or cared much about the place of origin of their neighbours or fellow villagers. This, however, did not mean that they were incapable of, or uninterested in, tracing out quite distant relationships between living people. Relationships between second or third cousins can be explained with considerable enthusiasm. But these relations are reckoned 'horizontally', in terms of siblingship, rather than 'vertically', in terms of descent. The point about such relations is that they exist in the present and they have a future. If the kin involved live fairly close to one another, then they or their children may well intermarry and thus be brought closer in the future.

Inquiring into distant kin connections is a different matter from asking about people's locality of origin. In Sungai Cantik such origins have little relevance to anything else. They are quite simply not a point of reference. People who originate from other parts of the Malay peninsula or elsewhere in the region do not live in distinct parts of the village or form endogamous groups.[9] They are not recognizable by costume, deportment, accent, cuisine, or the styles of houses they live in. I was quite willing to

[9] This account does not of course apply to the Chinese, amongst whom I did not conduct research.

believe that, as a foreigner, I might be blind to such details, but if so, the Malaysian history students who assisted me on this project were equally so. And indeed they expressed considerable surprise at the information they collected.[10]

In 1988–9 I collected detailed information on migration histories in Sungai Cantik. The figures I obtained only offer the most approximate guide to the actual *rates* of migration; what they do convey is a clear indication of the importance of migration as a general fact in the lives of villagers of Sungai Cantik. I had many informal conversations with older people about their early memories of Langkawi and about their family histories. In order to get a broader picture of the extent of migration and of the region involved I then carried out a household survey with the help of three research assistants. Information was collected from all married couples, widowed, or divorced people living in 110 houses distributed in four different hamlets of the village. These 260 interviewees were asked for their own place of birth, the names and birthplaces of their parents, and those of their grandparents. They were asked whether they had any ancestor apart from these who came from outside Langkawi, and if they knew of any immediate neighbours who came from elsewhere. Where informants or their ancestors had come from elsewhere they were asked for additional information about their reasons for migrating and the circumstances involved.

About one-fifth of the 260 adults interviewed (23 men and 25 women) were born outside Langkawi. 25 of these originate from the mainland state of Kedah, 7 from southern Thailand, the rest from other mainland states including Perak (5), Penang (4), Pahang (2), Perlis (2), Johor (1), Negeri Sembilan (1), Terengganu (1).

Almost all of those interviewed could recall the place of birth of both their parents. Of the 212 who were born in Langkawi, 48 (nearly a quarter) had either one or both parents who originated from elsewhere. 31 fathers and 28 mothers were born outside the island. In 11 of these cases *both* parents came from outside the island. These people mainly came from nearby areas on the mainland: many from Kedah, significant numbers from Pulau Pinang, southern Thailand, Perlis, and Perak. A few came from areas of the peninsula still further away: Johor, Terengganu, Negeri Sembilan. Others came from Aceh, Minangkabau, Java, India, or Hong Kong. A picture quickly emerges of a village where a relatively high

[10] Sharifah Masniah, Ibrahim Takip, and Cik Jamaliyah were then third-year history students at Universiti Sains Malaysia.

proportion of inhabitants at any time in the recent past have moved in from elsewhere, and where there is a very great diversity of origins.

Many villagers are rather less sure of the details of their grandparents' lives, particularly if they never knew them. Slightly more than half of the men and women interviewed could remember the first names of all four grandparents. In the cases where they could recall that they had grandparents who originated from elsewhere, they did not necessarily know their place of origin; and while they usually knew whether these were patrilateral or matrilateral grandparents, they did not necessarily recall whether it was the grandmother or the grandfather or both who originated outside Langkawi.

Out of the total of 164 interviewees who were themselves born in Langkawi and whose parents were also born there, I was told of 44 cases where either the father's parents or the mother's parents had come from outside the island, and a further 2 cases where the grandparents on both sides came from outside Langkawi. The most frequently cited localities of origin were Pulau Pinang, mainland Kedah, and Perlis; once again a few came from further afield: southern Thailand, Aceh, Minangkabau, and Java.

Very few people can recall genealogies beyond two or three generations. There is no systematic attempt to maintain traditions or memories of ancestors who have come from elsewhere. When villagers were asked whether they knew of any more distant ancestors than their grandparents who had come from outside Langkawi, the great majority replied in the negative. 19 could recall that they had an ancestor who had come to Langkawi from Aceh, 6 from Siam, 2 from Penang, 2 from Kedah, 1 from Java, and 1 from 'Indonesia'. The Acehnese cases were somewhat exceptional in that many of these 19 described themselves as descendants of two named brothers and a cousin of theirs who are said to have come to Langkawi around the time of the Acehnese wars towards the end of the nineteenth century. These were probably among the founding members of the village. In spite of the fact that in Southeast Asia the Acehnese are widely respected for their independence, religious learning, and extraordinary feats of resistance to external powers, no special claims are made by these descendants. Furthermore, my own research showed that very many more villagers were apparently descended from these early Acehnese immigrants but were either ignorant of this or regarded it as insignificant.

Once again the implications are telling. One's own and one's parents origins are recalled, but those of more distant ancestors are rapidly forgotten. A few people can name ancestors four or five generations back but this is exceptional. In two cases these were men who seemed anxious to display such knowledge and whose genealogies consisted of far more men than women. Even where it would seem that these origins might form the basis for status claims or exclusivity there is little evidence that this occurs.

When villagers were asked whether they knew of neighbours or fellow villagers who have come from outside Langkawi, the replies were even more striking. Almost everyone replied in the negative. Occasionally someone would recall one other person in the vicinity who had come from elsewhere. Given the very high proportion of households that actually have an immigrant resident in them (or whose members are directly descended from immigrants), this reported ignorance is impressive. There was no indication that villagers were trying to conceal this information, and whatever was remembered was willingly and openly offered in response to my queries. It simply seemed that this was not knowledge which was important to preserve or remember.

The frankness with which questions about migration were answered was especially striking when villagers were asked why they or their ancestors had come to Langkawi. The replies were straightforward and rather standardized: 'to gain a living' (*cari makan*, literally, 'to look for food'); 'to open land' (*buka tanah*); 'to seek property' (*cari harta*). Many explained how the land where they came from was all used up, 'the property was all finished' (*harta sudah habis*). In Langkawi it was still possible to open up new land. Many said that they came 'to look for work' (*cari kerja*); and to 'work as a fisherman' (*kerja nelayan*). One could gain a livelihood from fishing in Langkawi even without land on which to grow rice.

According to villagers' accounts, the main motivating force behind migration has been economic. Although other reasons are sometimes cited—quarrels with kin, fighting or warfare such as that in Aceh, Kedah, and Siam in the nineteenth century, the difficult conditions of the Japanese occupation in the 1940s—the chief concern was to make a living. These accounts suggest not only a great mixture of origins and influences in Langkawi, but that the island has been bound into a regional network and historical economy in which, at least since the middle of the nineteenth century (and probably for very much longer), people have been relatively mobile and land and resources in outlying areas more abundant than near the centres of power on the mainland.

When villagers talk about how they or their ancestors came to Langkawi, they often say, 'we came destitute, as migrants' (*kita mari bangsat*). The term *bangsat* is significant. In standard Malay it can mean 'vagabond', 'tramp', 'outcast' (Wilkinson 1959: 81) and even 'thief'

(Iskandar 1970: 71). But villagers I talked to seemed to use it without pejorative connotations and indeed with great matter-of-factness.[11] One man did once say to me it was better not to use the term *bangsat* because it was 'a little crude' (*kasar sikit*), and better to use *rantau*. But the general tone of their comments indicates that these villagers were not simply trying to underplay 'questionable' pasts, or keep them hidden, but that a sense of a shared history of poverty is central to their links with fellow villagers, and makes the term *bangsat* appropriate.

Migration appears to have occurred in a more or less continuous trickle from the mid-nineteenth century until today, and this coupled with the great diversity of origins may explain why people from the same localities have not formed distinct groups within the village.[12] Nor does this migration have any single dominant pattern. Men and women have described to me how they, their parents, or their grandparents came to the island as children accompanying their parents. Sometimes such a family group might be followed by one or other spouse's parents or an unmarried sibling. Others came as unmarried young men, on their own or with a brother, and married and settled on the island. A child might be taken by an uncle or aunt as a foster child to grow up on Langkawi. A young man or woman from the mainland might marry someone from Langkawi and come to live there. People of all ages came; some life histories show several movements back and forth between the mainland and Langkawi which are often linked to particular marital histories. For example, a couple with ties to Langkawi and a village in mainland Kedah might spend many years after their marriage on the mainland before coming to Langkawi. Divorce or death of one spouse and subsequent marriage of the other might be followed by further moves. The migration histories of individuals are very varied.[13] They are influenced by external political events, by economic constraints, by whom one marries, and by the many contingent factors

[11] The meaning of *bangsat* in this context seems more or less synonymous with *merantau*, the term used in Sumatra and other regions for to travel, migrate, wander (Iskandar 1970: 71). Karim writes: 'Occasionally the term *orang bangsat* is also used to refer to "outsiders" as "desperate destitutes." Significantly, only the children of such villagers may be accepted as "proper" villagers so that birth-rights are often used as an important criterion for acceptability' (1992: 86). This is not the case in Langkawi.

[12] In-migration has certainly been accompanied by a similar trickle of out-migration. However, detailed information on this is even more difficult to collect since, as many ethnographers of similar Southeast Asian groups have observed, relatives who move away are rapidly forgotten or become irrelevant unless their immediate descendants intermarry in the future.

[13] See Gullick (1987: 104–5) on the varied composition of migrant groups in late 19th-cent. Malaya.

that make one person's life different from another's. But in the way people talk and think about migration there is considerable consistency. These recollections are told in a manner which reveals that people in Sungai Cantik have a common way of thinking about their own past, and that this is an important part of their shared identity.

I have already referred to some stereotypical phrases: 'We came as poor migrants, to gain a living, to open land' (*kita mari bangsat, cari makan, buka tanah*). 'Descendants sold their property. It was finished. They looked for their own property' (*keturunan harta jual, sudah habis. Cari harta sendiri*). The image of a shared history of poverty is strong. Many people vividly described to me how the area where the village now stands seemed empty in the first part of the century. 'There weren't many people. Land was plentiful, you could clear and plant it or build a house, and then take out title-deeds. There were few houses where now there are many.' I was told how 'Fresh water was plentiful too, unlike in other places; the sources in Langkawi do not run dry and the water is pure, cool, and pleasant.' Even without land, men could survive by selling fish that they caught and buying rice. There were no big landowners in the village; 'Everyone had about the same, they were similar' (*kira semua se macam, se rupa*). There were no really poor or very rich people in the village. 'Nobody had very much but there was enough to eat.' Most people had to buy rice but sold fish.

One could survive but life was not easy. To travel from one part of the island to another meant walking or going by boat. Journeys to other villages or to the local town were long and arduous: it was a day's walk to Kuah, the main town. Going to sea could mean encountering smugglers and pirates. To combat smuggling from Siam there was a customs post at Sungai Cantik. On land too there were dangerous people about; villagers kept swords (*pedang*) and knives (*pisau*) in their houses which were confiscated by the Japanese in the early 1940s. There was poverty and sickness. I was told how villages were isolated during cholera epidemics, and their inhabitants conducted purification ceremonies and prayers at the perimeters to banish sickness, spirits, and the devil. Women died in childbirth because it was impossible to get help to them. Under the Japanese occupation there was no rice, but conditions on the mainland seem to have been even worse, and people settled both temporarily and permanently on Langkawi. Stories about these times are told with great emotion and vividly remembered.

Although people came to Langkawi in many different circumstances and at different stages of their life cycle, certain patterns stand out in people's minds. There are prototypical stories which in some cases take on aspects of myths of origin and in which Langkawi appears as a haven, a source of land, water, and women. Some people came simply because they 'liked to wander' (*suka merantau*); 'they liked to move' (*suka berjalan*). There are stories of shipwrecked travellers: one early immigrant from Aceh is reported to have drifted for three months in an earthenware vessel without food or water before fetching up on the shores of Langkawi.

Stories about men without parents, coming alone or with siblings, tell how new migrants were fostered by, or married, Langkawi women and so settled on the island and became part of the local population. Often villagers suggest that men are more mobile then women: 'Men wander more. They see a good-looking woman, stay, and marry' (*orang jantang merantau lebih. Tengok orang perempuan segok, duduk, kahwin*).[14] Groups of brothers are prototypical migrants. Many stories tell of two or three brothers coming to the island as young men without parents or wives. One man I knew well had come from Thailand after his parents died; then he brought his brother and sister; they came destitute (*bangsat*), and all married and settled in Langkawi. Such people 'come to Langkawi and they do not go back'. Of some it is said, 'people didn't let him go back' (*orang tak bagi dia balik*).

Even if they do not record genealogies, or preserve their differences of origin, villagers are conscious of their diversity. The village headman told me how people in the village were from all over: 'Penang, Java, Aceh, Bugis, Siam, and Kedah. But people don't keep records, they don't remember. Lots of them have died now, their children don't remember.' An older woman put it more directly: 'Everyone is from outside; where are there Langkawi people?' (*semua orang pada luar; mana orang Langkawi?*). When I asked one old man, himself a migrant from Kedah, who were the 'original' or 'native' people in the village, he explained, 'There aren't people from here. It's not thought of like that. If you stay for a long time, you become a Langkawi person' (*orang sini tak ada. Tak kira lagu itu. Kalau duduk lama, jadi orang Langkawi*).

Discussing my findings with the village headman again, shortly before I left the village in 1989, he concluded: 'People here are all people who have come. There aren't any native people' (*orang sini semua orang mendatang. Orang asli tak ada*). But they 'mix easily' (*mudah campur*), he

[14] The idea that men are more mobile than women, and associated with the outside of the house, recalls the way that, in the rites following childbirth, a boy's sibling placenta is tied up with rattan before burial, and a girl's with pandanus. This is because men use rattan to tie the steps of an exterior house ladder while girls weave pandanus for the interior mats.

said. They 'don't dig up their ancestry' (*tak bangkit keturunan*). These comments and observations emphasize diversity and mixing. In contrast, immigrant communities elsewhere on the mainland peninsula appear to have been either more homogeneous or more divided by differences of origin.[15]

Villagers' comments also highlight the significance of marriage and fostering as the means of drawing outsiders in, as I described in earlier chapters. New affines become connected to other villagers, especially once children are born. Marriage and the birth of children create interconnections in succeeding generations, but because of the emphasis on the co-substantiality of two sets of grandparents, this is also echoed in preceding generations. The full salience of these incorporative processes becomes clear in the light of the history of migration I have described. It is through hospitality, fostering, and marriage that new migrants become Langkawi people.

The fact that migrants are often described as having arrived in sibling groups can be linked to the general emphasis on siblingship which I described in Chapter 3. There I showed how siblingship is central to notions of kinship and how the wider community is conceived in many respects as an expanded sibling group. The theme of siblingship is echoed in myth in which spirits often appear as sibling sets without parents. In the migration stories which I collected these myths were evoked in another narrative frame. The mysterious filiation of spirit-siblings without parents becomes more meaningful in a context where siblings do sometimes arrive from foreign places without their parents. And, in a similar way, ideas about relatedness often seem to imply that ties of siblingship prefigure those of descent.[16]

There are other quasi-mythical aspects to the way migration stories are told. One woman described to me how her father had come to visit Langkawi from mainland Kedah as a young man, and how he had been a religious teacher. When I asked why he had not gone back, she replied simply, 'people ordered him to stay' (*orang suruh dia duduk*). The implication was of course that he was so well respected and liked that people would not let him leave. He merely complied with the wishes of others.

[15] Gullick (1987: 98) and Wilson (1967: 18–23) report antipathy among immigrant groups of different local origins, while Karim (1992: 86, 156–7) and Wilder (1982: 33–4) note the importance of distinctions between older, established families and newly settled migrants and difficulties in integrating the latter.

[16] See Errington (1989: 293), who notes the frequency in Southeast Asian foundation myths of the brother–sister pair who travel together, commit incest, and are separated.

But the story reveals how the process of integrating new migrants is obligatory. In the ideal image the newcomer's welcome is forceful: he is shown such overwhelming hospitality that there is no choice but to submit. A short stay becomes a long one, a foster home becomes as dear as one's home of origin, eventually one finds a spouse, has children, and is truly settled.

Memory and the Creation of Kinship

The problem of eliciting the memories with which I was concerned was that villagers themselves seemed to be engaged in forgetting them. Although experiences in the very recent past remain powerful and salient, more distant ones rapidly disappear. There is no sense that villagers are anxious to maintain traditions from their diverse places of origin. The emphasis is on absorbing and blending, rather than maintaining regional and cultural difference.

The tendency to forget rather than remember such differences meant that conducting research on this topic was sometimes a frustrating experience. Answers to questions were often brief or dismissive; people who in other contexts were more patient and forthcoming were rather mystified as to why I was asking such detailed questions. If these difficulties challenged the accuracy and validity of my research, they also encouraged me to think harder about the significance of the stories I was being told and the manner in which they were related.

References to an absence of knowledge of ancestors are a more or less standard feature of ethnographies of cognatic societies in Southeast Asia. With few exceptions (most notably that of Errington 1989: 203–31), this has been treated in negative terms as a lack, rather than as a positive feature of these societies. In Borneo, it has long been considered highly problematic to consider descent as an organizing principle (King 1978). Indeed, Freeman's (1961: 208) characterization of the Iban as a people suffering from 'structural amnesia' has come to seem almost stereotypical. Elsewhere in the region, Hildred and Clifford Geertz (1964) refer to the Balinese having 'genealogical amnesia', while Jay (1969: 171) mentions a lack of interest in tracing kinship and scanty genealogical knowledge in rural Java. In the Philippines, Gibson records that the Buid 'do not bother to remember genealogical connection past the level of their grandparents' (Gibson 1986: 88), while Jean-Paul Dumont discusses how Visayans enter 'into the business of forgetting relatives' (Dumont 1992: 146).

My own observation that slightly more than half of the Langkawi villagers interviewed could remember the names of all four of their grandparents is very much in the tradition of this ethnography. What is being described is a lack, a knowledge that is absent. And here Southeast Asian societies are implicitly or explicitly being compared with Africa or Europe (see Freeman 1961; Geertz and Geertz 1964; Gibson 1986: 61–7).

However, Freeman's essay on the bilateral kindred also drew attention to other features of such kinship in more positive terms. He noted how easy it was for the Iban to recruit large-scale associations of men especially for fighting (Freeman 1961: 213–14). Here diffuse links over a wide geographical area are seen to have a positive value. These two features of kinship seem to go together: diffuse horizontal ties spreading out in concentric circles are the positive side of 'structural amnesia'—although it is not quite clear from Freeman's analysis why such kin continue to be recognized.

In an equally positive spirit, Hildred and Clifford Geertz (1964) discuss how 'genealogical amnesia' among Balinese commoners enhances the flexibility of their descent groups, enabling these to expand and contract in response to changing circumstances. In Chapter 8 I mentioned the Geertzes' notion that teknonymy is an active process by means of which Balinese kinship is produced as a 'downward-looking' system (Hildred and Clifford Geertz 1964: 105). In this system 'a man sees himself, so to speak, producing structure below him rather than emerging from it above him' (1964: 105). The fact that the implications of this highly suggestive formulation have been little explored in the literature may have to do with the fact that, in another and rather better-known article, Clifford Geertz (1973) saw teknonymy in more negative terms. Here he linked it to a 'depersonalized concept of the person', a 'reduced sense of temporal flow' and the maintenance of a 'steady state' (1973: 406). In this rendition, a Balinese construction of an 'unperishing present' (1973: 379) has replaced the earlier evocation of an *active production* of children and grandchildren and an orientation towards the *future*.[17]

The idea that forgetting who your relatives are represents a loss, and is part of a negative process, a flattening of personhood, a diminution of kinship, a reduced temporality, has been far more prevalent in the litera-

[17] Geertz's theory of Balinese personhood has been extensively criticized by Hobart (1986), Howe (1984), and Wikan (1990). Jean-Paul Dumont argues that this process of forgetting has the effect of turning 'distant and vague relatives into potential affines', thus allowing Visayans to maintain their cultural identity through endogamy (Dumont 1992: 155). One reason to doubt his logic is that exactly the same phenomenon is observed in cognatic societies with far less restrictive marriage rules than are found in the Visaya Islands.

ture than more positive accounts. Here I suggest that this kind of forgetting is not only an active process, but that it is linked to other aspects of identity in Southeast Asia, most notably an emphasis on siblingship, and this point has been cogently made by Errington (1989: 203–31). 'Genealogical amnesia' can thus be viewed from another angle: as an intimate and detailed knowledge of ties of siblingship. It is because siblingship is logically prior to, and in some respects more important than, descent in this type of bilateral kinship (see McKinley 1981; Errington 1989: 207–17) that it is possible to have a very broad knowledge of quite distant ties with cousins (as Freeman (1961) and others have described) without being able to name one's forebears beyond about two generations.

This makes clear why thinking in terms of amnesia may be misleading, since it fails to convey the importance of other kinds of knowledge which people do retain. Knowledge of kinship in cognatic societies of Southeast Asia tends to be 'wide' rather than 'deep': it stretches outwards, following degrees of siblingship, rather than backwards into the past.

The obliteration of memory of different origins in Langkawi seems, similarly, to be an aspect of the horizontality of knowledge about genealogical connections which I have described. But it can also be linked to the migration history of people in Langkawi. A lack of interest in precisely who one's ancestors are correlates *both* with an emphasis on siblingship as the core of kinship, *and* with the fact that so many people have come to the island as impoverished migrants in the recent past. In this context kinship—or a sense of connectedness to place and people—is not derived from past ties but must be created in the future. The enormous emphasis on the production of children in marriage, the image of the community as one of shared grandchildren, the way in which the sharing of grandchildren creates kinship between two sets of grandparents, are all aspects of this forward projection. Hildred and Clifford Geertz's notion of 'downward-looking' kinship is thus particularly apt for Langkawi.

In Langkawi kinship—conceived as similarity of attributes and substance—is created both in the present and the future through the absorption and homogenization of difference. People 'mix easily'. In fact they are given no choice but to do so. Differences that characterize newcomers to the island are rapidly erased, partly through the emphasis on conformity and similarity which I described in Chapter 5. Behaviour, dialect, consumption patterns, house design and furnishings, style of dress may vary according to wealth and age but they are not expressions of individuality. Differences of taste are actively discouraged; they are not a means of distinguishing villagers of different origins.

I have suggested that the features of Langkawi which I have outlined in this chapter can be placed within a wider regional and political context. They can be linked to the nature of the Southeast Asian state, in which maritime trade and the movement of people have been associated for thousands of years. Migration is, in fact, an intriguing feature of several historical and anthropological studies in the region (see Gullick 1958; 1987; Adas 1981; Lim Teck Ghee 1977; Roff 1969; Wang Gungwu 1985). The Iban (Freeman 1970) and Minangkabau (Kahn 1980; Kato 1982) are two well-known ethnographic examples of societies in which mobility is clearly a central feature of social life. These examples suggest that on a regional scale such demographic mobility may be very significant, as may be its long-term interaction with kinship structures.[18]

For those people at the bottom end of the hierarchical order and in the outlying regions of the state (in other words the most mobile segments of the population), kinship seems to have taken a characteristic form. Here the features of kinship which anthropologists have noted as characterizing cognatic groups of Southeast Asia take on a crucial political importance.[19] For low-status groups or commoners, the most significant of these features are that one becomes related to previously unrelated people relatively easily through fostering and marriage, and that absolute distinctions between kin and non-kin tend to be avoided. Kin ties may be spread over a very wide geographic area, as Freeman and other ethnographers of the region have reported. But these features, which are merely puzzling when considered in the context of stable communities, mean something quite different when coupled with population mobility. They all make the attachment of migrants to new places and people rather easy.

Similarly, the cast to memory described here—in which knowledge of kinship is 'wide' rather than 'deep', produced in the future rather than derived from the past—takes on a different meaning. For when people are highly mobile, then it may be more important to create kinship out of new ties than to remember ancestors whose identity has become largely irrelevant.[20]

Anthropologists have recently emphasized the fluidity of Austronesian

[18] Errington (1989: 292) links the prominence of the journey in insular Southeast Asian societies to notions of potency in which the source of potency for ordinary people (as opposed to rulers who stay still) is external and far away.

[19] Of course the deep genealogies of high-status groups in hierarchical societies of Southeast Asia contrast with the shallow broad ones of commoners or egalitarian groups (see Hildred and Clifford Geertz 1975; Errington 1989).

[20] This of course is not always the case among migrants. One important factor may be that Langkawi people have not migrated in large groups, but have come in small numbers from diverse places over a very long period. The political status of immigrants in their new home might also be expected to play a role in the kind of ties these migrants maintain with their ancestors and places of origin.

notions of identity (see Fox 1987). Identity is not fixed at birth; people become who they are gradually through life as they acquire different attributes derived from the activities in which they engage and the people with whom they live. One important contributor to identity is place. People are shaped, and their bodies become marked, by the activities in which they engage in the particular locality in which they live. Identities, skills, and personal characteristics are acquired rather than innate.[21] Interestingly, the Ilongot of the Philippines actually remember their past in spatial terms, as a 'winding thread of continuous movement through space' (Rosaldo 1980: 16). History here becomes a succession of places (1980: 42), 'a movement through space in which . . . people walk along a trail and stop at a sequence of named resting places' (1980: 56). The idea that identity and place are closely associated once again has a different meaning in a context of demographic mobility. By settling in a new locality one can quite easily become *of that place.*

Clearly, there is room for further research on the regional significance of population mobility. I suggest that in Langkawi this kind of demographic movement can be linked to aspects of kinship and notions about community and to villagers' perception of themselves and their place in the social structure of Malaysia.

The sense of distinctiveness and difference from mainland society that pervades the self-perceptions of people in Langkawi which I discussed in Chapter 5 seems on one level to contradict their fundamental economic and social integration which was the starting-point for this historical analysis. However, these perceptions are themselves a product of the social and historical forces affecting the wider society. Certain characteristics of Langkawi—its location as a border region relatively remote from the political centre, the centrality of fishing rather than wet-rice agriculture, the absence of an indigenous aristocracy—may have encouraged the establishment of migrant communities in which similarity and closeness was valued above hierarchy and difference.

The long-term process of creating kinship that I have described here may be characterized as one of incorporation. It occurs through hospitality, feeding, fostering, marriage, and the birth of children. As I have emphasized, these are all processes which occur through the actions of women. The image of the Langkawi community is that of an enlarged house characterized by the unity and similarity that are the attributes of

[21] Astuti (1995) gives a finely drawn description of this process among the Vezo of Madagascar.

close kinship. It is this warm, enclosed house which, as I described in the Introduction to this book, I experienced so powerfully at the beginning of my fieldwork. This house can keep the divisive and threatening aspects of the external world of the state and the mainland at bay. It can also symbolically transform division and difference into shared substance.

Coercive Incorporation and the Process of Fieldwork

I conclude this chapter with a return to the conditions of my own fieldwork. I began this book by describing a tension between the warmth and intimacy which I experienced inside a Malay house, and more negative, and often overpowering, feelings of being taken over and controlled. While I was in Langkawi, I tended to think about what was happening to me in personal and emotional terms. But as my analysis of kinship progressed, it seemed to me that these powerful experiences revealed something about the processes that I was analysing. It is for this reason that I have left this subject to the end. It is necessary to have an understanding of kinship and history in Langkawi in order to make sense of what happened to me.

The way in which villagers in Sungai Cantik reacted to me taught me a great deal about their own concerns, underlining what anthropologists all know—that fieldwork is a two-way process. I therefore include my experience not so much to place '[t]he ethnographer, a character in a fiction, . . . at center stage', to 'speak of previously "irrelevant" topics: violence and desire, confusions, struggles and economic transactions with informants' (Clifford and Marcus 1986: 14). Rather, I introduce it for what it reveals about kinship in Langkawi.

In the discussion of the history of migration above, I mentioned a woman who related to me how her father had come to Langkawi from Kedah and stayed simply because he had been 'ordered to' by local people. The story captures the ideal image of proper behaviour on both sides. It also underlines the coercive nature of the process of integration. The polite guest must give in gracefully to the overwhelming hospitality of his or her hosts. And this marks the beginning of a long process which results in the stranger settling on the island.

Coming to Langkawi to do fieldwork I was, without realizing it, placing myself in a role similar to one that villagers were very familiar with: that of the new migrant. As I described in the Introduction, throughout my stay I lived together with a three-generational family, a husband and wife in their late middle age, their adult married daughter and her husband, and their four young children. Their house comprised two main rooms and a small kitchen. Living in such close contact with a family over a considerable period, I developed strong ties with them and gained a knowledge which it would have been difficult to acquire in any other way.

I described how I became a foster daughter to the senior couple in the house. It should by now be clear that this is a very common relation between older and younger people in the Malay world. It meant I was taken in, socialized, and integrated with an ease and to an extent which might not have been possible elsewhere. My relationship with my foster mother (*mak angkat*) became particularly warm and close. She took her responsibilities for my care and education seriously and also with good humour, attempting to give me a belated upbringing that would compensate for, and if possible supplant, my outlandish and often inappropriate or impolite ways. As foster mother, she tried to ensure that, at the very least, I would not shame the household or her own role in my upbringing.

Thus when guests came to visit I might be sent, in a quite peremptory manner, to make them coffee, or told to sit on the floor rather than continue writing my notes on a chair. Before going to visit another house, I would regularly be asked where I was going, and then have my clothing checked and, if necessary, be told to go and change into something more appropriate for visiting—to put on a better sarong and a headscarf or veil. I was encouraged to participate in most forms of household work. These included washing dishes, doing laundry, house-cleaning, occasional childcare, and agricultural work. On the day following my return to Sungai Cantik in 1988 after nearly seven years' absence, I received a visit from the man who had originally introduced me to the village. He was astonished to find me sitting on the ground with a group of women plucking chickens for a feast as if I had never been away.

In all these and many other ways, I learnt the appropriate forms of behaviour for a young adult daughter. These included humility, modesty, obedience, diligence, and respect. These are lessons not easily acquired by aspiring feminist academics from north London. Often I grew irritated or depressed by the restraints imposed upon me. I bridled at being sent into the *dapur* when male strangers from another village paid a visit. I felt clumsy and uncomfortable in the formal visiting clothes deemed suitable for a wedding. Learning (in public) to bathe at the well, having my toilet habits checked, or finding my last bastion of privacy—the mosquito net under which I slept—lifted when I was sleeping by a group of elderly women keen to see what I looked like asleep seemed like further assaults on my privacy. I found the constant enquiries about, and corrections to, my behaviour or dress irksome and restrictive, and some of the tasks which I was set tedious. I have vivid memories of long hours spent minding a sleeping baby when all the adults of the house seemed to have vanished; the heat and tiredness from washing my own and other clothes at the well; a particularly trying (and tearful) afternoon spent seeding dried chillies the day before I left the village in 1982.

But some kinds of work were more enjoyable. Outside the house, the constraints seemed lighter. I loved participating in the co-operative work parties in the rice fields, journeys round the island by fishing boat, planting or gathering in the vegetable gardens. The midday meals eaten outside on these and other occasions were often fairly riotous ones, greatly enjoyed by adults and children, and the food was quite delicious. I was pleased to be complimented on my rice-harvesting skills, fearlessness with leeches, or to receive my share of the watermelon harvest I had helped to plant. At such times I felt less useless, more 'myself', than when playing the demure young Malay woman.

Difficulties were always tempered by my mother's powerful empathy and imagination, and her ability to find comedy in the many bizarre circumstances and occurrences of my stay. Out on an excursion together, we were often questioned about our relationship by bemused strangers, and she would regularly relate with deadpan expression how I was her daughter by a previous marriage to a white man.

I described in the Introduction how, before setting out for fieldwork, I had wished to minimize the social distance between myself and those with whom I was living in Sungai Cantik. I now attribute any success in this endeavour entirely to the way my preferences accorded with those of villagers in Sungai Cantik. Ties with neighbours, particular friends, and relatives who visited frequently were indeed characterized by informality. But this was mainly because it would have been very difficult to conduct relations in any other way. As I developed close ties in a small number of households which I came to be very familiar with, my presence became a normal part of the daily routine. In this context conducting formal interviews would have been embarrassing and incongruous.

I was often struck by the elaborate courtesy with which urban Malay visitors to the village were treated—at least in their presence (after they had left, their behaviour was often the subject of sharp satirical scrutiny). But these visitors could be easily placed in the social hierarchy. In contrast, villagers showed no desire to accord me any particular respect as an outsider. My age and gender coupled with being a non-Muslim seemed on the contrary to ensure my low status. Villagers' perception of my background as extremely alien, coupled with a strong pride in their own culture and religion, meant that my status started low and on the whole remained so. In many respects, I found this attitude highly congenial although there were occasions (such as when I was sent into the *dapur* when a party of male schoolteachers came to visit, or when my foster mother allocated me a domestic chore when I had other plans) when it became an irritation.

My family and other villagers made their wish to integrate me as thoroughly as possible absolutely plain. In as many spheres as possible I was to adopt their ways of doing things to the complete exclusion of my own. My experience of fieldwork was thus one of very intense incorporation. The stress on conformity which I have described meant that my apparel, behaviour, consumption, physical posture, and mobility were all controlled to the very highest degree. At the beginning of my stay it seemed there was nothing of myself that I could be allowed to keep: name, clothing, bathing and toilet habits were all to be replaced. I was constantly told how to do things, or how not to. Constantly too, my foster mother or I were asked a crucial question concerning my humanity by villagers who were meeting me for the first time: did I eat rice? There were other questions too: how many siblings did I have? Did I get periods? But the amount of attention paid to feeding me, to what I ate and the manner in

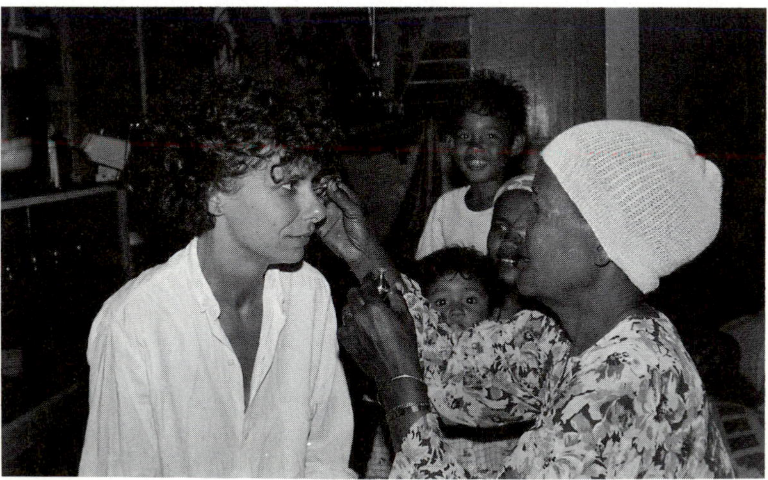

22. The author being made up

which I ate it, made it seem that I was to be transformed from the inside out as well as the outside in.

There was, then, no struggle on my part to become absorbed or accepted. On the contrary, I often found myself attempting to defend my sense of autonomy, culture, and self against what seemed a barrage of opposing forces. And this resulted in a paradoxical tendency to shut out the words, gestures, and experiences of those I was there to learn about. I experienced this as a sense of failure to conform adequately to both local and anthropological standards of behaviour—an inability to relinquish aspects of my own culture and to live up to the ideals of what I thought of as 'proper fieldwork'. However, as I described in the Introduction, anthropological visitors expressed considerable surprise at the extent of my integration.

As fieldwork progressed, the problems changed but they did not go away. The stronger and more affectionate my ties with villagers became, the more those around me showed their concern for my well-being. Those whom I knew best wished that I would stay, although they realized perfectly well that this was unlikely. I was uncomfortably aware that a religious conversion would have given relief to those who were worried about my spiritual welfare. The fragmentary nature of my knowledge of religious matters is partly a result of the strong pressure I felt to become a Muslim. My increasing discomfort resulted in a tendency to avoid matters pertaining to religion in conversation.

I felt these pressures intensely, but as time went on I also began to feel that there was a sense in which I could never adequately comply with either my own expectations or those of the people I was closest to in the village. My own preconceptions seemed increasingly naïve. The participation that is fieldwork, I belatedly realized, has inherent limits—or else it ceases to be fieldwork and becomes something quite different. And it also became clear to me that, for villagers in Sungai Cantik, the implicit and explicit logical conclusion of the process of assimilation which had been set in train when I began fieldwork would be religious conversion followed by marriage and giving birth in the village.[22]

It is significant that the process of absorption which I have described could be so easily initiated through mechanisms of fostering which I have

[22] Wazir Jahan Karim (1993*a*; 1993*b*) has described how, during her fieldwork among the Ma' Betise, an Orang Asli (aborigine) group in Malaysia, they attempted to incorporate her fully, while she herself became more distanced from them as she became progressively disillusioned with the role of anthropologist. Karim notes that this incorporation meant that by the end of fieldwork she 'was no longer "fictitious" in their eyes' (1993*a*: 79).

described as integral to kinship structures.[23] In this way my own attachment as foster daughter provided a means for me to be socialized in the manners appropriate to a young girl (*anak dara*), and was part of a process of integration which would in local terms imply eventual settlement and marriage. As I described in Chapter 8, the line between foster kin and consanguineal kin is blurred and highly permeable. Foster kin can easily be transformed into affines and kin. It is normal to address and refer to a foster mother (or other foster kin) using simply the consanguineal term *mak* (mother) without the marker *angkat*, 'raised', to signify fostering. To make the fostering explicit is to distance oneself from the kinsperson referred to, and this is highly impolite (just as is the case between affines, who also always use consanguineal terms). My internalization of these notions was so complete that I continued to refer to my foster mother as 'my mother' long after I returned to Britain (to my birth mother's considerable annoyance), and still feel quite uncomfortable with the term 'foster mother'.

While my experience of fieldwork was somewhat extreme by the standards of anthropologists, the experience that villagers in Langkawi had of me was in some respects a normal part, and consequence, of the historical processes I have described in this book. In Langkawi the absorption of newcomers through hospitality, feeding, fostering, and marriage is central to the process of constructing community. And this incorporation is so efficient that it may be completed within one generation. In Langkawi people say, 'Marry someone from here, become someone from here' (*kahwin orang sini, jadi orang sini*). The phrase may be used to describe someone's history or as an exhortation to the hesitant anthropologist. In either case it seems a succinct summary for a process I have called coercive incorporation and which is at the heart of the creation of social ties.

[23] See also Peletz (1988: xvii–xviii) on the importance of eating together, the kinship it implies, and informal adoption as modes of integration during fieldwork among Malays.

Conclusion

I have argued that, both in the past and today, incorporation has been the central process in the construction of community in Langkawi. The rapid absorption of outsiders through the mechanisms which I have described here—hospitality, feeding, fostering, marriage, and having children—has meant that people of diverse origins have been able to establish their homes and villages, and to create a sense of kinship with their co-villagers. In spite of the mobility of the local population, villagers of Sungai Cantik know that they are 'all kin'. This kinship is created out of memories of a shared past, living and eating together in the present, and having children and grandchildren in the future. Kinship is based on a shared history of poverty and migration, and on notions of shared substance which are derived both from present living arrangements and from genealogical ties. These genealogical ties are themselves projected both forward and backward in time from the present.

This sense of relatedness in Langkawi may challenge some traditional anthropological assumptions about kinship, to which I will return, but it is a powerful reality for those who live and create it. Kinship may have elusive qualities, it may be difficult for the anthropologist to convey its meanings, but this very elusiveness lends it power. It is because relatedness is always in the process of being created, without ever being a finished reality, that it can provide an idiom of attachment to place and people for those whose attachment is in fact often transitory and contingent.

I have shown how the house is central to notions of kinship and community in Langkawi. The house is the site of the process of incorporation and provides the means for it to occur. It is in the house that things which are different and which originate outside are made similar and part of the inside. It is in houses that women cook and provide the meals which are central to hospitality and to the shared substance of those who live together; it is in houses that fostering occurs; it is in houses that the difference of the in-marrying affine is gradually transformed into the shared substance of kin; it is in houses that women give birth to new sets of siblings who create a consanguineal link between their two sets of grandparents.

Incorporation is both a domestic and a political process. It occurs largely through the everyday activities of women—activities which in other contexts might be viewed as having a purely domestic import. Although many studies of Southeast Asian communities have drawn attention to women's prominence and autonomy in domestic life, and women of the region are often described as being economically active (see Rosemary Firth 1966; Hildred Geertz 1961; Strange 1981; Rudie 1994), these studies provide fewer clues about the wider significance of women's autonomy or its social concomitants. In Langkawi, the importance of incorporative processes, and the symbolic prominence of the house, which are linked to a history of demographic mobility, mean that the significance of the activities of women is different from what anthropologists might assume.

Indeed, these activities may be viewed as central to the most important political process. In a pioneer area with a mobile population, the incorporative processes I have described have allowed new migrants to be absorbed quickly and easily into existing communities. These communities have themselves been established and expanded through this process of incorporation. It is through the activities of women that new migrants have been integrated. When men emphatically participate at marriage feasts, which are a ritualized and expanded version of the domestic meal, they are asserting their place in a political process to which they seem, in at least some respects, rather marginal.

I have shown how the house in Langkawi is a 'private' and 'domestic' space—the locus of warmth and informality associated with close kin. But it can also be a 'public' and 'political' space—the locus of large-scale, formal gatherings which involve the entire village. In both these aspects the house is the focus and site of the process of incorporation. The image of the community is that of the expanded house, its central ritual an expanded version of the most central domestic activity: the consumption of a cooked rice meal. In these images, what we commonly think of as 'domestic' is in fact thoroughly 'political', and vice versa. The material I have presented invites us to rethink the division between these domains—as feminist scholars have long urged us to do.

In a similar manner, we can link a political ideology of egalitarianism in Langkawi to a more 'domestic' emphasis on similarity in kinship. These can be seen as two aspects of one phenomenon. Both have been fostered by the same historical processes. These have involved the combination of

Langkawi's geographic peripherality, as an island on the fringe of a Malay state, its mixed economy, based largely on fishing rather than rice cultivation, and its status as a refuge area for poor peasants migrating from more central areas of the state. But if we think of these factors in narrow terms as 'political', or 'economic', we miss a large part of their significance. In fact, the historical processes which have shaped the lives of people in Langkawi have not acted in a partial manner. Nor can the kinship which I have described here be understood in narrow terms, however faithful these may be to the analytic domains of anthropologists. The kinship I have described in fact involves every aspect of social life.

In demonstrating the centrality of the house and its multifacetedness, I have drawn upon the ideas of Lévi-Strauss (1983*a*; 1987), especially his fruitful suggestion that the house is the key to understanding certain Southeast Asian societies in which priciples such as residence, filiation, ownership of property, or ranking, taken alone, do not provide an explanation of social forms. However, I have departed from Lévi-Strauss in one respect. He seems to suggest that the houses in 'sociétés à maison' are inevitably ranked (1983*a*: 181), but in Langkawi the relation between houses occurs in an idiom of similarity and equality—echoing the emphasis on these principles in kinship and in the wider community. The unity of the sibling group is central to the image of the house. Siblings, whose relationships are premised on equality and similarity, inevitably divide in adult life and establish new houses whose relations are founded on these same principles.

In so far as I have argued that the house is central to social organization in Langkawi, this study follows recent work on other Southeast Asian societies (see Barraud 1979; Errington 1987; 1989; Macdonald 1987; Traube 1986; Waterson 1990; McKinnon 1991; Carsten and Hugh-Jones 1995). However, it is clear that in this case the symbolic and practical elaborations of the house take particular forms which differ from those in some other Southeast Asian societies and which can be linked to the other features of Langkawi's history and political economy that I have described.

The expansive nature of the house, its ability to incorporate outside elements and encompass them, is particularly crucial where the outside world is seen as divisive and threatening. The expanded house in Langkawi is the symbol of a community attempting to maintain its autonomy in the face of these external forces. An image of the warm house endlessly reproducing itself is one in which the external world can either be incorporated or kept at bay. The centrality of the house, the fact that it can symbolically incorporate external elements, and that it is conceived in an idiom of equality can all be linked, then, to the history of Langkawi as a pioneer area in which social forms have been kept distinct from the political hierarchy which characterizes mainland areas nearer the traditional centres of power.

In all these respects Langkawi both recalls other Southeast Asian societies and maintains its historic distinctness from them. While certain of the elements that I have described here occur elsewhere, their particular combination is specific to Langkawi. Houses among the Atoni (Cunningham 1964*a*), in Tanimbar-Evav (McKinnon 1991), Torajan noble houses or those of the Nias chiefs (Waterson 1990) are very prominent features of social organization; they are also a means of symbolizing and instituting the hierarchical differentiation prominent in these societies.

The emphasis on similarity and equality among Malays in Langkawi seems more marked than among paddy-farming peasants or urban people living nearer to the centres of power in mainland Southeast Asia. Geertz's study of the *Religion of Java* (1960) shows very clearly the elaboration of status markers in Modjokuto, where speech patterns, body posture, dress, music can all be used to express differential rank. Leach's (1954) classic study of highland Burma makes clear the thoroughgoing hierarchy that characterizes the lowland Shan state and the significance of this for swidden cultivators in the highlands. While some studies of peasants in agricultural communities describe an egalitarian ethos (see, for example, Jay 1969; Syed Husin Ali 1975), such ideologies may mask underlying social division. Scott's (1985) study of a peasant community in mainland Kedah shows how villagers there are highly conscious of differences of wealth and status in spite of an ideology of mutual aid (Scott 1985: 192–5). Nearer the royal centres, a greater value is placed on attachment to land and to hierarchies of rank and property ownership. Forms of deference are more marked, disputes often express the importance of maintaining minute status differences, people talk about 'following the customs of the rajah' (*ikut adat dirajah*).

Aspects of sociality in Langkawi seem, paradoxically, to recall swidden cultivators or hunters and gatherers in the region, rather than peasants. Thus the strong emphasis on personal autonomy, and egalitarianism, and the resistance to state structures and external sources of power are familiar from studies of the Buid (Gibson 1986) or the Iban (Freeman 1970).

Gibson has described how, in the Buid case, these features are a result of their historical enclavement by the lowland state. Faced with the choice of being incorporated into the state or running away, the Buid solution was to penetrate deeper into the forest and to reject lowland Hispanic peasant values of dependence and hierarchy (Gibson 1986: 225). Gibson describes how close ties of kinship imply a limitation on personal autonomy for the Buid and an acceptance of hierarchical values. Their social life can be viewed as an attempt to minimize these by placing a high value on sharing and companionship. Ties between parents and children show a strong attempt to limit hierarchy and dependency: children are never commanded by their parents; they are encouraged to spend most of their time with their peers, and their residence is quite mobile, partly as a result of remarriage rates (ibid.: 96–7). Marriages are serially monogamous, and individuals may contract several in the course of their lives; jealousy and possessiveness are disapproved of (ibid.: 78–80).

Although the economy and ecology of the Buid are very different from those in Langkawi, some of these aspects of their social life do not seem unfamiliar when compared with Langkawi. While the Buid have been in a far weaker position *vis-à-vis* the state than people in Langkawi, and have attempted to distance themselves more radically from it, the sense of an external world to be kept at bay is rather similar. Similar too is an emphasis on living and eating together, which Gibson (ibid.: 119–21) argues is part of a rejection of kinship as such among the Buid, but which I have argued is in Langkawi a core idiom of kinship. Here it becomes important to distinguish a difference of perspective between anthropologists from differences between the societies they have studied. Is 'kinship' as it is used here a meaningful indigenous category or only an analytic one?

My own view is that this difference arises from different analytic usages of 'kinship'. Precisely because we are here concerned with kinship as an analytic category, it is not particularly meaningful to say that the Buid reject it while people in Langkawi do not. From an indigenous point of view, people are concerned with a sense of relatedness with their co-residents and neighbours. This is phrased in culturally specific idioms. Those that Gibson describes for the Buid are in many ways similar to those I have described for people in Langkawi. What the Buid do reject is dyadic ties implying dependence and hierarchy (which they associate with lowland peasant values) but it is clear that siblingship, and ties between half-siblings, are very significant for them (ibid.: 84–8, 98–100). It is possible that this fact can be linked to the emphasis on sharing and companionship.

All this would encourage the anthropological redefinition of 'kinship' so that it is less bound by analytic assumptions and more open to indigenous diversity. I return to this point below but here I want to suggest that idioms of social life in Langkawi can as usefully be compared to those of Southeast Asian swidden cultivators or hunters and gatherers as to lowland peasants practising wet-rice cultivation. And that the similarities to be found can be attributed to some similarity of historical circumstances. First, swidden cultivators or hunters and gatherers have often been in contact with more powerful lowland states which pose a threat to their cultural autonomy. This situation can be compared to the way fishing people in Langkawi perceive themselves to be threatened by the outside world, although the threat in this case is certainly much less extreme. Secondly, swidden cultivators and hunters and gatherers are by definition mobile. This crucial facet of social life makes such people comparable to fishing people and peasants living in a pioneer region, and distinguishes both of these from more settled agriculturalists. It is to these two historical features that I would attribute the similar emphasis on equality and autonomy and on creating 'kinship' out of living and eating together.

These suggestions are to some degree speculative—there remains much comparative and historical research to be done on Southeast Asian societies. My final observations are also speculative. They are a reflection on the significance of the material I have presented for anthropological studies of the person and kinship more generally. As such, they are intended more as an encouragement to further research than as a final account of the present study.

One important aspect of the emphasis on incorporation in Langkawi is its implications for notions of the body and the person. I have described how, for persons, the process of incorporation occurs largely through feeding. It is the nature of the food consumed, and who it is consumed with, that determines the course of this process. Feeding creates and transforms kinship, and it does this by creating and transforming the blood of which bodies are largely composed. The ideas presented in Chapter 4 imply rather flexible concepts of personhood and of kinship which can be linked to ideas about blood. All of these are always in the process of being created and transformed.

I have also described how ideas about kinship and personhood reveal a fascination with boundaries—those of the 'life essence' (*semangat*), the person, the sibling set, and of the wider kindred. One is never quite sure where the boundaries of these various entities are. They may be drawn in one place at one moment, only to be erased and redrawn at the next. Notions about affinity have this ambiguity at their core. The status of affinity as a category of relation is always elusive, precisely because affines are at some level incorporated as consanguineal kin, but also—and simultaneously—distinguished from them.[1] This same fascination with boundaries is reflected in ideas about the house, the neighbourhood, and the village community, which are from one point of view merely the containers of the relations discussed here.

The speculation on boundaries can also be viewed as a reflection on the nature of similarity and difference and the possibility of transforming one into the other. From this point of view we can see it as another aspect of the emphasis on the process of incorporation which is at the heart of ideas of kinship. If kinship is created and transformed through incorporation, then people who are different can become similar. Conversely, those who are the same can become different, that is non-kin, by moving away or not maintaining their ties.

Thus the similar and the different, the inside and the outside, are always potentially subject to transformation into each other. The emphasis on incorporation as a central process of kinship necessarily implies very flexible concepts of personhood and relatedness. A corollary of this lack of fixity is a kind of cultural fascination or play with the notion of boundary itself. Since in this context boundaries must be alterable, the question of where they will be placed is always negotiable and therefore of immense interest. I would argue that this concern with boundaries is at the heart of what Errington (1987; 1989) calls the 'Centrist societies' of Southeast Asia. These cultures are not based around a systematic series of dualist oppositions, as are Eastern Indonesian cultures. Instead they are based on the idea of an 'encompassing centre' which can always absorb what is on their periphery (see Errington 1989: 252). Thus what is different, and on the outside, can always be encompassed and made similar, and this is at the heart of cultural processes.

This is most clear in notions of affinity. I have argued that affines can be viewed as people who are both similar and different. In fact they are a category of people who are almost visibly undergoing transformation from the one state into the other. There is no permanent category of affines. Affinity is itself merely a transition state, or boundary, between the different and the similar. Anthropologists who have tried to understand the

[1] The term 'consanguineal kin' is carefully chosen. It captures the emphasis Langkawi people place on blood in kinship. The sharing of blood, however, does not necessarily result from sexual reproduction as is assumed in Western notions and in anthropological usage; see below.

crucial importance of affinity in bilateral kinship in Southeast Asia have failed to elucidate its most important characteristic: its lack of fixity. Transformative processes are crucial to understanding kinship in this context.

The same flexibility is present in notions of personhood and the body. In Chapters 3 and 4 I showed how the identity of the person seems to contain the relation of siblingship, and how ideas about personhood reveal a considerable play on single and multiple aspects of identity. It is not surprising that these ideas should come to the fore during pregnancy and childbirth when one body literally contains another. In the material I have presented, it sometimes seems difficult to fix the boundaries of the person or the body, or to ascertain whether we are dealing with individual notions of personhood, such as have been asserted for modern, 'Western' cultures, or something more like the 'identical particular persons' that have been described for India (Dumont 1970: 11).

Marriott (1976: 113) has criticized Dumont for transposing Western dualistic models onto Indian thought. He describes a model of Indian transactions in which

> what goes on *between* actors are the same connected processes of mixing and separation that go on *within* actors. (1976: 109, original emphasis)

In Indian thought, Marriott argues, conduct alters bodily substance. Thus the separability of action from actor, code from substance, mind from body which pervades Western thought is absent (ibid.: 110).[2] In these ideas persons are not thought of as indivisible, bounded units, the individuals of 'Western' thought, but as 'dividual' or 'divisible' (ibid.: 111). Drawing on this formulation, Marilyn Strathern has argued that Melanesian persons

> are frequently constructed as the plural and composite site of the relationships that produced them. The singular person can be imagined as the social microcosm. (Strathern 1988: 13, footnote omitted)

In the ideas I have described for Langkawi we can discern both notions of 'multiple' or 'partible' identity, like those described for India and Melanesia, and more individualistic concepts of the person. That ideas about personhood should reveal both these aspects, and in fact be rather flexible, fits with the more general concern with similarity and difference

[2] For an ethnographic account which emphasizes the fluidity of bodily substance in the Indian context see Daniel (1984). There are a number of intriguing parallels between the material presented here and the Tamil case analysed by Daniel, for example the centrality of the house and its person-like qualities (Daniel 1984: 149–53).

which I have discussed. The possibility of transforming difference into similarity, the unified into the multiple, or vice versa, implies that both kinds of idea about personhood are important. Thus we find ideas about a unitary individual identity (for example, at the moment when the midwife cuts the umbilical cord and the child is given a name, or when men go fishing), and ideas about multiple identity expressed in terms of siblingship. At different moments one or other aspect may be more prominent, while ideas about childbirth express both concerns most vividly.

In Langkawi, then, people are thought of as both multiple and individual, and I suspect this may also be true in Melanesia, India, and Europe too. Following Bloch (1988), it seems likely that in most societies both kinds of idea will be present, however submerged one of them may be. Thus it is as possible to find traces of 'individualistic' notions among the Tallensi, who on the whole emphasize continuity between members of one lineage (see Fortes 1983), as it is to find a strain of thinking that emphasizes continuity between persons in the Western Christian tradition.

Parry (1989) has argued that in India itself ideas about personhood are not quite so systematic as Marriott maintains, and in fact the whole ideology of caste ranking is testimony to a certain contradiction in notions about the fluidity of personhood. He suggests that ideas about the fluidity of substance and identity both contradict and sustain a static ideology of caste. Parry points out that Marriott's contrast between Western dualistic thought and South Asian monism is even more radical than Dumont's opposition between 'homo aequalis' and 'homo hierarchicus'. It is

> more radical because it makes no explicit place, even at a secondary or 'encompassed' level, for any ideological recognition of the contrary value scheme. (Parry 1989: 496)

The Southeast Asian ideas I have discussed show very clearly how misleading it is to adopt a simple opposition between 'Western' and 'non-Western' societies in terms of notions of personhood. Here 'non-Western' dividualism seems to coexist quite happily with something like 'Western' individualism.

Ideas about relatedness in Langkawi also challenge us to look again at the significance of the relation between code and substance in kinship, and at the construction of 'substance' itself. In Langkawi we have seen how relatedness is created through the sharing of substance, both as a result of acts of procreation and through living and eating together. In the analysis of these notions I have been stimulated by Schneider's (1984) critique of the anthropological analysis of kinship, which he sees as thoroughly rooted in Western concepts, and of its status as a cross-cultural category, which both he and Needham (1971) have argued is untenable.[3]

Schneider argues that anthropological analysis defines kinship in terms of the shared substance that results from the act of procreation (see Schneider 1984: 187–96). He shows that both Western kinship and anthropological analysis rest on a key distinction between 'biological' ties (defined as the result of sexual reproduction) and their 'social' attributes. Both indigenous Western ideas and the analysis of kinship assume that social aspects of a relationship can be separated from, or added to, a biological substratum. Equally, '[b]iological kinship has been distinguished sharply from social kinship by most anthropologists' (ibid.: 189). The anthropological analysis of adoption and fostering arrangements provides a neat example of this (see Schneider 1984: 171–2).

For Schneider, the analytical significance of defining kinship in these terms lies in the universality it presupposes (ibid.: 195). His book is an explicit challenge to the idea that procreation is everywhere accorded the same high value as in Western cultures. He rejects a cross-cultural definition of kinship in terms of procreation because procreation may not be central in some cultures. Other kinds of relationship that do not derive (or are not perceived as deriving) from procreative ties may be important. But for Schneider these are necessarily 'social' rather than 'biological' and therefore not kinship as it has been defined. His central question, then, is: 'Given this definition of kinship, do these particular people have it or do they not?' (ibid.: 200). And he concludes by more or less rejecting the validity of kinship as a cross-cultural category.

Instead of rejecting kinship as such, I suggest that we would do better to ask: how do the people we study define and construct their notions of relatedness and what values and meaning do they give them? If we accept that both the definition and the meaning of kinship are culturally variable, then we certainly must reject a universal definition of kinship in terms of procreation. But this does not mean that we cannot compare both how people conceive of relatedness and the meaning they attribute it in different cultures. It seems to me that if we are to reject kinship in the sense which Schneider criticizes, then we would do better to adopt a term to characterize the relatedness which people act and feel. I would call this kinship.

[3] For a more detailed discussion of Schneider's argument see Carsten 1995*a*.

Here I refer to a non-anthropological source, *The Oxford Dictionary of Etymology*. The dictionary entry for *kin* gives 'family, race; class, kind', and also lists other derivations from the same Indo-European base. I quote these in full:

> agnate, cognate; benign, malign; nation, nature; genus, general; generate; generous; degenerate, regenerate; genius, ingenious; ingenuous, ingénue; indigenous; kind; progeny; -gen, gono-; gentile; genital, genitive, germ, germinate, germane'. (Onions 1966: 505)[4]

This very wide domain underlines the multifaceted significance of 'kinship'. Rather than drawing arbitrary boundaries around one particular subset of these terms, anthropologists should consider the full range of vocabularies of relatedness.

We can then ask whether relatedness seems to us 'biological'; but we can also ask whether that question makes any sense in indigenous terms, or more generally whether any indigenous differentiation might correspond to our biological–social distinction.[5] In the case of Langkawi, the key to relatedness is siblingship, and the key to siblingship is similarity of attributes and shared bodily substance. It is not clear whether any such distinction as social–biological is used. It is clear that the important relationships of kinship involve what we would regard as both. In Langkawi meals are understood to create shared substance and thus engender similarity. In this sense they might be considered as both social and biological.

Ideas about relatedness in Langkawi thus show very clearly how culturally specific is the separation of the 'social' from the 'biological' and the reduction of the latter to sexual reproduction. In Langkawi relatedness is derived both from acts of procreation and from living and eating together. But it makes little sense in indigenous terms to label some of these activities as social and some as biological, and certainly I never heard Langkawi people do so. If blood, which is the stuff of kinship and to some extent of personhood, is acquired during gestation in the uterus and, after birth, in the house through feeding with others as people in Langkawi assert, is it, then, biological or social? The impossibility of answering this question merely underlines the unsatisfactory nature of the distinction.

These points make clearer my difference with Gibson which I discussed above. I would suggest that it is because he implicitly defines kinship in terms of procreative acts and ties of filiation that he finds that

[4] I am grateful to Jonathan Spencer for bringing this reference to my attention.

[5] See Ingold 1991 for a critique of the anthropological use of this distinction.

the Buid reject kinship as such. It is only if we think about relatedness in indigenous terms—that is, for the Buid in terms of sharing and companionship, or for people in Langkawi in terms of siblingship, eating, and living together—that we may arrive at a more fruitful basis for the cross-cultural comparison of its idioms. The considerable lability of the notions of kinship and personhood that I have discussed here may be an encouragement to a new and more flexible approach to the study of kinship in anthropology.

This brings me back to my starting-point. At the beginning of Chapter 1, I recounted a conversation which took place in Sungai Cantik in 1989. In response to a question about how new houses are established, I was, to my considerable surprise, given what amounted to a recipe for chicken curry. A mother buys for her daughter's *dapur* all the ingredients for this dish. And then all the other things which furnish a proper hearth must also be bought. The subtlety of this response and all that underlies it can now perhaps be better appreciated. The establishment of a new house involves lighting its hearth and setting in motion the life-giving processes which take place there. And so *dapur* generates *dapur* as mothers generate daughters. Houses, far from being mere material objects, are the people that live in them and the activities which give them life. Boundaries between houses, people, and these processes of life are here merged.

And so the Malay fascination with boundaries, the subtle way in which distinctions are made only to be erased, may perhaps encourage us to question and refine the way in which, as anthropologists, we use our own analytic dichotomies such as those I have discussed here. If Malay thought on these subjects seems in many respects more subtle than ours, perhaps it is because kinship for them is part of a process of speculation as well as a process of becoming.

BIBLIOGRAPHY

ASEMI	*Asie du Sud-Est et Monde Insulindien*
JMBRAS	*Journal of the Malayan Branch of the Royal Asiatic Society*
JRAI	*Journal of the Royal Anthropological Institute*
JSBRAS	*Journal of the Straits Branch of the Royal Asiatic Society*

Adas, M. (1981), 'From Avoidance to Confrontation: Peasant Protest in Pre-colonial and Colonial Southeast Asia', *Comparative Studies in Society and History*, 23: 217–47.

Anderson, B. (1990 [1972]), 'The Idea of Power in Javanese Culture', in *Language and Power: Exploring Political Cultures in Indonesia*, Cornell: Cornell University Press.

Ardener, S. (1964), 'The Comparative Study of Rotating Credit Associations', *JRAI* 94 (2): 201–29.

Ariès, P. (1962), *Centuries of Childhood*, Harmondsworth: Penguin.

Astuti, R. (1995), ' "The Vezo are not a Kind of People": Identity, Difference, and "Ethnicity" among a Fishing People of Western Madagascar', *American Ethnologist*, 22 (3): 464–82.

Atkinson, J. M. (1989), *The Art and Politics of Wana Shamanship*, Berkeley: University of California Press.

——and Errington, S. (eds.) (1990), *Power and Difference: Gender in Island Southeast Asia*, Stanford: Stanford University Press.

Bailey, C. (1983), *The Sociology of Production in Rural Malay Society*, Kuala Lumpur: Oxford University Press.

Banks, D. J. (1972), 'Changing Kinship in North Malaya', *American Anthropologist*, 74: 1254–76.

——(1974), 'Malay Kinship Terms and Morgan's Malayan Terminology: The Complexity of Simplicity', *Bijdragen tot de Taal-, Land- en Volkenkunde*, 130 (1): 44–68.

——(1976), 'Islam and Inheritance in Malaya: Culture, Conflict or Islamic Revolution?', *American Ethnologist*, 3 (4): 573–86.

——(1983), *Malay Kinship*, Philadelphia: Institute for the Study of Human Issues.

Barraud, C. (1979), *Tanebar-Evav: Une Société de Maisons Tournée vers le Large*, Paris: Cambridge University Press.

——(1990), 'Kei Society and the Person: An Approach through Childbirth and Funerary Rituals', *Ethnos*, 3–4: 214–31.

Benjamin, G. (1968), 'Temiar Personal Names', *Bijdragen tot de Taal-, Land- en Volkenkunde*, 124: 99–134.

Bird, B. (1989), *Langkawi from Mahsuri to Mahathir: Tourism for Whom?*, Kuala Lumpur: INSAN.

Bloch, M. (1971*a*), 'The Moral and Tactical Meaning of Kinship', *Man* (NS) 6: 79–87.

——(1971*b*), *Placing the Dead: Tombs, Ancestral Villages, and Kinship Organization in Madagascar*, London: Seminar Press.

——(1978), 'Marriage amongst Equals: An Analysis of Merina Marriage Rituals', *Man* (NS) 13: 21–33.

——(1981), 'Hierarchy and Equality in Merina Kinship', *Ethnos*, 1–2: 5–18.

——(1986), *From Blessing to Violence: History and Ideology in the Circumcision Ritual of the Merina of Madagascar*, Cambridge: Cambridge University Press.

——(1988), 'Death and the Concept of the Person', in S. Cederroth, C. Corlin, and J. Lundstrom (eds.), *On the Meaning of Death: Essays on Mortuary Rituals and Eschatological Beliefs* (Uppsala Studies in Cultural Anthropology, No. 8), Stockholm: Almqvist and Wiksell International.

——(1991), 'Language, Anthropology and Cognitive Science', *Man* (NS) 26 (2): 183–98.

Bonney, R. (1971), *Kedah 1771–1821: The Search for Security and Independence*, Kuala Lumpur: Oxford University Press.

Bowen, J. R. (1991), *Sumatran Politics and Poetics: Gayo History 1900–1989*, New Haven: Yale University Press.

——(1993), *Muslims through Discourse*, Princeton: Princeton University Press.

Braudel, F. (1976), *The Mediterranean and the Mediterranean World in the Age of Philip II*, trans. S. Reynolds, 2 vols., New York: Harper Colophon Books.

Carsten, J. (1987*a*), 'Women, Kinship and Community in a Malay Fishing Village on Pulau Langkawi, Kedah, Malaysia', unpublished Ph.D. thesis, University of London.

——(1987*b*), 'Analogues or Opposites: Household and Community in Pulau Langkawi, Malaysia', in C. Macdonald (ed.), *De la Hutte au Palais: Sociétés 'à Maison' en Asie du Sud-Est Insulaire*, Paris: Éditions du CNRS.

——(1989), 'Cooking Money: Gender and the Symbolic Transformation of Means of Exchange in a Malay Fishing Community', in J. P. Parry and M. Bloch (eds.), *Money and the Morality of Exchange*, Cambridge: Cambridge University Press.

——(1990), 'Women, Men, and the Long and the Short Term of Inheritance in Langkawi, Malaysia', *Bijdragen tot de Taal-, Land- en Volkenkunde*, 146: 270–88.

——(1991), 'Children in between: Fostering and the Process of Kinship on Pulau Langkawi, Malaysia', *Man* (NS) 26: 425–43.

——(1992), 'Bisan, Equality and Community in Langkawi, Malaysia', in F. Husken and J. Kemp (eds.), *Cognation and Social Organisation in Southeast Asia*, Leiden: KITLV Press.

——(1995*a*), 'The Substance of Kinship and the Heat of the Hearth: Feeding, Personhood and Relatedness among Malays in Pulau Langkawi', *American Ethnologist*, 22 (2): 223–41.

——(1995*b*), 'Houses in Langkawi: Stable Structures or Mobile Homes?', in J. Carsten and S. Hugh-Jones (eds.), *About the House: Lévi-Strauss and Beyond*, Cambridge: Cambridge University Press.

——(1995*c*), 'The Politics of Forgetting: Migration, Kinship and Memory on the Periphery of the Southeast Asian State', *JRAI* (NS) 1: 317–35.

——and Hugh-Jones, S. (eds.) (1995), *About the House: Lévi-Strauss and Beyond*, Cambridge: Cambridge University Press.

Chandra Muzaffar (1987), *Islamic Resurgence in Malaysia*, Petaling Jaya: Penerbit Fajar Bakti Sdn. Bhd.

Cheah Boon Kheng (1981), 'Social Banditry and Rural Crime in North Kedah, 1909–1929', *JMBRAS* 54 (2): 98–130.

——(1988), *The Peasant Robbers of Kedah 1900–1929: Historical and Folk Perceptions*, Singapore: Oxford University Press.

Clifford, J., and Marcus, G. E. (eds.) (1986), *Writing Culture: The Poetics and Politics of Ethnography*, Berkeley and Los Angeles: University of California Press.

Coedès, G. (1968), *The Indianized States of Southeast Asia*, Honolulu: East-West Center Press.

Cowan, C. D. (1961), *Nineteenth-Century Malaya: The Origins of British Political Control*, London: Oxford University Press.

Cunningham, C. (1964*a*), 'Order in the Atoni House', *Bijdragen tot de Taal-, Land- en Volkenkunde*, 120: 34–68.

——(1964*b*), 'Borrowing of Atoni Children: An Aspect of Mediation', in J. Helm (ed.), *Symposium on New Approaches to the Study of Religion. Proceedings of the American Ethnological Society*, Seattle: University of Washington Press.

Daniel, E. V. (1984), *Fluid Signs: Being a Person the Tamil Way*, Berkeley: University of California Press.

Dirks, N. B. (1987), *The Hollow Crown: Ethnohistory of an Indian Kingdom*, Cambridge and New York: Cambridge University Press.

Djamour, J. (1965 [1959]), *Malay Kinship and Marriage in Singapore*, London: Athlone Press.

——(1966), *The Muslim Matrimonial Court in Singapore*, London: Athlone Press.

Douglas, M. (1975), 'Deciphering a Meal', in *Implicit Meanings*, London: Routledge & Kegan Paul.

Downs, R. E. (1967), 'A Kelantan Village of Malaya', in J. H. Steward (ed.), *Contemporary Change in Traditional Societies*, Illinois: University of Illinois Press.

Dumont, J.-P. (1992), *Visayan Vignettes: Ethnographic Traces of a Philippine Island*, Chicago: University of Chicago Press.

Dumont, L. (1970), *Homo Hierarchicus: The Caste System and its Implications*, Chicago: University of Chicago Press.

Embree, J. F. (1950), 'Thailand: A Loosely Structured Social System', *American Anthropologist*, 52: 181–93.

Endicott, K. M. (1970), *An Analysis of Malay Magic*, Kuala Lumpur: Oxford University Press.

Errington, S. (1987), 'Incestuous Twins and the House Societies of Southeast Asia', *Cultural Anthropology*, 2: 403–44.

——(1989), *Meaning and Power in a Southeast Asian Realm*, Princeton: Princeton University Press.

Esterik, P. van (ed.) (1982), *Women of Southeast Asia* (Northern Illinois University series on Southeast Asia, Occasional Paper, No. 9), De Kalb: Northern Illinois University.

Evans-Pritchard, E. E. (1940), *The Nuer: A Description of the Modes of Livelihood and Political Institutions of a Nilotic People*, Oxford: Oxford University Press.

Firth, Raymond (1966 [1946]), *Malay Fishermen: Their Peasant Economy*, London: Routledge & Kegan Paul.

——(1974), 'Relations between Personal Kin (*Waris*) among Kelantan Malays', in R. J. Smith (ed.), *Social Organization and the Applications of Anthropology*, Ithaca, NY: Cornell University Press.

Firth, Rosemary (1966 [1943]), *Housekeeping among Malay Peasants*, London: Athlone Press.

Fortes, M. (1958), 'Introduction', in J. Goody (ed.), *The Developmental Cycle in Domestic Groups*, Cambridge: Cambridge University Press.

——(1969), *Kinship and the Social Order*, Chicago: Aldine Pub. Co.

——(1983 [1959]), *Oedipus and Job in West African Religion*, Cambridge: Cambridge University Press.

Fox, J. J. (1980), *The Flow of Life: Essays on Eastern Indonesia*, Cambridge, Mass.: Harvard University Press.

——(1987), 'The House as a Type of Social Organisation on the Island of Roti', in C. Macdonald (ed.), *De la Hutte au Palais: Sociétés 'à Maison' en Asie du Sud-Est Insulaire*, Paris: Éditions du CNRS.

Fraser, T. M. (1960), *Rusembilan: A Malay Fishing Village in Southern Thailand*, Ithaca, NY: Cornell University Press.

——(1966), *Fishermen of South Thailand: The Malay Villagers*, New York: Holt, Rinehart and Winston.

Freeman, J. D. (1961), 'On the Concept of the Kindred', *JRAI* 91: 192–220.

——(1970), *Report on the Iban*, London: Athlone Press.

Geertz, C. (1960), *The Religion of Java*, Chicago: University of Chicago Press.

——(1962), 'The Rotating Credit Association: A "Middle Rung" in Development', *Economic Development and Cultural Change*, 10: 241–63.

——(1973), 'Person, Time and Conduct in Bali', in *The Interpretation of Cultures*, New York: Basic Books.

——(1980), *Negara: The Theater Sate in Nineteenth-Century Bali*, Princeton: Princeton University Press.

Geertz, H. (1961), *The Javanese Family: A Study of Kinship and Socialization*, Glencoe, Ill.: Free Press.

——and Geertz, C. (1964), 'Teknonymy in Bali: Parenthood, Age Grading and Genealogical Amnesia', *JRAI* 94: 94–108.

————(1975), *Kinship in Bali*, Chicago: University of Chicago Press.

Gibson, T. (1986), *Sacrifice and Sharing in the Philippine Highlands: Religion and Society among the Buid of Mindoro*, London: Athlone Press.

Gimlette, J. D., and Thomson, H. W. (1971), *A Dictionary of Malayan Medicine*, London: Oxford University Press (1st edn. 1939).

Good, B. J., and DelVecchio Good, M.-J. (1992), 'The Comparative Study of Greco-Islamic Medicine: The Integration of Medical Knowledge into Local Symbolic Contexts', in C. Leslie and A. Young (eds.), *Paths to Asian Medical Knowledge*, Berkeley: University of California Press.

Goodenough, W. H. (1970), 'Epilogue: Transactions in Parenthood', in Vern Carroll (ed.), *Adoption in Eastern Oceania*, Honolulu: University of Hawaii Press.

Goody, E. (1982), *Parenthood and Social Reproduction: Fostering and Occupational Roles in West Africa*, Cambridge: Cambridge University Press.

Gow, P. (1991), *Of Mixed Blood: Kinship and History in Peruvian Amazonia*, Oxford: Oxford University Press.

Gullick, J. M. (1958), *Indigenous Political Systems of Western Malaya*, London: Athlone Press.

——(1983), 'Kedah 1821–1855: Years of Exile and Return', *JMBRAS* 56 (2): 31–86.

——(1985), 'Kedah in the Reign of Sultan Ahmad Jajuddin II (1854–1879)', *JMBRAS* 58 (2): 102–34.

——(1987), *Malay Society in the Late Nineteenth Century: The Beginnings of Change*, Singapore: Oxford University Press.

Hall, D. G. E. (1964), *A History of Southeast Asia* (2nd edn.), London: Macmillan.

Harris, H. (comp.) (1764), *Navigantium atque Itinerantium Bibliotheca or a Complete Collection of Voyages & Travels*, vol. 1, London.

Harris, O. (1981), 'Households as Natural Units', in K. Young, C. Wolkowitz, and R. McCullagh (eds.), *Of Marriage and the Market*, London: CSE.

Hart, D. V., Rajadhon, P. A., and Coughlin, R. C. (1965), *Southeast Asian Birth Customs: Three Studies in Human Reproduction*, New Haven: HRAF Press.

Headley, S. (1983), 'Houses in Java: The Missing Kin', unpublished paper presented at seminar on *Cognatic Forms of Social Organization in Southeast Asia*, University of Amsterdam.

——(1987*a*), 'The Body as a House in Javanese Society', in C. Macdonald (ed.), *De la Hutte au Palais: Sociétés 'à Maison' en Asie du Sud-Est Insulaire*, Paris: Éditions du CNRS.

Headley, S. (1987*b*), 'The Idiom of Siblingship: One Definition of "House" Societies in Southeast Asia', in C. Macdonald (ed.), *De la Hutte au Palais: Sociétés 'à Maison' en Asie du Sud-Est Insulaire*, Paris: Éditions du CNRS.

Hill, R. D. (1977), *Rice in Malaya: A Study in Historical Geography*, Kuala Lumpur: Oxford University Press.

Hilton, R. N. (1956), 'The Basic Malay House', *JMBRAS* 29 (3): 134–55.

Hobart, M. (1986), 'Thinker, Thespian, Soldier, Slave? Assumptions about Human Nature in the Study of Balinese Society', in M. Hobart and R. H. Taylor (eds.), *Context, Meaning, and Power in Southeast Asia*, Ithaca, NY: Cornell Southeast Asia Program.

Hodgson, G. (1967), 'Malay Conventional Sib-names', *JMBRAS* 40 (2): 106–21.

Hooykaas, C. (1974), *Cosmogony and Creation in Balinese Tradition*, The Hague; Martinus Nijhoff.

Howe, L. E. A. (1984), 'Gods, People, Spirits and Witches: The Balinese System of Person Definition', *Bijdragen tot de Taal-, Land- en Volkenkunde*, 140: 193–222.

Ingold, T. (1991), 'Becoming Persons: Consciousness and Sociality in Human Evolution', *Cultural Dynamics*, 4: 355–78.

Iskandar, T. (1970), *Kamus Dewan*, Kuala Lumpur: Dewan Bahasa dan Pustaka.

Jabatan Perangkaan Malaysia [Department of Statistics Malaysia] (1984), *Banci Penduduk dan Perumahan Malaysia 1980* [Population and Housing Census of Malaysia], *Laporan Penduduk Daerah Pentadbiran* [Population Report for Administrative Districts], Kuala Lumpur.

Jay, R. R. (1969), *Javanese Villagers: Social Relations in Modjokuto*, Cambridge, Mass.: MIT Press.

Jayawardena, C. (1977), 'Women and Kinship in Acheh Besar, Northern Sumatra', *Ethnology*, 16 (1): 21–38.

Kahn, J. S. (1980), *Minangkabau Social Formations: Indonesian Peasants and the World Economy*, Cambridge: Cambridge University Press.

Karim, W. J. (1984), 'Malay Midwives and Witches', *Social Science and Medicine*, 18 (22): 159–66.

——(1990), 'Prelude to Madness: The Language of Emotion in Courtship and Early Marriage', in W. J. Karim (ed.), *Emotions of Culture: A Malay Perspective*, Singapore: Oxford University Press.

——(1992), *Women and Culture: Between Malay Adat and Islam*, Boulder, Colo.: Westview Press.

——(1993*a*), 'With *Moyang Melur* in Carey Island: More Endangered, More Engendered', in D. Bell, P. Caplan, and W. J. Karim (eds.), *Gendered Fields: Women, Men and Ethnography*, London and New York: Routledge.

——(1993*b*), 'Epilogue: The "Nativised" self and the "Native"', in D. Bell, P. Caplan, and W. J. Karim (eds.), *Gendered Fields: Women, Men and Ethnography*, London and New York: Routledge.

Kato, T. (1982), *Matriliny and Migration: Evolving Minangkabau Traditions in Indonesia*, Ithaca, NY: Cornell University Press.

Kedah Annual Report (1906–8), Bangkok.

Kemp, J. H. (1983), 'Kinship and the Management of Personal Relations: Kin Terminologies and the "Axiom of Amity"', *Bijdragen tot de Taal-, Land- en Volkenkunde*, 139 (1): 81–98.

Kessler, C. (1978), *Islam and Politics in a Malay State: Kelantan 1838–1969*, Ithaca, NY: Cornell University Press.

King, V. T. (ed.) (1978), *Essays on Borneo Societies*, Oxford: Oxford University Press.

Koentjaraningrat, R. M. (1957), *A Preliminary Description of the Javanese Kinship System* (Yale University Southeast Asia Studies Report), New Haven: Yale University.

——(1960), 'The Javanese of South Central Java', in G. P. Murdock (ed.), *Social Structure in Southeast Asia*, Chicago: Quadrangle Books.

Kratoska, P. H. (1985), 'The Peripatetic Peasant and Land Tenure in British Malaya', *Journal of Southeast Asian Studies*, 16 (1): 16–46.

Kuchiba, M., Tsubouchi, Y., and Maeda, N. (1979), *Three Malay Villages: A Sociology of Paddy Growers in West Malaysia*, trans. Peter and Stephani Hawkes, Honolulu: University Press of Hawaii.

Laderman, C. (1981), 'Symbolic and Empirical Reality: A New Approach to the Analysis of Food Avoidances', *American Ethnologist*, 8 (3): 468–93.

——(1983), *Wives and Midwives: Childbirth and Nutrition in Rural Malaysia*, Berkeley: University of California Press.

——(1992), 'A Welcoming Soil: Islamic Humoralism on the Malay Peninsula', in C. Leslie and A. Young (eds.), *Paths to Asian Medical Knowledge*, Berkeley: University of California Press.

Leach, E. (1954), *Political Systems of Highland Burma*, London: Athlone Press.

Lévi-Strauss, C. (1969), *The Elementary Structures of Kinship* (rev. edn.), Boston: Beacon Press.

——(1978), *The Origin of Table Manners, Introduction to a Science of Mythology*: 3, trans. John and Doreen Weightman, London: Jonathan Cape.

——(1983*a*), *The Way of the Masks*, trans. Sylvia Modelski, London: Jonathan Cape.

——(1983*b*), 'Histoire et Ethnologie', *Annales* (Nov.–Dec.): 1217–31.

——(1987), *Anthropology and Myth: Lectures 1951–1982*, trans. Roy Willis, Oxford: Basil Blackwell.

Li, Tania (1989), *Malays in Singapore: Culture, Economy, and Ideology*, Singapore: Oxford University Press.

Lim Jee Yuan (1987), *The Malay House: Rediscovering Malaysia's Indigenous Shelter System*, Pulau Pinang: Institut Masyarakat.

Lim Teck Ghee (1977), *Peasants and their Agricultural Economy in Colonial Malaya 1874–1941*, Kuala Lumpur: Oxford University Press.

Lundstrom, W. (1982), 'The Group of People Living in a House', in K. G. Izikowitz and P. Sorensen (eds.), *The House in East and Southeast Asia: Anthropological and Architectural Aspects*, London: Curzon Press.

Lundstrom-Burghoorn, W. (1981), *Minahasa Civilization: A Tradition of Change*, Gothenburg: Acta Universitatis Gothoburgensis.

Macdonald, C. (ed.) (1987), *De la Hutte au Palais: Sociétés 'à Maison' en Asie du Sud-Est Insulaire*, Paris: Éditions du CNRS.

McKinley, R. (1975), 'A Knife Cutting Water: Child Transfers and Siblingship among Urban Malays', unpublished Ph.D. thesis, University of Michigan.

——(1981), 'Cain and Abel on the Malay Peninsula', in Mac Marshall (ed.), *Siblingship in Oceania: Studies in the Meaning of Kin Relations* (ASAO Monographs, No. 8), Lanham, Md.: University Press of America.

McKinnon, S. (1991), *From a Shattered Sun: Hierarchy, Gender, and Alliance in the Tanimbar Islands*, Madison: University of Wisconsin Press.

Maeda, N. (1975), 'Family Circle, Community and Nation in Malaysia', *Current Anthropology*, 16: 163–6.

Marriott, McKim (1976), 'Hindu Transactions: Diversity without Dualism', in B. Kapferer (ed.), *Transaction and Meaning*, Philadelphia: Institute for the Study of Human Issues.

Massard, J. (1978), 'Un Retour à la Simplicité: L'Alimentation de la Jeune Accouchée en Malaisie', *ASEMI* 9 (3–4): 141–50.

——(1980), '"Les Moineaux avec les moineaux . . ." Rapport des Malais au Monde Animal', *Cheminements, ASEMI* 11 (1–4): 349–69.

——(1983*a*), *Nous Gens de Ganchong: Environnement et Échanges dans un Village Malais*, Paris: Éditions du Centre National de la Recherche Scientifique.

——(1983*b*), 'Le Don d'Enfants dans la Société Malaise', *L'Homme*, 23 (3): 101–14.

——(1985), 'The New-Born Malay Child: A Multiple Identity Being', *JMBRAS* 58 (2): 71–84.

Maxwell, W. E. (1884), 'The Law and Customs of the Malays with Reference to the Tenure of Land', *JSBRAS* 13: 75–220.

Maznah Mohamed (1984), 'Gender, Class and the Sexual Division of Labour in a Rural Community in Kedah', *Kajian Malaysia*, 2: 101–22.

Mintz, M. W. (1987), 'Gelaran Kampung: Nicknames in a Malay Village', *JMBRAS* 60 (1): 81–108.

Moore, H. L. (1988), *Feminism and Anthropology*, Cambridge: Polity Press.

Murdock, G. P. (1960), 'Cognatic Forms of Social Organization', in *Social Structure in Southeast Asia*, Chicago: Quadrangle Books.

Nagata, J. A. (1976), 'Kinship and Social Mobility among the Malays', *Man* (NS) 2 (3): 400–9.

——(1979), *Malaysian Mosaic: Perspectives from a Poly-Ethnic Society*, Vancouver: University of British Columbia Press.

——(1984), *The Reflowering of Malaysian Islam: Modern Religious Radicals and Their Roots*, Vancouver: University of British Columbia Press.

Nash, M. (1974), *Peasant Citizens: Politics, Religion and Modernization in Kelantan, Malaysia*, Athens, Oh.: Ohio University Center for International Studies.

Nathan, J. E. (1922), *The Census of British Malaya 1921*, London.

Needham, R. (1954), 'The System of Teknonyms and Death-Names of the Penan', *Southwestern Journal of Anthropology*, 10: 416–31.

——(1959), 'Mourning Terms', *Bijdragen tot de Taal-, Land- en Volkenkunde*, 115: 58–89.

——(1971), 'Remarks on the Analysis of Kinship and Marriage', in R. Needham (ed.), *Rethinking Kinship and Marriage*, London: Tavistock.

Ong, A. (1987), *Spirits of Resistance and Capitalist Discipline: Factory Women in Malaysia*, Albany: State University of New York Press.

Onions, L. T. (ed.) (1966), *The Oxford Dictionary of Etymology*, Oxford: Oxford University Press.

Parry, J. (1985), 'Death and Digestion: The Symbolism of Food and Eating in North Indian Mortuary Rites', *Man* (NS) 20: 612–30.

——(1989), 'The End of the Body', in M. Feher (ed.), *Fragments for a History of the Body, Part Two*, New York: Zone.

Peletz, M. G. (1985), 'Siblingship and Social Structure in Negeri Sembilan: Perspectives from Myth, History and the Present', in L. L. Thomas and F. von Benda-Beckmann (eds.), *Change and Continuity in Minangkabau: Local, Regional and Historical Perspectives on West Sumatra*, Athens, Oh.: Ohio University Press.

——(1988), *A Share of the Harvest: Kinship, Property and Social History Among the Malays of Rembau*, Berkeley: University of California Press.

Provencher, R. (1971), *Two Malay Worlds: Interaction in Urban and Rural Settings*, Berkeley: Center for South and Southeast Asian Studies, University of California.

——(1972), 'Comparisons of Social Interaction Styles: Urban and Rural Malay Culture', in T. Weaver and D. White (eds.), *The Anthropology of Urban Environments*, Society of Applied Anthropology Monograph, No. 11.

——(1979), 'Orality as a Pattern of Symbolism in Malay Psychiatry', in A. L. Becker and A. A. Yengoyan (eds.), *The Imagination of Reality*, Norwood: Ablex Publishing Corporation.

Reid, A. (1988), *Southeast Asia in the Age of Commerce 1450–1680, Volume One: The Lands Below the Winds*, New Haven: Yale University Press.

Reiter, R. R. (1975), 'Men and Women in the South of France: Public and Private Domains', in R. R. Reiter (ed.), *Towards an Anthropology of Women*, New York: Monthly Review Press.

Rodman, M. C. (1985), 'Moving Houses: Residential Mobility and the Mobility of Residences in Logana, Vanuatu', *American Anthropologist*, 87: 56–72.

Roff, W. R. (1969), 'Social History and its Materials in Malaysia', *Peninjau Sejarah*, 3: 13–20.

Rogers, M. L. (1977), *Sungai Raya: A Sociopolitical Study of a Rural Malay*

Community (Center for South and Southeast Asian Studies, Research Monograph, No. 15), Berkeley: University of California.

Rogers, M. L. (1993), *Local Politics in Rural Malaysia: Patterns of Change in Sungai Raya*, Kuala Lumpur: S. Abdul Majeed & Co.

Rosaldo, M. Z. (1974), 'Woman, Culture and Society: A Theoretical Overview', in M. Z. Rosaldo and L. Lamphere (eds.), *Women, Culture and Society*, Stanford: Stanford University Press.

Rosaldo, R. (1980), *Ilongot Headhunting 1883–1974: A Study in Society and History*, Stanford: Stanford University Press.

Rudie, I. (1993), 'A Hall of Mirrors: Autonomy Translated Over Time in Malaysia', in D. Bell, P. Caplan, and W. J. Karim (eds.), *Gendered Fields: Women, Men and Ethnography*, London and New York: Routledge.

——(1994), *Visible Women in East Coast Malay Society: On the Reproduction of Gender in Ceremonial, School and Market*, Oslo: Scandinavian University Press.

Sahlins, M. (1972), 'On the Sociology of Primitive Exchange', in *Stone Age Economics*, London: Tavistock Publications.

Schneider, D. M. (1984), *A Critique of the Study of Kinship*, Ann Arbor: University of Michigan Press.

Scott, J. C. (1976), *The Moral Economy of the Peasant: Rebellion and Subsistence in Southeast Asia*, New Haven: Cornell University Press.

——(1985), *Weapons of the Weak: Everyday Forms of Peasant Resistance*, New Haven: Yale University Press.

Shamsul, A. B. (1986), *From British to Bumiputera Rule: Local Politics and Rural Development in Peninsular Malaysia*, Singapore: Institute of Southeast Asian Studies.

Sharom Ahmat (1970*a*), 'The Structure of the Economy of Kedah, 1879–1905', *JMBRAS* 43 (2): 1–24.

——(1970*b*), 'The Political Structure of the State of Kedah, 1879–1905', *Journal of Southeast Asian Studies*, 1 (2): 115–28.

——(1984), *Tradition and Change in a Malay State: A Study of the Economic and Political Development of Kedah 1878–1923*, Kuala Lumpur: The Malaysian Branch of the Royal Asiatic Society.

Siegel, J. T. (1969), *The Rope of God*, Berkeley: University of California Press.

Siti Hasmah Ali (1979), 'Traditional Practices and Modern Medicine in Kedah', in Asmah Haji Omar (ed.), *Darulaman: Essays on Linguistic, Cultural and Socio-Economic Aspects of the Malaysian State of Kedah*, Kuala Lumpur: Penerbit Universiti Malaya.

Skeat, W. W. (1900), *Malay Magic: An Introduction to the Folklore and Popular Religion of the Malay Peninsula*, London: Macmillan & Co.

Snouck Hurgronje, C. (1906), *The Achehnese*, trans. A. W. S. O'Sullivan, 2 vols., Leiden: Brill.

Stivens, M. (1985), *Sexual Politics in Rembau: Female Autonomy, Matriliny and*

Agrarian Change in Negeri Sembilan, Malaysia (Centre of Southeast Asian Studies, Occasional Paper No. 5), University of Kent at Canterbury.

Strange, H. (1980), 'Some Changing Socio-Economic Roles of Rural Malay Women', in Sylvia Chipp and Justin Green (eds.), *Asian Women in Transition*, University Park, Pa.: Pennsylvania University Press.

——(1981), *Rural Malay Women in Tradition and Transition*, New York: Praeger.

Strathern, M. (1984), 'Domesticity and the Denigration of Women', in D. O'Brien and S. Tiffanny (eds.), *Rethinking Women's Roles: Perspectives from the Pacific*, Berkeley: University of California Press.

——(1988), *The Gender of the Gift: Problems with Women and Problems with Society in Melanesia*, Berkeley: University of California Press.

Swift, M. G. (1963), 'Men and Women in Malay Society', in B. Ward (ed.), *Women in the New Asia*, Paris: Unesco.

——(1965), *Malay Peasant Society in Jelebu*, London: Athlone Press.

Syed Husin Ali (1964), *Social Stratification in Kampung Bagan*, Singapore: Malaysian Branch of the Royal Asiatic Society.

——(1975), *Malay Peasant Society and Leadership*, Kuala Lumpur: Oxford University Press.

Syed Hussein Alatas (1968), 'Feudalism in Malaysian Society: A Study in Historical Continuity', *Civilisations*, 13: 579–92.

Tambiah, S. J. (1976), *World Conqueror and World Renouncer*, Cambridge: Cambridge University Press.

Tanner, N. (1974), 'Matrifocality in Indonesia and Africa and Among Black Americans', in M. Z. Rosaldo and L. Lamphere (eds.), *Women, Culture and Society*, Stanford: Stanford University Press.

Topping, M. (1850), 'Some Account of Kedah', *Journal of the Indian Archipelago and Eastern Asia*, 4: 42–4.

Traube, E. G. (1986), *Cosmology and Social Life: Ritual Exchange among the Mambai of East Timor*, Chicago: University of Chicago Press.

Wan Hashim (1978), *A Malay Community in Upper Perak*, Bangi, Malaysia: National University of Malaysia Press.

Wang Gungwu (1985), 'Migration Patterns in the History of Malaya and the Region', *JMBRAS* 58 (1): 43–57.

Waterson, H. R. (1986), 'The Ideology and Terminology of Kinship among the Sa'dan Toraja', *Bijdragen tot de Taal-, Land- en Volkenkunde*, 143: 87–112.

——(1990), *The Living House: An Anthropology of Architecture in Southeast Asia*, Singapore: Oxford University Press.

Wikan, U. (1990), *Managing Turbulent Hearts: A Javanese Formula for Living*, Chicago: University of Chicago Press.

Wilder, W. D. (1970), 'Socialization and Social Structure in a Malay Village', in P. Mayer (ed.), *Socialization: The Approach from Social Anthropology*, London: Tavistock Publications.

——(1976), 'Problems in Comparison of Kinship Systems in Island Southeast

Asia', in D. J. Banks (ed.), *Changing Identities in Modern Southeast Asia, World Anthropology*, The Hague: Mouton Publishers.

Wilder, W. D. (1982), *Communication, Social Structure and Development in Rural Malaysia: A Study of Kampung Kuala Bera*, London: Athlone Press.

Wilkinson, R. J. (1957), 'Papers on Malay Customs and Beliefs', *JMBRAS* 30 (4): 1–79.

——(1959), *A Malay–English Dictionary (Romanized)*, London: Macmillan.

Wilson, P. (1966), 'A Note on Descent in a Malay Village', *Behaviour Science Notes*, 1: 7–15.

——(1967), *A Malay Village and Malaysia: Social Values and Rural Development*, New Haven: HRAF Press.

Winstedt, R. O. (1936), 'Notes on the History of Kedah', *JMBRAS* 14 (3): 155–89.

——(1982), *The Malay Magician*, Kuala Lumpur: Oxford University Press.

Wolf, E. (1982), *Europe and the People without History*, Berkeley: University of California Press.

Wolters, O. W. (1982), *History, Culture, and Region in Southeast Asian Perspectives*, Singapore: Institute of Southeast Asian Studies.

Wong, D. (1987), *Peasants in the Making: Malaysia's Green Revolution*, Singapore: Institute of Southeast Asian Studies.

Yanagisako, S. J. (1979), 'Family and Household: The Analysis of Domestic Groups', *Annual Review of Anthropology*, 8: 161–205.

——(1987), 'Mixed Metaphors: Native and Anthropological Models of Gender and Kinship Domains' in J. F. Collier and S. J. Yanagisako (eds.), *Gender and Kinship: Essays Toward a Unified Analysis*, Stanford: Stanford University Press.

Zaharah Mahmud (1972), 'The Population of Kedah in the Nineteenth Century', *Journal of Southeast Asian Studies*, 3 (2): 193–209.

Zainal Abidin bin Ahmad (1947) , 'The Various Significations of the Malay Word *Sejok*', *JMBRAS* 20 (2): 40–4.

——(1950), 'Malay Manners and Etiquette', *JMBRAS* 23 (3): 43–74.

INDEX